Experiencing Rome

Culture, Identity and Power in the Roman Empire

EDITED BY JANET HUSKINSON

in association with The Open University

This book has been prepared for the Open University course AA309 *Culture, Identity and Power in the Roman Empire*. Details of this and other Open University courses can be obtained from the Course Reservations Centre, PO Box 724, The Open University, Milton Keynes MK7 6ZS, United Kingdom, tel: (00 44) (0)1908 653231.

For availability of other course components, contact Open University Worldwide Ltd, The Berrill Building, Walton Hall, Milton Keynes, MK7 6AA, United Kingdom, tel: (00 44) (0)1908 858585, email ouwenq@open.ac.uk

Much useful information can also be obtained from The Open University's website: http://www.open.ac.uk

First published 2000
by Routledge
2 Park Square, Milton Park, Abingdon, Oxon, OX14 4RN

Written and produced by The Open University
Walton Hall
Milton Keynes
MK7 6AA

Simultaneously published in the USA and Canada by Routledge
270 Madison Ave,
New York
NY 10016

Transferred to Digital Printing 2005

Edited, designed and typeset by The Open University

British Library Cataloguing in Publication Data
A catalogue record for this book is available from the British Library

Library of Congress Cataloguing in Publication Data
Experiencing Rome: culture, identity and power in the Roman Empire / edited by Janet Huskinson.
Includes bibliographical references and index.
1 Rome – Civilization. 2 Power (Social sciences) – Rome. 3 Romans – Ethnic identity. I. Huskinson, Janet. DG78.E95 2000
306' .0945–dc21

99–39870
CIP

ISBN 0 415 21285 5 hardback
ISBN 0 415 21284 7 paperback

21251B/aa309bki.1

Printed and bound by Antony Rowe Ltd, Eastbourne

Contents

Preface

The essays in this book were especially written for a third-level Open University course on 'Culture, Identity and Power in the Roman Empire' with the needs of undergraduate students primarily in mind. But we hope that they will be of interest and value to many other readers who want to read about these aspects of Roman society, whether or not they already have much knowledge of the Roman world.

As with all Open University publications, the authors have been supported by a team of people in producing this volume, and we would like to acknowledge with thanks the help of Kate Clements, Clare Butler and Nancy Marten (course editors), Ruth Cole and Debbie Ball (course managers), Sophie Reid (course secretary), Tony Coulson and Jane Lea (picture researchers), Rich Hoyle (designer), Ray Munns (cartographer), John Taylor (graphic artist), Robert Gibson (compositor), Isobel MacLean (indexer), and Gill Gowans and Jonathan Hunt (who made the arrangements for co-publication with Routledge).

Special thanks go to Professor Greg Woolf of the University of St Andrews for his detailed and constructive comments on various drafts of the essays, and for the generosity with which he gave them. Needless to say, any remaining errors are the responsibility of the authors.

Translations of passages quoted in the text are those of the essay author unless otherwise indicated.

Contributors

Dr Lorna Hardwick, Department of Classical Studies, The Open University

Dr Valerie Hope, Department of Classical Studies, The Open University

Dr Janet Huskinson, Department of Classical Studies, The Open University

Dr Paula James, Department of Classical Studies, The Open University

Dr Richard Miles, Department of Classical Studies, The Open University

Dr Dominic Montserrat, Department of Classics, University of Warwick

Dr Lisa Nevett, Department of Classical Studies, The Open University

Dr Phil Perkins, Department of Classical Studies, The Open University

Professor James Rives, Vanier College, York University, Toronto

Dr Margaret Williams, Department of Classical Studies, The Open University

Key dates

Periods in Greek history

The 'Archaic' period usually refers to the years from 800 to 500 BC. It saw the formation of Greek culture.

The 'Classical' period is generally used for the fifth and early fourth centuries BC. It is particularly associated with the politics and culture of city states (*poleis*).

The 'Hellenistic' period is usually taken to run from the accession of Alexander as king of Macedon in 336 BC to the first century BC. Alexander conquered the Persian empire and much of the near east, opening up those areas to a common Greek culture (*koine*), which continued even into the period of the Roman empire.

Periods in Roman history

753 BC   Legendary foundation of Rome: period of kings.

509 BC   The republic set up (in place of kings), with a ruling senate and two annually elected consuls.

'Early republic' usually relates to the fourth and third centuries BC. Rome was established as a leading Mediterranean power by defeating Carthage in the Punic Wars.

'Mid republic' usually means the second century BC. It saw continuing expansion of Rome's power in areas of the Mediterranean such as Greece and Asia Minor.

'Late republic' usually means the first century BC. This saw increasing tension in Italy, to do with citizenship rights for the Italian allies of Rome and the distribution of land; in mid first century Rome there was mounting rivalry between individuals (such as Pompey and Julius Caesar) with political and military power.

31 BC   Octavian defeated Mark Antony at the battle of Actium, and in 28 BC by a constitutional settlement took the title *princeps* (leading citizen). In 27 BC he took the title Augustus.

List of emperors, their reigns and their dynasties

Julio-Claudians

27 BC–AD 14	Augustus
AD 14–37	Tiberius
AD 37–41	Gaius, also known as Caligula
AD 41–54	Claudius
AD 54–68	Nero
AD 68–69	Galba
AD 69	'The year of the Four Emperors': Galba, Otho, Vitellius, Vespasian

Flavians

AD 69–79	Vespasian
AD 79–81	Titus
AD 81–96	Domitian
AD 96–98	Nerva
AD 98–117	Trajan
AD 117–38	Hadrian

Antonines

AD 138–61	Antoninus Pius
AD 161–80	Marcus Aurelius (co-emperor with Lucius Verus AD 161–69)
AD 180–92	Commodus (co-emperor with his father, Marcus Aurelius 177–80)
AD 193	Pertinax
AD 193	Didius Julianus

Severans

AD 193–211	Septimius Severus
AD 211–17	Caracalla (co-ruler with Geta AD 211–12)
AD 217–18	Macrinus
AD 218–22	Elagabalus
AD 222–35	Alexander Severus

Dynasties emperors from Augustus to Nero are known as Julio-Claudians; Vespasian to Domitian as Flavians; Antoninus Pius to Commodus as the Antonines; and Septimius Severus to Alexander Severus as Severans.

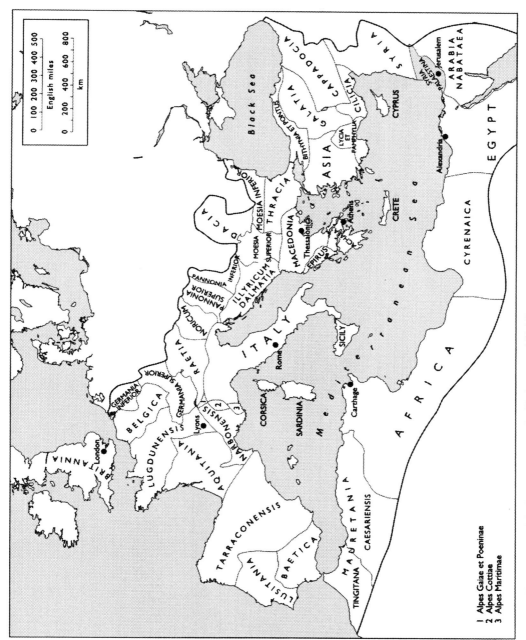

Map 1 The provinces of the Roman empire under Hadrian (AD 117–38)

1 Alpes Gaiae et Poeninae
2 Alpes Cottiae
3 Alpes Maritimae

xi

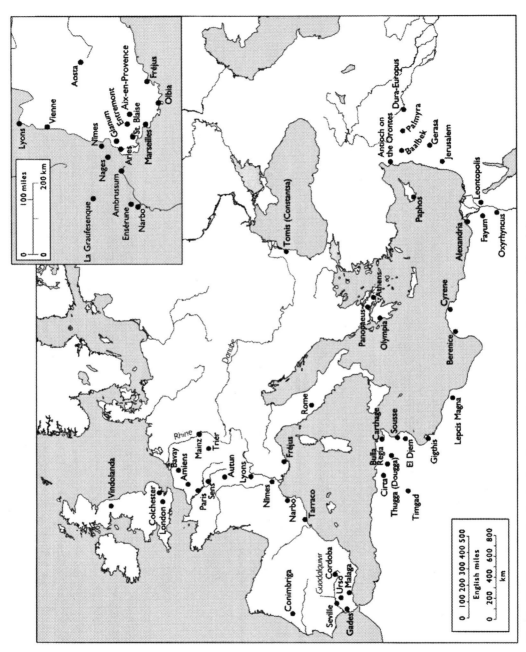

Map 2 The Roman empire showing key places mentioned in the essays (see also maps 3 and 4)

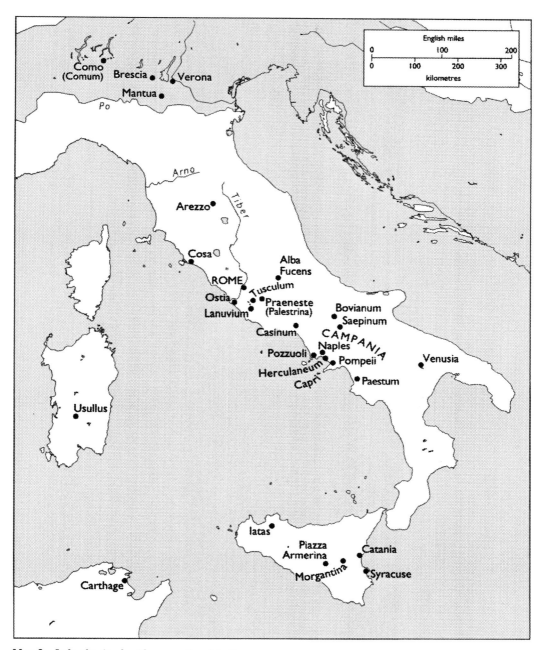

Map 3 *Italy, showing key places mentioned in the essays*

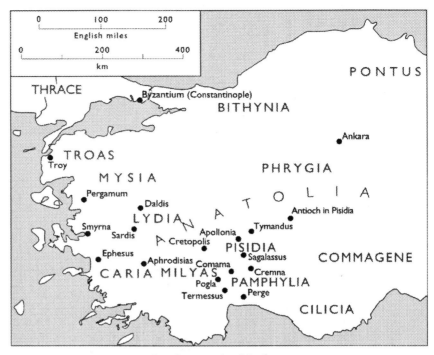

Map 4 *Asia Minor, showing key places mentioned in the essays*

Acknowledgements

Grateful acknowledgement is made to the following sources for permission to reproduce material in this book:

Text

The Odes of Horace, translated by James Michie, Penguin Books Ltd, 1967, copyright © James Michie, 1964; reprinted by permission of the publishers and the Loeb Classical Library from *Martial: Epigrams*, translated by W.C.A. Ker, Cambridge, Mass., Harvard University Press, 1919, 1920, revised 1968; Juvenal, *The Sixteen Satires*, translated by Peter Green (Penguin Classics 1967, revised edition 1974) copyright © Peter Green, 1967, 1974, reproduced by permission of Penguin Books Ltd; Williams, M.H. (1998) *The Jews Among the Greeks and Romans, A Diasporan Sourcebook*, pp.4–5, 11–14, 16–17, 26, © 1998 by Margaret H. Williams, reprinted by permission of Gerald Duckworth & Co Ltd., also by permission of Johns Hopkins University Press.

Figures

Figure 2.8 Private collection, courtesy of Tullie House Museum, Carlisle. *Figure 4.4* Boethius, A. and Ward-Perkins, J.B. (1992) *Etruscan and Early Roman Architecture*, Pelican History of Art/Yale University Press; *Figure 5.3* adapted from Alföldy, G. (1988) *The Social History of Rome*, translated by Braund, D. and Pollock, F., revised edition, Routledge; *Figure 7.1* Carandini, A. and Settis, S. (1979) *Schiavi e Padroni nell'Etruria Romana*, De Donato Editore; *Figure 7.4* Carandini, A. (1988) *Schiavi in Italia. Gli Strumenti Pensanti dei Romani fra Tarda Repubblica e Medio Impero*, La Nuova Italia Scientifica; *Figure 8.1* Waelkens, M. (1993) *Sagalassos I. First General Report on the Survey 1986–89 and Excavations 1990–91*, Leuven University Press; *Figure 8.2* Mitchell, S. (1995) *Cremna in Pisidia: an Ancient City in Peace and in War*, Gerald Duckworth & Co Ltd/Classical Press of Wales; *Figures 8.3 and 8.4* Duby, G. (1980) *Histoire de la France Urbaine, vol.1: La Ville Antique des Origines au IXe Siècle*, Seuil; *Figure 8.9* Gros, P. and Torelli, M. (1994) *Storia dell'Urbanistica. Il Mondoromano*, third edition, Laterza; *Figure 11.2* Fine, S. (1996) *Sacred Realm: the Emergence of the Synagogue in the Ancient World*, Yeshiva University Museum/Oxford University Press; *Figures 11.4 and 11.6* Hanfmann, G.M.A. (1983) *Sardis, from Prehistoric to Roman Times*, Harvard University Press, © Archaeological Exploration of Sardis/Harvard University.

Introduction

BY JANET HUSKINSON

How people experience a culture and identify themselves in relation to it is very much to the fore in current social debate. Much of this interest has been stimulated by changes that have occurred in the power structures that traditionally shaped communities at local and international levels. These had often determined culture and identity through relationships of social class or empire, but since the second part of the twentieth century gender and ethnicity, for example, have become more powerful as ways of defining identity. In a world of fast communications and globalized culture (perhaps a new kind of imperialism?) people have become more aware of cultural distinctions as well as values and beliefs which are shared.

These factors mean that we look at ourselves and our society from a viewpoint which is inevitably rather different from, say, that of the earlier twentieth century, and this approach also extends to reviewing the past. For the history of the Roman empire this change raises many questions which were not of such interest to previous scholars, whose views were inevitably formed by *their* cultural experiences and within their own historical context. And the changes go further: there are differences now not only in the subjects researched but also in how the outcomes are represented. Rather than presenting the ancient society as a unified totality (whether reconstructed through empirical research or some large-scale theoretical model), present-day scholarship on the Roman empire tends to consider diversity and the complexity of social factors, acknowledging that insights are more achievable than definitive answers.

In fact, these approaches offer a very fruitful way of studying the Roman empire, the history of which involves many issues which have modern resonances. It is particularly interesting to look at the diversity of the Roman experience and at how the assertion of power in various forms shaped concepts of culture and identity across a wide span of time and place. Studying the Roman empire raises questions to do with the impact of a major culture on others, and also about how the responses of the 'others' may be identified and interpreted from a historical record that inevitably privileges the Roman point of view.

So there are subjects of fresh interest, and also fresh critiques and theoretical perspectives for the interpretation of them. Over the last decades post-colonial studies have challenged earlier views of the benefits of empires and of the processes by which they were established.

Post-modernism, with its interests in problematization, deconstruction and diversity of viewpoint, encourages a positive assessment of cultural variability, while post-processual archaeology has turned to look at the social element of cultural change, including the ways in which contemporary societies 'write' these periods of their past. All these approaches bring a concern to hear the hitherto 'silent voices' in Roman society (of the conquered, or of minorities within the mainstream culture such as women and children) and to understand how power and reactions to it are symbolized in society. For the Roman empire such issues can be problematic to pursue because of the gaps and biases in the ancient evidence, so revisiting ancient sources with fresh frames of reference can often open up new interpretations of the material. Culture, identity and power make just such a fresh framework as they involve a wide range of human and social interactions: they provide a vivid means for looking at ancient ways of 'experiencing Rome'.

This is what the essays in this book explore. They cover a selection of key subjects which are treated in a multidisciplinary way, each taking its own approach. Some offer surveys and synthesis of existing material, while others raise new issues or divergent theoretical perspectives; but the point of them all is to introduce students and other interested readers to ancient material and current debates to do with various ways of 'experiencing Rome' in the first three centuries or so of its empire. The first essay provides an overview of the issues involved, introducing some of the terminology (such as Romanization). Of the rest, some deal with subjects that are central aspects of any society (such as gender, religion, communication and status) and set their issues in the historical context of the Roman empire. Others examine situations that are historically specific to the Roman empire: dissent, concepts of peace, the city of Rome, developments in élite culture, economic power, urbanism and the Jewish communities in the Roman empire. They include discussions of other topics such as education, literacy, minority cultures, and concepts of civilization and barbarism. Overall, the aim is to introduce aspects of Roman society in which culture, identity and power are embedded, and to show how they work together as factors in the hugely diverse world that was Rome's empire.

Essay One
Looking for culture, identity and power

BY JANET HUSKINSON

Sometime during the second or early third century AD mosaic pavements were laid in a wealthy house in the north African town of Thysdrus, the modern El Djem in Tunisia (Blanchard-Lemée et al., 1996, pp.18–34). One was decorated with personifications of Africa and the Seasons, while another, in an adjacent room, depicted a series of figures who have been identified as representations of Rome and the provinces (Figure 1.1). Six hexagonal panels containing alternately female busts and full-standing figures surround a seventh which shows the seated figure of Rome, armed and holding the orb of the universe (Figure 1.2). The outer figures are identified by their attributes as personifications of various provinces: Africa (the left-hand bust) in an elephant head-dress (Figure 1.3), Egypt

Figure 1.1 Mosaic showing Rome and provinces from a house in El Djem, Tunisia. Museum of El Djem, Tunis. (Photo: Gilles Mermet)

Figure 1.2 Detail showing the central figure of
Rome. Museum of El Djem, Tunis. (Photo: Gilles
Mermet)

Figure 1.3 Detail showing Africa. Museum of El
Djem, Tunis. (Photo: Gilles Mermet)

(the bust on the right) with hair in 'dreadlocks' and holding a rattle used
in the worship of Isis, and Sicily (bottom standing figure), who is shown as
a huntress and has triple 'feet' behind her head to denote the island's
triangular shape. The uppermost bust probably represents Asia since she
has a turreted crown like those worn by personifications of cities in Asia
Minor, but the others are less easily identified by surviving attributes (one
holds an olive branch, and another a sacrificial jug and dish). Together
these figures are linked in an arrangement which suggests the
geographical extent of the Roman empire and its diversity united under
the central control of Rome.

So here in this mosaic themes of culture, identity and power occur in
various ways – in the personifications and their identifying attributes, in
the arrangement of panels, and in the mosaic's very setting in a
provincial house. Here too are some of the issues that arise in
interpreting the themes from the ancient evidence – the problem that
some key knowledge is lost to us (for identifying the remaining
'provinces' from their attributes), and the fact that to an important
extent viewers would bring their own cultural values to their reading of
an image. In short, the mosaic provides a useful entry point for
considering many of the issues involved in looking for culture, identity
and power in the Roman world. These are concepts central to the
understanding of any society, and are currently much debated by
cultural historians, social scientists, and other academic analysts,
producing a large body of literature. Writing about Roman experiences
from such modern perspectives can be illuminating, but we need to be
clear about what we are looking for, and looking at, in the ancient

material. After all, Roman society differed from present western society in some fundamental ways, and these differences are crucial to our understanding of Roman culture: for example, the institution of slavery (see Essay Five) affected all kinds of cultural practices, while the low level of literacy gave a special value to non-written forms of communication (see Essay Two).

By focusing this essay on the mosaic from El Djem and its images I will show what is at stake in looking for culture, identity and power in the Roman empire and introduce some of the central questions. At the end of the essay some of these issues will be considered from a more distanced viewpoint, particularly the question of Romanization (that is, the process whereby Roman culture spread to other areas) and the wider contexts of time and space.

Looking for culture

We must start by defining 'culture'. This is notoriously hard to do, and the term is used in many ways, often just to mean the arts or interests of 'high culture' (see Essay Four). But in this essay something much broader is intended, and 'culture as shared meanings' makes a simple and effective working definition (Hall, 1997). People who belong to a particular culture share a set of assumptions and experiences, and this sharing is expressed by following certain common practices or by employing accepted representations of mutual identity.

Immediately it is possible to relate this back to the mosaic. This expensive form of pavement, together with its chosen subject matter and iconography, is a way in which the householders expressed their membership of a particular culture (affluent and 'Roman', like the group described in the quotation that opens Essay Four). Even the arrangement of the panels, concentrically and within a containing frame, reiterates the idea of a shared cultural experience, which is reinforced by the way in which the figures of Egypt and Africa turn slightly towards each other. Similarly, the 'provinces' are all dressed in the same fashion, rather like heroic figures in classical Greek art. This too suggests their shared cultural experience, expressed in traditional Graeco-Roman terms. There is nothing distinctive in that, yet it is clear from the variation in their hairstyles, attributes and head-dresses that some measure of distinctiveness is also meant to be an important part of the experience. This is particularly true for the figure of Rome, whose centrality to the whole cultural relationship is expressed by her position in the design.

In fact, the image can be summed up in terms of two issues which are at the heart of any search for culture, identity and power in the Roman world. One is cultural diversity within the empire; the second is the relationship of the central power (Rome) to societies on the periphery of the empire. Radiating out from these issues (somewhat like the configuration of the mosaic) is a series of further questions to do with identity, power and the practice of culture. These will be considered separately here to make their discussion clearer, although of course in historical reality they are closely interconnected: the social structures created in power relationships help to define cultural identity and determine how culture is expressed and practised. So, taking the mosaic as a starting point, let us look at some of the underlying questions.

Cultural diversity in the Roman empire

In the image of the mosaic the various 'provinces' appear to share a common culture (suggested by the overall setting, and by the dress they wear) but display some individual differences in their attributes. Visually, this produces a variety which is lively yet cohesive: all the differences are subsumed in the overall pattern and serve to enrich the group as a whole. But how far does this image represent the actual lived experience of cultural diversity in the Roman empire? Were different cultures treated as positively in reality as in the image, and how did they fit within the overall cultural framework of the empire? And what was the 'Roman' element in all this? Did the repeated representation of 'Africa' in the mosaics of this house mean that the owner felt particularly 'African', or perhaps 'Romano-African'?

These are complex questions, and in fact, as we shall see, Romans themselves may have been unable to answer them consistently. People experienced their identities in different ways, and what is more, many people can be described as 'Roman', from the inhabitants of Rome itself to Roman citizens who lived in far-flung provinces such as Syria or Britain. (This makes it hard to speak collectively of 'the Romans' as each time the particular group needs definition; but in this essay I use the term to refer to what in effect are the upper social strata of the city of Rome, and then from the first century AD onwards, of the empire.) In some parts of the Roman empire various cultures coexisted. This was true of the great cosmopolitan cities such as Rome (see Essay Three) and Alexandria, and especially in the east, where the legacy of Greek traditions inherited from the Hellenistic kingdoms which had succeeded Alexander overlay various local cultures (see Essay Eight). Jewish communities of the Diaspora, scattered as they were across the empire, experienced this pluralism in a different way, keeping their traditions within the wider Graeco-Roman cultural context (see Essay Eleven). In all these cases people would have demonstrated their cultural allegiances, consciously and unwittingly, by various means.

Representing shared values

So what are the means by which people demonstrate their membership of a particular culture, and how do they represent the values they share? Common language, religion, names, dress and diet are some of the media that spring to mind, but there are others which are fundamental and perhaps less obvious, such as ways of thinking about the world, and codes of morality and social behaviour: a key Roman social virtue, for instance, was *pietas* (a sense of dutiful obligation towards others), while 'ancestral custom' (*mos maiorum*) was much quoted in the early empire as a benchmark of social practice, harking back to a supposedly noble past.

Looking at the El Djem mosaic and its design, we can find some features that illustrate a range of these means. Firstly there is the role that the mosaic played in the overall design and decoration of the house. Floor mosaic was an expensive form of decoration and became something of a status symbol; and because it was used throughout most of the Roman world it was an effective way in which householders could associate themselves with others of similar tastes and standing across the empire (see Essay Four). The same could be said of the houses and their layout. They too were a way of articulating cultural values (indicating social status, for instance); we can look at them for influences of local traditions, as well as for design features that were more widely reproduced.

Secondly, there is the design of the mosaic itself: as noted in the opening description, its elements are carefully arranged in terms of a central feature and surrounding figures. With its alternation of full-length figures and busts this composition makes a pleasing impression, but its sum total is meant to be more than that: it aims to structure the relationship between the different features in such a way as to persuade the viewer of their conceptual relationship. This approach to design, as a means of giving order to experiences, could be described as 'rhetorical'. Rhetoric played a central role in the Graeco-Roman world of the élite and educated in shaping thought and expression, and although it was linked with the practice of oratory (and was a central element in ancient historiography and biography) it was not confined to the verbal arts, as this example shows. It was more than a matter of elaborate or persuasive phraseology; rather it was a way of representing experiences and events within some kind of moral or social framework – in short, a way of expressing some of the 'shared meanings' that underpinned the culture from which it sprang.

Thirdly, there are the representations of Rome and the provinces. The fact that female figures have been used here to stand for geographical and cultural entities is significant in the context of our questions about how cultural values are expressed. Personification was one of several options available to anyone trying to depict these places in the visual arts (or, indeed, in literature). Another solution would have been to represent the different places by landscapes, perhaps even rendered schematically in map-like compositions (as was commonly done in Roman depictions of Egypt and the Nile). But the choice of female figures is illuminating in what it reveals about the cultural background. Personifications of places or of social institutions, or even of particular vices and virtues, developed in the Hellenistic Greek world from the late fourth century BC, but they gained great popularity in Roman imperial art, where personifications of Rome, or Victory, or the Genius of the Roman People were frequently used. (Look at Figure 1.7, for example, the Gemma Augustea, which celebrates Augustus' rule by showing him with Rome and other figures, including the personifications of Earth and Ocean, which suggest the universality of his power.) These figures were almost always female, even when – as with the figure of Rome in the pavement – they were meant to signify 'male' qualities of military strength and prowess: in fact, the usual personification of *Virtus* (which literally means 'manliness', but translates more generally into 'courage' and 'conspicuous bravery') was a woman. Personifications of provinces were not uncommon in the context of imperial sculpture or coinage, where their obvious function was to reflect the nature of Roman rule; this meant that they were sometimes represented as captive subjects, but sometimes as apparently 'equal and free members of the Roman commonwealth' (Hannestad, 1986, p.197; cf. Smith, 1988).

What can be said of these figures, then, is that they show a particular mode of representing concepts that had a value commonly understood in the Graeco-Roman cultural tradition which became so much the culture of empire. This included a way of thinking about gender that allowed female figures to become effective symbols of certain 'male' qualities (like 'Rome' here) while at the same time suggesting a vulnerability (the provinces).

Finally, and remaining with these figures, we can look again at the use of dress to signify culture: like the various attributes (Egypt's Isis rattle, Rome's arms and armour, and so forth), the style of dress says something about the cultural associations to be made with these figures. In the El Djem mosaic it is rather a uniform garb, evocative perhaps of that worn by heroic characters in Graeco-Roman art, and so linking these figures to that status and cultural background. Headgear is used to the same effect: Rome's helmet shows her military power (Figure 1.2), Africa's cap is reminiscent of her wild beasts (Figure 1.3), the turreted crown evokes the strength of city states, and Sicily's symbol denotes the island's shape.

In fact, dress is an important way in which societies represent certain values: think of uniforms, badges, religious robes, academic hoods and gowns. Beyond its obvious basic protective function dress can carry symbolic meanings, to do with status, ethnicity or morality, for instance. This was certainly part of the Roman experience, where different types of toga, for example, were worn according to social status. The equivalent Greek robe, the *pallium* (or *himation* in Greek), had some conflicting connotations in Roman society. As it was traditionally associated with Greek philosophers some intellectual Romans apparently chose to wear it, usually in private, but here it appears in a portrait statue of the philhellene emperor Hadrian from Cyrene (Figure 1.4). Yet generally it was considered unsuitable to be worn by Romans, especially in the context of public business, because it represented all the negative qualities of self-indulgence and degeneracy which Romans pinned on the Greeks.

This example of the *pallium* and the different values attached to it by Romans is a reminder that objects in themselves are not intrinsically meaningful in cultural terms. All depends on the meanings that people give to them, and these may vary from one context to another. Reverting again to the representation on the mosaic, we can imagine how the image of Rome's relationship to the provinces (and particularly to the 'home' province of Africa) could have been read in quite

Figure 1.4   *Statue of Hadrian from Cyrene, c. AD 122. The British Museum. (© British Museum)*

different ways by different viewers, especially, say, by visiting Roman officials and local Africans. In this case, however, we have no hard evidence to prove this variation, but one subject on which diverse reactions survive in the ancient sources is the amphitheatre games. These games included fights between gladiators, wild beast shows and the execution of prisoners and criminals, and involved a good deal of death and violence. In evaluating them we may have to make our own cultural leap to understand them in the context of ancient values and not of ours. Gladiatorial combat seems to have begun in Roman society as a display of aristocratic valour, but by the time of the empire had been developed by the state as a means of expressing imperial power. In this context it is not hard to understand the executions, the displays of animals from far-flung parts of the empire, and even the seating arrangements (which were allocated according to social status) as symbols of state control (Wiedemann, 1992). Amphitheatre shows were hugely popular across the empire, although in the Greek-speaking east they seem to have found a place within a rather different set of communal values, to do with the local city rather than the empire as a whole (Woolf, 1994). But there is also evidence (largely from the writings of an educated élite) that some people objected to them, particularly for their dehumanizing effect on spectators, and for what this said about contemporary society. So although it is easy to point to the amphitheatre as a distinctive expression of Roman culture, it is impossible to define its ancient meaning in a single way: it has a multiplicity of possible values.

Multiplicity of values is also important to bear in mind as we turn now to consider individuals and their cultural identity.

Cultural identity: relative or essential?

The possibility that individuals have more than one identity in cultural terms should not surprise us, as we operate on this assumption from day to day. If identity can be described as a way of placing people – individuals and communities – within a particular cultural context, then it can involve various different modes of definition such as gender, race, age, social status, job or religion. People belong to several such categories at once; so a woman may be simultaneously wife, mother, lawyer, British-born Afro-Caribbean, and 'Thirtysomething', and see herself as all, or some, or none of these at any given moment. Furthermore, it is not just a case of how people see themselves, but how they are seen by others, particularly when those relationships cross cultural boundaries, and the perceived, or their perceivers, are 'insiders' or 'outsiders' of a cultural group. Thus a person may claim one identity but have another one (or more) imposed by other people's views. So in looking at cultural identity we meet with constantly changing or multiple definitions, and need to look carefully at the way they are expressed or signified. (Essay Five discusses examples of this from the Roman world.)

However, some fundamental aspects of identity, such as gender and ethnicity, have been seen as determined by various 'essential', non-negotiable factors (by biology, for instance), and not as relative to circumstances. This 'essentialist' or 'primordial' argument has often been used in discussions about the formation of identity, in present-day and historical societies, but it has now been largely superseded by the 'relational' view which, as Essay Six on gender shows, is clearly sustainable from the ancient evidence. In the Roman world, gender was far from being regarded as a constant determined by the 'given' of biological sex, but was treated instead as a fluid category, set partly by social context; certain types of situation or behaviour constructed identities as male or female, but even these could be overriden in the presence of other social hierarchies.

As for ethnicity, the essentialist argument has been important in some discussions of modern nationalism as it sees particular races or nations as distinct and objective entities, identified by observable physical characteristics and common cultural features (such as language, customs and beliefs: Renfrew, 1996, p.130). This view was also important in the 'culture history' generated by archaeologists who linked a particular material culture with a particular people (such as 'the Celts' and 'Celtic culture'; cf. Renfrew, 1996). But here too recent views of ethnic identity prefer to see it as relative to a given situation, being often constructed by the group's own definition of its ethnicity in opposition to others. Even so, the essentialist line continues to shape certain approaches to archaeology, particularly those which may have some nationalistic sub-agenda (Graves-Brown et al., 1996); and, as we shall see, it is partly behind arguments in the modern 'Romanization' debate, which tend to imply that there was a single homogeneous and identifiable 'Roman culture'.

But 'essentialism' is not just a modern view. There are also some indications of it in the Roman world: for instance, where indigenous groups claimed a distinctiveness in terms of their past, usually as a survival strategy in the face of a majority culture. They did so by promoting the myths attached to the foundation of their cities, depicting local gods or heroes in public ritual and art, such as Androclus at Ephesus. The relief from the city of Cyrene (Figure 1.5) shows the local nymph of the same name being crowned by Libya.[1] Another way indigenous groups could claim distinctiveness was to make much of their own cultural heritage, as did intellectuals in Greece and Asia Minor during the second century AD. In the movement known as the 'Second Sophistic', these intellectuals drew on many facets of the Greek cultural past – literary themes and styles, and antiquarianism – as if to reaffirm the identity of Greek culture in the face of the Roman empire (Bowie, 1974; Swain, 1996).

Even the Romans (who saw themselves as instigators of the 'global' culture) used the past to set out their essential right to rule. Divine

1 According to one myth Cyrene slew a lion which was terrorizing the kingdom of Libya and was rewarded with part of the territory. The Greek inscription below the scene reads: 'Making this dedication in token of great hospitality, Karpos placed over the architrave Cyrene, mother of cities and lion-slayer, crowned by Libya herself, who has the glory of being a third continent.'

ancestry, for instance, could give an unassailably strong and exclusive identity, and in the *Aeneid* Virgil set out Rome's legendary descent from the Trojan heroes, interweaving Rome's past, present and future to create the idea of a given role and identity. Leading individuals did it too: witness Augustus, who could trace his family back to the goddess Venus (Zanker, 1988).

In cases like these individual people or communities promoted their identity as 'given' to suit their particular purposes and situation. But was it a view that was generally held? As Essay Eleven will show in greater detail, the case of the Diaspora Jews is particularly interesting in this respect. In defining itself this minority culture placed a high value on observant behaviour (rather than birth); as a result its identity was surprisingly open and tolerant of outside influences. As for the majority cultures of Greece and Rome, a recent discussion of Greek identity in the Roman world made a relevant contrast between the two peoples:

> Romans did not conceive of their identity as underwritten by a unique language or a common descent in the same way that some others (including Greeks) did, and their traditions of origin stressed the progressive incorporation of outsiders. Roman identity was based to an unusual degree on membership of a political and religious community with common values and *mores* [that is, customs, morality and way of life]. Cultural change, especially acculturation, posed a special threat to a self-definition framed in those terms.
>
> (Woolf, 1994, p.120)

This is an interesting point: it suggests that while Greeks may have had an essentialist approach to their cultural identity, Romans defined themselves in a way which was potentially more inclusive of outsiders. Yet because it depended on the continuation of certain social codes and institutions, this self-definition could be jeopardized by the same outsiders if they brought too much cultural change with them. In the context of the Roman empire, with its many peoples, this was a very real threat to the traditional sense of identity originally formulated in the small community of the early city of Rome. So the question must be, how did Romans keep their own sense of identity distinct and preserve the integrity of their traditions?

One answer is that they evolved boundaries of various kinds, which essentially served to exclude foreign influences from particular traditional areas of their society and culture. In the city of Rome, expulsion was one method of exclusion: Jews, Isis-worshippers, actors, astrologers and philosophers were all at some time told to leave town when their presence was interpreted as presenting a particular threat. Other strategies preserved Roman values alongside imported practices by acting out a division between the two. For instance, Dionysius of

Figure 1.5   *Relief of Cyrene crowned by Libya, second century AD. The British Museum.*
(© *British Museum*)

Halicarnassus, writing at the end of the first century BC, observed that even in the celebration of foreign cults Romans still managed to preserve aspects of their own identity through practising their traditional rituals and refraining from 'foreign' behaviour: in the worship of the Phrygian Great Mother goddess (*Magna Mater*) a Roman magistrate performed Roman sacrifices and games in her honour, but her priests were Phrygian and no native-born Roman was allowed to walk in the procession (*Roman Antiquities* 2.19). And looking out to the wider context of empire, perhaps it would not be too far-fetched to see in the design of the El Djem mosaic another version of this practice. The 'foreignness' of the individual provinces is kept separate and peripheral to Rome in the circle of self-contained panels; this not only allows Rome to exercise control from the centre, but keeps any threat of cultural contamination at bay.

Perceiving identity

More clearly perhaps the mosaic illustrates well the point I made earlier about cultural identity being as much to do with the perceptions of other people as with one's own. It offers a Roman view of the provinces, as *included* in the culture of empire. Africa and Egypt (to take the most easily identified cases) are represented very much within the traditional Graeco-Roman artistic form of personifications, as women, with idealized features and wearing rather nondescript, classical dress; in this context their 'ethnic' features (Africa's symbolic elephant-skin head-dress and Egypt's dreadlocks and rattle) seem like a token concession to distinctiveness. They are being identified as exotic and distinctive entities, who have been brought 'inside' the orbit of Roman imperial culture and made to conform to a degree. This is particularly interesting to note in the case of Africa, since the other mosaic image of her found in the house emphasizes more 'ethnic' features by giving her corkscrew curls, large eyes, and darker skin (as described by Blanchard-Lemée et al., 1996, pp.19–22).

Other peoples were not so privileged, and elsewhere in Roman art and literature there are many examples where they are shown as 'barbarian outsiders'. Yet here again this is a Roman view, and one that paradoxically needed an 'uncivilized other' as a foil for the qualities of civilization which Romans wanted to claim for themselves. Roman writers identified peoples such as the Britons and the Germans with all the hallmarks of barbarity – wild habitat (that is to say, not in 'civilized' towns), fierce looks enhanced with body-paint, unsocialized practices such as wife-sharing and human sacrifice – yet at the same time drew them into the Roman concept of empire with its ideas of a 'civilizing' mission, and used them sometimes as a mouthpiece for their own dissent (see Essay Ten).

In a similar way Romans looked at Greeks and their civilization with ambivalence, relative to their particular interests and experiences. On one hand, they identified them with an ancient Greece, which was the source not only of high, classical culture (see Essay Four), but of civilization itself (Cicero, *Letter to his Brother Quintus* 1.1.27); yet on the other they berated Greek immigrants to Rome as full of vices (Pliny, *Natural History* 15.5) and a threat to traditional Roman virtues (Juvenal, *Satires* 3.62–118). In general Romans regarded Greek contemporaries as tending to bother only with their own concerns (Tacitus, *Annals* 2, 88, 4); and this seems to be borne out by the evidence. Greeks were often less than willing to identify with the culture of the Roman empire of which they were now part: some even went so far as to resist using official Latin terminology (Bowie, 1974, pp.200–01). Although some individual writers, such as Dionysius of Halicarnassus, Strabo, Plutarch and Appian, actively engaged with the existence of the Roman empire and could praise its virtues in relationship to Greek culture, few Greeks seem to have been interested in Latin literature, or Roman history, or even (until the mid second century) in holding high public office.

What these examples emphasize is how identities can be created and imposed according to different contexts; in other words they are relative to particular historical situations or viewpoints. Furthermore they are often expressed in terms of similarity and difference: Roman compared with barbarian or Greek, or, in the mosaic, one province compared with another. So much depends on the viewpoint, and here we have to remember just how much of the source material for our knowledge of the Roman empire offers the world-view of the élite Roman and Greek. There is little about how other peoples saw themselves, with the important exception of the Jews. This means that 'belonging' to particular cultural elements, or relative 'similarity' and 'difference', may be very much constructed in terms of the mainstream Graeco-Roman culture of the empire, according to a Roman imperial agenda. And inevitably the question of agenda does not stop there, as it also comes into interpretation of ancient events and images. It is a matter in which no one can really be objective and, indeed, as respectively reader and writer of this essay, you and I will bring our own identities to bear as we look for cultural identity in the ancient material.

Representing identity

Looking for identity as something shaped by context makes it important to consider the factors that affect its representation. Not only do we need to look for the kinds of signifiers that were discussed earlier (such as dress, names, food and beliefs) by which people are identified with one particular cultural group or another, but we also need to look at how these are used and why. For this reason representation and self-representation are important sources for studying identity in the Roman world because they are to do with perceptions of self and others; they also show the values claimed by a particular cultural identity, and show how an identity is (sometimes literally) constructed from a selection of particular features.

Probably the most useful place to look to understand this clearly is at the image of an emperor such as Augustus. Here all kinds of identity needed to be conveyed, from a physically recognizable individual, to religious leader, invincible soldier and merciful conqueror. The motive for such representation was primarily political, and to this end a whole series of set scenes or poses were evolved in art to identify unmistakably the emperor's roles and the particular virtues that were attached to them (cf. Figure 1.7). Variations in their usual iconography can indicate a preference for one identity over another; thus Hadrian was shown in Greek (rather than Roman) dress in Greek-speaking Cyrene (Figure 1.4), while Trajan was depicted in Egyptian style, subduing enemies of Greece, at the Temple of Khnum at Latopolis on the Nile (Bowman, 1996, Figure 25).

As these last two cases show, similarity and difference remain important themes to look for in the representation of identity. In the context of the overall culture of the Roman empire they can suggest the degree to which difference was seen as a quality to be noted and respected. Earlier on I noted how attributes were used to differentiate the figures on the El Djem mosaic in a limited but significant way. Representations of soldiers provide some more examples: scenes on Trajan's column (erected AD 113) show Roman soldiers from different units in their own distinctive dress, as if to represent the wide ethnic range contained within the Roman army. These images depict people included in the Roman world-view; for representations of those excluded it is necessary only to look back at the representation of 'barbarians' in the literature quoted earlier, or at some Roman military tombstones which show the soldiers as distinctly Roman, whatever their own ethnic background, but the conquered barbarians as long-haired, wild and often naked, as if they had no hope of a place in the civilized Roman world.

As the different images of the emperor showed, it is quite possible to represent multiple identity, either through a series of images which express different facets of the same person (portraits of Augustus provide an excellent example: Zanker, 1988), or through a combination of attributes or allusions within a single image. Representations in visual art have, inevitably, to indicate identity at a single point in time, and often resort to showing a hierarchy of symbols which signify the various different identities experienced by the individual in the course of life; so different features are included in the iconography or through inscriptions to extend the scope of the central image. This happens on many Egyptian mummy portraits of the Roman period, such as that of Artemidorus (Figure 4.2), where Greek, Roman and Egyptian elements are shown together but separated out as if to indicate the various cultural identities that had coexisted in his life.

In sum, looking for cultural identities in the Roman world almost inevitably opens up a world of relative definitions; when reading sources, written or material, it is important to notice details of representation and to understand the context. Ultimately, though, some things may elude us: does this portrait (Figure 1.6) show an individual (and if so who) or is it generic? Was it consciously shaping up a 'black' identity, and if so what might that imply? Is it a portrait of 'the other'? Or of someone perceived as belonging to a multi-ethnic empire?

Representations and power

When we look at the context of cultural representations and at their motives, power emerges as a key factor. It is present at almost every level. The El Djem mosaic shows this so vividly that it

Figure 1.6 Portrait of a man of African origin, first century AD. Boston Museum of Fine Arts. (Museum of Fine Arts, Boston, inv. no. 88.643, Benjamin Pierce Cheney Fund)

is worth looking at in detail. First of all the image depicts a power relationship between Rome and the provinces, articulating it by the radial design of the panels and in the iconography of the figures. Rome at the centre is the only figure who is armed, which illustrates her supreme military power. She carries an orb, the globe of the world, and her shield is decorated with the Medusa head, a motif with the power to ward off death and evil by its terrible gaze. But the power relationship is a two-way affair. Africa and Spain, in particular, had great economic power in respect of their exports of grain and oil to Rome (note the olive branch which the figure holds here) (see Essay Seven). The choice of this subject for the mosaic also expresses Rome's influence in the provinces, as experienced in the lives of rich householders like these: it shows the prestige attached to Graeco-Roman art and its images (to the extent that even the 'home' province of Africa is represented in these terms), and suggests that the patron may have drawn on this as a way of identifying himself with imperial culture and its connotations of power, rather than with anything local. Producing the mosaic was an act of power, involving patron and craftsman. Even the position of the room within the house would have had implications in terms of social power. Decorated with this impressive scene of political power, this room was probably a reception room in the more public part of the house where the owner as *patronus* (head of household) met and dealt with visiting *clientes* (dependents or retainers). In fact the 'social structure' of a Roman house can be seen as a way in which power relationships were articulated in terms of different social functions (Thébert, 1987). (The distinctions that can be established for many élite Roman houses serve as a reminder that 'public' and 'private' often operated differently in Roman culture from how they work in the West today.) The house itself can be set in a wider context of power, that of the owner's social status and influence (Essay Five) and of a flourishing economy in Rome and north Africa (Essay Seven). Finally, as an artefact that has survived for centuries, the mosaic is a reminder that it is usually material associated with the powerful that has lasted for our interpretation: the powerless in the ancient world are generally hard to trace in the surviving records.

This analysis of a single mosaic suggests that power is omnipresent as a factor in the creation of culture and identity, particularly where the context involves a set of social hierarchies or decisions to be made: who chose the mosaic, who saw it, and who paid for it all basically stem from power relationships. Looking at other sources would have added further examples: for instance, in the personal and domestic context, power relationships exist within the family structure, in the master–slave relationship, and even in the intimacy of sexual encounters where passivity and penetrability were regarded as defining gendered roles. The relationship of humans to the supernatural and elemental (such as the seasons and the weather) was experienced as an issue of power which required strategies for negotiation (see Essay Nine; and note too the sacrificing figure on the mosaic). And in interpreting the ancient past today, whether through written histories or museum displays, power is exercised in selecting and presenting the material. In short, power relationships condition the kind of culture that is created and the identities that people find for themselves within it.

But the specific historical context of the Roman empire adds another important collection of issues to do with power, particularly the power of the state and its institutions (such as the emperor, army and legislation). Not only does it mean that people get identified as 'rulers' or 'ruled', when they act in certain ways (seizing, imposing, resisting, losing or justifying power, for instance), but it throws into sharper focus the relationship between ideology and power (usefully summarized by Millett et al., 1995, p.2).

As we have already seen in our analysis of how it treats issues of culture and identity, the El Djem mosaic is a highly ideological statement. The image of the empire it constructs has Rome at the centre of a relationship in which various important provinces offer goods and services (if that is the meaning of the sacrificing figure). All this is contained within a definite boundary. Is this perhaps the world united in peace and civilization that Romans had seen as a justifying vision for their earlier expansionism (cf. Virgil, *Aeneid* 6.851–3; Pliny the Elder, *Natural History* 3.39)? Or does it perhaps celebrate the effects of peace won by war (see Essay Twelve), whereby provinces may flourish so long as Rome is at the centre? The fact that it was laid in a town house is perhaps also important when considering power structures in the Roman empire. Qualities symbolized by the city of Rome at the empire's centre (see Essay Three) were often replicated in towns and cities throughout the provinces, and in their civic institutions, formal culture and appearance, these communities articulated the central values of the empire and reinforced them in their locality: 'the city was both the major cultural construct and conveyancer of Roman imperialism abroad' (Whittaker, 1997, p.145; cf. Essay Eight). Certainly this can be seen elsewhere in Thysdrus (the Roman town at El Djem), which boasted an enormous amphitheatre like the Colosseum and many wealthy town houses with superb mosaics. Local élites could enjoy a 'Roman style' culture and so buy into the power and status it afforded them over the rest of the indigenous population. In fact, in the early days of the empire, this instinct for imitation, if not competition, was actively exploited by the Roman authorities as one of the ways in which they worked through local structures in a newly conquered territory, as Tacitus (*Agricola* 21) cynically observed in Britain. But by the second century AD, at the time this mosaic was laid, it was not so much a case of 'locals' imitating 'Romans' as élites across the empire sharing a similar culture (as argued in Essay Four).

A major problem with an artefact like the mosaic from El Djem, and the imagery it presents, is that it survives as evidence for one group in Roman society, while, as I said, the powerless within it are often voiceless in the ancient record. It would seem that this householder was happy to conform to the ideology of empire and accepted this rather 'public' subject matter in his private house, almost, it might seem, with pride. But conforming does not necessarily mean that there were no objections to the ideal, or no resistance; as Essay Ten will show, dissent from the empire could be couched in 'insider' terms. Perhaps it is possible to see the repetition of Africa in the two mosaics in the house as something more than local pride, especially since the other image puts her in the centre of the design, and emphasizes more her ethnic features, but this can only remain a very tentative suggestion. The fact remains that there is little clear evidence for the reactions of other peoples in the Roman empire (apart from the Greeks and the Jews) to the cultural power of the empire; for the majority it represented something to be taken up, copied, and used for their own purposes of expression.

At this point in the essay I want to move away from the mosaic to take a wider view of two particular issues. One is the question of Romanization, which follows on from some of the matters of power which we have just been considering, and the other is the way time and space relate to some of these aspects of culture, identity and power.

Romanization

Earlier I offered a definition of 'Romanization' as the process whereby Roman culture spread to other areas. At that point only a simple explanation was needed, but its words were carefully chosen. For the fact is that 'Romanization' is quite a problematic term, and though invented to facilitate the interpretation of ancient material, it needs to be approached with caution; yet the dynamic of cultural change which it seeks to express is central to any discussion of culture, identity and power in the empire (cf. Woolf, 1998, pp.13–16).

The first difficulty is that scholars use the term in different ways. Some use it to describe more the processes by which local peoples assimilated Roman culture (cf. Hingley, 1997, p.84), while others reserve it more for the final outcome. It can be used to mean some two-way process: 'We must see Romanization as a process of dialectical change, rather than the influence of one "pure" culture upon others' (Millett, 1990, p.1). Or it can be seen more as a move in a single direction: 'Romanization is generally applied to all those processes whereby diverse indigenous peoples were either incorporated in or aligned themselves with the Roman Empire' (Barrett, 1997, p.51). Others ask how far 'romanization was deliberate and how much an accidental by-product of Roman conduct, resulting from actions like the imposition of a taxation system' (Millett et al., 1995, p.3). Some may concentrate on its economic facets, others on such aspects as literacy, ideology, or the spread of Graeco-Roman culture from the élites.

The second is a much more substantial problem. Implicit in the idea of Romanization (however it is used) is some notion that there was a homogeneous 'Roman' culture, and that this culture was both superior (in strength and quality) to the indigenous cultures it encountered, and has some unmistakable characteristics which can be found in the surviving evidence (see Freeman, 1993 and 1997). But this view of

Roman culture has become outmoded in many respects: there is now greater awareness of how diverse it was, and how different provinces responded to it in different ways and at different times. Questions are now being asked, for instance, about how far 'Romanization' was an underlying purpose of Roman expansion, what the signs of resistance to it were, what its negative effects were, and how much variation is to be found across the empire (is what happens in the north-western provinces, for instance, at all useful for understanding the very different situation in the Greek east?). (See, for example, Woolf, 1994, 1995, 1998; Webster and Cooper, 1996; Mattingly, 1997). Any answers to these questions have to acknowledge nuances and variations in cultural situations, and this is where close analysis of the evidence, written as well as material, becomes so important: observations at grass-roots level across the empire build up a wider picture and offer a productive way to proceed. But there is now a question mark hanging over the usefulness of the concept of Romanization, with its absolute tones, as a model for considering cultural change initiated by the Roman empire: can it provide a way of understanding the relationship between local provincial cultures and Rome?

At the heart of the concept of 'Romanization' is the question: was a Rome-centred culture imposed on provinces, or was it spread by locals, from below? Certainly a large amount of material survives across the empire which is to do with what might be termed 'official Roman culture' or 'imperial culture'; and it is not unreasonable to ask whether this could be seen as a 'homogeneous Roman culture' operating within a process of 'Romanization'. It involves the army, civil institutions (religious, legal and administrative) and their buildings and ceremonies, town planning and facilities such as baths and amphitheatres, as well as tokens of the imperial presence in the form of honorific statues, cult centres and coinage. It was underpinned by economic systems (see Essay Seven) and communication networks (see Essay Two).

Although 'Romanization' is itself a modern term, various ancient writers seem to describe a similar process (though usually for reasons of their own), with elements like these brought by Rome. Tacitus represents the introduction of such a lifestyle and its seductive 'improvements' as a deliberate aspect of Roman policy, at least in the case of newly conquered Britain (*Agricola* 21), while the sophist Aelius Aristides of Smyrna, writing later in the second century and from a very different part of the empire, eulogized the benefits and prosperity brought by Rome to reinvigorate the ancient cities of Asia Minor. But it would be wrong to see all these features as imposed by Roman authorities on the local communities. Many were created by local leaders themselves, albeit in the Roman vein: at Aphrodisias in Asia Minor, for instance, two local families were responsible for erecting an imperial shrine, with its images of emperors alongside scenes of classical mythology (Smith, 1987), just as at Olympia Herodes Atticus built a large fountain, decorated with portraits of the imperial as well as his own family (Vermeule, 1977, p.84). (And the householder at El Djem used an 'official' Roman theme for his floor mosaic.) This pattern of imitation (*aemulatio*) is another factor in the complex processes of assimilation and acculturation, whereby local élites adopted for themselves some of the Roman practices, giving them further currency.

But despite the apparent similarity of much of what survives in the material record across the Roman world, behind it lies a diversity of actual cultural experience (as we have glimpsed). Some of this was inherent in the central 'Roman' culture itself: not only did it involve much that was and had been Greek, but it was regularly affected by the local cultures with which it was in contact across the empire (see Essay Four). It often reached more peripheral regions through intermediate provinces or via the army, thus passing through various cultural filters en route, and processes like this led to the development of 'hybrid' cultures. The same 'Roman' institutions might be invested with rather different cultural values in different places: for instance, in the Greek-speaking eastern part of the empire, the emperor cult was linked much more to a local civic context than to central Roman ideology (Price, 1984). Furthermore, some areas must have always remained multicultural in background despite being officially 'Roman'; these would include the great city of Rome itself, and military communities in forts such as those on Hadrian's Wall, where the 'Roman' soldiers in fact came from many lands.

It could be argued, then, that this 'centralized' imperial culture was more diverse than it might at first appear, and there are further arguments to be made as to how far it was actually imposed on the provinces (cf. Whittaker, 1997; Webster, 1997). A complicating factor is that it is so often difficult to establish the experiences of the local communities faced with this intervention: did they accept it, or resist, passively or actively? How can we tell? The sources usually show the Roman perspective (even when, like Tacitus, they purport to be addressing local reactions), and for some parts of the empire the evidence is sparser than others. This can be tantalizing for places such as Britain where the surviving evidence is primarily material, but for the eastern empire there is a good deal of evidence from literature (overt and otherwise) about Greek reactions to being in the Roman empire. For instance, it has been suggested that various religious cults based in the eastern Greek world were developed partly to counteract the propagation of the imperial cult across those areas (Elsner, 1997, p.189).

From both sides, then, the overall picture involved in 'Romanization' is complex. What is clear, though, is that a number of different processes was involved, whereby Romans and locals adjusted in varying degrees to each other's cultures. Obviously there was some direct assimilation. But there are many signs that the cultural changes were not always just a one-way process, with locals taking on, for example, Roman cultural symbols. Romans too picked up on local characteristics, as is shown by their receptivity to local institutions (such as the dedications to local gods on Hadrian's Wall). Cultural contacts and exchanges of this kind must have served to build up the differentiated cultural patterns of the empire, producing a characteristic flexibility.

Time and space

This variability in the culture of the Roman empire makes it especially important to note the role of time and place in shaping change and diversity. So, to conclude, here are some brief comments and questions which they raise, as so far most of the themes and examples in this essay have been treated synchronically.

One of the major factors to note in relation to place is the cultural division between east and west of the empire. Not only did they use different languages (Greek in the east and Latin in the west), but they had different cultural histories, and were confronted by different experiences in their provinces. The north-west, for instance, contained territories which had had only limited experience of Graeco-Roman culture before their conquest, while the Greek east included many cities, ancient in their foundation, which flourished anew under the Roman empire. It is also important to remember so far as 'Romanization' is concerned that the cultural division was not just an issue for peripheral regions, but had affected Italy itself.

Then there is the relationship of the city of Rome to the rest of the empire: just as immigrants moved to it, attracted by its promise of wealth and power (Seneca, *Consolation of Helvia* 2.6), so others travelled out from it on various kinds of business. And when emperors themselves came from places other than Rome, how did that affect the capital and their home province? 'The city of Rome – capital and symbol' is the topic of Essay Three, which looks at realities and ideologies that underlay this critical relationship.

One of the key issues to consider regarding time is periodization, or how we divide past time into 'significant' periods, and what implications and consequences follow from this. A classic way of doing this for the empire has been in terms of the reigns of emperors, and is useful even now (see the list of key dates at the beginning of this volume). This approach was shaped very much by available ancient sources (Wells, 1992, p.31), but it also fitted in with a modern style of writing history that privileged events in political or military history. Of course, it can be justified as a way of writing the political history of the Roman empire, since different emperors seemed to have had different interests in the empire at various times, as in its military defence, or in defining its limits; and sometimes these did affect cultural developments (witness Hadrian's philhellenism). Yet by and large these reigns are not really appropriate in looking for culture, identity and power as they are irrelevant to most of the source material. Perhaps a more effective way is to chart chronological developments as they occur in particular areas of the empire and then cross-relate them. For instance, one general picture that this might produce would suggest that two particular periods – in

Figure 1.7 *The Gemma Augustea, cameo, first century* AD. *Kunsthistorisches Museum, Vienna.*

the late first century BC and the mid second century AD – saw a formative momentum in developing the culture of empire (Woolf, 1995; Whittaker, 1997, p.158).

These are some issues for real time and space; but the Roman empire also operated in their symbolic dimensions. The ambiguity of the great phrase 'empire without end' (*imperium sine fine*) promised to the Romans by Jupiter in the *Aeneid* blurs the end of time and space, and this reinforces the concept of universality which was so potent in Roman imperial imagery. It celebrated aims and achievement, and was repeated time and again in official and in private spheres. In the cameo shown in Figure 1.7, the emperor Augustus is depicted among the gods and cosmic personifications, presiding over a Roman triumph that was, it is implied, unending.

What the El Djem mosaic shows, however, is that as the real time of the Roman empire moved on, the image of Rome at the centre of the world might remain, but surrounded now by other parts of the empire with their own distinctive cultural identities, albeit contained in the context of imperial power (cf. Smith, 1987, especially pp.76–7). Culture, identity and power remain inextricably interconnected even though the way they are represented may shift over time. Tracing movements like these requires close attention to the ancient sources, and the essays that follow combine this with discussion of wider questions and contexts.

References

BARRETT, J.C. (1997) 'Romanization: a critical comment' in Mattingly (ed.) pp.51–64.

BLANCHARD-LEMÉE, M., ENNAÏFER, M., SLIM, H. and SLIM, L. (1996) *Mosaics of Roman Africa* (trans. K.D. Whitehead), London, British Museum Press (first published in France (1995) as *Sols de l'Afrique romaine*, Imprimerie nationale éditions).

BOWIE, E.L. (1974) 'Greeks and their past in the Second Sophistic' in M.I. Finley (ed.) *Studies in Ancient Society*, London, Routledge and Kegan Paul, pp.166–209.

BOWMAN, A. (1996) *Egypt after the Pharaohs 332 BC–AD 642: From Alexander to the Arab Conquest*, London, British Museum Press.

ELSNER, J. (1997) 'The origins of the icon: pilgrimage, religion and visual culture in the Roman east as "resistance" to the culture' in S.E. Alcock (ed.) (1997) *The Early Roman Empire in the East*, Oxford, Oxbow Monograph 95, pp.178–99.

FREEMAN, P.W.M. (1993) ' "Romanisation" and Roman material culture', *Journal of Roman Archaeology*, 6, pp.438–45.

FREEMAN, P.W.M. (1997) 'Mommsen through to Haverfield: the origins of Romanization studies in late nineteenth-century Britain' in Mattingly (ed.) pp.27–50.

GRAVES-BROWN, P., JONES, S. and GAMBLE, C. (eds) (1996) *Cultural Identity and Archaeology: the Construction of European Communities*, London and New York, Routledge.

HALL, S. (ed.) (1997) *Representation: Cultural Representations and Signifying Practices*, London and Thousand Oaks, Open University and Sage.

HANNESTAD, N. (1986) *Roman Art and Imperial Policy*, Jutland Archaeological Society Publications, XIX, Aarhus University Press.

HINGLEY, R. (1997) 'Resistance and domination: social change in Roman Britain' in Mattingly (ed.) pp.81–102.

JONES, S. and GRAVES-BROWN, P. (1996) 'Introduction: archaeology and cultural identity in Europe' in Graves-Brown et al. (eds) pp.1–24.

MATTINGLY, D.J. (ed.) (1997) *Dialogues in Roman Imperialism: Power, Discourse, and Discrepant Experience in the Roman Empire*, Journal of Roman Archaeology Supplementary Series no.23, Portsmouth, Rhode Island, Journal of Roman Archaeology.

METZLER, J., MILLETT, M., ROYMANS, N. and SLOFSTRA, J.(eds) (1995) *Integration in the Early Roman West: the Role of Culture and Ideology*, Dossiers d'archéologie du musée national d'histoire et d'art, IV, Luxembourg.

MILLETT, M. (1990) *The Romanization of Britain: an Essay in Archaeological Interpretation*, Cambridge, Cambridge University Press.

MILLETT, M., ROYMANS, N. and SLOFSTRA, J. (1995) 'Integration, culture and ideology in the early Roman west' in Metzler et al. (eds) pp.1–5.

PRICE, S. (1984) *Rituals and Power: the Roman imperial cult in Asia Minor*, Cambridge, Cambridge University Press.

RENFREW, C. (1996) 'Prehistory and the identity of Europe, or, don't let's be beastly to the Hungarians' in Graves-Brown et al. (eds) pp.125–37.

SMITH, R.R.R. (1987) 'The imperial reliefs from the Sebasteion at Aphrodisias', *Journal of Roman Studies*, 77, pp.88–138.

SMITH, R.R.R. (1988) '*Simulacra gentium*: the *Ethne* from the Sebasteion at Aphrodisias', *Journal of Roman Studies*, 78, pp.50–77.

SWAIN, S. (1996) *Hellenism and Empire: Language, Classicism and Power in the Greek World, AD 50 – AD 250*, Oxford, Clarendon Press.

THÉBERT, Y. (1987) 'Private life and domestic architecture in Roman Africa: some theoretical considerations' in P. Veyne (ed.) *A History of Private Life. I: From Pagan Rome to Byzantium* (trans. A. Goldhammer), Cambridge, Mass., The Belknap Press of Harvard University Press, pp.319–23.

VERMEULE, C.C. (1977) *Greek Sculpture and Roman Taste: the Purpose and Setting of Graeco-Roman Art in Italy and the Greek Imperial East* (Jerome Lectures, Twelfth Series) Ann Arbor, University of Michigan Press.

WEBSTER, J. (1997) 'A negotiated syncretism: readings in the development of Romano-Celtic religion' in Mattingly (ed.) pp.165–84.

WEBSTER, J. and COOPER, N. (eds) (1996) *Roman Imperialism: Post-colonial Perspectives*, Leicester Archaeology Monographs no.3.

WELLS, C. (1992) *The Roman Empire*, Fontana History of the Ancient World (second edition, first published 1984), London, Fontana.

WHITTAKER, C.R. (1994) *Frontiers of the Roman Empire: a Social and Economic Study*, Baltimore and London, Johns Hopkins University Press.

WHITTAKER, C.R. (1997) 'Imperialism and culture: the Roman initiative' in Mattingly (ed.) pp.143–63.

WIEDEMANN, T. (1992) *Emperors and Gladiators*, London and New York, Routledge.

WOOLF, G. (1994) 'Becoming Roman, staying Greek: culture, identity and the civilizing process in the Roman East', *Proceedings of the Cambridge Philological Society*, 40, pp.116–43.

WOOLF, G. (1995) 'The formation of Roman provincial cultures' in Metzler et al. (eds) pp.9–18.

WOOLF, G. (1998) *Becoming Roman: the Origins of Provincial Civilization in Gaul*, Cambridge, Cambridge University Press.

ZANKER, P. (1988) *The Power of Images in the Age of Augustus* (trans. A. Shapiro), Ann Arbor, University of Michigan Press.

Essay Two
Communicating culture, identity and power

BY RICHARD MILES

Any study which takes communication as its main focus finds itself faced with the problem of definition. This is summed up very neatly in the introduction to Sian Lewis' book *News and Society in the Greek Polis*:

> When the project was still in its early stages as a D. Phil thesis, my supervisor Robin Osborne warned me against using the term 'communication' in any description of the project, because, as he said, 'Communication is about everything'.
>
> (Lewis, 1996, p.vii)

Everything that we profess to know about the past has been articulated in some way, whether it be a text that has been written, a fresco that has been painted, or a pot that has been manufactured. A process of communication has taken place on one or more levels.

Human communication can be summarily defined as a basic social function that ultimately involves interaction between two or more persons. It may develop through both verbal and non-verbal symbols, and usually aims to influence another's beliefs or behaviour. Communication involves at least two basic concepts: the articulation of ideas and their transmission. The communication process involves: 'Who?' 'Says what?' 'How?' 'To whom?' 'With what effect?'

This volume has been organized around culture, identity and power. It is therefore important that we begin by exploring the complex set of relationships that exist between these terms and communication.

Remembering Philopappos

Sometime between AD 114 and 116, the funerary monument of an important Roman citizen was completed on an imposing hill which overlooked much of Athens, the city which he had made his home. The tomb itself was a most impressive structure: on a clear day it was visible from several miles outside the city. Indeed, the uppermost part of the tomb was higher than the urban acropolis itself. Built on a platform, it

Figure 2.1 *The funerary monument of Philopappos, Athens. (Photo: Craig and Marie Mauzy)*

was a fine two-storey structure. The first storey was covered with a magnificent frieze depicting what the dead man must have considered to be the most prestigious event of his life, his inauguration as consul in Rome a few years previously. The upper storey, divided into three parts by four Corinthian pilasters, contained a seated portrait of the dead man, flanked on either side by seated portraits of his paternal grandfather and another distinguished ancestor (Kleiner, 1986, pp.12–14).

There is nothing unusual in the description above. Many impressive funerary monuments commemorating important Roman officials were set up throughout the empire, although this particular tomb's exclusive location within the city walls and magnificent construction would have set it slightly apart.

What makes this monument a particularly suitable case study for the often complex relationship between communication and constructions of culture, identity and power in the Roman empire is that the man commemorated was Roman consul (the highest Roman magistracy), Athenian archon (the highest magistracy in democratic Athens, although by this time it bestowed no real power), dispossessed ruler of a small kingdom in Asia Minor and god. All of these cultural influences, identities and positions of power are represented on his tomb.

Philopappos was a grandson of Antiochus IV, the last reigning monarch of Commagene, a small kingdom in eastern Anatolia, west of the Euphrates river between Cappadocia and Syria. Commagene was annexed by Rome in AD 72, but earlier good relations between the two meant that the emperor Vespasian brought Antiochus IV and his family to Greece and then to Rome with the due honour that befitted their status. Philopappos himself enjoyed a high position in society because of his noble birth. In Rome, he was admitted into the senate by the emperor Trajan and was appointed consul in AD 109. Later Philopappos moved to Athens, where he was made an honorary citizen and was also appointed to the senior honorific position of archon (Kleiner, 1986, p.11). Although he was destined never to reign over Commagene, his circle of friends continued to address him as 'King Philopappos' (Plutarch, *Table Talk* 1.10.628; *How to Tell a Flatterer from a Friend* 27, 32, 59, 76).

It would be easy to dismiss the funerary monument of Philopappos as some kind of freakish anomaly. In many ways his ancestry and the positions that he held make him a unique figure. However, many of the observations that can be made concerning the construction and representation of culture, identity and power on this startling monument are applicable to countless more mundane examples across the Roman empire. Let us now look more closely at the narratives presented by the tomb of Philopappos.

The inscriptions, sculpture and frieze on the monument offer what on the surface would seem to be a plethora of contradictory images. On the upper storey a colossal seated portrait shows Philopappos in heroic nudity in the Greek tradition. He is flanked by a portrait on his left of his grandfather, the last reigning monarch, Antiochus IV, and on his right by king Seleucus Nicator, founder of the Hellenistic Seleucid empire, with whom he claimed distant kinship. Here it would seem the viewer is confronted with Philopappos, king of Commagene. However, on the lower storey of the monument there is a frieze which presents a striking contrast to the images above. Philopappos the Roman consul stands in a four-horse chariot, clad in a Roman tunic and toga and

Figure 2.2 *Eighteenth-century drawing of the restored view of the façade of the funerary monument of Philopappos, Athens. From J. Stuart and N. Revett,* The Antiquities of Athens, *1762. (Photo: The University of Sheffield)*

accompanied by his official entourage. In his left hand he holds a sceptre, with his right he makes a salute. The picture is further complicated by the fact that there is not a straightforward distinction between the 'Commagenian' upper storey and 'Roman' lower storey. Each of the images has stylistic idiosyncrasies which further complicate the picture. For instance, the portrait of Philopappos' grandfather, the last king of Commagene, has him dressed in the tunic and toga of a Roman magistrate. Even more extraordinary is the portrayal of Philopappos wearing a rayed crown, which denoted divinity, on the consular frieze. It would have been absolutely unthinkable for a Roman consul to wear such a thing: only the imperial family had the chance of divinity. His chariot is ornamented with a statue of the demi-god Hercules, with whom the kings of Commagene had long associated themselves. In this scene Philopappos was not only demonstrating his investiture as Roman consul as the highpoint of his career, but was also directly proclaiming that he had not lost sight of his ancestry and his right to divinity as king of Commagene (Kleiner, 1986, pp.12–17).

The inscriptions on the tomb also add to this richly diverse set of narratives. There are five inscriptions on the monument (if you discount those left by modern day lovelorn Athenian teenagers), four in Greek and one in Latin. Below the central niche housing the seated portrait of Philopappos, a Greek inscription reads 'Philopappos, son of Epiphanes, of the Deme [voting tribe] Besa'. This is an articulation of Philopappos' honorary citizenship of the city of Athens and indicates the high status which made such a conferral possible. A Latin inscription on the left pilaster gives his Roman titles: 'Caius Iulius Antiochus Philopappus, son of Caius, of the Fabian tribe, Consul and Arval brother, admitted to the Praetorian rank by the emperor Caesar Nerva Trajan Optumus Augustus Germanicus Dacicus'. A Greek inscription proclaims his Commagenian birthright: 'King Antiochos Philopappos, son of King Epiphanes, son of Antiochos'. Two other Greek inscriptions give the names of his grandfather and his illustrious Hellenistic ancestor respectively underneath their portraits (Kleiner, 1992, pp.233–5).

The monument itself contains elements of Greek, Commagenian and Roman styles. Its lofty position and artistic representations of ancestors and companion deities correspond with royal funerary monuments in Commagene. However, the concave façade of the building and the design of its frieze parallel Roman designs for commemorative arches and city gates, the most striking being the arch of the emperor Titus, built sometime after his death in AD 81. Again, this architectural parallel is not as straightforward as it first seems. The arch of Titus, which commemorated the emperor's victorious campaigns in Judaea, must have had particular resonance for a Commagenian prince as his father and uncle had both assisted Titus in that war (Kleiner, 1986, p.15). (See Figure 11.9 for one of the reliefs on the arch of Titus.)

Philopappos' tomb, with its Roman, Commagenian and Greek influences, is not some whimsical 'mix and match' made up of elements gleaned from secure cultural locations. Rather, it indicates that all cultures are involved in one another: rather than being single and pure, all are hybrid and heterogeneous (Said, 1993, pp.xix, 15 and 262; Wintle, 1996, p.6). 'Culture' has been described as an ever-changing construct, a multifarious mental conditioning which is communicated through oral transmission, gesture and text (García, 1993, p.67). In the case of Philopappos' funerary monument we are concerned with text. For our purposes the term 'text' includes other forms of visual media as well as writing. These texts not only reflect but also add to the cultural traditions that spawned them. With the funerary monument of Philopappos, architecture, art and writing combine to form a 'world' with its own particular parameters and dynamic. What this tells us is that culture is produced *performatively*, as narrative, in a constant state of contestation, revision and reformation (Bhabha, 1990, pp.296–7; 1994, p.2).

The fact that Philopappos can represent himself as a Roman consul, an Athenian archon, a Commagenian king and even a god on the same monument shows that identity is a constructed rather than a fixed reality. Consequently, the formation and assertion of identity is fundamentally about *power*, the power to *represent*, and representation is obviously intrinsically linked to communication. Philopappos can be an important Roman dignitary, a citizen of Athens, a Commagenian king and a god because he has the means to articulate himself as such, both in writing and in visual imagery on his tomb. In other words, his identity can only be represented through communication.

Philopappos' funerary monument clearly indicates that the creation and wielding of power relies predominantly on its *representation*. Although in many cases it would be true to say that the writing and images on such monuments would not have been visible to the viewer on the ground (this is discussed later), this does not negate either the author's desire to represent himself and others, or the symbolic authority derived from the creation of text or its size and magnificence. The inscriptions, sculptures and friezes on the tomb clearly indicate the importance of written and visual images in the construction and representation of power.

The use of different languages on the monument not only represents Philopappos' construction of his own identity, but also denotes clear delineations in the way that his power is represented. When articulating the power that he held in the Roman state, Philopappos used the Latin language even though the monument stood in a Greek-speaking area of the empire. He reverts back to his native Greek when describing his prestigious honorary citizenship of Athens and his kingship of Commagene.

Much the same can be said about the names recorded on the monument. The names and titles of the emperor who bestowed the consulship on Philopappos show in clear terms how the past was used to justify the present. The legitimacy of Trajan's power is emphasized through the use of the titles Caesar, Optumus and Augustus and the inclusion of the name of his adoptive father, the emperor Nerva. His military achievements in extending the power of Rome over new areas are also included in his nomenclature (Germanicus and Dacicus). The nomenclature and titles associated with Philopappos and his family also emphasize the importance of language in the representation of identity and power. Whereas in the inscription proclaiming his citizenship of Athens it was deemed sufficient to include his Greek name and the name of his father, Epiphanes, the inscription that addresses his kingship of Commagene not only prefixes his own name with 'king' but also adds the name of his grandfather, the last monarch of that kingdom, to that of his father. However, the most striking contrast is between the Greek inscriptions and the Latin one; here both Philopappos' and his father's names are 'Romanized'. Not only is this a construction of a very different type of identity, but the configuration of power that is represented is unlike that found in the Greek inscriptions. In an arrangement typical of Roman nomenclature, Philopappos' Latin name contains the names of the emperor who had bestowed Roman citizenship on his family; his father's name is recorded simply as Gaius, with no mention of his Commagenian/Greek name. Their Commagenian ancestry is ignored: only the Roman tribe that they belonged to is named. The high rank and priesthood that Philopappos had attained in Rome are recorded, but what is made clear at the end of the inscription is that these honours were obtained under the patronage of the Roman emperor, Trajan. Consequently, although the inscription portrays Philopappos as a powerful man, at the same time it displays the superior power of the Roman emperor himself.

The dominant position of the emperor in the Latin inscription on the funerary monument of Philopappos raises another important point, namely that the creation and wielding of power relies to a great extent on the ability to control the means of communication. Power is attained by placing limits on the creation and reception of information. These include restrictions on those with the skills to use communication media, on access to and possession of texts, and on the legitimate uses that the written and spoken word can be put to.

The invocation of this power can be both implicit and explicit. Philopappos' choice of his elevation into the Roman consulship as the subject of the frieze on his funerary monument – with its explicit reference to the triumph scenes on the arch of Titus in Rome, the representation of his grandfather, the last king of Commagene, in Roman tunic and toga, and the Latin inscription that charts his political career – is significant. These were as much a recognition of the political realities of the age as was the fact that 'king' Philopappos no longer had a kingdom to rule. Power is often wielded by changing the way that texts are created and language is used. Political authorities might simply make it impossible to participate in political, social or economic life without acquiring some form of linguistic competence in the language of the ruler.[1] Power exercised *over* the creation, dissemination and reception of channels of communication allows power to be exercised *through* those very same media. Art, architecture, written text and speech are all useful tools with which to legitimize power.

Communication, however, is always a two-way process. Power often involves imposing an *authorized* reading of such texts and images as have been made available. This authorized reading will always be ranged against the power of its receivers to generate new interpretations. By creating new meanings, the languages and images of the ruler can also be a source of power for the ruled. So through the same set of channels we are able to witness not only the configuration of different forms of power, but also *resistance* to it (Said, 1993, p.253). Philopappos, although an individual who had held high office in the Roman imperial administration, was also, as the Greek-speaking dispossessed ruler of a small kingdom in Asia Minor which had been converted into a Roman province, part of the subjugated 'other'. Hence it is illuminating and perhaps somewhat gratifying to see that most Roman of scenes, the consular procession, being subverted by the image of Philopappos, with his rayed crown and his ornamented chariot, laying claim to divine status as befitted a Commagenian monarch.

The power of the written word

The modern world is inconceivable without the written word, the illiterate is excluded. Illiteracy, in a culture so dependent on the accumulated wisdom of books, is tantamount to backwardness and barbarism. For most people who read with complete ease, the application and uses of writing seem obvious and inevitable (so inevitable that it is difficult to imagine a world where they are not central).

(Thomas, 1992, p.2)

1 For a useful discussion of the relationship between power and the written media, see Bowman and Woolf, 1994, pp.6ff.

As students of the ancient world we are all confronted by the mirage that is the written word. In terms of verbal communication only the written and not the spoken word survives. The spoken word only survives at all because it has been *written down.*

One question that we need to address is the extent to which literacy as a technology helps to define culture and the construction of identity and power. (We will explore just what we mean by 'literacy' later in this essay.) How far is literacy an agent of change? During the twentieth century the dominant academic discourse has been one that maintains that the presence of literacy is the single most determining factor for logical and scientific thought, bureaucracy, the modern state and law.[2] The classical world has been an important case study for the propagation of such ideas. In their seminal article 'The consequences of literacy', Goody and Watt (1968) argue that literacy must be seen as the main reason why Ancient Greece produced democracy, rational thought, philosophy and historiography.

However, there has been a move away from these determinist models of literacy to models which see literacy as much more fluid, its uses, implications and effects being largely determined by the habits and beliefs of the society already in place.[3] In other words, literacy does not change society, but rather is changed by the societies on which it is imposed.

As will become clear in our case study of the Roman empire, neither stance is satisfactory in that although literacy is not a single definable skill with definite uses and predictable results, it can act to either *exaggerate* or *minimize* certain facets of a society (Bowman and Woolf, 1994, pp.3–4). Literacy is not a universal tool above culture, but is itself conditioned by culture and is therefore inseparable from the education that accompanies it. I now want to take a closer look at the role of writing in Roman constructions of culture, identity and power.

The emperor

For the emperor, the representation of his power was as important in the maintenance of his rule as passing laws and commanding armies. The written word played a central role in this process. Text was also an essential medium in the actual governing of the empire, for the emperor exercised power over his absent subordinates mainly through correspondence, and used texts on a large scale to deal with his subjects. In addition, most of the information that he received about the army, about revenues, and about all affairs outside Rome was transmitted

2 See, for example, Goody, 1986.

3 For a useful discussion of this see Thomas, 1992, pp.15–28.

through writing. Without a wide diffusion of writing, political and administrative control of the empire would have been impossible. So to a great extent imperial power rested on the successful use and control of the written word.

Knowledge is power; the emperor, therefore, needed to maintain well-structured channels to maintain the flow of information to and from the imperial palace. Official channels of information had first been set up by Julius Caesar during his consulship of 59 BC, with the establishment of official transcripts of the meetings of the senate and other records of public affairs, important speeches and processes. Under the emperor these records were used to strengthen his hold on power: births, marriages, deaths, and other events such as accidents, numbers in the circus, eclipses and new buildings in the city of Rome were now officially registered. It is doubtful that this information was used in any practical way, but its significance lies in the emperor's monopoly of information that it represents. This control is well illustrated by the temporary suspension of the senatorial records by Augustus (Tacitus, *Annals* 16.22.8).

It was important that the emperor stayed in constant contact with the senatorial élite, and the most effective way to achieve this was through a network of communications of which he was the hub. This was particularly important when he was away from Rome. Nero discovered a plot against him while away on a musical tour of Greece only because a freedman, Helius, wrote to inform him (Suetonius, *Nero* 23). When in Rome the emperor would still communicate through the written word with the senate even though he could have talked to them in person (see 'Tiberius' in Cassius Dio, *Roman History* 63.21; 'Nero' in Cassius Dio, *Roman History* 62.33). This was because of the permanence and legitimation afforded by the written word. When Hadrian had been proclaimed emperor by his troops in Syria, he wrote a letter to the senate asking them to confirm his position and authority also by letter (Cassius Dio, *Roman History* 79). It was through the written word that the emperor could enlist and maintain support for his rule; and members of the imperial household could exert power by withholding information. During the principate, along with the theoretical votes of the public assemblies and senatorial decrees, imperial writings came to constitute a third, and undoubtedly the most significant, legislative power – no legislation could be passed without imperial consent. The actual administration of the empire created a mass of written material to and from the emperor and his subjects: letters, written petitions, answers and edicts.[4]

4 For a comprehensive summary of these documents, see Millar, 1977.

It was important that the emperor kept control of the officials who administered the empire in his name. This meant maintaining his central position in communication networks between Rome and the provinces. A system had to be enforced whereby senior provincial officials recognized the importance of consulting the emperor on a whole range of matters. Consultation of the emperor by the governor was also an important indirect channel by which individuals, groups and cities in the provinces communicated with him. This culture of consultation was recognized by contemporaries as a central facet of imperial power. Here is an excerpt from Aelius Aristides' second century AD treatise, *The Ruling Power*.

> And if the governors should have even some slight doubt whether certain claims are valid in connection with either public or private law suits and petitions from the governed, they straightaway send to him [the emperor] with a request for instruction what to do, they wait until he renders a reply, like a chorus waiting for its trainer.
>
> (Aelius Aristides, *The Ruling Power*, trans. Oliver, 1953, p.899)

This is further evidenced by the tenth book of the letters of Pliny the Younger, which include a unique documentary source for the government of the Roman empire – a series of 116 missives addressed by the governor of a Roman province to the reigning emperor, together with the latter's replies. Pliny was governor of the province of Bithynia/ Pontus on the north coast of Asia Minor in approximately AD 109–111. Pliny was renowned as a prolific letter writer, and while it is not known whether it was normal for the emperor and a provincial governor to be in such close contact, the letters themselves cover almost every aspect of administering a province. These include the security arrangements for prisoners (*Letters* 18), the building of bath houses (23, 70), recommendations of individuals (26, 94), the setting up of a fire brigade (33), the building of an aqueduct and a theatre leading to suspected embezzlement and fraud (37, 39, 90), the building of a canal (41, 61), the restoration of temples (49), legal matters (56, 58, 74, 75, 83, 110), embassies from client kings (67), membership of local senates (81), the punishment of Christians (96), grants of Roman citizenship (104, 106) and the public provision for athletes (118).

However, it was not normal practice for the emperor to write official letters himself; rather, they would be dictated. Each emperor would appoint an *ab epistulis*, an official whose sole responsibility was to oversee the imperial correspondence. The extreme importance of the written word as a tool and signifier of imperial power is borne out by the seniority of the post: the *ab epistulis* would accompany the emperor on all his travels, unlike other senior members of his secretariat. It was generally considered that the holder of that post wielded considerable influence with the emperor. For instance, here is a comment made about Cornelianus, *ab epistulis* to one of the Antonine emperors: 'Therefore the kings of the Romans considered you worthy of the highest honours, directed you to manage all the affairs of the Greeks, setting you beside them as guardian, in theory appointing you as *ab epistulis*, but in reality choosing you as a partner in their kingship' (Phrynichus, *Eclogue* 393). Indeed, the right to send letters in the emperor's name was a sign of great favour or even succession: the wives and freedmen of Claudius, for instance, effectively ruled the empire by using the seal of the emperor to issue orders (Suetonius, *Claudius* 29).

Such delegation meant that the emperor had to make use of certain strategies in order to maintain control over the communication process if it were not to be a serious threat to his own power. This often manifested itself in the form of written addenda attached to the end of official correspondence. Not only did this indicate that he had control over his bureaucracy and maintained a personal bond between himself and the correspondent, but it was also an effective way of displaying imperial praise or censure. For instance, Philo mentions that Gaius added a sentence in threatening terms in his own hand to a letter to Petronius, the provincial governor of Syria (Philo, *On the Embassy to Gaius* 42.333–4). For the emperor to write a letter with his own hand it had to belong in the context of entirely private correspondence, be a formal diplomatic act, or be a deliberate indication of special goodwill or favour. For example, Cassius Dio makes a special point of mentioning that Marcus Aurelius wrote most of his letters to his closest friends by hand (Cassius Dio, *Roman History* 70.36.2).

In order to maintain his hold on power and ensure the efficient running of the empire, it was essential that the emperor maintained a steady flow of information to and from the provinces. The *cursus publicus*, the imperial postage system with its regular staging posts and senior officials to maintain its smooth running, ensured this. It has been calculated that government couriers travelled from station to station at an average of five miles an hour for a total of fifty miles in a normal day's travelling. Thus a dispatch from Rome would reach Brindisi in about seven days, Byzantium in twenty-five, Antioch in forty and Alexandria in fifty-five. During emergencies this speed could be trebled by travelling day and night. For instance, the news of the death of Nero in AD 68 got to Galba in Spain in seven days, and when the armies mutinied on the Rhine in the following year the news reached Rome in eight or nine days. This is in contrast to the situation facing private individuals, whose couriers would have to wait to find ships going in the right direction. A letter that Cicero wrote to his son in Athens took seven weeks, while another from Rome to Athens took only three, which, Cicero remarked, was very quick indeed. A letter sent from Africa to

Rome could be there in three days, but one for Cicero once took twenty. Some letters from Syria to Rome took fifty days, some double that (Cicero, *Letter to his Friends* 16.21.1; 12.25; 12.10.2).

Imperial decisions on particular cases were often further disseminated. Edicts and letters would be either inscribed on stone or posted up in the emperor's place of residence and relayed to the important centres of the empire. Take, for example, this general edict released by Claudius protecting the rights of Jewish communities of the Diaspora:

> This edict of mine I wish the magistrates of the cities and the *coloniae* and *municipia* of Italy and outside, and also kings and dynasts through their own representatives, to have copied up, and to display for not less than thirty days in a place where it can easily be read from the ground.
>
> (Josephus, *Jewish Antiquities* 19.5.3)

Here again we see the importance of communication not only as a means of making the emperor's subjects aware of imperial decisions, but also as a more abstract representation of his power.

Through the written word, the emperor could promote the ideology of his rule throughout his huge empire. Perhaps the most striking example of this is the *Res Gestae*, a text set out as an inscription documenting the achievements of the reign of the emperor Augustus (27 BC–AD 14). Inscribed in bronze in front of the tomb where its author was buried in Rome, and exported, translated and inscribed on the walls of temples dedicated to the imperial cult in the provinces, the *Res Gestae* is organized into several distinct sections (Figure 2.3).[5] The earlier parts set out Augustus' political actions, the honours conferred on him and the dispensations and generosities bestowed by him on his subjects. The later parts, the account of his military victories and diplomatic successes, constitute in sum an explanation and justification of the conquest of the known world. The text is concluded with two chapters revisiting the establishment of the new regime in 27 BC and its culmination with the bestowal of the title *Pater Patriae* (Father of the Country). As one commentator has argued:

> ... it was the signature of empire, a written contract for the relations of centre and periphery and an articulation of the place of individual citizens within a new world system defined by the imperial 'I' which governs the verbs of the document.
>
> (Elsner, 1996, p.52)

5 As well as in Rome itself, fragments of copies of the *Res Gestae* have been found at Antioch in Pisidia, Apollonia in Asia Minor and the main bulk of the text in Ankara. For the two best studies of the document see Nicolet, 1988, chapters 1 and 2; Elsner, 1996.

Figure 2.3 *A detail from the* Res Gestae *inscription. (Deutsches Archäologisches Institut, Rome)*

The *Res Gestae* is also an example of how inscriptions were not just insular texts; they were often framing devices which provided a narrative for the architecture or art around them. The *Res Gestae* gave an important context to the group of imperial dynastic buildings around it; the Horologium (the largest sundial ever constructed), the Ustrinum (the crematorium where Augustus' remains were burnt and the apotheosis was meant to have taken place) and the mausoleum itself. As Elsner has argued:

> In effect by surveying the city topographically and by cataloging a carefully selected group of monuments constructed or restored by Augustus, the *Res Gestae* framed the viewing of Augustan Rome. For it told Romans how their city should now be seen.
>
> (Elsner, 1996, p.40)

This contextualizing role is also common to another important medium which expressed the emperor's power: coins. All coinage was issued in the emperor's name and was therefore a channel of communication through which the emperor had exclusive control. Here images and writing combine in articulating particular aspects of the imperial virtues or powers, whether associated with the political or religious offices traditionally held or more abstract representations of individual qualities. The obverse ('heads') side of the coin normally consisted of a portrait, usually of the emperor, empress, or some other member of the imperial family. This was accompanied by a legend which usually consisted of imperial names, titles and offices, frequently in abbreviated form, such as *Imperator, Augustus, Pontifex Maximus* (high priest), *Consul, Tribunicia Potestas* (holder of tribunician power), *Pater Patriae* and *Censor* (Figure 2.4). On the reverse of the coin the portraits were either depictions of major Olympian deities – Jupiter, Juno and Mars being the most common – or demi-gods such as Hercules. These served to show the divine sanction of the imperial house. Other popular alternatives were personifications of abstract ideas associated with the emperor's qualities or the achievements of the Roman empire. These were often elevated to the status of minor deities, the most common being depictions of *Victoria* as a winged female figure carrying a wreath and a palm (Figure 2.5).

Other categories of representation included imperial occasions such as the *Adventus* (the arrival of the emperor in Rome), the *Profectio* (the emperor's departure), the *Adlocutio* (the emperor addressing his troops), distributions of largesse, imperial building programmes and illustrations of or allusion to visits to the provinces. Often the legend on the reverse was a description in words of the representation. For example, Titus

Figure 2.4 *Obverse side of a gold* quinarius *depicting the head of the emperor Tiberius with the superscription* TI DIVI F AUGUSTUS *('Tiberius, son of the Divine Augustus'). British Museum.* (© *The British Museum*)

Figure 2.5 *The reverse side of the* quinarius *in Figure 2.4 depicting the winged figure of Victory seated on a globe with a diadem in her hands with the superscription* TR POT XXVI *(Tribunicia Potestas 26 – the twenty-sixth year that Tiberius had held tribunician power). British Museum. (© The British Museum)*

used *Aeternitas* (Eternity) to emphasize the longevity and hence the legitimacy of the Flavian dynasty; Nerva after the tyranny of Domitian used *Libertas publica* (Freedom of the people). Although it could be argued that many of the finer points of imperial propaganda must have gone unnoticed, these images had a powerful symbolic value as a representation of the legitimacy and success of a particular emperor's reign. Thus coins, like inscriptions, were common currency in the legitimization of imperial power.[6]

The emperors may have tried to control all forms of written media, but communication being a two-way process, the monopoly was never absolute. Anti-imperial writing did exist: Thrasea under Nero and Maternus under Vespasian both wrote pointed eulogies about the arch-republican Cato (Tacitus, *Dialogue on Orators* 3). There was also political graffiti: on a wall in Pompeii was written the slogan 'The poison, minister of finances of Nero' (*Corpus Inscriptionum Latinorum*, 4.8075). Tacitus informs us that the wills of many of the condemned senators in the time of Nero contained abuse of the emperor which caused great embarrassment when read out (Tacitus, *Annals* 16.19).

Retribution was severe: Augustus banned the publication of anonymous tracts, and promised rewards for people who informed on those putting up critical posters (Suetonius, *Augustus* 31.1, 55). The emperor Tiberius burnt all the copies of a eulogy of Cassius and Brutus (Suetonius, *Tiberius* 61.3). Domitian put to death not only Hermogenes of Tarsus because of several critical allusions in his history, but also all the booksellers who had copied the book (Suetonius, *Domitian* 10). It is hardly surprising that in such an environment many authors chose to censor themselves.

Bureaucracy and officialdom

The exchange of written documents was an essential process linking rulers and ruled. The administration of the Roman empire was heavily bureaucratized; this bureaucracy made extensive use of the written word. Forms, claims, reports, orders, proclamations, files and archives convey something of how the government of the Roman empire depended on paperwork both for its knowledge of events and as a means of influencing their course. Consequently bureaucratic documentation is another manifestation of power. Imperial administration sometimes imposed its power through the written word quite literally, as is shown by the official stamp of the Procuratorial office impressed on the wooden writing tablet shown in Figure 2.6.

Nowhere is the importance of the written word for administrative purposes more evident than in Roman Egypt (although this is untypical

6 See Carson, 1990, pp.276–83.

Figure 2.6 *A wooden stamp from the office of the Procurator of Britain with the superscription* PROC AUG DEDERUNT BRIT PROV *('The imperial procurators of the province of Britain issued this'), from Walbrook, London. British Museum. (© The British Museum)*

of the empire as a whole, in terms of both administrative arrangements and the unique survival of papyrus documents). One edict of a prefect holding assizes in Arsinoe in Egypt in the early third century AD reveals that over the three days he received no fewer than 1,804 petitions from those seeking legal redress. Every civil servant in Roman service was expected to keep a daily journal of his official transactions. This journal would be written by a secretary, signed by the official, publicly exhibited and then filed in duplicate, one locally and one in Alexandria.

A huge amount of correspondence was generated. For example, the *strategus* (chief official) of the Panopolite Nome (administrative area) in the late third century had six clerks who wrote his letters. We know that on one day alone seventeen letters were dispatched from his office: to the president of the local municipality, the head of financial administration, the *strategus* of the neighbouring nome, the procurator, the head of the night police and the prefect. Officials would also receive a flood of lists and reports, and would send reports on to their superiors.

All administrative documents were meant for submission, whether they were journals, correspondence, declarations, lists or reports on judicial business. Municipal record offices held the minutes of the debates of the local senate in Oxyrhynchus as well as the town clerk's correspondence. This system gradually increased in sophistication and complexity. By the first century AD each nome had a public depository. In AD 72 this was subdivided into a depository of public records and property records. Under Hadrian the central depository in Alexandria was yet further elaborated.

Insistence by the authorities on the documentation and archiving of even the most simple transactions, of which we have prolific evidence in Roman Egypt, again brings us back to the point that in the administration of the Roman empire power could be wielded not only over, but through, texts. Officialdom insisted on contracts being written up by a professional notary and undergoing registration at a public office, the legacy of which is a mass of documentation pertaining to the lives of citizens from various socio-economic groupings. These include documentations of marriage, divorce, apprenticeship, sales, leases, loans, invitations to weddings, payments on credit, reports of public meetings, trials and enquiries, declarations such as births and deaths, registrations of property and return of livestock.

The written word was an essential tool for the functioning of the Roman army. Reams of documentation survive: rosters, pay records, military material, records, letters about personnel on papyri, ostraka (potsherds) and wooden tablets (Figures 2.7 and 2.8). The documents from the fort at Vindolanda in northern Britain, dating from AD 90–120, just before the building of Hadrian's Wall, record numerous different aspects of military life on the frontier, such as unit strength, building and construction work (for instance the building of the bath house), collection and processing of lead, plastering and work in the kilns, and accounts, including receipts or disbursements of commodities and cash (Bowman and Thomas, 1994, pp.77–101).

Many of the Vindolanda documents were generated or retained in the house of the commander of the fort, the largest archive being that of Flavius Cerialis, prefect of the ninth cohort of Batavians. Several striking observations can be made about the Vindolanda material. Firstly, it shows that literacy was introduced by the Roman army within a very short time of its occupation of an area that had previously been illiterate. Secondly, these soldiers are not Italians or Romanized Gauls but Batavians from the lower Rhine area; even their commander Flavius Cerialis was likely to have been only a first or second generation Roman citizen, yet he and his men are introducing Latin literacy into this area of Britain. Thirdly, the Roman army recorded its operations and administration in a mass of paperwork. Records down to the smallest

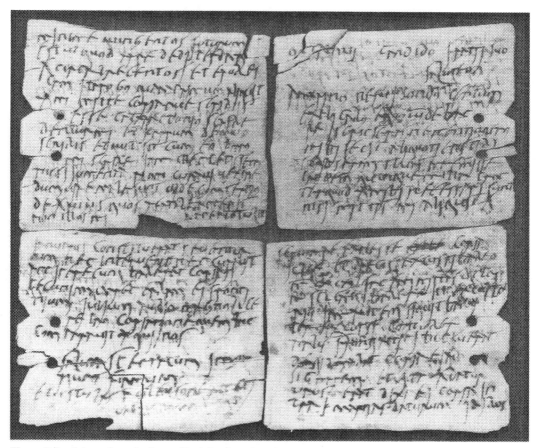

Figure 2.7   *A letter from the fort at Vindolanda written by a certain Octavius to Candidus, asking for the latter to send the money that he had promised for a business transaction. British Museum. (© The British Museum)*

Figure 2.8   *Drawing of a fragment of a wooden tablet from the fort at Castle Street, Carlisle, bearing the misspelling BRITANIA. Tullie House Museum, Carlisle.*

detail were an essential means of keeping track of what was going on. This in many ways explains how the Roman military presence exerted such control over a large area with so few troops.

The élite

The Graeco-Roman élite, wherever they lived within the Roman empire, considered that through education they were linked with one another in a universal brotherhood. In the Greek world, and to some extent in the Latin west too, this was called *paideia*. This sense of shared culture and identity communicated through the written word served to generate and reinforce power.

In his considerable corpus of letters, Marcus Aurelius Fronto (*c.* AD 100–167), man of letters, senator and lawyer, demonstrates that he places himself at the centre not only of the Latin literary world but, as a man with considerable connections with the *literari*, of the Greek east too. His *Epistulae ad Amicos* (*Letters to his Friends*) are in essence a series of letters of commendation, which allow us to explore the extraordinarily interconnected élite networks of the second century AD.

A surprising number of Fronto's letters are addressed to prominent figures from the Greek east. There are several to Tiberius Claudius Iulianus of Smyrna, an ex-consul and eastern magnate. Iulianus is himself the epitome of this empire-wide network constructed around *paideia*: he was a friend not only of Fronto but also of Herodes Atticus, the most prominent man of letters in the Greek east at this time.

Fronto's first missive to Iulianus was a letter of commendation for a young man, Calvisius Faustinianus, who had to fulfil his military obligations in the provincial army of Iulianus. But Fronto, rather than concentrating on his military talents, emphasizes his learning and literary elegance: let Iulianus test his new officer not only in his military duties but also in literary affairs. Here we find *paideia* and patronage combining to strengthen bonds between members of the provincial élite. To compound this, Faustinianus' father Caius Calvisus Statianus, prefect of Egypt and another man of letters, had been *ab epistulis latinis* (a high-ranking official who dealt with the Latin correspondence of the emperor). Fronto duly praises Statianus' *paideia* in his letter (Fronto, *Letters to his Friends* 1.17).

The commonality of language not only serves as a linking device but becomes formalized into structures of power and influence. Thus we see the system of patronage exercised through literacy. How better could geographically dispersed individuals be integrated into a system of reciprocal favours than through a network which allowed them at once to discharge duty and render it visible through an eloquent display of *pietas* (dutifulness)? In a letter to his son-in-law Aufidius Victorinus, twice consul, Fronto recommends Antoninus Aquila as a learned and eloquent man. It turns out that Fronto has never heard the man declaim, but is merely acting as an intermediary for other patrons of Aquila, who are Greeks like Aquila himself. These unknowns are the true recipients of Fronto's favour: 'I want this to be done for Aquila for the sake of those who are promoting him so strongly.' Victorinus in turn is to use his influence with yet another party, a city council within his province, which will select Aquila as 'a public instructor of its youth'. Here we witness close interweaving between the Greek and Latin literary worlds, and a chain of patronage stretching back from an unknown city council to the provincial governor, to the governor's father-in-law, to that man's learned friends, to their client, the pedagogue (Fronto, *Letters to his Friends* 1.8) (Champlin, 1980, pp.29–44).

These letters also served another purpose, again linked with *paideia*, namely the furtherance of Fronto's own reputation as a cultured man of letters with a large entourage of like-minded, powerful friends. They were published probably within his lifetime. His *sermones* (speeches) were not only delivered to an audience but also published. For example, in a letter to his son-in-law he discusses the preparation of his speech *On Behalf of the Bithynians* for the public in an expanded and enhanced version (Fronto, *Letters to his Friends*, 1.14). Fronto also remarks that he had often praised Hadrian in the senate 'and those speeches were constantly in everyone's hands' (Fronto, *Letter to Marcus Aurelius* 2. 1.1). In the east the emperor, Lucius Verus, had requested copies of several of his speeches, including one that attacked a friend of the emperor: 'As soon as I became aware of this, I was myself anxious to suppress the speech, but it had already circulated too widely to be recalled in' (Fronto, *Letter to Lucius Verus* 11.9.1).

A vehicle for the display of intellectual and linguistic competence, the deployment of literacy operated as a defining characteristic of the sophists in the Greek east. Relations between the sophists themselves were often theatrically tense: there are a huge number of references to academic quarrels. There came into being a form of polemical literature by warring sophists denouncing each other with wit and erudition. One particular dispute had arisen between Apasius of Ravenna and Philostratus of Lemnos: sophists from both east and west took sides. Philostratus, in an attempt to belittle Apasius, had produced a book on how to write letters, the joke being that at the time Apasius was *ab epistulis graecis* (Philostratus, *Lives of the Sophists* 627–8) The most abundant documentation of professional quarrels can be found in accounts of the career of Herodes Atticus. His biographer, Philostratus, actually comments on the fame of one particular piece by a certain Demostratus attacking Herodes (Philostratus, *Lives of the Sophists* 563). We also hear of Fronto sending another speech attacking Herodes to the co-emperors Lucius Verus and Marcus Aurelius (Fronto, *Letters* 130, 166).

The medium is the message?

> The medium is the message because it is the medium that shapes and controls the scale and form of human association and action. The content or uses of such media are as diverse as they are ineffectual in shaping the form of human association. Indeed it is only too typical that the 'content' of any medium blinds us to the character of the medium.
>
> (McLuhan, 1964, p.9)

The medium itself often has a significant effect on the message, or indeed in some instances the medium is a more powerful means of articulation than the written message it contains. One or other of the these statements is applicable to all forms of written media in the Roman world.

In the Roman world, the cities, towns, villages, palaces, villas, military camps and religious complexes boasted countless inscriptions carved ornamentally on to stone of all different types. For those who both were literate and understood the complex rules by which epigraphy works, one could say that the information imparted by the text would be the most significant factor. However, several other considerations make the reception of inscriptions in the ancient world a rather more complicated business than one would think. A recent study of the prytany (magistracy) of Caius Vibius Salutaris of Ephesus makes some interesting observations on this matter. Salutaris was a very wealthy Roman citizen of equestrian status who lived in Ephesus on the cusp of the first and second centuries AD. Salutaris had decided to make a very large public foundation to his native city. This included the dedication of certain statues and money to Artemis, the patron of the Ephesus, and to various civic bodies and individuals (Rogers, 1991, pp.41–3).

The inscription was inscribed on the marble wall of the theatre, at such a height that almost all the inscription would have been well above human eye level. The small size of the letters (between 1 and 4 cm), the variable height of the engraved stones (left 208 cm, right 403 cm) and their breadth (494 cm), together with the length and complexity of the text of the seven documents (568 lines in six columns), makes one conclude that the text was not intended to be read. In fact people simply could not do so physically.

So what role did this enormous display of writing have in the city? The answer lies in how the inscription was matched to specific architectural and topographical contexts in the city. The text actually says that Salutaris chose the places where the inscriptions should go. His choice of the theatre, a building designed architecturally and used socially for public performances such as plays, public meetings and rituals, can be justified by the fact that these were precisely the kinds of public ceremonies that his foundation would fund. In addition, these ceremonies took place literally underneath the inscription. It has also been argued that the inscription was a symbolic validation of the legal process by which Salutaris transferred some of his wealth to the beneficiaries. In a case where heirs were being passed over in preference to various civic groups there was a need for a symbolic statement which would allow peace between the donor and his heirs. At the same time the inscription functioned within the city as a public and permanent validation of the power of the *boule* and the *demos* (city councils) to transfer the property of Salutaris to the various beneficiaries by means of a legal process. It also symbolized and legitimated the various power relationships in the city and the province which made such a transfer of property and such endowed rituals possible (Rogers, 1991, pp.19–24). Hence the most important function of Salutaris' inscription and countless others in the Roman empire was a symbolic rather than a textual one.

This is also true of bronze tablets on which laws were recorded. The text on those that survive was often complex and convoluted and the lettering cramped, making them very difficult to read. Since public proclamation or temporary posters were the common ways of making laws known, with the élite relying on private archives, this has led to the conclusion that it was the bronze that they are made from which was important, rather than the texts themselves. Bronze was eternally lasting, hence its symbolic worth. It advertised permanence and authority. So these tablets were created as eternal monuments of the laws passed, which were rendered sacred and inviolable by the material they were made in, even though the text was virtually unreadable (Williamson, 1987, pp.167–80). But as there is evidence that bronze tablets and other inscriptions were consulted, this was a process where symbolic significance and reference combined to provide the public copy with legal force (Crawford, 1988).

Although there is much evidence for care in the production and maintenance of Roman bureaucratic documentation, accessibility was limited. The more important documents would go on display on temporary whitened boards for a limited amount of time, or were read out by heralds (Harris, 1989, p.161). Copies of state documents were dispersed among numerous buildings in Rome, which made access difficult, and were inscribed on wax tablets, which must have given them a limited life. Even for edicts whose provisions were intended to be of indefinite application, we have no evidence of them being recorded in any permanent public form in Rome. Equally, where imperial pronouncements, of whatever kind, survive on inscriptions, they do so only because cities or private persons had them inscribed as being of direct interest to themselves (Millar, 1977, pp.255–6).

It is also clear that the official dissemination of even the most important documents could be extremely slow. An edict of the emperor Caracalla concerning the restoration of exiles was posted up in Rome on 11 July 212. It was then copied in the office of the prefect of Egypt in Alexandria on 29 January 213, and only posted up there on 10 February: the whole process had taken seven months (Millar, 1977, p.256).

So what was the purpose of these documents if accessibility was so difficult? Thomas makes this very important observation: 'Making documents and using them later were quite separate stages which by no means followed inevitably from one another' (Thomas, 1992, p.94). The same holds true for the Roman empire. Although there were central state and provincial archives, little use was made of them. Most individuals still tended to rely on memory and oral communication where one might have expected written proof. It seems that after these documents had served their immediate purpose, their function was not really as a reference for administrative purposes but was more a symbolic and an exemplary one, protecting and confirming the values of the society that they were meant to represent.[7]

Culture, power and identity in an oral world

Much of this essay so far has concerned itself with demonstrating that the written word was a central medium in constructions of culture, identity and power in the Roman empire. Yet here lies a paradox, in that ancient Rome was in many ways an oral society in which the written word took second place to the spoken. Harris (1989) argues that although Rome, with its senatorial and equestrian orders and their dependents, praetorian guard and imperial household, had a large number of literate individuals, there is no evidence that this literacy spread down to the ordinary citizenry. Indeed, he calculates that less than 5 per cent of the population of Italy were likely to have been literate. In the western provinces by the first century AD it is probably right to think that levels of literacy in Baetica in Spain, Narbonensis (southern France) and north Africa were roughly the same as in Italy. In the less 'Romanized' provinces such as Germany, northern Gaul and Britain the numbers of literate individuals would be far fewer. In the Greek-speaking east, most of the males of the 'gymnasium class', that is, Greek townsmen of

7 See Culham, 1989, and Talbert, 1984, pp.303–7, in reference to senatorial documents; Coles, 1966, p.16, for the proceedings of town and district councils.

substantial property who were sons of similar individuals, were literate and were part of an élite who made a great effort to assert their Hellenism. In towns and villages some artisans were literate. However, many more, although they used writing, were semi-literate or illiterate. Almost all the freeborn poor were illiterate. In the countryside there was less literacy than in the town.

There is also the problem of how one defines 'literacy'. As Rosalind Thomas writes, 'We might define literacy as the ability to read and write, but read and write what?' (Thomas, 1992, p.8). Reading a simple message scratched on to a wall is very different from reading a book of poetry. Within the Roman world we should reckon there have to have been many degrees of reading ability and reading contexts.

It must also be remembered that reading, writing and oral comprehension are three distinct processes, which are not necessarily mastered equally by the same individual. It seems likely that more people could read than write. The ability to read or write very simple messages, often in capitals, was probably not rare, and in cities, where there would probably be more exposure to documents, most individuals would have some basic reading skills. But written texts of poetry and literature had a reading audience confined to the highly educated and wealthy élite and their secretaries. Roman definitions of literacy were evidently different from those of the modern world. Otherwise what are we to make of the prosperous freedman, Hermeros, in Petronius' *Satyricon*, who only knows 'lapidary writing' (the capitals of inscriptions) (Petronius, *Satyricon* 58.7), or of Petaus, the second century Egyptian village clerk (Lewis, 1983, p.81), who although he could sign his name with a standard formula was unable to read or write?

So the Roman world remained highly dependent on oral communication and non-written visual communication. The written word always remained less vital to the individual than in practically any early modern culture. Although literacy was always virtually universal among the men who made up the political and social élite, most people could live out their lives without the use of reading and writing. This is recognized implicitly by the extensive use that the imperial authorities made of art and architecture in their efforts to convey messages to the general population of the empire. However, illiterates and semi-literates were often able to make use of the written word through intermediaries – having legal documents written or read by others, having an inscription explained, listening to a speech given by someone relying on a script (Harris, 1989, pp.33–4). From this it can be concluded that oral communication played an important role in constructions of culture, identity and power in the Roman world and also in the dissemination of the written word.

It becomes evident that the Roman empire was strictly neither a totally 'literate' society nor an 'oral' one. Any study of communication in the Roman world is necessarily an exploration of the relationship between oracy and literacy. What is clear is that often the lines between the two cannot be clearly drawn.

Even among those for whom literacy was a central part of their identity, the élite oral traditions remained paramount. The most important indication of this can be found in the definition of the word *eloquentia*, an attribute at the very heart of Roman élite self-definition and an important co-ordinate in the world of élite culture. In an oration to the emperor Marcus Aurelius, his former tutor, Fronto, imparted the following advice.

> Therefore consider whether in this second category of duties the study of eloquence should be incorporated. For the duties of emperors are: to urge necessary steps in the senate; to address the people on a multitude of matters in public meeting; to correct the injustices of the law; to send letters to all parts of the world; to bring compulsion to bear on kings of foreign nations; to repress by edicts the faults of the provincials, give praise to good actions, conquer the seditious and terrify the aggressive ones. All these are assuredly things to be achieved by words and letters. Will you therefore not practise a skill which you can see will be of great service to you on many and such important occasions?
> (Fronto, *On Eloquence* 2.7)

The mark of a civilized man was not just that he should be able to read and write but, as importantly, *to have the ability to speak well in public*. Power and élite self-representation still relied heavily on the spoken word.

This stress on the value of oral performance alongside that of written texts is found throughout the educated élite of the empire. It was through a brilliant display of public speaking that Apuleius, a wealthy lawyer of equestrian status, was able to appeal successfully to the *paideia* of his trial judge, the proconsul of Africa, and gain an acquittal (Apuleius, *Apologia* 36.5, 41.4, 25.10, 38.1, 91.3). The Second Sophistic, the second century AD cultural renaissance of the Greek world, was itself centred on production of archaizing speeches and highly theatrical declamations to huge audiences in the theatre. Skill in improvised public speech was considered one of the most highly valued commodities that a sophist could possess (Russell, 1983, pp.74–82). Audiences could be very large, and a visit from a well-known sophist was a special occasion. Here is Aelius Aristides' account of his arrival in the city of Smyrna.

> Before I even entered the city, there were people coming to meet me because they had heard about me, the most accomplished of the young

men were giving themselves to me, and there was already a definite plan for the lecture ... Despite the fact that my appearance was impromptu, and most people knew nothing about it, the council chamber was so full that you could see nothing but human faces and you couldn't have thrust your hand between [them]. The noise and the goodwill, or rather the enthusiasm, were so universal that there was no one to be seen sitting down either during my preliminary speech or when I stood up and declaimed. From the very first word they stood there, excited, joyful, amazed.

(Aelius Aristides, *Oration* 15.29–34)

The same bias towards the spoken word can be found among the philosophical schools, where the true teachings of its founder were considered to reside in the traditions continued by the school rather than in the founder's original writings (Alexander, 1990).

However, despite the disapproval of the teachers of rhetoric (Quintillan 10.7.30–2, 11), many unofficial transcripts of speeches were in circulation. Indeed, a certain Philagrus of Cilicia found himself in the embarrassing situation of having his speech chanted back at him by the audience because texts of it had already reached Athens (Philostratus, *Lives of the Sophists* 579).

One also finds the same configuration of the written and spoken word in the practice and representation of imperial power. At the beginning of the second century AD, Pliny the Younger delivered a speech in praise of the emperor Trajan. The following extract illustrates well the importance of the spoken word to the image of the virtuous emperor.

When the prince moves among his subjects they are at liberty to stay still or approach him, to accompany him or pass ahead, for you do not walk among us to confer a benefit by your presence, nor put us in your debt if we enjoy your company. Anyone who approaches you can stay at your side, *and conversation lasts till it is ended by his discretion, not by any loftiness of yours.*

(Pliny, *Pan* 24, 3–4)

Pliny is referring to the emperor's relationship with his *amici* (friends), members of Rome's aristocratic élite, rather than with the general populace. The model being propagated is one that was important for the imperial image in this period, namely that although all-powerful, the emperor should behave as nothing more than *primus inter pares* (first among equals) with fellow members of the senatorial élite. Free and easy conversation was an important component of this.

It was not just with the senatorial élite that the spoken word was a crucial structuring device for the articulation of imperial power. The emperor's method of propagandizing soldiers (at the *adlocutio*), as with ordinary citizens (by the use of heralds), was predominantly oral. Written communications from his subjects were presented in person by the interested parties and would usually involve formal or informal verbal exchanges with the emperor himself. The emperor would find himself inundated with personal petitions. Embassies and petitioners from all over the empire would come to where the emperor was. Cassius Dio mentions that when an earthquake struck Antioch when Trajan was there in 114–15, the whole empire suffered because people had gathered there from all over the empire (Cassius Dio, *Roman History* 68.24.1–2).

The spoken and written word would combine when one chosen member from the embassy would make a suitable oration which accompanied the actual handing over of the letter or decree of the city or other body. For instance, in 7 BC, when Gaius Caesar assumed the *toga virilis*, the council and people of Sardis voted 'to send ambassadors from among the most distinguished men to offer greetings from the city, to hand over to him [Gaius] a copy of this decree, sealed with the public seal, and to address Augustus on matters of common concern to Asia and to the city' (*Sardis* 7.1.2.17–20, trans. Millar, 1977, p.217).

The spoken word was also important in the dispensation of imperial justice. In Rome many of the emperors up to Hadrian gave judgement in public from a tribunal, which was probably a deliberate procedure to evoke popular favour and avert rumour. It could also be a forum through which the emperor's subjects could show their dissatisfaction. In AD 51 Claudius had to be escorted to safety by his soldiers when an angry mob used such an occasion to complain about corn prices (Tacitus, *Annals* 12.43.1; Suetonius, *Claudius* 18.2).

'Romanization': language and the written word

The previous sections of this essay have been concerned with how power was exercised both over and through the written media by different individuals and groups within the Roman empire. However, the question needs to be asked whether there is congruity in the uses of the written word which points to a common cultural outlook. Is there anything that we can pinpoint as being specifically Roman?

The term 'Romanization' has been used for what has been perceived as the gradual subsumption of the values and customs of subject peoples to those of the Roman conquerors, in other words to denote that some sort of cultural standardization took place. The inherent problems of such a monolithic model of culture and identity are well illustrated by a study of the use of written media in the Roman empire.

Inscriptions are often taken as the written medium which, more than others, indicates 'Romanization'. But it is clear that the extensive use of inscriptions as a medium in different areas of the empire was not an exclusively Roman practice. The epigraphic habit was strong in the Greek world (Thomas, 1989), and even in areas such as Gaul, where urbanization had not really existed before the conquest, there are inscriptions (Woolf, 1994, pp.94–5). However, the Romans did use inscriptions for new purposes, for example the career inscription, giving a list of the subject's public offices in great detail. Such inscriptions often show how provincials had access to Roman offices and thereby to positions of power (Millar, 1983, pp.127–8). Epitaphs have also been seen as deliberate statements of Romanization or an upward quest for Roman status, especially where they highlight the deceased's status as a Roman citizen.

What is not in dispute is that with the advent of Roman political hegemony, there is a marked increase in the number of inscriptions found in all the provinces including the Greek east (Millar, 1983, p.124). In first century AD north Africa, there is a direct correlation between the emergence of a Romano-African élite and the growth of an epigraphic tradition (Rives, 1995). Other indications of a connection between the putting up of inscriptions and acculturation to a Roman way of life can be found in Spain, where the areas most directly influenced by Rome, such as the Mediterranean coast, have many more inscriptions than the north-west region, which was relatively untouched by Graeco-Roman patterns of life. The same pattern can be found throughout all the western provinces of the Roman empire (Millar, 1983, pp.124–5).

Epigraphy is a useful tool with which to gauge Romanization not only through practice but also through *language*. Although not an absolute determinant, language is an important indicator of identity. It is not only the medium through which power is articulated, but also provides an important control over access to power.

In regard to the imperial administration there was an important linguistic dichotomy. The language of government was Latin in the western provinces and Greek in the eastern. Imperial powers not only impose their own language on their subjects, but also appropriate the language of those they rule for their own purposes, thereby neutralizing any potential threat to their hegemony. Greek, as the language of government throughout the east since the time of Alexander, was therefore recognized as an imperial language. Many of the emperors in our period were familiar with Greek literature and could converse in Greek. Its importance as a language of Roman rule in the east is shown by the great lengths to which the emperors went to ensure that imperial texts would live up to the exacting standards of grammar and vocabulary expected of public pronouncements in the Greek world. Suetonius tells us that Augustus, although he knew Greek, would write a speech in Latin and then have it translated into Greek for delivery (Suetonius, *Augustus* 89.1).

In the west, where there was no such pre-existing and unifying culture, the reverse occurred: the language of the ruler was imposed on the ruled. The Latinization of the west is a phenomenon that is closely connected to Roman conquest. As a new configuration of power was established, the language of the conqueror was superimposed to articulate it. Those who wished to gain access to this new power structure could only do so through the Latin language. It is no coincidence that the inscriptions put up by bureaucrats and soldiers from the provinces are written in the language that had gained them access to their positions. When the town council of Bulla Regia in north Africa wished to honour one of its most successful sons, Quintus Domitius Marsianus, who had risen to the rank of procurator in the reign of Marcus Aurelius (AD 161–80), it did so in Latin, the language of Roman imperial rule (Millar, 1983, pp.127–8). In Gaul, the very localized linguistic differences that existed between autonomous groups disappeared: there was a sudden and complete disappearance of Iberian and Gallo-Greek scripts by the mid first century AD. Such local written languages were relegated to a position as barbarian, 'other' to Roman civilization (Woolf, 1984, pp.94–5).

However, although it is possible to conclude that by the end of the first century AD the dominant *written* language was Latin in Italy and the western provinces (extending as far east as Dacia and lower Moesia), and Greek in the eastern provinces, at least a dozen other languages were used in written form within the empire. In Italy itself, Oscan inscriptions have been found at Pompeii that date to around the time of the town's destruction in the late first century AD. The last Etruscan inscription found in Italy dates from around the same time. In north Africa Punic and Libyan were widely used in inscriptions throughout the period of the empire. Such was the importance of Punic that it was partly used on some coin legends until the reign of Tiberius (AD 14–37) and is found on public buildings until the late second century AD. In Asia Minor inscriptions have been found in Phrygian, Pisidian and Galatian Celtic (Harris, 1989, pp.175–9).

Although these inscriptions are far outnumbered by those written in Latin or Greek, they point to the existence of local identities and power structures which are articulated through local languages. A good example of this can be found in Roman Judaea, where those scribes who copied out Hebrew sacred texts gained power and prestige through their roles as writers and interpreters (Goodman, 1994, pp.99–108).

The new political realities of the Roman empire were reflected in the use of written languages. In north Africa, with the emergence of a Romano-African élite in the first century AD, bilingual inscriptions in both Latin and Punic reflect this élite's need to not only maintain its local power base with a self-consciously constructed 'African' cultural identity, but also to articulate its position as an important group of people within the framework of the Roman empire (Rives, 1995). In Gaul the same concerns are reflected in the evolution of a Gallo-Roman text that used the Roman language to write Celtic languages. Gallo-Latin inscriptions flourished alongside Latin texts. As Woolf has argued, this was neither a popular pidgin used by semi-Romanized groups nor the language of the culturally disenfranchised, but rather a text created by a Gallo-Roman élite whose self-definition of their identity was in some ways both Gallic and Roman (Woolf, 1994, pp.95–7). The assimilation of local and imperial language was an important articulatory tool for the creation of new élites within the Roman empire. In areas where literacy does not predate Roman influence, we find the language of the conqueror being adopted as a useful tool of communication.

So by the end of the first century AD, all the western provinces contained not only the descendants of Roman colonists, but a segment of the truly indigenous population which was acquainted with the Latin language and other aspects of Roman culture. Writing, in one aspect or another, was a routine part of their experience. Such provinces had never before experienced the degree of literacy that they now attained. It was not just confined to the aristocratic, clerical or priestly élite. In cities everywhere there were literate artisans as well as literate property owners. However, this new literacy was numerically restricted and generally refers to literacy in the Latin language.

Epigraphic evidence, though, gives the historian no real indication of the diffusion and extent of *spoken* languages within the Roman empire. It seems likely that the number of individuals who could speak these local languages was far greater than those who could read or write them. In many provincial communities different languages served different purposes. For instance, in the rural areas of Roman Egypt, although the predominant written language was Greek, it is likely that Demotic (an Egyptian/Greek patois) was the language spoken in the villages. In Britain, although most inscriptions are in Latin, the vast majority of the inhabitants continued to speak British dialects. What has to be remembered is that the inability to speak, write or read Latin or Greek did not exclude an individual from Roman citizenship, but the evidence suggests that a certain degree of bilingualism may have been common. Many things might have encouraged individuals whose first language was not Greek or Latin to learn one or the other – cultural prestige, commercial advantage, social contact or wishing to communicate with officialdom.

The relationship between Romanization and language is a complex one. However it can be said that to equate Romanization with the complete eclipse of local cultures and their languages is hopelessly simplistic. The meeting of the respective cultures of conquerors and conquered not only involved the subsumption and appropriation of old languages, but also threw up new ones with which to articulate the changed circumstances and possibilities created by Roman hegemony.

Conclusions

Several points emerge from this essay.

- Power, culture and identity are constructed, maintained and contested through communication.
- Control over and through the written word was a central component of imperial rule and élite self-definition.
- The written word fulfilled an important ritualistic and symbolic purpose as well as a referential function in constructions of power, culture and identity in the Roman world.
- The Roman empire was a predominantly oral society. Oral communication played an important role not only in constructions of culture, identity and power but also in the dissemination of the written word.
- The paucity of literate individuals in the Roman empire ensured that non-written visual media were an important component in the representation and formation of culture, identity and power; non-written and written media were often combined to create particular narratives.
- Romanization does not represent a complete takeover of local cultures and the languages which were used to articulate them. Rather, it was a process that involved appropriations by both rulers and ruled in the creation of new imperial narratives.

References

ALEXANDER, L. (1990) 'The living voice: scepticism towards the written word in early Christian and in Graeco-Roman texts' in D.J. Clines, S.E. Fowl and S.E. Porter (eds), *The Bible in Three Dimensions: Essays in Celebration of Forty Years of Biblical Studies in the University of Sheffield*, Sheffield, Journal for the Study of the Old Testament Supplement Series 87, pp.221–7.

BHABHA, H.K. (1990) 'Introduction: narrating the nation' in H.K. Bhabha (ed.) *Nation and Narration*, London and New York, Routledge.

BHABHA, H.K. (1994) *The Location of Culture*, London and New York, Routledge.

BOWMAN, A.K. and THOMAS, J.D. (eds) (1994) *The Vindolanda Writing Tablets II*, London, British Museum Press.

BOWMAN, A.K. and WOOLF, G. (eds) (1994) *Literacy and Power in the Ancient World*, Cambridge, Cambridge University Press.

CARSON, R.A.G. (1990) *Coins of the Roman Empire*, London and New York, Routledge.

CHAMPLIN, E. (1980) *Fronto and Antonine Rome*, Cambridge, Mass., Harvard University Press.

COLES, R.A. (1966) *Reports of the Proceedings in Papyri* (Papyrilogica Bruxellensia 4), Brussels.

CRAWFORD, M. (1988) 'The laws of the Romans, knowledge and diffusion', in J. Gonzalez and J. Arce (eds) *Estudios sobre la Tabula Siarensis*, Madrid, Consejo Superior de Investigaciones Científicas, Centro de Estudios Históricos, pp.127–40.

CULHAM, P. (1989) 'Archives and alternatives in Republican Rome', *Classical Philology*, 84, pp.100–15.

ELSNER, J. (1996) 'Inventing *Imperium*: texts and the propaganda of monuments in Augustan Rome', in J. Elsner (ed.) *Art and Text in Roman Culture*, Cambridge, Cambridge University Press, pp.32–53.

GARCÍA, S. (ed.) (1993) *European Identity and the Search for Legitimacy*, London, Pinter Publishers.

GOODMAN, M.D. (1994) 'Texts, scribes, and power in Roman Judaea' in Bowman and Woolf (eds), pp.99–101.

GOODY, J. (1986) *The Logic of Writing and the Organisation of Society*, Cambridge, Cambridge University Press.

GOODY, J. and WATT, I. (1968) 'The consequences of literacy' in J. Goody (ed.), *Literacy in Traditional Societies*, Cambridge, Cambridge University Press, pp.27–68.

HARRIS, W.V. (1989) *Ancient Literacy*, Cambridge, Mass., Harvard University Press.

KLEINER, D.C.E. (1986) 'Athens under the Romans: the patronage of emperors and kings', in C.B. McClendon (ed.) *Rome and the Provinces: the Transformation of Art in the Mediterranean*, New Haven, Conn., Yale University Press, pp.8–20.

KLEINER, D.C.E. (1992) *Roman Sculpture*, New Haven, Conn., Yale University Press.

LEWIS, N. (1983) *Life in Roman Egypt under Roman Rule*, Oxford, Clarendon Press.

LEWIS, S. (1996) *News and Society in the Greek Polis*, London, Duckworth.

MCLUHAN, M. (1964, reprinted 1987) *Understanding Media: the Extensions of Man: the Medium is the Message*, London, Ark.

MEYER, E.A. (1990) 'Explaining the epigraphic habit in the Roman Empire: the evidence of epitaphs', *Journal of Roman Studies*, 80, pp.74–96.

MILLAR, F. (1977) *The Emperor in the Roman World*, London, Duckworth.

MILLAR, F. (1983) 'Epigraphy' in M. Crawford (ed.) *Sources for Ancient History*, Cambridge, Cambridge University Press.

NICOLET, C. (1988) *L'Inventaire du Monde: Géographie et Politique aux Origines de l'Empire Romain*, Paris, Fayard.

OLIVER, J.H. (trans.) (1953) *Aelius Aristides: The Ruling Power*, Philadelphia, American Philosophical Society.

RIVES, J. (1995) *Religion and Authority in Roman Carthage from Augustus to Constantine*, Oxford, Clarendon Press.

ROGERS, G.M. (1991) *The Sacred Identity of Ephesos: Foundation Myths of a Roman City*, London, Routledge.

RUSSELL, D.A. (1983) *Greek Declamation*, Cambridge, Cambridge University Press.

SAID, E.W. (1993) *Culture and Imperialism*, London, Chatto & Windus.

TALBERT, R.J.A. (1984) *The Senate of Imperial Rome*, Princeton, N.J., Princeton University Press.

THOMAS, R. (1989) *Oral Tradition and Written Record in Classical Athens*, Cambridge, Cambridge University Press.

THOMAS, R. (1992) *Literacy and Orality in Ancient Greece*, Cambridge, Cambridge University Press.

WILLIAMSON, C. (1987) 'Monuments of bronze: Roman legal documents on bronze tablets', *Classical Antiquity*, vol.6, no.1, pp.160–83.

WINTLE, M. (1996) 'Cultural diversity and identity in Europe' in M. Wintle (ed.) *Culture and Identity in Europe: Perceptions of Divergence and Unity in Past and Present*, Aldershot, Avebury.

WOOLF, G. (1994) 'Power and the spread of writing in the West' in Bowman and Woolf (eds), pp.84–98.

Essay Three
The city of Rome: capital and symbol

BY VALERIE HOPE

An empire without Rome?

> What made matters worse was a persistent rumour that Caesar intended to move the seat of government to Troy or Alexandria, carrying off all the national resources, drafting every available man in Italy for military service, and letting his friends govern what was left of the city.
>
> (Suetonius, *Julius Caesar* 79, in Graves, 1989, p.48)

Julius Caesar was assassinated dramatically in 44 BC. One of the reasons subsequently propagated by the assassins to justify his death was that Rome was no longer good enough for Caesar. Caesar, so the story went, was enticed by Cleopatra and by the east with its tradition of kingship and ruler gods. The idea that a Roman leader could contemplate abandoning Rome was unthinkable and unforgivable. Rome lay at the historical, political and symbolic heart of the empire and no one should challenge this. The whispers concerning Caesar's intentions were probably no more than rumours. Yet in the highly charged atmosphere of the late republic attacks on the reputation of the city served to undermine the very definition of Roman identity and power. But why were Julius Caesar and his successors so bound to the city of Rome?

This essay will explore some of the reasons why ancient Rome was perceived and constructed as the ultimate city. This will entail focusing on the city of Rome as both a physical and a symbolic entity. It was at Rome that the power of empire was manifested; the city was the seat of administration and the home of the emperor. This aura of power, derived from the empire, imbued the city with a unique culture and identity. But the city was not monolithic or static and this essay will also explore how the identity and culture of the city were renegotiated to match both the empire and the emperor. How did Rome influence the empire and the emperor, and how did the empire and emperor, in their turn, influence Rome?

Locating ancient Rome

Information concerning the foundation of Rome and its early development is derived from two major sources: the traditional historical

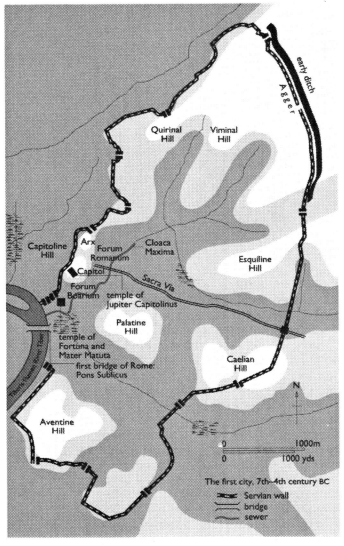

accounts composed by authors such as Livy several centuries later, and archaeological discoveries. According to legend, the Romans traced their ancestry back to Aeneas, the hero who escaped from Troy. Aeneas settled in Latium where his son founded the city of Alba Longa. Tradition held that Rome was founded in 753 BC by twin boys, Romulus and Remus, who were descended from the kings of Alba Longa. Archaeological evidence suggests that Rome began in the ninth or eighth century BC as a series of small farmsteads on a group of hills overlooking the River Tiber. Between the 'Seven Hills' were marshy areas which were utilized as cemeteries (Holloway, 1994; Cornell, 1995). This early informal settlement overlooked a convenient crossing point on the Tiber and had ready access to the coast.

Crucial changes which began the transformation of Rome from village to city occurred in the later seventh century BC under the six semi-legendary Tarquin kings. The Forum valley, between the Palatine and Capitoline hills, was reclaimed by the construction of a large drain, the Cloaca Maxima. The

Figure 3.1 *Plan showing the location and early development of Rome. (From Scarre, 1995, p.21. Map copyright of Swanston Publishing Ltd, Derby)*

Forum (Forum Romanum) became a public square and remained as such throughout Roman history. On the Capitoline hill a temple was built and dedicated to the god Jupiter Capitolinus. This temple, which would be rebuilt on several occasions, became the spiritual heart of the city. A wooden bridge was placed across the Tiber and a town wall may have been constructed. Tradition maintained that the Romans evicted their last king, Tarquin the Proud, in 510 BC. Rome then became a republic governed by a pair of annually elected magistrates, the consuls, drawn from an assembly of leading citizens, the senate. Over the following five centuries, under the republican system of government, this small town evolved to become mistress first of Italy and then of a vast empire. Rome became the leading city of the known world.

The physical impact of territorial expansion was substantial: Rome became large, densely populated and ultimately a grand city. In the fourth century BC the so-called Servian Wall was constructed which enclosed approximately 400 hectares, and in 312 BC the first aqueduct was built by Appius Claudius Caecus. From the second century BC Rome came into increasing contact with the Greek east and Hellenistic influences were felt in the city. It was during the first century BC, however, and at the hands of prominent men such as Sulla, Pompey and Julius Caesar, that the city increasingly gained the physical symbols of power. Aristocratic competition encouraged such men to embellish Rome as a means of increasing their own prestige. For example, Pompey provided Rome with its first stone theatre in 55 BC, while Julius Caesar planned a new forum adjacent to the existing Forum Romanum (Stambaugh, 1988, pp.39–45). Such acts of munificence would set the scene for the relationship that would develop between the emperor and the city. But Rome's success made the city more than a physical entity: it also became an abstract symbol and an ideal, the figurehead and embodiment of the empire.

Much of this essay will explore the relationship between the emperor and Rome and the impact of the empire upon the city. But initially the continuity of Rome both as a place and symbol needs to be stressed. The ultimate disintegration of the empire that Rome had established did not mark the end of the city. Rome soon acquired a new identity as the Christian capital, the heart of the Roman Catholic church. Popes and political leaders have looked to the ancient city for inspiration and have sought to resuscitate the splendour of the city. In the latter part of the nineteenth century, for example, Rome became a symbol for the new Italy, united for the first time since the collapse of the Roman Empire. Beyond the city itself the legacy of Rome has been pervasive in much of the western world for centuries. The idea of Rome has fuelled revolutions and revivals in artistic, literary and political contexts.

Rome's long history, continuing influence and changing face can make it difficult to isolate ancient Rome: three thousand years of continuous occupation have made it a complex urban site. To what degree is it possible to reconstruct the city of the emperors? The striking physical remains of the ancient city such as the Roman Forum, the Colosseum, the arch of Titus (Figure 3.8) and Trajan's column (Figure

3.9), are still prominent landmarks in modern Rome. But these structures represent, in general, isolated public buildings and provide limited insights into the overall townscape. Additional evidence can help with the reconstruction of the topography of the ancient city (Richardson, 1992; Steinby, 1993): coins may carry representations of now lost buildings celebrating their inauguration or restoration; similarly inscriptions record structures – their building, repair or maintenance; literature describes the city and the events for which it provided a backdrop; and unique evidence sometimes survives, such as the fragments of a marble plan of the city (*Forma urbis*), commissioned by the emperor Septimius Severus at the beginning of the third century (Figure 3.2).

Uniting this evidence into a coherent picture is a complex process. In particular the attempt to match archaeological and literary evidence is fraught with difficulty. Are anachronistic and partial texts a valid tool for interpreting and understanding extant physical remains? For example, can Livy's descriptions of the early settlement help to identify the archaeological remains of early Rome? Recreating the physical appearance of Rome is also complicated in terms of chronology; the city was constantly evolving throughout its history. The Rome of the republican orator and politician Cicero would have contrasted sharply with that, say, of the first Christian emperor Constantine. This would have been true not just of the appearance of the ancient city but in many other aspects; the urban image entailed more than just buildings. We need to search not just for the shifting appearance of the city but also changes in its organization, administration, in its populace and its feel or atmosphere.

The legacy of ancient Rome has fuelled imaginations for generations with the desire to reconstruct not only the events and spaces of the city but also to recapture the essence of the city at its height. This is often best illustrated in cinema, novels and art rather than through historical and archaeological studies. For example, the paintings of Lawrence Alma Tadema sought to capture a sense of the grandeur of Rome without relying on known physical structures or historical or legendary events. *An Audience at Agrippa's*, which was painted in 1875, seeks to bring to life many aspects of Rome as it was perceived in popular Victorian culture (Figure 3.3). The painting suggests the grandeur of the buildings covered in gleaming marble, the opulence of the interior furnishings and decor, the power of empire as enshrined in the emperor's statue, and the inequalities and hierarchies of Roman society. A depiction such as this is fanciful: a condensing of buildings, people and events. Such paintings may also contain a moral message: that despite and because of its power and opulence Rome became corrupt

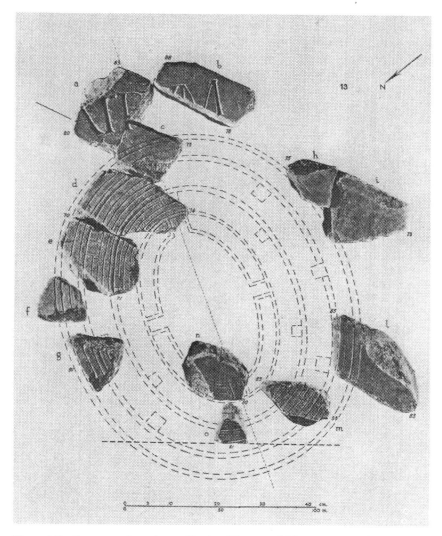

Figure 3.2 *Fragments from the marble plan* (Forma urbis) *representing the Colosseum. (Reproduced from Carettoni et al., 1960, plate 19, by permission of Commune di Roma Sovraintendenza ai Beni Culturali)*

and ultimately fell. Nevertheless, despite the moral dialogue, the nineteenth-century fantasy evokes what factual plans and pictures often fail to do.

To be in ancient Rome was an experience that appealed to all the senses – note the crowd of people, the whispered comments, the texture of the tiger-skin rug. People as well as buildings make up a city, and how

67

Figure 3.3 *Sir Lawrence Alma-Tadema,* An Audience at Agrippa's *(1875). (Dick Institute, Kilmarnock. Photo: East Ayrshire Council Museums and Arts)*

people viewed Rome was coloured by their own experiences of what life was both like and should have been like within the city, and by what Rome meant to them.

Rome was always and continues to be a city very conscious of its past. The ancient city was often described in terms of the past, and buildings and places by their old associations. Stories about Aeneas, Romulus and Remus are part of the shared Roman heritage. The image of Aeneas escorting his father and son from the ruins of Troy became an emblem for common Roman values, while the image of the wolf suckling the infant Romulus and Remus was used as a symbol for Rome itself. Of course, buildings, statues and inscriptions continued long after the creators had vanished, and thus monuments such as the Roman Forum, the arch of Titus and the Colosseum evoked the past. All this serves as a reminder that we cannot isolate a single view, moment or interpretation of ancient Rome. The city has always evolved, shaping its present from the remains of the past.

Rome, the perfect place

What makes a city great? Is it impressive architecture, industrious people, a fair political system, economic power, high culture or a reputation for good food? Or perhaps the key to greatness is more emotive – friendly inhabitants, the feel of the city, its atmosphere or personality. Latin and Greek authors, struck by Rome's rapid rise to power, tried to pinpoint what it was that made Rome special. Summarizing what Rome meant and stood for was almost beyond words.

> About her [Rome] not only is it impossible to speak properly, but it is impossible even to see her properly. In truth it requires some all-seeing Argos – rather the all-seeing god who dwells in the city. For beholding so many hills occupied by buildings, or on plains so many meadows completely urbanised, or so much land brought under the name of one city, who could survey her accurately? And from what point of observation?
>
> (Aelius Aristides, *To Rome* 6, trans. Oliver, 1953, p.896)

This did not, however, prevent people from tackling the basis of Rome's greatness. That the answer was not an easy one to find is well illustrated by the range of factors identified in contemporary literature which praise everything, from Rome's location to its buildings and amenities. The aspects identified by the different authors were often dictated by the specific purpose of the literature composed and the period in which it was written. Yet they all share a fascination with the city of Rome as an entity. The role of individuals in promoting Rome was acknowledged, but in general there was a lack of differentiation between the reasons why the Romans as a people should rule and why Rome as a place stood at the head of an empire. Rome itself was looked to as a collective entity and the city as a whole was imbued with qualities and its own personality.

Indeed Rome was often presented as a female or mother figure (for example, Martial, *On the Spectacles* 12.21, 9–10; Livy, *Histories* 2.40).

In the late republic and early empire authors often suggested that the beauty of Rome and the essence of its power lay not in its appearance or physical structures but in the stature of the city (Favro, 1996, p.45). Authors when describing Rome of this period were forced to focus on more abstract features than fine buildings, efficient amenities and expedient town planning. Emphasis fell on the physical advantages conveyed by the location of the city, its easy access to the sea, its fertile territory, its healthy springs and easily protected hills (Cicero, *On the Republic* 2.3, 5–6; Livy, *Histories* 5.54.4). That there was undoubted truth in these claims is illustrated by looking at a plan of the site of Rome (Figure 3.1). The proximity to the river of the plain surrounded by hills provided a sound site for a settlement. In lauding the physical advantages of Rome's location, however, such accounts inevitably failed to note the disadvantages of the site, such as the poor harbour at Ostia and the frequent flooding of the city. Rome was held up as the ideal place for the centre of an empire, as if the first founders of the city knew it was destined for greatness. Indeed the choice of the site of Rome was not viewed as purely human; it was claimed that those who established and founded Rome were divinely inspired and many places within the city were imbued with religious significance (Livy, *Histories* 5.51–2; Vitruvius, *On Architecture* 6.1). The true greatness of Rome and key to success lay in its receipt of divine favour. If Rome was not destined for great physical beauty, it was destined through the intervention of the gods to rule and govern the world (Virgil, *Aeneid* 6.849–54).

With the consolidation of the empire and the shift to autocratic power Rome attained more and more of the material symbols of greatness. Descriptions of Rome could now focus on the beauty of its architecture, the scale of its buildings and the opulence of its appearance. Strabo, describing the improvements to the city under the emperor Augustus, stressed the splendours of the Campus Martius. This area, which lay beyond the city walls and was thus less encumbered by structures than the central city, provided the perfect display area for the new regime. Grand buildings judiciously laid out in this spacious quarter captured the might and glory of both Rome and the emperor (Strabo, *Geography* 5, 3.8). Equally for the absent Ovid, who pined for Rome in his exile enforced by Augustus, the splendid city was defined and described not by its location (however divinely inspired) but by its grand buildings, marbles and fine views (Ovid, *Letters from Pontus* 1.8.33–8).

But for all its splendour and opulence emphasis continued to fall on the city as a practical place as well as a city of beauty. Rome was not just a show city but the seat of government of a vast empire which, like the city itself, needed to be well run and organized. Thus for some authors of the imperial period the real physical greatness of Rome lay not in imposing structures such as temples, fora and amphitheatres. These were mere frivolities compared to the practical amenities of the city – its roads, aqueducts and sewers. These impressive feats of engineering were to be marvelled at because of the sheer scale of the undertakings – the extent of the underground tunnels, for example, or the distance from which water was piped into Rome – but above all because of the benefits which they conveyed (Frontinus, *On Aqueducts* 1.4; Dionysius of Halicarnassus, *Roman Antiquities* 3.67.4; Pliny the Elder, *Natural History* 3.103; 3.121–4; Strabo, *Geography* 5.3–8). Such things added to the grandeur of Rome. In terms of scale Rome was the biggest city, or at least people could measure and calculate it to be so. This sense of scale is captured nowhere else so forcefully as in the summary of the size of Rome by Pliny the Elder written in the first century AD.

> A measurement running from the milestone set up at the head of the Roman Forum to each of the city gates – which today number thirty-seven if the Twelve Gates are counted as one and the seven of the old gates that no longer exist are omitted – gives a total of 20.765 miles in a straight line. But the measurement of all the thoroughfares block by block, from the same milestone to the outermost edge of the buildings including the Praetorian Camp, totals a little more than sixty miles. And if one should consider in addition the height of the buildings, he would assuredly form a fitting appraisal and would admit that no city has existed in the whole world that could be compared with Rome in size.
>
> (Pliny the Elder, *Natural History,* 3.5.66–7, in Lewis and Reinhold, 1990, pp.135–6)

The account becomes a numerical extravaganza as Pliny lists the lengths of the streets, the number of gateways, the circumference of the walls. Here is the factual and undeniable statistical proof that Rome is the greatest city (Purcell, 1992, pp.242–3).

Whether the authors of the imperial period dwell on Rome's location, temples or sewers, they all share the desire to define and describe Rome; to pinpoint the special features of the city. All the descriptions were informed and influenced by the author's knowledge that Rome had established a vast territorial empire. The empire was great: thus Rome must be the greatest city not only by association but also in appearance and attributes. People may have differed in opinion as to what Rome's greatest features were, but the cumulative effect was the impression that Rome deserved to stand at the head of the empire it had created. The perspective implies that it was Rome's greatness which made the empire and there was less acknowledgement that the empire had played its part in making Rome. Nevertheless the message was clear: Rome may not have been the most physically beautiful city that the world had ever known but it was undoubtedly, like its empire, the biggest and best.

Rome, the seat of power

The rumours that circulated following the death of Julius Caesar indicated that the prominence of Rome was not beyond question. The seeds of empire may have been sown in Rome but its pre-eminence was not guaranteed especially since there were other cities in the Mediterranean world which had claims to fame. In particular Alexandria, the capital of the Egyptian Ptolemaic dynasty, had a high reputation augmented by the prestige of being the foundation of Alexander the Great. Alexandria was often connected with the alleged plans of Roman rulers such as Julius Caesar, Mark Antony, Caligula and Nero, to find an alternative to Rome as the capital of the empire (Edwards, 1996, p.19). Yet during the unsettled times in which he was pre-eminent, Julius Caesar was probably more than aware of the political value of Rome. The actions of the *dictator* are far from suggesting that he intended to abandon the city. In some respects Caesar may have been dissatisfied with Rome. He was a well-travelled man, familiar with the great cities of the empire, and he may have found the mediocre appearance of Rome unsuited to its place as the capital of a great empire (Zanker, 1988, p.20). But rather than abandon Rome Julius Caesar sought to improve the city. He aligned himself with Rome, he proclaimed himself its saviour, he associated himself with the legendary founder of the city, Romulus, and undertook extensive building projects (Favro, 1996, pp.65–7). Some of his more grandiose schemes, such as plans to reroute the Tiber, coupled with his arrogant nature, may have alienated some of his peers (Suetonius, *Julius Caesar* 44; Cicero, *Letters to Atticus* 13.33; 13.35), and have contributed to the rumours of his opponents that the city was not good enough for him (Suetonius, *Julius Caesar* 79). The trouble was that in revamping the image of Rome, both politically and physically, Julius Caesar did too much too quickly, and there may have been a perceived danger that the very identity of the city was becoming obscured through the vision of one man.

The preservation of the centrality of Rome and the safeguarding of the elusive phenomenon of Roman identity continued to be a point of manipulation in the final years of the republic. Octavian, the young heir of Julius Caesar who was later named Augustus, aligned himself with the city and all its traditions. The propaganda of Octavian counterpoised this with the disloyalty of his opponent Antony who fell under the eastern sway of Cleopatra and kingship. The resulting battles and political intrigues often occurred hundreds of miles away from

Figure 3.4 *Coins dating to the years before the battle of Actium (31 BC) which show heads of Roman divinities on the obverse (Peace and Venus) and images of Octavian in military dress. Each coin has the legend* CAESAR DIVI F, *the son of the divine Caesar. (Reproduced by permission of the Trustees of the British Museum)*

Italy but the spotlight never completely left Rome. Octavian's strategy was to maintain Rome as the centre of the Roman world, with himself at the centre of republican Rome. By contrast Antony, removed from the traditional heart of the Roman world, could no longer monitor popular opinion and could easily be portrayed as having abandoned his Roman identity. Augustus promoted his own image through buildings, statues, and coinage (Zanker, 1988, pp.33–77). He was presented as the saviour of Rome, devoted to its people and its gods. On coins, for example, the portrait of Octavian was associated with that of Roman gods and goddesses or victories which Octavian had won on behalf of the Roman people (see Figure 3.4). On the other hand Antony was seen as favouring eastern deities and enjoying a life of luxury and decadence. The decisive battle of Actium (31 BC) was portrayed as the ultimate conflict between Roman refined and civilized qualities and the barbaric traditions of Egypt and the east. The battle was not between two Romans but between Rome and Octavian on the one hand, and Egypt and Cleopatra on the other.

> Not long ago it would have been high treason
> To fetch the Caecuban [a type of wine] from the family store-rooms,
>   When the wild Queen was still
> Plotting destruction to our Capitol
>
> And ruin to the Empire with her squalid
> Pack of diseased half-men – mad, wishful grandeur,
>   Tipsy with sweet good luck!
> But all her fleet burnt, scarcely one ship saved –
>
> That tamed her rage; and Caesar, when his galleys
> Chased her from Italy, soon brought her, dreaming
>   And drugged with native wine,
> Back to the hard realities of fear
> (Horace, *Odes* 1.37.1–12, trans. Michie, 1967, p.87)

The final battle, in literary images, was brought almost to Rome itself. Note Horace's reference to Italy in the third verse; it is almost as if the battle of Actium had been fought on the shores of the Italian peninsula. The reference to Cleopatra 'plotting destruction to the Capitol' in the first verse also suggests that the conflict threatened the heart of Rome, the Capitoline hill, where the sacred temple of Jupiter was located. The contest ceased to be a battle fought on a distant shore between fellow Romans and became instead a battle between good and evil, between west and east, a battle for the protection and defence of Rome itself.

With the advent of the imperial system the symbolic role of Rome increased. Rome, as a collective entity, in practice no longer ruled the empire since power was in the hands of one man. And to this one man Rome was the ultimate political prize. Thus the significance of the city and all that it stood for did not diminish. The rule of Octavian, now termed Augustus, saw the consolidation of Rome's position. By highlighting Antony's fatal mistake in his alleged abandonment of Rome, Augustus put his own cards squarely on the table. Augustus underlined that the empire was Roman and that only Rome could be the true centre of the Roman world. Augustus championed Rome as a symbolic representation of his power and that of the empire which he ruled. Augustus intertwined both his own and Rome's divine destiny; he promoted the history and traditions of Rome and sought to match these by improving the appearance and organization of the city (see below). Future emperors generally followed his lead – Rome was an arena which the emperor dared not ignore. Rome had to be funded and embellished and its people fed, clothed and entertained. Wherever the emperor was, Rome maintained the image of home and of power and authority as enshrined in the senate, even if the latter as a governing body was effectively defunct.

The power struggles of the end of the republic and the development of autocratic government revealed, however, a contradiction which faced all future emperors. On the one hand the emperor promoted Rome as the seat of power and as a physical representation of that power. On the other hand it was apparent that the true seat of power was wherever the emperor was and that was not necessarily in Rome. For any emperor to put all his energies into Rome alone and contemplate the empire from the confines of the capital city would be a mistake. Good emperors travelled the empire; it was beneficial to their image to be seen as proactive rather than passive. The emperor Trajan, for example, spent extended periods away from the capital city campaigning on the frontiers and extending the empire. His successor Hadrian passed more than twelve of his twenty-one-year reign away from Rome viewing and exploring his domain. But although the emperor and the court could be mobile, Rome retained its symbolic role as the centre of the empire.

What the emperor did while he was away was still interpreted by reference to the capital city and how it benefited. Any unnecessary or unjustified distance between emperor and capital could damage the reputation of the *princeps* (the first or leading citizen); when absence was necessary family and/or trustworthy deputies were essential to monitor the pulse of the capital and to act as frontline reminders of the absent power. The emperor Tiberius preferred the island of Capri to Rome, and his prolonged absence, although he was geographically not far removed from the city, alienated the populace and allowed his deputies too much sway (Tacitus, *Annals* 4.39–5.2; Suetonius, *Tiberius* 41–5; 60–5). Nero was condemned for travelling in the east for the wrong reason: that the excursion was for his own pleasure rather than for the good of Rome or the empire (Suetonius, *Nero* 22–4). By contrast Trajan was a hero because his absences from the city brought glory to Rome by the extension of the empire. Real power might be with the emperor wherever he went, but in accepting the city of Rome as his capital the emperor could not ignore the city or leave it to fall into the hands of others who might exploit the potent symbol of power. The emperor's relationship with the city and its people was parallel to his relationship with the whole empire and its people. If the emperor could not control Rome, how could he control a vast empire?

Rome, the showcase of the emperor

Augustus claimed to have refounded Rome. Images of fertility and rebirth pervaded the imagery and literature of his reign. Augustus created a paternalistic image of himself providing for and meeting the needs of the people. He took a holistic approach to the city, focusing not just on rebuilding the physical fabric of Rome but reorganizing its administration, its amenities and its religious facilities. Roads and aqueducts were improved, the supply of food was monitored and the inhabitants provided with facilities for worship, bathing and entertainment. The overall impact on the city of Rome was great. Augustus converted Rome into a place worthy of both the emperor and the empire, embellishing and improving the city. This was not in absolute terms something new. During the late republic ambitious citizens had competed to leave their mark on the city by funding buildings and providing for the needs of the populace. Often these up-and-coming politicians had emulated the architecture and facilities of other great cities and in the process had aggrandized Rome. Yet Rome of the republic, as was noted earlier, was not a city of great beauty or style; it was badly planned and lacked cohesiveness. In the final years of the republic the fabric of the city had increasingly come to represent the power struggles of individuals and the disintegration of the state. Augustus now took the aggrandizement of the city by an individual to a new level in which the city became the showcase of not many men but one man, and in the process it became more unified. The city ceased to be an arena for aristocratic competition, becoming instead the focus for the display of the emperor. Others were not completely precluded from adorning the city; buildings might also be set up in the name of the heirs or family of the *princeps*; but even if indirectly most of the glory still fell to the emperor. If Rome was perceived as the emperor's chosen city then it must outshine its rivals. It must be bigger, brasher, louder and more glorious. Rome was to be better than Alexandria and more famous than Troy.

Augustus may have transformed Rome but the transition had to be selective and tactful. Just as Augustus was forced to introduce his political changes in a subtle way he could not afford to treat the fabric of the city in an autocratic fashion. Certain areas of Rome and its environs provided considerable scope and space for the construction of extensive united structures which celebrated the new regime. In the Campus Martius, an area outside the city walls, structures funded by Augustus and his son-in-law Agrippa, or voted by the senate in honour of the emperor, such as the mausoleum of Augustus, the huge sundial and the Ara Pacis, were spatially united to give physical expression to the new

Figure 3.5 *Reconstruction of the northern end of the Campus Martius showing the spatial relationship between the mausoleum of Augustus, the sundial (Horologium Augusti) and the Ara Pacis. (Reproduced from Buchner, 1982, by permission of Professor Buchner)*

regime (see Figure 3.5). But the Campus Martius was not simply filled with empty display monuments: instead the area was redesigned to provide the people of Rome with public spaces, amenities and religious centres (Favro, 1996, p.207). Indeed in much of the city the scope for new structures was limited, and Augustus had to work within the existing framework. He did not change Rome by demolishing what he disliked, confiscating property and redesigning the city. Suetonius records that Augustus made his forum narrower than planned because he did not wish to eject people from their houses (Suetonius, *Augustus* 56). In Augustus' own biography, the *Res Gestae*, which was originally placed outside the mausoleum, the emphasis fell on restoration and rejuvenation rather than on a policy of 'out with the old and in with the new'. Augustus repeatedly describes how he repaired and rededicated buildings; his alterations and additions were entwined with the existing Rome and its structures. Modern commentators may speak of Augustan Rome almost as if it were a new city created in his own image, but Augustus was aware that Rome had to stay Roman and maintain its own unique identity even if that identity was given an Augustan slant. The *Res Gestae* itself was a monumental inscription about the city which helped interpret Rome and Augustus' impact upon it. Through his buildings Augustus became part of the geography of Rome (Elsner, 1996, pp.40–4).

The need to work within the existing framework of the city was also seen in Augustus' treatment of the practical problems that plagued Rome. Augustus could not overthrow the haphazard street system with all its hindrances. He did, however, divide the city into fourteen regions and 265 districts. Each district had a small-scale administration of officials with religious duties and practical responsibilities for supervising buildings, fire fighting and security. The major problems to afflict the residential areas, which were often aggravated by the narrow streets and shoddily constructed buildings, were fire and flood. In an attempt to alleviate these problems Augustus introduced building regulations, shored up the banks of the Tiber and created his own fire brigade (Zanker, 1988, p.155; Favro, 1996, pp.133–40). Improving Rome entailed more than visual spectacles: the city needed to be healthy and well ordered. The appearance of the residential districts of the city may not have changed dramatically but the infrastructure felt the emperor's touch.

One major aspect of how individual emperors recreated Rome in their own image was through the appropriation of the past, and Augustus was adept at entwining himself in Rome's history. For example, he associated himself with the mythical founders of Rome, Aeneas and Romulus, emphasizing how he too was the founder of a new age for Rome. This appropriation of the past was also apparent in Augustan building schemes. Augustus restored and repaired many of the pre-existing buildings of Rome which were then often adorned with inscriptions that recalled his generosity. Even when he declined a written record of his actions, those places and structures became connected in the popular knowledge with the name of the emperor. This adaptation of Rome's existing fabric to suit the image of the new regime is best illustrated by the Roman Forum (Figure 3.6). The traditional hub of the city was given a new gloss which celebrated Augustus and his family by the manipulation of both old and new structures. Among the many changes were the dedication by Augustus of a temple to his father, the

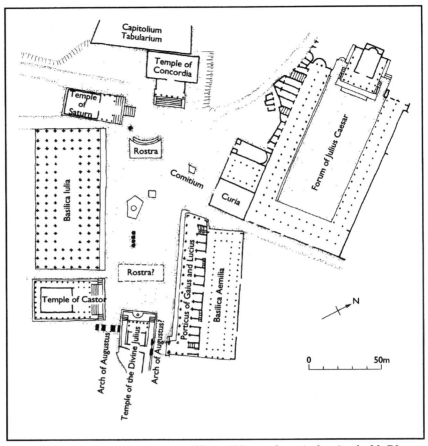

Figure 3.6 *The Forum Romanum, c. 10 BC. (After a schematic drawing by M. Pfanner. Reproduced from Zanker, 1988)*

divine Julius, and a new *curia* or meeting place for the senate which bore the family name of Iulia. The senate also dedicated at least one triumphal arch for Augustus' military victories while Augustus enlarged both of the existing basilicas, naming the extensions after his grandsons. This is not to mention the numerous statues, trophies and ornamental decorations which were probably added to the forum and the completion of the adjacent Forum of Julius Caesar which had been begun by Julius Caesar. This reordering of the Roman Forum gave it greater unity and grandeur but in the process created a new environment and experience (Favro, 1996, pp.195–9). The Roman Forum, the traditional emblem of republican government, still retained 'reminders of a glorious past, but one which was now overshadowed by the dazzling splendour of the present' (Zanker, 1988, p.82). Many of Augustus' successors similarly exploited the associations of old buildings and places. Nero, for example, placed images of the Ara Pacis of Augustus on his coins, which emphasized his descent from the first emperor and played on the themes of peace and stability (Elsner, 1994, p.115). Hadrian extensively overhauled the Campus Martius, restoring many of the buildings of Augustan date including the Pantheon which had been originally constructed by Agrippa (Boatwright, 1987, pp.33–73) and thus aligning himself with the image and projects of his predecessor. The reuse and restoration of specific structures underlines the significance of places in Roman political history (Edwards, 1996, p.22). Monuments triggered memories which gave access to the past, which in turn could gain potency in the present.

Rome and emperor, between human and divine

In the centuries following Augustus, Rome's physical appearance increasingly reflected and matched its extensive power, or perhaps more accurately the power of the emperor or ruling dynasty. Visitors were to be overawed by the city, its scale, its impressive buildings and amenities. Augustus set the pace for future emperors and the majority sought to embellish Rome and leave their mark on the city in some form. The emperor walked a careful line, however, between the display of his individual power and the power and might of the empire. Glorification of the emperor as an individual had to be counterbalanced by buildings and acts which glorified the gods and the might of Rome and which advantaged the general populace. Buildings could be interpreted as a sign of the greatness of both Rome and the emperor, but equally if taken to excess the same buildings could be interpreted as the egotistical fantasies of a bad emperor. Constructions such as fora and aqueducts might be named after individual emperors and members of their families but they were intended for the use of all. Gifts of money, food and shows promoted the emperor's name but benefited the people. Palaces were allowable but they needed to be modest, at least on the exterior, or built away from Rome. There was an inherent contradiction present in the emperor's position: he maintained the city, he controlled the city, but he could not portray himself as greater than the city.

Many emperors who followed Augustus claimed to refound Rome. They portrayed themselves as the saviours of the city, restoring it to past glories. Such claims had a particular potency at the beginning of an emperor's reign, especially if his predecessor had fallen short of expectations. After Rome's bad experiences under emperors such as Nero, Domitian and Caracalla, who were perceived as tyrants that used the city for selfish ends, the new dynasties looked to rejuvenate Rome and to revive the old values embodied in the city. Rome, its appearance and well-being, became a political pawn to be manoeuvred by emperors and used either to associate or distance them from their predecessors. Building schemes were part of the rhetoric of emperor evaluation. The biographies of the first twelve emperors composed by Suetonius contained lists of the new structures and repairs executed by each emperor accompanied by assessments of the worth or value of the schemes undertaken. One emperor who was assessed negatively in terms of his plans for Rome was Nero. The last emperor of the Julio-Claudian dynasty was presented as having failed Rome, and as having put himself before the city and the empire, seeking pleasure and flattery. When Rome suffered a catastrophic fire aid was insufficient and Nero allegedly provided for his own housing before that of the people (Tacitus, *Annals* 15.38–43; Suetonius, *Nero* 38). Nero was depicted as having taken over the city, displacing other Romans in the process (Elsner, 1994). Nero's successors, the Flavians, reclaimed the land that Nero had devoted to his extravagant palace (the *Domus Aurea*) and restored it to the people of Rome through communal structures such as the Colosseum. The following extract is from a poem written to celebrate the inauguration of the Colosseum as an amphitheatre by the emperor Titus. It contrasts the generosity of the Flavians with the selfishness of Nero:

> Where the starry colossus sees the constellations at close range and lofty scaffolding rises in the middle of the road, once gleamed the odious halls of a cruel monarch, and in all Rome there stood a single house. Where rises before our eyes the august pile of the Amphitheatre, was once Nero's lake. Where we admire the warm baths, a speedy gift, a haughty tract of land had robbed the poor of their dwellings. Where the Claudian colonnade unfolds its wide-spread shade, was the outermost part of the palace's end. Rome has been restored to herself, and under your rule, Caesar, the pleasances that belonged to master now belong to the people.
>
> (Martial, *On the Spectacles* 2, trans. Shackleton-Bailey, 1993, pp.13–15)

The building schemes of both Nero and the Flavians are assessed in moral terms. Nero fell victim to the rhetorical abuse of his successors; if he had not been overthrown the evaluation of the physical impact of his reign upon Rome may have been somewhat different (Elsner, 1994). Instead by their victory the Flavians could claim that Rome had been saved and restored. The generous gestures of the Flavian emperors symbolized their claim to sound government not just in Rome but for the whole empire.

Rome acted as the showcase of each emperor. It was primarily in Rome that the emperor funded buildings, provided shows and celebrated victories. Some emperors liked to beautify the city through ornate buildings; others to tackle practical problems such as improving the food supply. Some emperors made more extensive use of the city than others, but all neglected it at their peril. The city as a collective entity was treated almost as a person; it was a living, breathing thing that needed to be clothed, fed, entertained and embellished. Roma had traditionally been personified as a woman who stood for the city and the state and this female figure gradually came to be worshipped as a goddess (Mellor, 1981, p.956). The goddess Roma was promoted by emperors who wished to depict themselves as the servants of the city and its people. The image of Roma the deity was a powerful one, placed on coins issued by emperors to celebrate victory or peace and stability. Under the emperor Hadrian the worship of Roma was given a physical centre in Rome through the building of a temple. The Greek-style temple was jointly dedicated to Roma and the goddess Venus. The latter was associated with fecundity and prosperity and was a goddess from whom many earlier emperors had claimed descent. The building of the temple exalted the strength and origins of the city and its people and thus Hadrian was seen to be promoting the city rather than himself and any dynastic aspirations (Boatwright, 1987, p.129).

Although Rome was pre-eminent, many emperors could call upon their own divine connections. In the capital itself the living emperor was not a god; that honour could only be conferred after death and those who aspired to divine status while alive, such as the emperor Caligula, were denigrated. But for many imperial subjects the line between the human and divine aspects of the emperor was a hazy one. The emperor as the actual or adopted son of a previous emperor might be called the son of a god, and in certain parts of the empire he might be treated as a god. Augustan coins, for example, included the legend that Augustus was the son of the divine Julius (see Figure 3.4). The ambiguity in the emperor's position was at least partially resolved through the imperial cult which allowed the worship of the name and spirit of the emperor if not his actual person. To render this less distasteful to the over-sensitive the name of the emperor was linked to that of Rome. Roma and the emperor were worshipped together; the inhabitants of the empire prayed for the well-being of a city and of a man who seemingly could not survive without each other. The imperial cult underlined once and for all the interdependency of Rome and emperor.

After death the emperor could attain divinity in his own right. If he was deemed worthy, the deceased emperor was voted divine honours by his fellow men. But whatever the destiny of his spirit his physical remains were earth bound. The emperor was buried on the edges of the city of Rome; the imperial dynastic tombs of Augustus and Hadrian dominated the Roman skyline (see Figure 3.5). In death as in life the emperor's

Figure 3.7 Sculptured relief from the arch of the Argentarii which shows Septimius Severus and his wife Julia Domna. There is a gap to the side of Julia Domna where the figure of Geta originally stood. This was chiselled away after the latter was killed by his brother Caracalla. (Photo: Alinari)

home was at Rome, his remains merging with the soil of the city, linking and intertwining their identities ever closer.

The opposite of deification was *damnatio memoriae*. For those emperors who drastically failed Rome and its subjects or, perhaps more accurately, failed to provide for the succession and the protection of their memory, damnation took the place of deification. This was the fate of the emperor Domitian, the last of the Flavian emperors. The senate celebrated his death, tearing down his statues, effacing inscriptions which referred to him and destroying all records of his reign (Suetonius, *Domitian* 23). The most graphic illustration of *damnatio memoriae* occurred in the reign of the emperor Caracalla and involved his brother Geta. At the death of his father, Septimius Severus, Caracalla murdered his brother and co-heir and sought to remove his name and face from Rome. On the triumphal arch in the forum which had previously been dedicated to Septimius Severus and his two sons, the name of Geta was deleted (Keppie, 1991, pp.50–5). On a second arch which had been dedicated to the imperial family by silversmiths (the arch of the Argentarii) not only was the name of Geta removed from the inscription but his figure was also erased from the associated sculptured panels (see Figure 3.7). The ultimate posthumous punishment was for the name of the emperor to be obliterated from the city which he had striven to serve. The emperor of Rome did not automatically become as immortal as the city.

The empire in Rome and Rome in the empire

The city, once beautified by the emperor, impressed the visitor and served as a reminder of the power of Rome, empire and emperor. The visual impression aimed at the visitor is apparent in the attention which was focused on the major access routes to the city – the River Tiber and the roads. Before anyone entered Rome they were presented with its grandeur through the villas, tombs and trophy monuments of the suburbs (Champlin, 1982; Purcell, 1987, pp.187–90). Even the roads themselves, built and funded by prominent men, were monuments to the greatness of the city. All roads led to Rome, but where did the city begin and end? The boundaries and edges of Rome were permeable and changeable. By the time of Augustus the city had spread beyond the republican walls, hence Augustus' creation of new districts which encompassed at least some of the urban sprawl. Yet the old wall was not demolished and a new one was not built until the third century AD. In addition to the town wall there was also a spiritual boundary that encircled the city, called the *pomerium*, which marked the area where no armies could gather, no dead could be buried and no foreign cults worshipped. This was not a physical barrier since it was only loosely marked by small boundary stones. The *pomerium* could be moved to reflect not only the growth of the city but also the political ambitions of its rulers. The emperors Claudius and Vespasian extended the *pomerium*, thus symbolically increasing the territory of the city just as they had increased the territory of the empire. This flexibility in defining the outer limits of Rome created the impression that the city stretched out indefinitely and that like its empire it was limitless (Dionysius of Halicarnassus, *Roman Antiquities* 4.13, 4–5). The extent of the city mirrored the extent of the empire and the boundaries between that city and the empire were often indistinct (Champlin, 1982, p.97).

The idea of Rome might be limitless but Rome and its inhabitants needed to be reminded of the significance of the city and the significance which each emperor had given it. Rome was shown to the empire but the empire was also shown to Rome. Emperors presented themselves as world rulers, advertising the extent of the territories that they controlled and maintained on behalf of Rome and, where appropriate, the territories and wealth that they had acquired for Rome. Maps were erected in the capital city to show the extent of the empire and to list the strange names of the foreigners and countries that Rome controlled (Nicolet, 1991). The riches and novelties of the empire were displayed in the city – exotic animals, coloured marbles, obelisks from Egypt and architectural ornaments from the east. Conquests and victories that occurred miles away in remote parts of the empire or on its fringes were celebrated in Rome by triumphal processions: prisoners and spoils were paraded through the streets of the city bringing the wonders of Rome's might to the symbolic heart of the empire. Permanent reminders of these victories and triumphs were constructed. Triumphal arches were symbolic gateways covered in ornamentation recalling the victories of individual emperors and the glory they had brought to

Figure 3.8 *The arch of Titus, which was set up to celebrate the victory over the Jews in* AD *70. (Photo: Alinari-Anderson)*

Rome. For example the arch dedicated to the emperor Titus was decorated with relief panels recalling the sack of Jerusalem and the parade of the Jewish prisoners through the streets of Rome (see Figures 3.8 and 11.9). Similarly, Trajan's column presented the military prowess of Trajan and his impressive victories against the Dacians (Figure 3.9). If

Figure 3.9 *Trajan's column which stands in Trajan's forum. The detailed reliefs represent scenes from Trajan's campaigns in Dacia. (Photo: Alinari)*

the majority of the inhabitants of Rome strayed no further than the city walls during their lifetime they were still presented with the empire. Rome was '*urbs et orbis*', the city and the world. Ovid said 'The world and the city of Rome occupy the same space' (Ovid, *Fasti* 2.684). Rome was presented throughout the known world and simultaneously the world was concentrated in Rome (Edwards, 1996, p.100). On coins the goddess Roma was depicted holding a globe or with her foot upon the globe, emphasizing that Rome both controlled and stood as a symbol of the known world (see Figure 1.1).

The empire was present in Rome through more than just spectacle and verbal and pictorial images of varied peoples and lands. Rome was not distant from its empire nor was it an unattainable ideal separated from the lived reality of the provincials. Across the empire there were thousands of people who could call themselves Roman citizens who had never been to Rome. Aelius Aristides, writing in the second century AD, captured the expansiveness of the idea of Rome:

> What another city is to its own boundaries and territory, this city is to the boundaries and territory of the entire civilized world, as if the latter were a country district and she had been appointed the common town.
>
> (Aelius Aristides, *To Rome* 61, trans. Oliver, 1953, p.901)

Throughout the empire the idea of Rome was powerful. Rome as a model – politically, socially and architecturally – pervaded the empire. A shared sense of belonging to the empire and being 'Roman' must have provided a unifying principle to the diverse empire. But this is not to say that the empire became a homogeneous mass. There was no simple definition of what being Roman meant or entailed in the city of Rome itself let alone across the wide expanse of the empire. Many of the emperors, and also the authors from whom our impressions of life in the city are drawn, were not born and bred in Rome. For example, Seneca was from Cordoba in Spain and the Younger Pliny from Como in Italy. Such individuals regarded Rome as home and themselves as Roman, although this did not mean that they severed all ties with their place of origin. To be a true Roman required knowledge of the city, and familiarity with its buildings, history, religion and culture. Such knowledge could make a foreigner in the city truly Roman while lack of this knowledge could render an inhabitant of the city less than Roman. But the basics of this knowledge could be acquired secondhand without even visiting the city since the idea of Rome was readily exported (Edwards, 1996, pp.17–18).

If Rome pervaded the empire, the empire also pervaded Rome, and in the process changed the city. On an economic level this was more than apparent. It was the wealth of the empire that financed much of the display in Rome. But the empire brought more than just cash and novelties. At least some of the inhabitants of Rome, whether it was their native or adoptive home through military and administrative duties or economic interests, experienced the diversity of empire or selected parts of it at first hand. This is apparent in the public careers of authors and their families who were senators and equestrians. The Younger Pliny served as a governor in the province of Bithynia; the father-in-law of Tacitus, Agricola, served as an administrator and general in Gaul and Britain. Others such as Ovid and Seneca were forced to experience life away from Rome through disgrace and exile. What they saw and heard may have influenced the lifestyle of these individuals and their perceptions of Rome. Equally people from the empire and the territories beyond flocked to Rome, whether of their own free will or forcibly through the institution of slavery. Some may have been temporary visitors, such as the two German kings who, according to Tacitus, took in the sights, including the theatre of Pompey, on a visit to the city (Tacitus, *Annals* 13.54). Others never left and were swallowed up by the metropolis. The cultural variety to be found in Rome was well represented in the cemeteries where epitaphs were composed in Greek as well as Latin and recalled people of diverse origins and faiths. A striking example is the inscriptions found in the Jewish catacombs which suggest that Jews formed a sizeable and distinct minority within the population, a view that is also supported by the eleven synagogues known in the city (Rutgers, 1995) (see Essay Eleven). The extent of interaction and integration between the different groups that made up Rome is difficult to establish. Indeed it was often possible to have dual identities: to be, for example, Roman and Jewish or Roman and Greek. What is more apparent is that Rome was a cosmopolitan city. Differences in race, culture and religion were all united in Rome and thus Rome itself came to symbolize the diversity of empire.

Rome provided a potted experience of empire. The people of Rome were presented with a spectacle of empire brought to them courtesy of the emperor: exotic beasts in the arena, defeated prisoners on display, varied tongues and modes of dress in the street, inscriptions and maps listing distant places and peoples, and monuments and sculptures which through their designs, materials and scale recalled the wealth and extent of the empire. But the people of Rome were not just bystanders or spectators; they too were part of the spectacle.

An alternative Rome

Modern impressions of ancient Rome most often entail the public side of the city. The striking images involve buildings, shows and opulence and the people brought to life in literature and art mainly represent the élite. The public side of Rome, its success and greatness, are more visible than individual experiences of life in the city. It is unclear how ordinary people reacted to the city in which they lived and the extent to which the public image of the city either mirrored or engaged with the private sentiments of its inhabitants. How much attention did the inhabitants of

Rome pay to the constructed public image of the city? Did people read the inscriptions, look at the carved reliefs, wonder at the exotic marbles? The level of literacy in ancient Rome is a matter of speculation; pictorial language may have been more understandable but it is easy to pass by statues and the like with scant regard for their significance; besides, the 'reading' of these images often required a level of historical, mythical or religious knowledge. The builder or creator of a building or series of buildings could not control how people responded to what they saw. To many people monuments may have been little more than landmarks to help negotiate a city with few street names and no addresses, or have provided basic facilities while the subtleties of the inherent messages were little regarded. The poems of Ovid capture the subversion of the imperial ideals when grand and hallowed buildings become the backdrop for erotic encounters (Ovid, *The Art of Love* 1.73–4; 1.492; 3.389). Yet it may be too cynical to claim that beyond the élite, who might grasp or even deliberately misread the messages, no one noted or cared about the overall impression created by the city or what an individual emperor did for Rome. If the city was relatively clean, tidy and impressive, if only in its public spaces, this may have engendered a feeling of well-being which would be absent from an altogether shabby city. If the majority of the inhabitants were relatively well fed, employed and entertained this counted for even more.

Individuals must have been conditioned by their own unique experiences of life both inside and beyond the city. How people perceived or related to the city was influenced by whether they were slaves or free, rich or poor, natives or immigrants, citizens or non citizens. How can we access this diverse population when our sources reflect only a minority? For the city of Rome it is public rather than domestic architecture that survives, and any impressions of life in the city are mainly drawn from literary evidence mediated by an élite perspective. In short the voice of the poor is not audible in Latin literature and dwellings constructed of flimsy material do not survive in the archaeological record. Attempts have been made to reconstruct daily life in Rome and to consider aspects such as housing, work, dining, dress and status by drawing upon the available literature and analogies from comparatively well-preserved archaeological sites such as Pompeii and Ostia (Carcopino, 1941; Balsdon, 1969; Dupont, 1993). But such a methodology has limitations especially in terms of its applicability to the Roman population in general and its chronological specificity. Similar difficulties also beset attempts to evaluate standards of living, hygiene and sanitation, which often create a negative impression of life in Rome (Scobie, 1986). This is not to dispute that it is sometimes possible to catch occasional glimpses of an alternative Rome far removed from the public ideals.

Myself, I would value
A barren offshore island more than Rome's urban heart:
Squalor and isolation are minor evils compared
To this endless nightmare of fire and collapsing houses,
The cruel city's myriad perils – and poets reciting
Their work in August!

(Juvenal, *Satires* 3.5–10, trans. Green, 1974, p.87)

Thieves, beggars and prostitutes haunted the streets of Rome. People lived in fear of substandard housing, flood and fire (Seneca, *On Benefits* 4.6.2; *On Anger* 3.35.4–5; Strabo, *Geography* 235; Juvenal, *Satires* 3, 194–245). It is not difficult to imagine the slums, the homeless, the exploited and the general dirt and poverty which were excluded from Rome's public image; large cities always have their seedy as well as glamorous side. There is a danger, however, that in painting a negative picture of life for the poor we may fall prey once more to the biases of the literary sources. Rome was often portrayed as a city of extremes. Juvenal in *Satire* 3 creates a negative impression of Rome because he wants to contrast life in the city with a rural idyll (Braund, 1989); it suits his literary purposes to make Rome hell rather than heaven (Laurence, 1997, pp.14–17).

There were inherent contradictions about life in Rome and the city of Rome itself. On the one hand city life was the symbol and definition of civilization and Roman culture, the urban dream which was exported to the provinces (Strabo, *Geography* 4.1.5; Tacitus, *Agricola* 21; *Germania* 16). Yet life in the city was not always perfect. Rome might be a great city but it was not necessarily the best place to live. Among the wealthy and well-to-do doubts were raised about Rome which challenged its status as the epitome of beauty and greatness. Those who could afford to escaped to the countryside especially during the oppressive summer months.

> You should take the first opportunity yourself to leave the din, the futile bustle and useless occupations of the city and devote yourself to literature or to leisure.
>
> (Pliny the Younger, *Letters* 1.9, trans. Radice, 1969, p.43)

The city was associated with dirt, work and unpleasantness; the countryside with relaxation and tranquillity. Rome could also be unhealthy in a moral as well as physical sense. The city of Rome was often portrayed as corrupt and evil. The same things that made it great – the magnificent buildings, the splendid shows, the wealth and opulence – also made Rome suspect. Just as Rome's beauty was described in exaggerated form, so was its evil. Herein lies the difficulty of interpretation: between both the positive and negative hyperbole, where does the true Rome lie? Rome in so many aspects – in its topography, buildings, and the life of its inhabitants – ceased to be simply a city and became a moral exemplar.

The eternal city?

For much of the imperial period Rome stood as a symbol of greatness, a city that engendered loyalty across the empire. But in some respects the things that made Rome great ultimately undermined its identity and centrality. You did not need to live in Rome to be Roman, nor did you need to be in Rome to wear a toga or go to an amphitheatre. Furthermore the emperor did not have to live in Rome continually and could be absent for extended periods. For the first emperor, Augustus, it was important in terms of political stability to champion the position of Rome as the centre of the empire. An emperor needed a capital and the legacy of Augustus was that Rome became eminently suited to this role. Augustus had perceived the potential danger and divisions of a multi-capital empire; if one city was the clear and distinguished capital of the empire it would be difficult for rivals to establish alternative power bases. It was centuries before Rome's position as the head of empire was undermined. In the defeat of Antony and Cleopatra, Augustus had also highlighted what was special about Rome and Romans, aspects such as practical skills and attributes, divine favour and the ability to govern. Rome was created as a symbol of all these things. But as the empire pervaded Rome more and more the exact nature of what it symbolized was obscured. Rome continued to be the focus of emperors. The majority of Augustus' successors glorified the idea of Rome and saw the city as a symbol of power. But increasingly Rome became just that – an empty symbol rather than a true heart.

The symbolic power of the empire lay in Rome but the true power lay with the emperor and the army. Decisive political and military decisions often happened away from Rome. In the civil wars of AD 69 the power struggle focused on the frontiers where men could win over the army to their cause. As the historian Tacitus made clear, 'the truth was out; emperors could be made elsewhere than Rome' (Tacitus, *Histories* 1.4). The emperor Vespasian, who triumphed in AD 69, counted the years of his reign from the moment he had been declared emperor by the troops in Alexandria rather than from when he was formally accepted by the senate in Rome. The emperor's Roman pedigree became more and more spurious. Not all emperors were born and bred in Italy let alone in Rome; with time emperors came from across the empire. Rome was not the sole focus of these emperors' attention. The pan-Hellene Hadrian was fascinated by the city of Athens, while the home town of Septimius Severus, Lepcis Magna, prospered because of the association. This is not to say that Rome had no value to emperors such as Vespasian, Hadrian or Septimius Severus whose natal origins or initial power base lay away from the city; Rome still stood as the central political prize well into the third century AD. But gradually the emperors' dependency upon the army rather than the city became more apparent, and as the empire struggled for survival the danger of other cities leading the way became an increasing reality. Competing dynasties of a divided empire needed their own centres, and provincial capitals fulfilled this role. In the third century Herodian placed in the mouth of an adviser to the emperor Commodus the words 'Rome is wherever the emperor is' (Herodian, *A History of the Empire after Marcus Aurelius* 1.6.5), thus expressing what had long been known but rarely articulated. Power lay in the hands of a man not in the hands of a city. Rome was no longer unrivalled. Towards the end of the third century the emperor Diocletian divided the empire and shared power with a co-emperor; Diocletian chose to base himself in Nicomedia rather than in Rome. And then the first Christian emperor, Constantine, created a new city on the Hellespont, Constantinople (now Istanbul), which would come to challenge Rome's supremacy. The sack of Rome in AD 410 marked a turning point; the city was not destroyed and life continued but the eternity of Rome had been challenged.

In the following centuries Rome would suffer many more indignities: barbarian invasions and the despoiling of its treasures. Yet Augustus and his successors had been so successful in promoting the primacy of Rome that its greatness never completely left her. Rome is still associated with a sense of permanence, longevity and immortality. Rather than lying vanquished the idea of Rome persists and is constantly reinvented.

References

BALSDON, J.P.V.D. (1969) *Life and Leisure in Ancient Rome*, London, Bodley Head.

BOATWRIGHT, M. (1987) *Hadrian and the City of Rome*, New Jersey, Princeton University Press.

BRAUND, S.H. (1989) 'City and country in Roman satire' in S.H. Braund, *Satire and Society in Ancient Rome*, Exeter, University of Exeter.

BUCHNER, E. (1982) *Die Sonnenuhr des Augustus*, Mainz, Verlag Philipp von Zabern.

CARETTONI, G., COLINI, A.M., COZZA, L. and GATTI, G. (1960) *La pianta marmorea di Roma antica*, Rome, Comune di Roma Sovraintendenza ai Beni Culturali.

CARCOPINO, J. (1941) *Daily Life in Ancient Rome: the People and City at the Height of the Empire*, London, G. Routledge & Sons Ltd.

CHAMPLIN, E. (1982) 'The Suburbium of Rome', *American Journal of Ancient History*, 7, pp.97–117.

CORNELL, T.J. (1995) *The Beginnings of Rome: Italy and Rome from the Bronze Age to the Punic Wars (c.1000–264 BC)*, London and New York, Routledge.

DUPONT, F. (1993) *Daily Life in Ancient Rome*, Oxford, Oxford University Press.

EDWARDS, C. (1996) *Writing Rome: Textual Approaches to the City*, Cambridge, Cambridge University Press.

ELSNER, J. (1994) 'Constructing decadence: the representation of Nero as imperial builder' in J. Elsner and J. Masters (eds) *Reflections of Nero: Culture, History and Representation*, London, Duckworth, pp.112–30.

ELSNER, J. (1996) 'Inventing Imperium: texts and the propaganda of monuments in Augustan Rome' in J. Elsner (ed.) *Art and Text in Roman Culture*, Cambridge, Cambridge University Press, pp.32–53.

FAVRO, D. (1996) *The Urban Image of Augustan Rome*, Cambridge, Cambridge University Press.

GRAVES, R. (trans.) (1989) *Seutonius – The Twelve Caesars*, Harmondsworth, Penguin, The Penguin Classics (first published 1957, revised edition 1979, reprinted with a new bibliography 1989).

GREEN, P. (trans.) (1974) *Juvenal – The Sixteen Satires*, Harmondsworth, Penguin, The Penguin Classics (first published 1967, reprinted with revisions 1974).

HOLLOWAY, R.R. (1994) *The Archaeology of Early Rome and Latium*, London and New York, Routledge.

KEPPIE, L. (1991) *Understanding Roman Inscriptions*, London, Batsford.

LAURENCE, R. (1997) 'Writing the Roman metropolis' in H. Parkins (ed.) *Roman Urbanism: Beyond the Consumer City*, London and New York, Routledge, pp.1–19.

LEWIS, N. and REINHOLD, M. (eds) (1990) *Roman Civilization: Selected Readings. Volume II The Empire* (third edition), New York, Columbia University Press.

MELLOR, R. (1981) 'The goddess Roma' in *Aufsteig und Niedergang der Römischen Welt: Geschichte und Kultur Roms im Spiegel der Neuern Forschung 11.17.2*, Berlin, Walter de Gruyter, pp.950–1030.

MICHIE, J. (trans.) (1967) *The Odes of Horace*, Harmondsworth, Penguin, The Penguin Classics (first published 1964).

NICOLET, C. (1991) *Space, Geography and Politics in the Early Roman Empire*, Ann Arbor, University of Michigan Press.

OLIVER, J.H. (1953) 'The ruling power: a study of the Roman empire in the second century after Christ through the Roman oration of Aelius Aristides', *Transactions of the American Philosophical Association*, vol. 43, no. 4, pp.871–1003.

PURCELL, N. (1992) 'The city of Rome' in R. Jenkyns (ed.) *The Legacy of Rome: a New Appraisal*, Oxford, Oxford University Press.

PURCELL, N. (1987) 'Town in country and country in town' in E. Macdougall (ed.) *Ancient Roman Villa Gardens: Dumbarton Oaks Colloquium on the History of Landscape Architecture,* 10, pp.185–203.

RADICE, B. (trans.) (1963) *The Letters of the Younger Pliny,* Harmondsworth, Penguin, The Penguin Classics (reprinted with a select bibliography 1969).

RICHARDSON, L. (1992) *A New Topographical Dictionary of Ancient Rome,* Baltimore, Johns Hopkins University Press.

RUTGERS, L. (1995) *The Jews in Late Ancient Rome: Evidence of Cultural Interaction in the Roman Diaspora,* Leiden and New York, E.J. Brill.

SCARRE, C. (1995) *The Penguin Historical Atlas of Ancient Rome,* Harmondsworth, Penguin.

SCOBIE, A. (1986) 'Slums, sanitation and mortality in the Roman world', *Klio,* vol. 68, no. 2, pp.399–433.

SHACKLETON-BAILEY, D.R. (trans.) (1993) *Epigrams of Martial: Vol.I,* Cambridge, Mass., Harvard University Press, Loeb Classical Library.

STAMBAUGH, J.E. (1988) *The Ancient Roman City,* Baltimore, John Hopkins University Press.

STEINBY, E.M. (ed.) (1993–) *Lexicon topographicum urbis Romae,* Rome, Edizioni Quasar.

ZANKER, P. (1988) *The Power of Images in the Age of Augustus* (trans. A. Shapiro), Ann Arbor, University of Michigan Press.

Essay Four
Élite culture and the identity of empire

BY JANET HUSKINSON

> Among the rich élite ... there developed a high degree of cultural
> consensus, such that a provincial aristocrat from one corner of the empire
> would have a great deal of cultural common ground with his counterpart
> in the furthermost reaches of Rome's domains.
>
> (Goodman, 1997, p.149)

This 'common ground' in the artistic and intellectual tastes of the élite
(which is what 'culture' is intended to mean here; cf. Essay One) is
something quite easy to infer from the surviving evidence of the Roman
world. Here Goodman sees it in the architecture of towns, but there are
many other examples in the material record, such as floor mosaics
(Kondoleon, 1994, p.323) and portrait fashions (Walker and Bierbrier,
1997, p.14). For commentators ancient and modern this shared cultural
experience was a crucial factor in the cohesion of the empire: Pliny the
Elder, for instance, writes of it as part of Rome's god-given role (*Natural
History* 3.39), and Goodman (1997, p.149) goes on to say 'Such cultural
agreement was of high value in cementing the political co-operation of
the upper classes in the government of the empire'.

But behind the immediacy of this picture are some complex issues
which form the agenda for this essay. One is the actual nature of this
élite culture: Goodman, in the same passage, calls it 'Graeco-Roman',
and so in many ways it is. But to get the fuller picture this term needs to
be unpacked so that we can consider how the Greek and Roman
elements worked together. This process forms a central part of this
discussion. I shall look first at the historical background to the close
cultural relationship between Greece and Rome in the republic, then at
how this was developed by Augustus and experienced by various
individuals in their lives; the last part of the essay will move on to look at
the 'common cultural ground' of the empire to see how the Graeco-
Roman elements in it were fostered by various links such as education
and the built environment.

Secondly, and as a theme that runs in and out of the relationship
between Greek and Roman, is the question of how to define the 'élitism'
of this culture and its participants. This is more than just a matter of
charting the rise and fall of those with social influence and wealth;
rather it is a case of being clear about whom we mean by 'the élite' at

any given time in terms of cultural pursuits. For instance, we could be looking at a small group of leading Romans in the late republic, engaged in serious Greek intellectual pursuits and concerned to balance these in their lives with the demands of Roman public service. But equally the term could apply to a more general highbrow interest in the arts enjoyed by the upper classes; after its promotion by the imperial court this fed down to other social groups, who in turn adopted and adapted it for their own particular needs. As Roman society broadened out, so this became much more of a popular culture, widely accepted and understood: it was 'in a sense an ancestor of the "jeans and coca cola" phenomenon universally recognized today' (Walker and Bierbrier, 1997, p.14). Yet the empire also included other élite groups who stood outside the Graeco-Roman tradition. Their situation is not always easy to trace (often because of the very dominance of the mainstream culture) yet involves important questions about local cultural identity in relation to Rome.

A third theme of this essay is the interaction of 'public' and 'private' (which, as we need to remember, divided on rather different lines in Roman society from those in the modern West). The relationship between the kinds of intellectual and artistic values prioritized in each context can be revealing, particularly when 'official' culture impinged upon the private sphere.

So it is important to keep these different strands distinct – or rather, distinctly described – in the course of argument, drawing them together at the end to see how they relate in the context of the empire. For the key question must be to what extent the culture of the Roman empire came to be identified with an élite Graeco-Roman culture that did in fact extend across the empire, and whether this can be meaningfully described in terms of *romanitas*, that is, of some quintessential 'Romanness'.

The following two passages from Tacitus' literary portrait of Agricola sum up many of the issues. The first gives his biographical details:

> Gnaeus Julius Agricola was born in the old and famous colony of Forum Julii [modern Fréjus]. Both his grandfathers were procurators in the imperial service – the crowning dignity of the Equestrian Order. His father Julius Graecinus was a member of the Senate and won fame by his devotion to literature and philosophy ... Agricola's mother was Julia Procilla, a paragon of feminine virtue. Brought up under her tender care, he passed his boyhood and youth in the cultivation of all the liberal arts. He was shielded from the temptations of evil companions, partly by his own sound instincts and partly by living and going to school from his very early years at Massilia [modern Marseilles], a place where Greek refinement and provincial puritanism are happily blended. I remember how he would often tell us that in his early youth he was tempted to drink

deeper of philosophy than was allowable for a Roman and a future senator, but that his mother in her wisdom damped the fire of his passion.

The second passage describes Agricola's strategy in dealing with the local British populations (it is a passage that you will find often quoted in these essays):

> Furthermore, he educated the sons of the chiefs in the liberal arts ... The result was that instead of loathing the Latin language they became eager to speak it effectively. In the same way, our national dress came into favour and the toga was everywhere to be seen. And so the population was gradually led into the demoralizing temptations of arcades, baths, and sumptuous banquets. The unsuspecting Britons spoke of such novelties as 'civilization', when in fact they were only a feature of their enslavement.
>
> (Tacitus, *Agricola* 4 and 21, in Mattingly, 1970, pp.53–4 and 72–3)

Together these passages introduce themes of culture and status, of the place of Greek traditions within a Roman élite identity, and of how élite culture (of varying kinds) operated within the empire. These topics recur throughout this essay.

The evidence

The evidence for these topics comes from a wide variety of sources. They cover the arts and intellectual movements, the material culture of buildings and artefacts, and modes of representation (such as rhetoric and mythology) by which society's values are articulated. Much of the material is urban, not just because the élite were usually to be found in cities but because the provision of arts, such as buildings, statues, games or competitions, was all part of the fabric of urban power structures and control. Even in the countryside wealthy landowners could express their social values by urban symbols (Woolf, 1998, pp.165–9, on Gaul). Through spending their surplus wealth on public arts or on goods for their private homes the élite could reinforce their status in the community, and their lifestyle was in turn copied by the upwardly mobile.

Inevitably, though, evidence from such sources is often hard to assess. The first problem is that many documents of élite culture are monuments of self-representation: interior decoration, funerary memorials, even domestic tableware, were meant to say something about their owners, just as biographies and the *res gestae* (achievements) of public men were couched in terms that promoted their image. Understanding the element of self-advertisement – and the role of élite cultural values – in these is crucial. Secondly, the sources are also biased in that most represent the position of the educated Roman male, so that it is harder to reach the experiences of those outside this privileged group. This is particularly true for literary sources; more of the 'silent lives' can be retrieved from material evidence as archaeologists ask questions about gender, for instance (see Essay Six).

Finally, isolated pieces of source material are often hard to assess yet can raise important questions about the depth of the cultural experience they suggest. The single line from the *Aeneid* quoted on a writing-tablet found at Vindolanda in northern England (Bowman, 1994, p.91) exemplifies this problem: does it come from a solid literary knowledge or is it a token gesture? Research on literacy in the Roman world warns that outside the small number of the highly educated, people were unlikely to have a deep knowledge of classical literature (if they could read at all), but the ability to make the odd quotation from famous authors allowed them to show their allegiance to mainstream Graeco-Roman culture (Harris, 1989). This may make it hard for us to distinguish cultural aspiration from actual practice. So although the upper-class Roman culture described in this essay is relatively accessible in the ancient sources (compared, for instance, with indigenous cultures in many parts of the empire), the evidence may need careful questioning to reveal its standpoint. Its agenda may be hidden: it may voice dissent as well as conformity, aspiration as well as actual ownership.

Roman and Greek culture during the republic

The relationship between Greek and Roman culture was the subject of much discussion and analysis in the Roman world. The Romans were fascinated with the similarities and differences between the Greeks and themselves, and although they also explored what distinguished their culture from that of other races, it was interest in this relationship that predominated. Greeks living in the Greek-speaking eastern part of the empire also speculated on it and how it defined their own cultural identity.

Their mutual indebtedness was an aspect that received particular attention. In what has now become a famous quotation, the poet Horace (*Letters* 2.1.156–7) made the paradoxical comment that 'Captive Greece took her rough conqueror captive and introduced the arts to rustic Latium'. The theme was taken up again in the second century AD by Aelius Aristides, a sophist from the Greek city of Smyrna in Asia Minor, in an extravagant eulogy on the Roman Empire: he praised Greece for having introduced the arts of civilization, and Rome for strengthening them (*Roman Oration* 101). This view – that Rome took on the arts that Greece had invented and spread them across the world by the power structures of its empire – was often repeated, and can be found even during the late republic (Woolf, 1994, pp.119–25; for example, Cicero, *Letter to his brother Quintus* 1.1.27).

As both Horace and Aelius Aristides imply, by the time of the early empire Roman culture owed much to Greece. In fact Roman experience of Greek culture went back a long time. In the fourth and third centuries BC Rome had had links with cities of mainland Greece and their colonies in southern Italy and also with Hellenized communities in Etruria. Later came contact with the Hellenistic kingdoms that flourished after the death of Alexander, and it was then that upper-class Romans became aware of what Greek culture had to offer. They valued it for its own sake, and also for the role it could play in the competitive society of mid and late republican Rome. The wealth of these patrons allowed them to import, buy, or commission Greek art of all kinds.

Greek traditions and artists played an important part in the developing arts in Rome. This process began with the acquisition of Greek work (sometimes enforced), which was then adapted and, later still, used as a basis for Roman innovation (Beard and Crawford, 1985). Thus the first Latin literature seems to have been translated from the Greek; later, Greek works were adapted to make Latin versions (the comedies of Plautus and Terence, for instance), and even in the empire Latin poets continued to use Greek literary forms as the basis of their own creations. There were similar developments for the visual arts. From the late third century BC paintings and sculptures were brought from Greece, sometimes as military booty, but also because they were valued as works of art. Art galleries were set up and private houses adorned. Following this Greek work was copied, and finally, certain Greek art forms (portraiture is an example) were recast to meet the particular needs of Roman aristocratic society.

At the same time Greek learning was highly prized in some Roman circles. Greek intellectuals lectured in Rome, Romans went to study in Athens, and others built up private libraries of literary and philosophical works (such as the collection of Epicurean texts found at the Villa of Papyri in Herculaneum) and decorated their homes with images of great intellectual figures – philosophers and poets – of Greece. Greek was the language of rhetoric and philosophy; in short, at this time 'any Roman with cultural pretensions would have a mind filled with Greek learning' (Fantham, 1996, p.27).

Yet there was ambivalence towards Greek culture, shown up in a strand of aristocratic Roman ideology that rejected it as decadent *luxuria* (extravagant living). Together with a view of the Greeks themselves as self-indulgent and prone to philosophizing, this was to be a recurrent theme in Roman literature. Whereas intellectual ideas had played such a public role in Greek societies (in the city states of the fifth century BC, for example) in republican Rome, there was a strong sense that they belonged to the private sphere, and to an individual's leisure (*otium*) rather than to the world of public business (*negotium*). This can be seen clearly in the opening of the philosophical work in Latin, *De finibus bonorum et malorum* ('the ends of good and evil'), which Cicero wrote in 45 BC: there he sets out – in order to refute them – the various criticisms he expects. Their range is wide and shows how the practice of philosophy by a Roman intellectual could be criticized on many scores: that it was a total waste of time, that it was tolerable only as a leisure pursuit, that Greek writing was preferable to Latin, and that the subject was unworthy.

So there were mixed reactions. Romans appropriated arts from Greece yet at the same time were aware of their own distinctive culture. The values of its archaic agrarian past were still reflected in many of its social structures and ancestral customs (*mos maiorum*); Romans looked back on the supposedly simple morality of their past with pride and many saw Greek ideas as a real threat.

In fact from early on the Roman élite had had some particular interests which were not always best expressed through forms favoured by the Greeks. One was the desire to record particular men or events, which it did through fairly literal historical depictions rather than by idealization or allegory. Maplike paintings of battle sites were made to show military triumphs and the aristocratic dead were commemorated by funerary masks (which may have contributed to the realism of late republican portraiture). Such examples show how much Roman aristocratic culture was linked with ideas about *virtus* (conspicuous bravery), and with a mind-set that related more easily to the concrete than to the abstract. This same interest in people, actual and particular, and in how they behave, may also explain why Roman literary talent for satire developed and, in the area of philosophical thought (in which the Romans were not great innovators), account for the attraction of Stoicism with its ethical interests.

The individualism, if not rivalry, of many wealthy patrons in the late republic stimulated the development of Roman culture to a lively diversity. Greek and Roman cultural elements existed side by side or were combined: new, specifically Roman subject matter was expressed through forms that were originally Greek, and a whole new vocabulary of artistic media was deployed. But for many Romans at the time the political and social turbulence seemed a sign that both culturally and morally their society had lost its ancient way. As well as experiencing the impact of Greek culture, they were faced with a social challenge as communities of the Italian peninsula, with varied cultures of their own, were given Roman citizenship after the Social Wars of 91–89 BC. It is not surprising, perhaps, that some Romans felt their own traditions were a spent force.

Yet the reality was that Roman culture as such had truly developed. It had moved on to a point where it was able to draw on its own traditions as well as those of Greece, and it had proved itself able to offer the élite in Rome a common means of identifying – and promoting – their interests in society. In short it had reached a confidence and maturity which could meet the particular demands of the times.

Augustus and Greek and Roman culture

Under Augustus the demands took a new and lasting turn: élite culture was called upon to carry the values of the new empire and a new age. Augustus had political needs, urgent at first, to consolidate his own power and authority and to bring back stability to society; this he did by promoting themes of 'renewal of religion and custom, *virtus* and the honour of the Roman people' (Zanker, 1988, p.101). The arts were used for this end and in a wide range of media and contexts which brought the forms of classical culture to people who would not have seen them before; they not only shaped society but reflected some of its fundamental changes, and so were firmly set in a central position in imperial power politics.

Augustan culture was less diverse and more conformist than that of the late republic, yet it was suited to fit the new context of empire. The degree to which its developments were orchestrated in some masterplan is arguable. Virgil and Horace were not propaganda writers although their poetry is full of the great Augustan themes of leadership, prosperity and peace; but there seems to have been some co-ordination, as in the monumental rebuilding of Rome by Agrippa and Augustus himself. Although scholars disagree about the degree of cultural uniformity involved (compare Zanker, 1988, and Wallace-Hadrill, 1989), the overall result was a powerful cohesiveness which came to permeate both the public and the private sphere. The same basic themes were given various forms of expression which were repeated and interlinked in the literary and visual arts.

Many of these themes were Greek in origin. For instance, much of the victory imagery generated by the battle of Actium in 31 BC evoked the god Apollo, with whose help Augustus (then Octavian) had defeated Antony. This event had both cultural and religious value which the god and his imagery was well suited to express. Culturally the victory could be seen as the defeat of the 'new' indulgences associated with the Hellenistic east, to which Antony had come to be linked through his Egyptian connections. In religious terms, it reaffirmed 'old' values of order and purity which the god Apollo had traditionally represented. In addition Apollo was also the god of arts, and the temple dedicated to him in Rome in 28 BC contained appropriate masterpieces of Greek art.

The ancient past was also given a significance in this imperial context, and drew on classical gods and heroes and on the legendary history of early Rome. To confirm his position Augustus promoted his own family history, tracing it back through Julius Caesar to Julus (Ascanius), son of the Trojan hero Aeneas and the goddess Venus. Rome too needed a heroic past, and was brilliantly supplied with one. The *Aeneid*, on which Virgil was still working when he died in 19 BC, contrived to mix Roman-foundation myth with a Homeric-style epic narrative of the Trojan hero Aeneas, and to show how this great heroic past anticipated the Augustan present and the new age to come. A similar combination of themes and characters was used for the programmatic decoration of the Temple of Mars Ultor ('Mars the Avenger') dedicated by Augustus in 2 BC. Here again ancestors were depicted who were significant for Augustus and for Rome. Its principal cult statues were of Venus, Mars and the Divine Julius (Caesar), while the niches in the colonnades contained the figures of Aeneas and Romulus (the legendary founder of Rome), flanked by other 'ancestral' figures such as the legendary kings of Alba Longa, the Julii family and various great men of Rome.

If these works had a specific 'Roman' function, Greek art forms were also used by Augustus for deliberate effect. It seems as if he played upon a current critical belief that the various styles of Greek art had different historical and moral implications (Zanker, 1988, pp.240–63). So while Hellenistic Greek art came to be associated with a (supposedly) self-indulgent and individualistic style of leadership defeated at Actium, classical styles recalled the high moral aspirations of the democratic city states (*poleis*) which suited the Augustan image.

Such allusions were presumably appreciated by many members of élite society; and one of the major developments under Augustus was the way in which aspects of élite culture were opened up for the rest of society. Not only did the use of the arts for imperial ends create some common reference points, but the very fact of the stable principate allowed space for the arts to flourish, and for elements of them which had become politicized in the rivalries of the late republic to be used in private settings. So developments that began as imperial initiatives were picked up by the wealthy classes (for the decoration of their houses or in portraiture, for instance), and some fashions percolated to the lower ranks of society. One example is the way in which freedmen in Rome (presumably wealthy ones) developed their own style of funerary monuments during the reign of Augustus, copying the practice of portraiture from their social superiors and often including the attributes of their own particular trade (see Essay Five, Figure 5.1).

The élite culture of four Romans in the later first and early second centuries AD

As Roman society broadened out in the early empire such trends continued, and were reflected in the lives of particular individuals. To illustrate this, here are four examples which date to the late first and early second centuries AD, some seventy years after the death of Augustus. One is a fictitious character, but there is a sense in which the others are also 'creations' since they are consciously constructed representations. Together they show that aspects of Greek culture and learning were still highly prized in Roman society.

The lives of the two Plinys, uncle and nephew, reveal a deep interest in classical learning combined with the benefits of landed wealth and the demands of a conventional Roman education. Pliny the Elder (c. AD 23–79) came from a leading family in the town of Comum (modern Como) in northern Italy, and spent some of his education in Rome. In his public-service career he travelled much, ending up in charge of the Roman fleet in the Bay of Naples. He died trying to rescue survivors from the eruption of Vesuvius, a fate that in many ways summed up what seemed to have been important in his life. For alongside his various public offices he devoted himself to scholarly research in natural sciences and produced the encyclopaedic *Natural Histories*. His nephew (and adopted son) Pliny the Younger (c. AD 61–114) described him as rather a stern workaholic, a follower of Roman Stoicism, who managed to show how a life as a polymath need not exclude the virtues of active public service.

This same integrated view – of learning and public life – is presented by Pliny the Younger for himself. He had the more distinguished public career: he entered the senate, gained fame as an orator in the law courts, and was sent by the emperor Trajan as governor of Bithynia. He had contact with several prominent writers in Rome, but devoted much of his personal time to cultural pursuits. Pliny, with his active public life, his wealth, country estates, and cultivated circle, is often taken to be the very model of a Roman gentleman. Writing to a friend (*Letters* 9.36, in Lewis and Reinhold, 1990, pp.163–4) he describes a typical summer day at his Tuscan villa: he thinks, writes, reads aloud a Greek or Latin speech, exercises, bathes, and dines to the accompaniment of a reading, ending the day with music and good conversation.

Confirmation that indeed these are the habits of a cultivated gentleman comes in the parody of which the third example, Trimalchio, is the star. He too dines, reads, writes poetry and listens to music, but all to rather different effect. Trimalchio is the unforgettable creation of the satirist Petronius, who wrote in Rome in the mid first century AD. From the little that is known about him it seems likely that Petronius was once a favourite of the emperor Nero (AD 54–68), and part of the fun of this comic narrative set among Roman lowlife are the veiled allusions to the extravagant imperial lifestyle. In the case of Trimalchio the parody is primarily aimed at the culture of wealthy ex-slaves (Petronius, *Satyricon* 37 and 38), and operates on the classic scenario of great wealth but little taste. So it offers useful insights into the value attached to certain cultural forms at the time, not just by Trimalchio and his cronies but by their more critical observers.

According to the epitaph he composed for himself (*Satyricon* 71), Trimalchio was the freed slave of a certain Maecenas, a name that conjures up memories of the friend of Augustus and patron of Horace and thereby arouses some expectations of highbrow culture. But these are certainly not fulfilled in the happenings at his dinner party (Lewis and Reinhold, 1990, pp.158–60; 158–70). Although this is described as endlessly lavish and sensuous, its intellectual conversation falls very flat. Trimalchio likes to show his learning: he claims Greek and Latin libraries (*Satyricon* 48) and a troupe of professional actors (*Satyricon* 53). Yet he uses them to play Latin farce rather than classic drama, and he misquotes famous Homeric stories. Despite his literary pretensions he is scornful of philosophy and wishes his epitaph to record him as a man who made a fortune but 'never once listened to a philosopher' (*Satyricon* 71). In fact he is very proud of being a graduate of 'the University of Life', and records his meteoric rise to riches in a picture in the hallway of his house, just as Roman patricians illustrated the honours of their career (though Trimalchio adds in a few gods to support him; *Satyricon* 29).

Here, then, the parody shows Trimalchio as someone 'who knows the price of everything but the value of nothing'; high culture is something to be bought into for effect. But it is important to remember that much of the effect depends on the ability of Petronius' audience to follow some learned allusions for themselves, and that behind Trimalchio and his friends is a further level of cultural experience to note.

The fourth example is an eleven-year-old boy, Quintus Sulpicius Maximus, depicted in a funerary memorial in Rome (Kleiner, 1987, no.45; see Figure 4.1). He had died c. AD 94, exhausted because 'day and night he thought only of the Muses', but he had been successful in a Greek poetry contest organized by the emperor Domitian. His verses frame his portrait where his parents have had him depicted like a middle-aged orator, dressed in the Roman toga and declaiming from an opened scroll. Here highbrow learning is used to express a child's precocity and his family's pride.

Figure 4.1   *Funerary monument of the boy poet, Quintus Sulpicius Maximus, c. AD 94. Palazzo dei Conservatori, Rome. (Photo: American Academy in Rome Photographic Archive and Fototeca Unione)*

These four portraits, fact and fiction, are illuminating about the Greek and Roman elements in élite culture of the time. They show Roman professional needs linked with oratory and the law courts. Pliny the Younger studied under Quintilian, who wrote a treatise on the education of an orator, *Institutio Oratoria*. Trimalchio and his friends also hanker after this professional life: one guest, for instance, has clear faith in legal training as a way to get rich (Petronius, *Satyricon* 46). The examples also show the continuing importance attached to Greek learning. For Pliny the Elder it is reflected in his encyclopaedic scholarship and his interest in Stoicism. Poor Quintus Sulpicius Maximus allegedly gave his life for it (while the contest in which he had done well had had imperial sponsorship). And lower down the social scale Trimalchio, despite his aversion to philosophy, claimed knowledge of Greek literature, enjoying some of the more ostentatious trappings of Greek culture such as Alexandrian singing.

All these examples are male. I have already mentioned the difficulty in identifying the cultural experience of women in the evidence, although women frequently appear as subject matter. What so often conceals their real historical role is the rhetoric used by male writers who work with stereotypes. Culture plays a part in this, not least because of its links with control and social empowerment. Thus the ideal wife practises some arts, appreciates her husband's work and learns from him (for example, Pliny, *Letters* 4.19; Plutarch, *Advice to Bride and Groom* 145c–d), and the ideal mother, like Agricola's, is cultivated and wise (Tacitus, *Agricola* 4, quoted above). Other women are set up as dangerous and subversive through allegedly immodest displays of intellect and culture (cf. Sallust, *Catiline* 25 on the late republican Sempronia; Juvenal, *Satires* 6.445–56). If such scenarios are to do with 'urban male fantasies' (Fantham, 1994, p.384) there is patchy evidence which shows historical women actually practising the arts (even if this tended to be music-making rather than the philosophy that their menfolk pursued, as contemporary visual images suggest; Zanker, 1995, p.271, fig.146). But even so it is clear that other social factors, such as wealth and status, affected the cultural experience of women.

The exclusiveness of élite culture was an important issue because social empowerment was at stake: outsiders might strive for inclusion, while participants questioned how they could apply it in their lives. Trimalchio and Quintus Sulpicius Maximus seem to have pursued it so hard (or, for Trimalchio, the appearance of having it) as to suggest that they feared missing out. On the other hand the Plinys, despite their provincial origins, reproduced a life of old-fashioned élite virtues, combining a serious intellectual life with active public service and dedication to the emperor and empire.

The context of empire gave a new dimension to traditional élite pursuits. Public service could require travel away from Rome which allowed encounters with other cultures and a chance to appreciate one's own. But more than that it focused questions on the role of Roman culture in the purposes and functions of empire. A powerful vision of this is articulated by Pliny the Elder, who described Rome's role as unifying and civilizing mankind (*Natural History* 3.39). As Romans themselves had once learned these qualities from Greece, so, the argument ran, they were now in their turn to extend them to the uncultivated world.

The rest of this essay will focus on how élite Graeco-Roman culture worked in the wider context of the empire, bringing together some central issues for communities and for individuals. It looks at the place of this culture within imperial policy, and at longer-term processes involving its transmission and reception in the public and private spheres across the empire.

Élite cultures within the empire

As time progressed social boundaries shifted and the culture of the old élites was effectively taken up by an expanding middle sector: their culture may have been élite in style, but their personal backgrounds were not necessarily so. Provincial origins could mean that even those who stood at the top of the Roman hierarchy were not always fully at home with Graeco-Roman culture. Allegedly Hadrian (AD 117–138), that most cultivated of emperors, had problems speaking Latin in the senate, coming as he did from Spain (Scriptores Historiae Augustae, *Hadrian* 3.1); the emperor Septimius Severus (AD 193–211) was said to have been fluent in the Punic of his native Lepcis, but his sister could scarcely manage Latin (Harris, 1989, p.179).

Graeco-Roman culture may have prevailed across the empire, but it was far from being the only élite tradition within it. Historical factors varied across time and place in the empire, and so did the impact of a centralized Roman 'official' culture. In particular, there was a major difference between regions in the east and west: the old Hellenistic kingdoms in the east had a lot to offer their 'rough conqueror' in terms of an existing artistic heritage, as Horace observed, but there was nothing comparable in most of the north-west. In Britain, for instance, the élites of pre-Conquest Iron Age communities were involved in a warrior culture which produced highly skilled metalwork, yet had no tradition in stone carving, so initially Romans had to import sculptors and sculptures of their own.

Figure 4.2 *Painted mummy and portrait of Artemidorus from Hawara, Egypt,* c. AD *100–20. British Museum. (Photo © British Museum)*

Individual communities too could be mixed in their make-up. Within the geographical empire new settlement and immigration, especially to the great cities, led to a mixing of traditions which gave individual communities a distinctive culture of their own: remember how Tacitus described the Massilia of Agricola's youth (Tacitus, *Agricola* 4, quoted earlier). The culture of a single area was often multi-layered. This is perhaps most clearly seen in the provinces in Asia Minor and the Near East, where the Greek culture which the Romans encountered was itself 'an alien importation' (Millar, 1981, p.197). This produced three different cultural layers: Roman officialdom, the local Greek-speaking élite, and an indigenous element which may or may not have preserved traditions of its own. Although in some places native languages were occasionally used in official written contexts, evidence for local traditions is often scanty, obscured by the Greek and Roman overlay.

Sometimes the various layers were used to mark out different aspects of cultural identity. Mummy portraits from Roman Egypt show this for individuals who often came from local élites of Greek cultural background: hairstyles, dress and jewellery reflect Roman imperial fashions, but religious imagery is traditionally Egyptian and names and inscriptions are usually Greek.

In the example shown in Figure 4.2, the young man Artemidorus claims an élite identity for himself through the Roman portrait, a Greek family through the inscription, and a local allegiance through the traditional religious scene. Institutions provide examples of a comparable separating-out of cultural elements. A list from Ancyra (Ankara) records the Galatian priests of the Divine Augustus and the Goddess Roma and their benefactions. These Galatian priests were apparently leading Celts, some with Hellenized names. Their benefactions reveal 'a mixture of Greek, Roman and Celtic traditions which was presumably characteristic of the behaviour of the Galatian aristocracy taken as a whole at this period' (Mitchell, 1995, p.109): olive oil for the gymnasium (a Greek tradition), public feasts (Celtic), and gladiatorial or wild-beast shows (Roman).

All these factors point to the huge variety of cultural experience contained in the empire, in which local élites found different forms of self-expression and identity. What, then, is the part played by the élite culture that had evolved in Rome and how did it work within this context? These are complex questions and the material is subject to constant debate, but the aim here is to outline some of the central issues. The starting point is with Augustus because of the issue of imperial policy, although cultural contacts between Rome and other regions which became the empire clearly antedate the principate.

Élite culture as an instrument of empire

Earlier we saw how facets of the prevailing élite culture in Rome were drawn in by Augustus to his policy of empire. This means that it was heavily and consciously linked in role to the official cultural language of the empire as an instrument of power. A prominent factor in this was the careful co-ordination of selected themes that defined and celebrated the status and purposes of the emperor and of Rome. These were worked out through buildings, the treatment of urban space, coinage and monumental public art, that is to say media that were traditionally associated with the élite of the republic, and with the ownership of power. These were also taken up in the poetry of writers close to the emperor such as Virgil (whose influence long after his death is also important here). Associated with this is a conscious choice of styles, with 'classical' Greek being used to evoke a timeless moral order with which the emperor aligned himself (as in his statue at Primaporta, which was based on a statue of the fifth century BC by Polyclitus).

From these themes and styles a new vocabulary of motifs and symbols emerged. These articulated such ideas as victory and prosperity, often using allusions to the past. In visual terms they contributed to the development of various 'set-piece' scenes in which the emperor was shown in some recognizable act of virtue. This imperial iconography laid down certain patterns that were continued by successive emperors for years to come. It formulated portrait-types for the emperor and his family, and conventional scenes of suitable imperial activities, which were added to, or given fresh emphases over time, but their essential function continued; they used the forms of élite artistic traditions and operated from a power base which in itself was inevitably élite.

Certainly in provincial cities it must have been hard for anyone to move far from the élite qualities encapsulated in the imperial image. The dominance of this was unavoidable. The official images of emperors and members of their family were circulated in an organized fashion throughout the empire. Their portrait statues were erected in public places including theatres and amphitheatres, and smaller images were presented as significant gifts. This was not only by official instigation; local élites also promoted the practice by setting up imperial images alongside their own (as Herodes Atticus did on the fountain he built at Olympia) or by adopting similar styles for self-representation (for example, Marcus Holconius Rufus at Pompeii). Others brought imperial images into the settings of their own home, as for instance, the ivory frieze found in a house in Ephesus showing the emperor Trajan and scenes of warfare (Figure 4.3). Here, then, the very forms of 'official culture' have been taken up by influential provincials for purposes of their own.

Figure 4.3 *Detail of an ivory frieze, used as furniture or wall decoration, from a house in Ephesus, early second century AD. Ephesus Museum. (Photo: BBC/OUP)*

The 'language' of these imperial arts played a major part in transmitting Graeco-Roman élite traditions across the empire. This élite culture became an instrument of empire, but not simply to promote Roman imperial domination; for being primarily urban in its values it was part and parcel of the civilizing vision. But it is not so easy to see how this worked because evidence is sometimes hard to interpret. One problem is that, generally speaking, processes of cultural assimilation or imitation may be scarcely conscious, and forms and attitudes of an élite, central culture may be appropriated by locals without imposition. A second, particular, problem is that it was a major part of early imperial policy to encourage local leaders to identify with Roman interests and then to manage the locality for themselves, promoting Roman culture as they did so; this is what Agricola did in Britain according to Tacitus (*Agricola* 21, quoted earlier). As a result the central culture was then the culture of the local élites and it becomes increasingly hard to speak of (let alone identify) distinct categories that interact.

Cultural links in the second century AD

As a result of these developments, experience of the Graeco-Roman culture which had originally been confined to the élite was extended to other social groups across the empire. As we have seen, different regions had their own cultural histories, and the long-established culture of Hellenistic Greece continued in the east of the empire and in north Africa as far west as Cyrenaica. But all this was linked together, into the 'cultural common ground' which Goodman described in the opening quotation, by a number of factors.

Buildings and spectacles

As we have seen, public buildings had an important role to play, for in both function and design they articulated Roman ideals and signified Roman power (see also Essay Eight). Roman urban culture usually involved a range of public buildings such as fora, temples, baths, amphitheatres and basilicas, for which there were regular designs. Some of these drew on types of buildings that had originated much earlier in Greece (temples, for instance), but others (such as baths and amphitheatres) had developed during the late republic and early empire to meet particular Roman social activities.

Across the empire they presented a high degree of uniformity and at face value indicate a 'Roman' town. Yet there is an interesting diversity to explore in terms of their design and distribution.

The design of buildings might vary for a number of reasons, an obvious one being the strength of local architectural traditions. This can be seen in Asia Minor, where Hellenistic styles were still very much alive in the flourishing cities of the west, in contrast with the greater use of imported designs in areas like coastal Cilicia which had been largely opened up by the Romans (Ward-Perkins, 1981, pp.273–306). Still further east sites such as Baalbek, Gerasa and Palmyra show the influence of oriental styles from outside the Roman empire: the temple of Bel at Palmyra, dedicated in AD 32, shows how extraordinary the effects of this might be (see Figure 4.4).

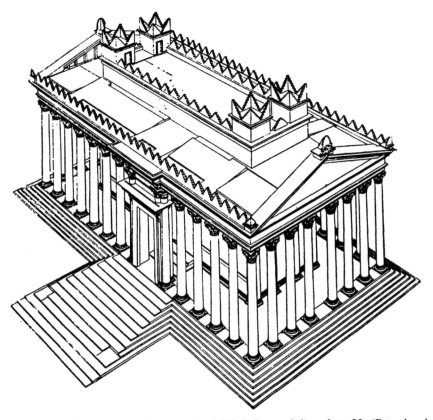

Figure 4.4 *Reconstruction of the temple of Bel, Palmyra, dedicated AD 32. (Reproduced from Boethius and Ward-Perkins, 1992)*

Another reason for variations in building design was the availability of natural resources. Western Asia Minor had marble and stone which supported traditional classical styles, while Rome and Campania were blessed with a local volcanic sand used to make concrete. Mixed with lime, this sand (pozzuolana, named after the Campanian town of Pozzuoli, the ancient Puteoli) made a strong mortar which hardened on exposure to water; it led to the use of concrete to form a structural core to be faced with dressed stone or brick. This enabled some major changes in Roman architecture at the start of the empire: the strength of this material supported new shapes and spaces which burst through the rectilinear patterns of traditional classical architecture. Vaults, curvilinear walls, and a new interest in interior spatial effects became a regular possibility, and the classical orders (which included supporting columns) were made structurally redundant. In Rome some of the most striking early examples of this new architecture are found in imperial palaces, such as the Golden House (Domus Aurea) built by Nero in AD 64–8, and Domitian's palace on the Palatine in Rome of AD 92. Here the stunning new spaces were decorated with wall paintings, stuccoes and inlaid marble: both architecture and decoration were to be much copied in upper-class houses.

The distribution of certain building types across the empire suggests variations in their popularity, and is an indication of just how far local communities had embraced the interests of the central culture. Greeks, for instance, came to appreciate Roman-style baths, and these were built in great number in Asia Minor during the late first and early second centuries AD (Mitchell, 1995, pp.216–7). But they retained other tastes of their own (as Trajan exclaimed to the younger Pliny, 'Those Greekies love their gymnasia!' (Pliny, *Letters* 10.40)), and rejected the western-style amphitheatres.

Central similarities and local differences are also to be found in the lived cultures of these towns. Communal events and activities instigated by central authorities were often developed by local dignitaries for their own cities. This bound central and local cultural enterprises within the same power structure. Many of these were religious, such as the celebrations put on by cities as part of the imperial cult in the east; these regularly included elements which were essentially élite yet affected the community at large – games, competitions, gladiatorial displays and displays of imperial statuary all drew local people into the empire-wide honouring of the emperor (Price, 1984).

Similar factors can be seen in the case of gladiatorial games, which show how various elements of élite and popular culture, of Roman power and local identities, could work dynamically together. As first recorded in republican Rome, such combats were part of the funerary commemorations of individual aristocratic families, but during the early empire they were brought firmly under imperial control by Augustus and became a vehicle for articulating power and cultural identity across society. This policy was made even more effective by the sheer popularity of the games, and by the fact that the people who enacted them – the gladiators, criminals, and even the wild beasts – were outsiders in Roman terms. 'Roman' power could be displayed by audience and emperor alike. The erection of the Colosseum shows how even in Rome an amphitheatre was a popular benefaction to the city, and this was followed up by the building of amphitheatres and staging of games across the Roman world. Communities anxious to identify themselves with the interests of the emperor and of the Roman élite used this as a means to proclaim their Romanness. There was scope for local leaders to give benefactions and to reap the benefits of the general passion for the games; the spread of artefacts decorated with images of gladiators (for

Figure 4.5 Terra sigillata *cup showing gladiators.* Colchester and Essex Museums. *(Photo: Colchester Museums)*

example, Figure 4.5) shows how popular these events were across the empire. Yet their essential 'Romanness' prevented total enthusiasm. In the Greek east there was rather a different response: gladiatorial combats were staged but usually within the context of civic ceremonial and in adapted theatres rather than in the specially designed amphitheatres of the west (Wiedemann, 1992, pp.43–4). And when in Judaea Herod included amphitheatre shows of wild-beast combat as one of his Roman-style benefactions, Jewish hostility was marked (Josephus, *Jewish Antiquities* 15.267–79).

Private houses are another important source of information about cultural priorities among local élites (Elsner, 1998, pp.95–113). Their design can articulate the value placed on public and private spaces, and the themes of their interior decoration can reveal the importance to many owners of displaying allegiance to the tastes of an empire-wide élite. Subjects may come from classical literature (the Virgil mosaic shown in Figure 4.7, for instance), from particularly Roman activities (such as gladiatorial games), or from significant episodes from classical mythology. The floor mosaics of the second century House of Dionysus at Paphos in Cyprus are a good example of 'deliberate choices intended to associate the inhabitants with the governing classes from other parts of the empire' (Kondoleon, 1994, p.323). Luxury artefacts were used and displayed to similar effect. Many were traded across the empire from particular centres of manufacture (such as the Rhineland for glass and Gaul for 'Samian ware', a high-class pottery probably made to imitate even higher-class silver tableware). Sculptures, paintings and other collectables were also brought to wealthy customers, sometimes from considerable distances (as material from shipwrecks attests).

Education and learning

Obviously literacy and the ability to respond to cultural references were in themselves empowering, just as conversely, to be illiterate and surrounded (as in a city like Ephesus) with the inscribed memorials of the powerful might have been an excluding experience. A degree of learning could help to locate a person within the civilized society of the empire, which is why there are so many instances where tokens of culture were taken up and shown by the upwardly mobile.

As we have seen, philosophy and poetry, the principal pursuits of Greek learning, were practised by many adult Romans in the republic and the early empire, but rarely in the context of public life. This may have been because they had no place in traditional Roman professional training, which focused instead on public oratory and rhetoric as a preparation for a career in public service or the law; and it is also possible that since Greece had fallen to Roman rule they were seen as somehow belonging to 'losers'. (Is this, perhaps, why Trimalchio steered clear of Greek philosophy?) But by the second century AD attitudes started to change: Romans began to represent themselves as intellectuals in the context of public life, and as it was espoused by emperors such as Hadrian (see Essay One, Figure 1.4) and Marcus Aurelius the theme of the Roman intellectual became extremely popular. Quite ordinary people wanted to show how much they valued this learning in their lives, even at the expense of downplaying their 'Roman' status: on their sarcophagus the centurion Lucius Pullius Peregrinus and his wife (*c.* AD 250) portray themselves as one of the Muses and Seven Sages complete with appropriate dress and portrait features (unfinished in the case of his wife) (Figure 4.6).

Figure 4.6   *Sarcophagus of the centurion Lucius Pullius Peregrinus and his wife,* c. *AD 250. Museo Torlonia, Rome. (Photo: German Archeological Institute in Rome)*

But in the contemporary Greek world it had another value: after the Roman conquest of Greece, pride in the local intellectual heritage became a powerful means of asserting identity. In the provinces of the Greek east, and especially in Greece itself, referencing to the Greek past became a crucial way for the people to reaffirm their cultural identity under Roman rule. This is part of the background to the local literary and philosophic movement known as the 'Second Sophistic', which flourished especially in the second century AD. For some Greeks, though, it was important to try to reconcile the two cultural aspects of their lives within the empire: a notable example was the Greek scholar and essayist, Plutarch (c. AD 46–120). He was also a member of the Roman equestrian class and held important public offices, but he lived most of his life in his provincial home town of Chaeronea in Boeotia, travelling to lecture and study in Athens and Rome. Greek traditions, intellectual and religious, were central to his personal identity, but a major concern of his work was to reconcile Greek and Roman, often using the past to mediate concerns of the present as in his *Parallel Lives* of famous Greeks and Romans.

Athens remained probably the foremost intellectual centre for scholars to visit, but Rome and other cities such as Alexandria and Carthage also attracted many students. Across the empire intellectuals felt bound together by the shared background of learning (*paideia*) and travelled to meet and keep in touch (see Essay Two). The spread of literary knowledge was helped by the sheer physical portability of written texts, despite the apparent rarity of booksellers and libraries in the cities of the empire (Harris, 1989, pp.222–8). Although the works of the greatest Latin writers such as Virgil, Horace and Livy were to be found in libraries soon after their deaths (Suetonius, *Life of Gaius Caligula* 34) or used as school textbooks (Juvenal, *Satires* 7.227), most literary works relied on readings for their circulation. Something of the status accorded to these literary 'classics' in the private sphere is suggested by their appearance in scenes chosen to decorate houses; themes of 'high' literary culture might reflect on the owner's aspirations, and perhaps repeat visually the kinds of cultural activities that happened in the house. This was most probably the background to the scene depicted on the floor mosaic from a second century house at Sousse in Tunisia (Figure 4.7): here Virgil (unnamed) is shown sitting between two Muses, with his scroll opened at a passage from the *Aeneid* (1.8) that calls on a Muse as his inspiration.

Other performance arts propagated the knowledge of major dramas (entire or as excerpts), while festivals and competitions must have been a regular way of bringing music and poetry to the wider public.

Figure 4.7   *Mosaic of Virgil and Muses from Sousse, Tunisia, c. AD 200. Bardo Museum, Tunisia. (Photo: Scala)*

Artists and patrons

Little is known about individual artists in the Roman world, even those who produced major works. This may seem surprising when compared with our knowledge of Roman literary figures, or of artists of other ages. The reason is not simply that so few signatures or ancient attributions survive, but rather the low importance Romans accorded to their artists.

Many artists working in Rome and southern Italy in the early days of the empire were from the Greek east and brought their skills and traditions to supply the local market, but by and large these were anonymous, low-status workers employed by particular patrons. Occasionally individuals are named: a fascinating case is that of Zenodorus, the leading sculptor of Nero's age who is credited with making the infamous colossal statue of Nero which stood in his 'Golden House' in Rome, and also a colossal Mercury commissioned by the people of Arverni in Gaul (modern Auvergne) (Pliny, *Natural History* 34.45–7). Here a Greek sculptor was working not only for the emperor but for a provincial community. Later on, and across the empire, there is evidence for artists operating together in local workshops or travelling further to work in other areas. Many of the designs they used were tried and tested compositions or motifs from the very conservative repertory of Graeco-Roman art; so while it is often possible to differentiate the work of particular craftsmen on points of technique, general styles and subject matter remained remarkably unchanging. The use of an unusual iconography may be the result of a patron's request (or perhaps of the artist's misunderstanding).

The relationship with a patron was important for the work of many artists. Patrons provided practical help but generally required something (such as eulogies) in return, which often gave them power over the artistic outcome. How far Virgil and Horace felt bound in their work to praise Augustus and Maecenas who were their powerful patrons remains unclear, but they must have found the material support that came with the relationship invaluable (particularly since they were not high-born or from Rome).

Patronage also worked for communities. In cities it was often linked with the practice of benefaction, so that the patron's chief relationship was with the community rather than with an individual artist. Wealthy men and women gave facilities to their home cities to be rewarded not only with the chance to advertise their generosity but also by honorific statues and inscriptions. This was a widespread practice. There are innumerable cases of buildings given by individuals, from the Temple of Isis at Pompeii rebuilt by the six-year-old Numerius Popidius Celsinus, to the library at Comum, which was yet another benefaction of the younger Pliny (Lewis and Reinhold, 1990, pp.269–71), the library of Celsus at Ephesus (which, honorifically, also housed his tomb) and the city gate rebuilt by Plancia Magna at Perge (Boatwright, 1993). An inscription of AD 112/117 from Sabratha shows how the reciprocal relationship could be expressed almost entirely in terms of civic monuments: to honour Gaius Flavius Pudens, who had given an aqueduct, fountains and gladiatorial games, the council of his native town voted to put up a four-horse chariot statue to him from public funds, but content with just the honour he paid for the statue as well (Goodman, 1997, p.283). Towns could end up bristling with such honorific statuary; one solution to the problem this might present was recycling (as it seems the Rhodians did, simply changing the inscriptions on existing statues: Dio Chrysostom, *Orations* 31.9–10).

Patrons might also sponsor events. For instance, during the reign of Hadrian, Gaius Julius Demosthenes endowed his native city of Termessus with a lavish music competition, the 'Demosthenia' (Lewis and

Reinhold, 1990, pp.264–8). It was to have its own festival director and be the occasion for special financial payments and the suspension of taxes. The donor was to pay for all this and more. The central role of wealth in such provisions is nicely depicted in a mosaic from Smirat, Tunisia, which commemorates in no uncertain terms the donation of a wild-beast show made by a certain Magerius, whose munificence is represented by the central figure of a boy holding money-bags.

Power, status and mythological subject matter

In the mosaic shown in Figure 4.8, Magerius enhanced the status of his activities by depicting two gods, Diana (left of the central figure) and Dionysus (right, and facing the other way), alongside the images of the beast fighters: this neatly illustrates a relationship between power, status and mythology that underlies many images in Roman art of the empire. We have seen it used by Augustus in his choice of 'historical' images for

Figure 4.8 *Detail from the mosaic of Magerius, from Smirat, Tunisia, AD 240–250. Sousse Museum, Tunisia. (Photo: Ancient Art and Architecture Collection Ltd)*

the Temple of Mars Ultor, and by the centurion L. Pullius Peregrinus and his wife on their sarcophagus to express the value of learning in their lives. In fact mythology was one of the major unifying themes in the subject matter of Graeco-Roman culture and provided a common framework for reference and representation. As well as recalling well-known stories it allowed ideas to be expressed indirectly (which might be useful if they seemed too radical or subversive for open display), and effectively identified humans with the world of immortals.

The private sphere provides some vivid examples, especially in the decoration of houses and domestic goods belonging to the wealthy élite across the empire. They are used to represent the various interests (religious, learning, leisure) of the owners, and to suggest their status and source of wealth. Dionysiac motifs were particularly common, and are open to a number of interpretations. In some circumstances they may reflect a particular cultic interest, but overall may be read as allusions to abundance and fertility which reflect on the wealth and comfort of the household. Scenes of the triumph of Dionysus are paralleled by scenes of the triumph of other gods, such as Neptune and Venus. These were frequently located in the principal rooms of the house, often open to visitors, which confirms their role in articulating the important social status of the owner. Other mythological subjects in floor mosaics have been interpreted as alluding to spectacles staged by the patron, for instance as mythological hunts or wild-beast displays. Moral values were another theme: the Labours of Hercules, for example, were the subject of various allegorical interpretations which cast him as a Stoic-type hero, and one genre of Greek writing, *ekphrasis*, had a narrator commenting on imaginary works of arts, usually in terms that related their appearance to a moral message.

All these examples show how mythological themes could play a central role in articulating identity and power relations in the decoration of houses of the élite. In parallel, what might be termed 'new mythologies' evolved to express the value of particular cultural activities. For instance, in late republican circles, when men met in their private homes for intellectual discourse, portraits of the great Greek philosophers were prominently displayed, as if they were cult statues in temples. Cicero had a statue of Plato and Atticus one of Aristotle (Zanker, 1995, p.205). And in north African floor mosaics from the second century AD, scenes of hunting, farming, and circus and gladiator shows gradually took over from traditional mythological subjects as a way of presenting the ideals and interests of wealthy patrons (Dunbabin, 1978).

Conclusions

At the beginning of this essay two key questions were identified: how far did élite Graeco-Roman culture become the culture of empire, and where does the concept of *romanitas* fit in? It is time to find some answers.

For the first question, the most important factor must be change over time (not surprising perhaps since we have been reviewing developments across three or four centuries). Although in many respects élite Graeco-Roman culture was conservative and traditional, it was exposed to constant revision and re-emphasis. The advent of empire brought new social groups and regions into regular contact with the culture that had originally supported the Roman élite. However, these new practitioners did not simply absorb or adopt the Graeco-Roman traditions, but usually changed or reinvented them in the process (Elsner, 1998, pp.117–26). Thus the culture of empire became something more than the culture of the Roman élites. At one level, that of its own élite, this empire culture relied on a 'common ground' to display recognizable values, but the presence of other strong traditions outside the Roman culture created many local cultural variations. Individuals, institutions, and even cities found their own ways of negotiating identities for themselves within this variety of traditions.

So where is *romanitas*, the Roman element in this picture? Certainly many aspects of the Roman aristocratic culture of the republic are recognizable in the empire, such as the interest in commemoration, in spectacle, and the value placed on action and experience, as well as the learning and literature drawn from Greek culture. But by the late first or early second century it ceases to be meaningful to talk of distinctive Roman or Greek elements in the overall view.

By then another cultural quality had emerged which seems to signify the *romanitas* of the empire: its flexibility and tendency to inclusiveness. This enabled people to identify with the empire and its élites, not so much by having a central culture imposed on them as by the provision of ways in which they could link their traditions with its own. From a Roman imperial standpoint this may have been a more effective way of managing the far-flung empire, while from a local viewpoint it offered a way of finding a particular cultural identity within it. The élite culture of Rome provided an overarching context to all this.

References

BEARD, M. and CRAWFORD, M. (1985) *Rome in the Late Republic*, London, Batsford.

BOATWRIGHT, M. (1993) 'The city gate of Plancia Magna in Perge' in E. D'Ambra (ed.) *Roman Art in Context*, Englewood Cliffs, Prentice Hall, pp.189–207.

BOETHIUS, A. and WARD-PERKINS, J.B. (1992) *Etruscan and Early Roman Architecture*, Pelican History of Art, New Haven and London, Yale University Press.

BOWMAN, A. (1994) *Life and Letters on the Roman Frontier*, London, British Museum Press.

DUNBABIN, K. (1978) *The Mosaics of Roman North Africa: Studies in Iconography and Patronage*, Oxford Monographs on Classical Mythology, Oxford, Clarendon Press.

ELSNER, J. (1998) *Imperial Rome and Christian Triumph: The Art of the Roman Empire AD 100–450*, Oxford History of Art, Oxford, Oxford University Press.

FANTHAM, E. (1994) *Women in the Classical World: Image and Text*, New York, Oxford University Press.

FANTHAM, E. (1996) *Roman Literary Culture from Cicero to Apuleius*, Baltimore and London, Johns Hopkins University Press.

GOODMAN, M. (1997) *The Roman World 44 BC–AD 180*, London and New York, Routledge.

HARRIS, W.V. (1989) *Ancient Literacy*, Cambridge, Mass., Harvard University Press.

KLEINER, D.E.E. (1987) *Roman Imperial Funerary Altars with Portraits*, Archaeologica 62, Rome, Bretschneider.

KONDOLEON, C. (1994) *Domestic and Divine: Roman Mosaics in the House of Dionysios*, Ithaca, Cornell University Press.

LEWIS, N. and REINHOLD, M. (eds) (1990) *Roman Civilization: Selected Readings. Volume II The Empire*, New York, Columbia University Press.

MATTINGLY, H. (trans.) (1970) *Tacitus: The Agricola and The Germania*, Harmondsworth, Penguin (first published 1948).

MILLAR, F. (1981) *The Roman Empire and its Neighbours*, second edition, London, Duckworth (first published 1968).

MITCHELL, S. (1995) *Anatolia: Land, Men, and Gods in Asia Minor. Vol.I The Celts in Anatolia and the Impact of Roman Rule*, Oxford, Clarendon Press.

PRICE, S.R.F. (1984) *Rituals and Power: the Roman Imperial Cult in Asia Minor*, Cambridge, Cambridge University Press.

WALKER, S. and BIERBRIER, M. (1997) *Ancient Faces: Mummy Portraits from Roman Egypt*, London, British Museum Press.

WALLACE-HADRILL, A. (1989) 'Rome's cultural revolution', *Journal of Roman Studies*, 79, pp.155–64.

WARD-PERKINS, J. B. (1981) *Roman Imperial Architecture*, Harmondsworth, Penguin (first published 1970 as Parts 2–4 of *Etruscan and Roman Architecture*, Harmondsworth, Penguin).

WIEDEMANN, T. (1992) *Emperors and Gladiators*, London and New York, Routledge.

WOOLF, G. (1994) 'Becoming Roman, staying Greek: culture, identity and the civilizing process in the Roman east', *Proceedings of the Cambridge Philological Society*, 40, pp.116–43.

WOOLF, G. (1998) *Becoming Roman: the Origins of Provincial Administration in Gaul*, Cambridge, Cambridge University Press.

ZANKER, P. (1988) *The Power of Images in the Age of Augustus* (trans. A. Shapiro), Ann Arbor, University of Michigan Press.

ZANKER, P. (1995) *The Mask of Socrates: the Image of the Intellectual in Antiquity* (trans. A. Shapiro), Berkeley, University of California Press.

Essay Five
Status and identity in the Roman world

BY VALERIE HOPE

Living in order

> I happened to be dining with a man – though no particular friend of his – whose elegant economy, as he called it, seemed to me a sort of stingy extravagance. The best dishes were set in front of himself and a select few, and cheap scraps of food before the rest of the company. He had even put wine into tiny little flasks, divided into three categories, not with the idea of giving his guests the opportunity of choosing, but to make it impossible for them to refuse what they were given. One lot was intended for himself and for us, another for his lesser friends (all his friends are graded) and the third for his and our freedmen. My neighbour at table noticed this and asked me if I approved. I said I did not. 'So what do you do?' he asked. 'I serve the same to everyone, for when I invite guests it is for a meal, not to make class distinctions; I have brought them as equals to the same table, so I give them the same treatment in everything.' 'Even the freedmen?' 'Of course, for then they are my fellow-diners, not freedmen.'
>
> (Pliny the Younger, *Letters* 2.6; trans. Radice, 1963, pp.63–4)

Pliny the Younger, writing at the end of the first century AD, recorded how social distinctions were articulated at a particular dinner by the food and drink supplied to those present. Pliny did not approve of such behaviour and described his own egalitarian dinner parties where the quality of the refreshments was not intended to reflect differences in the perceived worth of his guests. Accounts of other authors suggest, however, that the incident described by Pliny was not an isolated one (Martial, *Epigrams* 9.2; Juvenal, *Satires* 5.24–155; Horace, *Satires* 2.8; Pliny the Elder, *Natural History* 14.91). The dinner party, an event with both public and private overtones, was used by some hosts to display not only their wealth but also how they valued and rated their associates. The seating plan, types of food, quality of the wine and nature of the entertainment could be manipulated to show social relationships and to underline that in a given situation people were not perceived as equal. Simultaneously, these social occasions and their description (and condemnation) in literature, such as Pliny's letter, suggest that there was an on-going debate about both social etiquette and status evaluation.

To hold a dinner party required a degree of wealth. The majority of the inhabitants of Rome and the empire would have had few opportunities to partake in such social events. These occasions were the preserve of the well to do, and provided an opportunity for them to display their superiority to the wider world and simultaneously to differentiate and debate superiority within their own circles. But there is substantial evidence that differences were also articulated in more public places. Seats in the amphitheatre and theatre were graded and certain modes of dress were restricted to the élite. Such visual ordering and dividing of the populace served to underline that the Roman world was full of social inequalities. This essay will explore the basis of these inequalities especially in relation to the themes of culture, identity and power. The relative power and influence of the individual was conferred by the evaluation of his or her status within the Roman cultural framework. Yet, as will become apparent, the definition of an individual's status involved complex and sometimes contradictory and contested factors, which could be compounded by the geographic and chronological breadth of the empire. It is thus often impossible to provide a finite definition of an individual's status; instead it is more appropriate to consider how individual identity was constructed and perceived.

Inequality is a major part of people's lives (Berreman, 1981, p.4). It is human nature to evaluate ourselves and others and to create a pecking order, even if the specific criteria for evaluation vary between and within societies.[1] For the Roman period, variations in the material evidence, such as houses, public monuments, tombs and personal possessions, are suggestive of inequalities but not the basis of those inequalities. Furthermore there is no surviving definitive or systematic description of the constituent elements or groupings within Roman society. The evidence is indirect and drawn primarily from literature and inscriptions. The relevant literature is diverse in form – letters, legal documents, satire, poetry and so forth can all help to illuminate the criteria by which people were distinguished. This literature often represents a perspective that is élite, urban and male, and thus does not give access to all people and places. Inscriptions provide insights, albeit brief ones, into more lives, but still represent a minority, and not necessarily a representative minority since they cannot have been cheap to inscribe and they show a marked urban over rural bias. In short, inscriptions and literature often present selective views of those named and identified; they construct identities for individuals and groups which fulfil specific purposes. For

---

1 There is a debate over whether human society has always been hierarchical or if hierarchy arose at some point in prehistory. For a summary of the debate and differing ranking systems see Wason (1994).

example, the composition of an epitaph was a subjective process: some information might be prioritized while other things were left unsaid. Equally a letter such as Pliny's was written with a certain audience in mind and articulated specific views.

Despite all the evidence, whether literary or epigraphic, it remains impossible to compile definitive statistics on status distinctions. In the modern world figures and quantification are taken for granted, especially in demographic studies. For the Roman period we do not know the size of the population or relative levels of income, or how many people were slaves or how many people were citizens. Finding language and terms which are suitable to describe distinctions and divisions is also complex. In the translation of the letter of Pliny the Younger with which this essay began, reference is made to 'class distinctions'. Employing the terminology of class with its Marxist overtones, however, is problematic in the Roman context (Alföldy, 1988, pp.148–50; Garnsey and Saller, 1987, p.109). Labels such as upper, middle and lower class had no equivalent in the ancient world and attempting to equate groups to these modern categories can create more problems than it solves. Even the use of more general terms such as 'social groups' raises difficulties of how membership is to be defined. This is not to dispute that people could be grouped together by categories based, for example, on wealth or legal condition, but one-dimensional classifications risk ignoring the multiple factors and interactions that affected people's lives. There was no simple or single system which ordered society and thus evaluating status is a complex process.

To acknowledge the difficulties in evidence and language is not to dispute that the Roman world was a hierarchical place, but it serves to emphasize instead that the basis for distinctions could be diverse and involved both legal and social factors. It is worth stressing – since we live in a society where everyone is, in theory, equal before the law – that legal distinctions were a reality. A person living in the Roman empire was born into a certain legal condition and had to live with the consequences, although there were opportunities for those of inferior legal condition to improve their lot and occasionally for others to be demoted. Legal status was of substantial importance, but other social advantages, such as wealth, power and honour, could also be conveyed by birth, as well as disadvantages. But as with legal status there were possibilities that fortunes could change, and in addition many elements of social status involved personal judgements and evaluations. The dinner party anecdote reveals that people were rated by the host not only in terms of their legal condition, such as free birth or former servitude, but also by the closeness of their friendship. One may suspect that this man evaluated his friends according to wealth and connections rather than affection and loyalty. But by using both publicly acknowledged social and legal factors and his own more personal criteria the host was able to create his own social hierarchy which was given physical expression at the dinner table.

The following sections will explore the basis of both the legal and social distinctions present in the Roman world and their impact on the individual. How was one person differentiated from another? And to what degree did social and legal advantages and handicaps colour the lives of the inhabitants of the empire? Initially the basic legal distinctions between slaves, freed slaves and Roman citizens will be explored. This will be followed by an evaluation of the privileges, both legal and social, conveyed by rank, profession, property and wealth. Finally the possibilities for social mobility and the understanding of an individual's overall status rating will be assessed.

Slave or free

> The principal distinction in the law of persons is this, that all men are either free or slaves. Next, free men are either freeborn, or freedmen. Freeborn are those born free, freedmen those manumitted from lawful slavery.
> (Gaius, *Institutes* 1.9–11, in Lewis and Reinhold, 1990, p.500)

Gaius, an author of a handbook on Roman law, dwells on the legal distinctions between men. All men were not equal: they differed not only in whether they were free or slave but also, if free, in whether they were born to or acquired this status. The sharpest distinctions, both legal and social, within the Roman system were those created by the institution of slavery. Roman society, at least within Rome and Italy, was a slave society in which the major source of labour was provided by those who were bereft of their freedom: they were born into slavery, sold into slavery or forced into slavery by defeat in war (Hopkins, 1978; Bradley, 1994, pp.31–54). This is not to say that all labour was performed by slaves and in many provinces slavery may not have been widespread. Nevertheless, within Italy of the imperial period a substantial proportion of the population was probably servile. Slaves (*servi*) were the tools and possessions of their masters; they lived at the command of masters who had the power of life and death over them. Slaves could not own property, nor establish legitimate marriages, and any children born to slaves automatically became the property of their masters. For many slaves, especially those employed in agriculture on large rural estates, life must have been harsh and often short. The urban slave may have fared somewhat better. The household slaves were regarded as part of the *familia* and their own relationships with fellow slaves, although not legally recognized, were often tolerated and even encouraged (Bradley, 1987, pp.47–80). Some slaves might also be allowed a level of independence and the right to accumulate savings (*peculium*), although this technically remained the property of the master.

Many masters may have treated their slaves humanely. Legislation was gradually introduced to control physical cruelty (Bradley, 1987, pp.127–30; see Lewis and Reinhold, 1990, pp.181–2) and literature often underlined that the slave was a human being deserving of reasonable treatment (e.g. Seneca, *Epistles* 47, in Lewis and Reinhold, 1990, p.179). In his letters Pliny the Younger portrayed himself as a caring and responsible master. He spoke of individual slaves and ex-slaves with concern and kindness and stressed that by allowing his slaves certain rights and freedom a sense of community was engendered among them (*Letters* 5.19; 8.16). But such sentiments should not blind us to the exploitative and oppressive nature of slavery. All masters invested money in their slaves and would gain little by physically abusing this investment. Masters expected loyalty and obedience, and reasonable treatment was one method of ensuring this (Bradley, 1987, pp.140–3). Even Pliny the Younger was forced to acknowledge, after the death of a cruel master at the hands of his slaves, that kindness was a control mechanism, if not always a very adequate one.

> There you see the dangers, outrages, and insults to which we are exposed. No master can feel safe because he is kind and considerate; for it is their brutality, not their reasoning capacity, which leads slaves to murder masters.
>
> (Pliny the Younger, *Letters* 3.14; trans. Radice, 1963, p.101)

A fundamental and humanizing aspect of Roman slavery was that slavery was not automatically a life-long state. Slaves could be and regularly were given their freedom. The widespread manumission of slaves was a distinctive feature of Roman slavery. The willingness to free slaves probably had less to do with humanitarian concerns and more to do with control; the prospect of freedom may have encouraged the slave to be obedient and hard working. Once free, provided the slave's master was a Roman citizen and the slave was formally manumitted, the former slave also became a Roman citizen. In other words, the system sought to integrate the former slaves into Roman society rather than creating a permanent underclass. The freed slave could now own property, marry legally and have legitimate children. It was even possible for ex-slaves to marry their former owners and become slave owners in their own right.[2]

---

2 The freeing of female slaves by their masters in order that the latter could marry the former is particularly well attested.

The freed slave (male *libertus*, female *liberta*) did, however, remain bound to the former master, now termed a patron (*patronus*), by certain legal obligations (Gardner, 1993, pp.20–51); if the ex-slave prospered, the former master also stood to gain. In many respects former slaves (*liberti*), despite freedom and citizenship, continued to be stigmatized by former servitude; not only did they retain a debt of gratitude to their former masters but they were also excluded from certain honourable pursuits, such as service in the army and the holding of magisterial and governing offices; and if found guilty of a crime ex-slaves would often face more severe penalties than their freeborn counterparts (Garnsey, 1970, p.262). Such legal handicaps did not, however, affect any freeborn children of the freed slave, although some social stigmas could remain. Under the emperor Claudius a son of a freedman was even admitted to the senatorial order, but only after his adoption by an *eques* (Suetonius, *Claudius* 24.1). By the first century AD it seems probable that a large proportion of the freeborn citizens of the city of Rome could trace their origins to freed slaves. Tacitus claimed that it was reported in a senatorial debate that freed slaves were everywhere and that even many senators and knights were descended from former slaves (Tacitus, *Annals* 13.27). Such a claim may well have been exaggerated, serving to fuel anxieties about the dilution of 'Roman' blood. Nevertheless the freeing of slaves was accepted and the *liberti* formed part of the population profile, even if few freed slaves and their immediate offspring actually rose to great social heights.

Civis romanus sum[3]

In terms of the law of persons the principal distinction might be between freedom and servitude, but legal differences did not end there. The free man or woman could benefit by holding Roman citizenship. The free non-citizens, or *peregrini*, of the empire were in legal terms disadvantaged compared with Roman citizens. Only citizens could hold positions in the administration of those cities organized as municipalities and colonies, only citizens could serve in the legions, and only citizens enjoyed privileges in private law and the ability to compose a legally binding will (Crook, 1967, pp.253–9; Garnsey, 1970, pp.261–2). Furthermore, if they were found guilty of the same offences the punishments meted out to citizens and non-citizens could differ. In AD 17, for example, the senate took action to stamp out astrology in Rome: those astrologers who were Roman citizens were exiled, and those who were foreigners were put to death (Tacitus, *Annals* 2.32–5). The story of

3 'I am a Roman citizen.'

St Paul illustrates how citizenship could also advantage the holder in the provinces. Paul avoided summary justice at the hands of Roman officials by emphasizing that he was a Roman citizen and ultimately was able to appeal to the emperor (*Acts of the Apostles*, 22.25–29; 25.10–12).[4] Not all the freeborn inhabitants of the empire were as privileged as Paul and thus in the fullest sense they were not 'Roman'.

In a given province Roman citizens would initially represent the alien presence – they were the administrators, soldiers and colonists. With time the circle of citizenship gradually expanded; citizenship was given to individuals, families and whole settlements as a reward for service to Rome or assimilation to Roman ways. It was probably through such a grant that the family of St Paul gained citizenship. In addition, slaves who were formally manumitted by citizens became citizens themselves, and non-citizens who joined the Roman army became citizens on their discharge. Once attained, providing both parents were citizens, citizenship was passed on to the next generation. Citizenship was sought after for the advantages and privileges that it conveyed throughout the first two centuries of the empire. But the spread of citizenship also brought advantages to central government since it united the empire and helped to make it more uniform. Rome populated its empire with citizens who had never seen the city of Rome; it was less citizenship of a city than of an ideal.

> You have not made Rome a world's conceit, by letting nobody else share in it. No, you have sought out the complement of citizens it deserves. You have made the word 'Roman' apply not to a city but to a universal people.
>
> (Aelius Aristides, *To Rome* 59–60, in Lewis and Reinhold, 1990, p.59)

Citizenship became increasingly widespread until in AD 212 the emperor Caracalla extended citzenship to the freeborn population of the whole empire.[5]

Roman citizens were physically marked by their right to wear the toga. Its use was prohibited to non-citizens. Attempts by emperors such as Augustus to encourage the wearing of the toga in public places suggest that although the mode of dress retained a symbolic value it may have been little employed in daily life (Suetonius, *Augustus* 40; Juvenal, *Satires* 3.172–8). Citizenship and its associated privileges, whether legal advantages or styles of dress, were most celebrated by new citizens who found a sense of pride and superiority in the freshly acquired identity. The attainment of citizenship was often marked in visual and verbal

---

4 The reasons why the governor, Festus, allowed Paul to be sent for trial in Rome were probably multiple (see Garnsey, 1970, pp.75–6).

5 For an account of the diffusion of citizenship across the provinces and the reasons and mechanisms for its spread, see Sherwin-White (1973).

forms, especially during the first two centuries AD. This is well illustrated by funerary memorials set up to mark the graves of new citizens. Epitaphs contained the *tria nomina* or three names which were a symbol of citizenship, and contrasted with the single names generally associated with slaves and *peregrini*. The images that accompanied the inscriptions often depicted the new citizen wearing the toga and contained symbols associated with affluence and success. Lucius Ampudius Philomusus, for example, was commemorated in an epitaph that revealed him to be a freed slave (Figure 5.1).

Figure 5.1 *The funerary relief of the freedman Lucius Ampudius Philomusus from Rome. Augustan. The British Museum. (© The British Museum)*

The letter L in the middle of his name stood as an abbreviation for Libertus and was placed next to the first initial of his patron's or former owner's name. As a slave Lucius Ampudius Philomusus would have been known by the single name of Philomusus, but on manumission he adopted the family names of his former master thus acquiring three names (the *tria nomina*) which stood as a symbol of citizenship.[6] The epitaph was accompanied by a portrait of Lucius Ampudius Philomusus, wearing the toga, flanked by two women who were probably his wife and daughter. Overall the monument proudly celebrated the status symbols of Roman citizenship – name, dress and the right to a legitimate marriage and children (Taylor, 1961).

6 Freed slaves did not automatically become Roman citizens. If their master did not hold citizenship or if they were freed informally or below the legal age they did not attain citizenship. There is some evidence that freed slaves who were not citizens adopted the *tria nomina*. Thus the latter is not in itself an automatic indication that the holder was a Roman citizen.

A similar emphasis on citizenship and its advertisement was found among the soldiers who served on the Roman frontiers at forts and settlements where the natives had often not yet received the franchise. Gaius Faltonius Secundus was a legionary soldier based in Mainz in Germany during the first century AD (see Figure 5.2). His epitaph proudly declared his Roman and military identity by inclusion of the *tria nomina*, the name of his father indicating free birth and the voting tribe into which he was enrolled. The epitaph was complemented by a full figure depiction of the deceased wearing a cloak and military dress including weapons. The central figure of Gaius Faltonius Secundus was flanked by two lesser figures who were not identified in the epitaph. It seems probable that these represented the slaves of the soldier, their diminutive stature emphasizing their social inferiority and thus the superiority of their citizen and military master.

It would not be true to say that all Roman citizens were equal. The advantages conferred by wealth, connections and influence and the disadvantages for the non-privileged will be explored below. In terms of inequality within the overall citizen body it is worth noting here that some citizens were automatically handicapped by their past or gender. The restrictions that applied to former slaves have already been noted. The *libertus* might attain citizenship but the associated privileges were restricted. Others found themselves stigmatized by profession and pursuits. Those who were regarded as polluted, such as undertakers, or those who sold themselves for the pleasure of others, such as actors,

Figure 5.2   *The tombstone of the soldier Gaius Faltonius Secundus from Mainz (Germany), first century AD. (Photo: Landesmuseum Mainz)*

gladiators and prostitutes, were, if they were citizens, legally handicapped (Gardner, 1993, pp.110–54; Edwards, 1997). Other social groups – notably women and children – also did not benefit from all the advantages of the franchise. Roman society was patriarchal and male oriented. Women could hold the citizenship but were always, technically at least, under male authority. Within the family the *paterfamilias*, the eldest living male, was head, and all members of the family were in his *potestas* or authority. This included, it should be noted, not only women, slaves and young children but also adult sons (Gardner, 1993, pp.52–83). In theory a mature son who held citizenship remained dependent on his father. In practice few fathers probably lived long enough to see their offspring reach adulthood and those that did may rarely have utilized the full weight of their powers (Saller, 1987). But *potestas* serves as a reminder that citizenship was not the only prerequisite for freedom of thought and action.

The extent to which all male citizens wished or were able to benefit from all the advantages of the franchise and were treated as equals by fellow citizens may also be queried. Would a citizen born and bred in Rome really regard himself as the same as or equal to a recently enfranchised man from northern Gaul? Literature suggests that 'old' Romans could be condescending towards new citizens and that grants of citizenship to those who seemed ill-experienced in Roman ways could cause consternation (Tacitus, *Annals* 3.40; Sherwin-White, 1973, pp.258–9). Juvenal complained of Romans of Greek origin who were transforming the capital city (Juvenal, *Satires* 3, in Lewis and Reinhold, 1990, p.151). Martial spoke with disdain of Cappodocians and Syrians (Martial, *Epigrams* 10.76.1). Prejudice existed against certain ethnic and religious groups of people whether they held citizenship or not. Jews, for example, rarely attained high office in the Roman world and Egyptians were stereotyped as irresponsible and barbaric (Alföldy, 1988, p.113; Alston, 1996).

To many inhabitants of the empire citizenship of Rome may have been significant, but citizenship often coexisted with other regional and ethnic identities. Roman citizenship may have been only one element out of many used by individuals to define themselves. It was possible, for example, to be simultaneously a citizen of Rome and a citizen of a city such as Athens. This duality may have been of particular significance in the well-developed settlements of the Greek east where a strong sense of identity already existed. In Alexandria during the first century AD there were serious arguments between the Greek and Jewish inhabitants over who was eligible for Alexandrian citizenship. Although this gave access to Roman citizenship, the arguments were centred on the more immediate privileges that citizenship of the city conveyed; citizenship of Rome was not the priority. (Incidentally, how the Egyptians who were not Greeks, Jews or Roman citizens perceived themselves is unclear.) Equally, St Paul made full use of his Roman citizenship when his activities brought him into conflict with other 'Romans', but before this his citizenship may have been of secondary importance. Thus the relevance and benefits of holding citizenship may have varied according to individual circumstances. In a settlement where the majority of inhabitants were not citizens, citizenship may have conferred substantial social prestige but few practical advantages. Simultaneously, in a settlement where the majority of people did hold citizenship it conferred many practical advantages, but it was perhaps little noted and celebrated.

Privilege and power

In the Roman world there were numerous legal conditions into which an individual was either born or promoted, such as slave, ex-slave, citizen and non-citizen. But such distinctions could be further reinforced or ameliorated through wealth and prestige. The polarity between the distinguished and non-distinguished was a real one and from the mid second century AD onwards it was increasingly acknowledged through the terms *honestiores* and *humiliores*. The former were those with money, power and influence and the latter were those

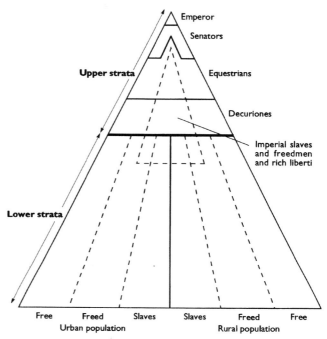

Figure 5.3   *A schematic representation of Roman social structure under the principate. (Based on Alföldy, 1988, Figure 1)*

without (Garnsey, 1970, pp.221–3). This division became even more pronounced during the third century AD when the privileges of citizenship were effectively undermined by the universal grant of Caracalla. Yet throughout the Imperial period, whether the terms *honestiores* and *humiliores* were employed or not, the Roman population was polarized into an upper and a lower strata with little in the way of what might be termed a middle class. A pyramid has been used as a graphic representation of the situation (see Figure 5.3). The lower part of the pyramid was made up of the bulk of the population, who might be differentiated by legal conditions such as slavery or citizenship, and even by social factors such as types of employment and income, but were united by their lack of rank, power and prestige. At the top of the pyramid was the emperor, surrounded and supported by the privileged classes who formed the upper strata of Roman society.

To be numbered among the upper strata required money (especially that invested in land), power through office holding, social prestige and membership of one of the leading orders (Alföldy, 1988, p.106). That is to say, the upper strata consisted of senators, equestrians and the *decuriones* of the local communities. The senate was the traditional ruling body of Rome from which the governing magistrates of the republic were drawn. In the empire the senate continued to represent the citizen élite of the empire as well as Rome, although service to the state now meant increasingly service to the emperor (Alföldy, 1988, p.102). For much of the Imperial period the senate was limited to 600 members whose entrance was dependent on property qualifications and election to key offices. The senate was not a hereditary body, but sons of senators were encouraged to follow in their father's footsteps; they might attend meetings with their father (Suetonius, *Augustus* 38) and the privileges of the office endured for three generations (*Digest* 23.2.44). Despite the incentives senatorial families often failed to reproduce themselves. The senate might be a small and exclusive body but it remained open to new men.

All senators were distinguished not only by extreme wealth but by a sense of privilege and respect which pervaded all aspects of life. A senator stood out through his mode of dress, specifically a broad purple stripe on his toga, and by his occupancy of the best seats at public spectacles held in the amphitheatre and theatre. The senator also held a privileged legal position: if he was found guilty of a crime he was unlikely to face severe penalties, and what would be a capital offence for others often resulted in voluntary exile for the senator (Garnsey, 1970, pp.221–3). The senate, however, also had its own internal hierarchy. The successful senator progressed through a series of offices which entailed administrative, military and religious duties (*cursus honorum*). The titles attained and the power and authority associated with them were a source of senatorial prestige. Honorary inscriptions inscribed on statue bases and funerary monuments focused on the career of the commemorated individual, emphasizing his most important achievements. The lengthy honorary inscription to Gaius Ummidius Durmius Quadratus from Casinum in Italy, for example, lists the attainment of the most prestigious office of *consul* first before recording the other many and varied posts that he had held (*Corpus Inscriptionum Latinarum* 10.5182, in Lewis and Reinhold, 1990, p.44). Success within the senatorial order was dependent, however, not just on personal ability and ambition but also on the quality of one's connections. Family background and/or imperial favour were of the greatest significance for senatorial status and elevation within the order.

The equestrian order, traditionally those who were entitled to a public horse, gained in prominence during the early empire, when the equestrian *cursus* (career) was more clearly defined so that those wishing to pursue a public career held military and administrative posts. As with the senatorial order, membership was dependent on meeting certain monetary requirements and brought privileges and status symbols. The property qualification was considerably less than for a senator but was still indicative of substantial wealth. Like the senator, the equestrian (*eques romanus*) could wear distinctive clothing (a narrow purple stripe on the toga and a gold ring), had access to choice seats at shows and spectacles and was legally privileged (Garnsey, 1970, pp.237–42). The equestrian order was considerably larger than the senatorial order and many wealthy provincials qualified for membership, although only a minority chose to pursue a political or military career. Strabo, writing in the early first century AD, noted, for example, that the Spanish town of Gades had as many as 500 men who qualified for equestrian status (Strabo, *Geography* 3.5.3; 5.1.7).

The social hierarchy found in the towns and cities of the provinces often mirrored that in Rome. Power and authority lay in the hands of a small wealthy élite who provided the magistrates and governance for the town. Entrance requirements for membership of the town council, the *ordo* of *decuriones*, included free birth, citizenship and wealth. The *decuriones* enjoyed distinctive dress, dined at public expense, had reserved seats in the local theatre and, like the senators and equestrians, were privileged before the law (Garnsey, 1970, pp.242–5). The town councils provided the provincial communities with a high level of autonomy and thus central government was concerned that those holding posts were responsible. Town charters provided rules and regulations for the running of the communities including guidelines for membership of the *ordo*. The charter for the Spanish town of Malaga, for example, specified that the *decuriones* should be of free birth and aged over twenty-five (*Corpus Inscriptionum Latinarum* 2.1964, in Lewis and Reinhold, 1990, pp.233–6). In return for their titles and prestige the local magistrates, in addition to their official duties, were expected to plough money back into their local communities by undertaking building projects and providing entertainment for the population. A public career could therefore prove expensive but it also could bring great prestige. Local benefactors might be honoured by their communities through the erection of a statue. Marcus Servilius Draco Abucianus from Gigthis in north Africa was honoured by a statue and an inscription which recorded his munificence and services to the town, which included several trips to Rome to promote the status of the community (*Corpus Inscriptionum Latinarum* 8.22737, in Lewis and Reinhold, 1990, p.274). No doubt he elevated his own profile in elevating that of the town.

In focusing on the upper section of the hypothetical social pyramid we should not forget the inherent diversity involved. Just as when citizenship was considered it was noted how the term encompassed peasants, aristocrats and soldiers, so the senatorial, equestrian and decurional labels cover a multiplicity of types of people. These people might be united by shared characteristics in terms of wealth and legal status but their backgrounds, experiences and ambitions might be diverse. Would the equestrian from Gades have much in common with the equestrian from Rome? Equally, we may also wish to question the real value of these titles. A degree of prestige might have been derived, especially on a local level, in describing yourself as a senator, an equestrian or a decurion, but did it really confer any power and authority? Were these offices often no more than empty titles rather than emblems of true power?

Money and connections

Money could not buy everything and some who were wealthy were excluded from holding office. Women, where appropriate, were classed as being of senatorial or equestrian status on the basis of the status of their male relatives; women could also amass substantial fortunes but they could hold no posts in the imperial administration. Wealthy women could, however, act as priestesses in certain cults and also become patrons and benefactors, which entailed a certain amount of prestige and influence. The restrictions which divided the upper strata from the lower most notably affected freed slaves. The *libertus* never completely lost the stigma of his past and was debarred from senatorial and equestrian status and could not serve as a decurion. But during the period of the empire the talents of those freed slaves who amassed fortunes were channelled to the advantage of their local communities. Some freed slaves were granted honorary titles entitling them to the symbols of privilege if not the actual office; thus freed slaves could become honorary *decuriones*. Wealthy freed slaves were also often to be found among the ranks of the *augustales* or priests of the imperial cult. The office fulfilled social as well as religious functions, giving the former slaves access to the trappings of office such as titles and privileged seats at public events (D'Arms, 1981, p.127). In return, like the *decuriones*, the *augustales* were expected to put money back into the local communities through acts of public generosity. Gaius Munatius Faustus, a freed slave and *augustalis* of Pompeii, for example, who was commemorated by his wife, received a funerary memorial which recorded his title of *augustalis* and his receipt of a privileged double seat (*bisellium*). The funerary monument was decorated with the image of the *bisellium* but also included a sculptural panel depicting Gaius Munatius Faustus distributing money or corn to an assembled crowd (see Figure 5.4). The monument sought to celebrate not just the titles and honours of the deceased but also the public good that he had done.

In Rome itself a minority of freed slaves also played a prominent role in the administration. The slaves and freed slaves of the emperor could

Figure 5.4
The front and side
panels of the
funerary altar of
Gaius Munatius
Faustus from
Pompeii, first
century AD.
(Photo: German
Archaeological
Institute, Rome.
Reproduced in
Kockel, 1983)

become especially privileged and command considerable influence. The majority of imperial slaves were employed in menial tasks but a few had access to the emperor as advisers and experts. These slaves could never become senators or equestrians or be described as *honestiores*, but their proximity to the seat of power allowed them, indirectly, to wield considerable authority (Weaver, 1974). In many ways it was their very servile status that made the imperial slaves and ex-slaves so well suited for these roles. The freed slave was at the mercy of the emperor: he could be removed or punished with ease and, unlike members of the élite, did not represent a serious rival for imperial power (Hopkins, 1978, p.124). Nevertheless, close proximity to the emperor was a source of status and prestige and some imperial freed slaves could be praised and rewarded (Pliny the Younger, *Letters* 7.29, 8.6). At death, service to the emperor might be recorded with pride in the epitaphs of imperial slaves and *liberti* – the designation of servitude accompanied by the name of the emperor became almost like an office or honorary title. The positions held by these slaves and freedmen were not without controversy and criticism, especially among the élite. It was one of the inconsistencies and ironies of life that those who held prestigious titles often had little real power, while those with power, at least in terms of access to the emperor, had access to few titles or honours.

The question of access to the emperor and the privileges that this could convey raises the issue of the real basis for the emperor's power – the control of the military. The emperor's position was highly dependent on maintaining the support of the vast number of men who served in the Roman army. The emperor relied on representatives in the field to maintain his authority, and this underlined his need for close relationships with the senatorial and equestrian orders from whom the military commanders were recruited. Control of the army thus lay in the hands of the upper strata. The average rank and file soldier was not among the highly privileged; that is to say he was not a senator or an equestrian. Yet military service did bring certain advantages, especially regular pay and gifts of money from the emperor. Soldiers and ex-soldiers also had some legal advantages over non-military counterparts. Veterans could not, for example, be punished for crimes by being beaten or thrown to wild animals in the arena; and, if accused of a crime, serving soldiers probably benefited from trial in a favourable military court (Garnsey, 1970, pp.245–51; Juvenal, *Satires* 16). The army looked after its own and created a sense of community and dependency among its men (MacMullen, 1984). Simultaneously, the army maintained a hierarchical structure through which the average soldier could progress by hard work and commitment, advantaging himself both financially and in terms of prestige. The tombstone of Gaius Faltonius Secundus (Figure 5.2), for example, records pride in military identity and also suggests a degree of wealth for the deceased and his commemorators who could afford such a monument.

The army provided a support system for its members, the equivalent of which was not available to the civilian population. Nevertheless, informal dependency relationships were a marked feature of Roman life. The upper strata were connected to the lower strata through a dense and complex patronage network. The emperor functioned as the ultimate patron, for without his support and favour the ambitious senator was unlikely to reach the highest offices. Equally, lesser senators looked to more eminent colleagues to promote their interests. A successful man was marked by the number of dependent clients (*clientes*) who formed his retinue. Yet such relationships were not restricted to the élite and instead pervaded all aspects of Roman society, with people looking to their 'friends' for support, whether they were wealthy office holders or poverty stricken artisans. Such networks provided access to authority and the wheels of power even if in an indirect fashion. The lower strata may have had little political voice, but by way of the patronage system they gained some access to the higher levels of the imperial system. Towns and whole communities might also seek influential patrons who would provide them with a voice in Rome. People could also organize themselves into clubs or *collegia*, associations often based on trade or religious affiliations, which might be supported by patrons. After extensive exploitation by politicians during the late republic, the *collegia* were strictly regulated during the imperial period. Most performed the role of burial clubs – for a small subscription members were guaranteed a decent burial in the association's communal tomb. But the *collegia* also fulfilled social roles: they provided opportunities for people to meet informally and their internal organization often accorded to a hierarchical principle. In the *collegia* people could hold office and obtain titles whereas in the wider world they could not.

Internal hierarchies, whether within the senatorial order or a *collegium*, ordered people's lives and their relationships with others. We should not forget, however, the marked polarity between the haves and have nots. There must have been a highly visible contrast between the wealthy who owned vast houses and estates which Martial likened to kingdoms (Martial, *Epigrams* 12.57.19), and the very poor who endured appalling housing conditions and food shortages (Juvenal, *Satires* 3.194–218, in Lewis and Reinhold, 1990, p.153). The critical comments of authors such as Martial and Juvenal suggest that questions could be raised about the appropriate and inappropriate use of wealth. Yet money could talk and buy the individual status symbols and privileges and even a degree of power and influence through the patronage system. However, wealth and connections were not enough to overcome the most persistent social stigmas such as those based on gender and lowly birth.

Social mobility

A pyramid (Figure 5.3) is in some respects a useful way of summarizing Roman social structure but, as with all such models, it has its limitations and can be challenged. In particular it tends to simplify the nature of the interaction between the differing levels. The law did underpin distinctions between people. A freed slave could not become a senator; a *peregrinus* could not serve in the Roman legions. But the hierarchical pyramid was not as set as it might at first appear. It may have been difficult for an individual to move upwards by leaps and bounds, but equally the separate strata could not and did not remain static. This is apparent among the senatorial order. The senate may have had the appearance of a hereditary body, but leading families regularly died out and thus the senate had to be constantly regenerated from below (Hopkins, 1974 and 1983). Inherited birth rites were important, but these were not the only criteria for admittance into the senate: money and military and/or administrative skills were also a factor, which for the ambitious could counter the lack of family connections (Hopkins, 1974, p.109). Throughout the Imperial period men with no senatorial background and men from the provincial aristocracy entered the senate. Ultimately recruitment to the highest position in the state – that of emperor – reflected the cosmopolitan nature of the senate. The emperor Trajan (AD 97–117), for example, was from a Spanish family, and Septimius Severus (AD 193–211) came from north Africa. The stigma of a dubious past was not completely removed and stories readily circulated about the pedigree of senators. Publius Vitellius, for example, an *eques* and procurator under Augustus, who was the father of four senators and the grandfather of the emperor Vitellius (AD 15–69), was said to be the son of a prostitute and the grandson of a freed slave and a baker (Suetonius, *Vitellius* 2). Such a story may have been propagated by the opponents of Vitellius but it still illustrates that the ideal was that advantages were conveyed by birth. Thus, although some emperors and their families advanced rapidly, exploiting military connections rather than birth connections, many others inherited power. As the Vitellius anecdote illustrates, upward advancement could take several generations rather than a single lifetime. Barriers might be overcome one at a time: a freed slave, for example, was debarred from holding office but there were no legal barriers, even if there were some social ones, against his son or grandson becoming a local decurion and then he or future generations could gain access to the equestrian order and higher.

Across the empire the extent of social mobility is difficult to quantify with any accuracy. For the majority of the inhabitants of the empire little may have occurred to change their lot from the cradle to the grave. A man born to poverty may have struggled to make any real improvement in his economic circumstances. Nevertheless social mobility was at least a possibility for all, however distant. The Roman system may have been based on the privileges of birth and on the currying of favour, but it also promoted the ideal of rewards for hard work, commitment and ambition. Even the man born with the advantages of senatorial status needed to be determined in his self-promotion if he wished to reach the highest position of consul. At the lower levels of society certain fundamental institutions actively involved changes to a person's social and legal status. A poor citizen, for example, could enter the army and receive pay, food and training, and if he lived long enough his position as a discharged veteran conveyed certain social and monetary benefits. The role of the army in promoting the individual in terms of his legal position is most apparent among the auxiliary units. The auxiliary forces were primarily recruited from *peregrini* and if the recruit survived his long period of army service he left as a Roman citizen. It was the institution of slavery, however, which had the greatest potential for rags to riches stories. A man born a slave could by dedication and loyalty to his master gain his freedom and thus become a Roman citizen. If the ex-slave accumulated wealth, whether by hard work, stealth or patronal connections, he could acquire many status symbols and even office in the imperial cult. Such success stories, however, should not lead us to believe that all ex-slaves were so fortunate. In terms of their change in legal status all ex-slaves were upwardly mobile – even the slave who was informally manumitted and who did not gain citizenship still attained his freedom. But beyond the change in legal status the fortunes of many ex-slaves may have improved little. The majority of freed slaves probably remained dependent on their former masters and some may have found themselves economically worse off since their patrons were no longer obliged to support them.

The fact that social mobility was a reality, even if only for a minority, is evidenced through literature which hints at the jealousy occasioned by those who benefited from an upturn in their fortunes. The *nouveaux riches* were often mocked and despised for copying their social betters and their forgetfulness of their humble origins. Imperial slaves who had access to the emperor's ear could in particular be a source of resentment, especially among the senatorial élite (Pliny the Younger, *Letters* 7.29, 8.6; Suetonius, *Claudius* 29). What right did a man born to slavery have to exert so much influence in the corridors of power? The plight of the freed slave in many ways captured the hypocrisy and ambiguity inherent in the Roman world. On the one hand the slave was encouraged to work hard in order to gain his freedom; on the other hand once free he was despised for his former servitude, and however successful he became was never allowed to forget that servile blood coursed through his veins. Pliny the Elder tells of an ex-slave who at his death owned over 4,000 slaves, 7,200 oxen and 60 million sesterces in cash (Pliny the Elder, *Natural History* 33.135). The cash sum alone was sixty times the minimum fortune required of a senator, yet this man would never be able to become one. To break into high society took more than just money and citizenship. This type of inconsistency in how people were evaluated by others has been described, borrowing from the language of sociology, as status dissonance. 'Social mobility may usefully be seen as a process of status dissonance, that is a process in which the social riser rates highly on some status dimensions but not on others' (Hopkins, 1974, p.119). The slaves and freedmen who served the emperor provide a striking example: these imperial servants were stigmatized by their servitude but had access to great power and influence, that is to say that they scored highly in some status areas and lowly in others (Weaver, 1974, p.124). The reversal in the fortunes of successful ex-slaves in general could be perceived as almost unnatural and could lead to scorn and resentment. For the freed slaves the attitudes of others and the contradictions in their position could create social difficulties. Some of these are captured in the character of the larger than life Trimalchio, the literary creation of Petronius (see Essay Four). Trimalchio had triumphed over slavery, becoming a wealthy and successful man who could afford to throw a sumptuous dinner party. He sought every opportunity to advertise his superiority, learning and wealth (Petronius, *Satyricon* 31–4, in Lewis and Reinhold, 1990, pp.158–60). But in fact the dinner promoted the opposite impression: Trimalchio was crass, egotistical and crude. The humour in Petronius' writing lay in the fact that Trimalchio played the gentleman but still had the heart of a slave. Yet it would be wrong to think that Trimalchio sought to disguise his humble origins. He was far from ashamed of his past and instead gloried in his own rags to riches story (Petronius, *Satyricon* 75–7, in Lewis and Reinhold, 1990, pp.168–70).

In planning his tomb Trimalchio was at his egotistical height. His tomb was to be big and brash, just like the living man. It was to be decorated with scenes from his life suggestive of opulence and high living, but also with images of ships, which hinted at how he had come by at least some of his money. The epitaph was to state the size of his fortune and that he was a self-made man, and detail the titles he had held and those he had magnanimously refused – the latter a gesture that only a literary creation would indulge in. The monument constructed and celebrated those aspects of identity selected by Trimalchio; others might have summed up his life in different terms. In the cemeteries of many Roman towns we find grandiose funerary monuments, although there are admittedly few to rival the extreme plans of Trimalchio. Nevertheless many of these tombs were set up to and by freed slaves. Through images and texts these freed slaves celebrated their economic and personal success. Lucius Ampudius Philomusus, for example, was depicted with members of his family emphasizing his legally recognized marriage and children – a future generation of Roman citizens (Figure 5.1). The portraits were flanked by symbols of his trade, corn measures, suggesting how he had earned a fortune sufficient for an impressive commemoration. Gaius Munatius Faustus from Pompeii was commemorated by a large and impressive funerary monument prominently located adjacent to the roadside just outside the walls of the town (Figure 5.4). The monument was decorated with scenes that captured his public generosity and status, but also with the image of a ship, suggesting his involvement in trade of some kind. In both cases servile origins and associations with trade and labour were not disguised; it was the humble background that made their memorials and their lives impressive. The tombstones celebrated the successes of the freed slaves and gave them prominence in the cemetery, a prominence that they had not so readily found in life. The memorials were a product of the mixed and contradictory status that was the successful ex-slave's lot. It would be too extreme to describe the ex-slaves as social misfits: indeed organizations such as the *augustales* aimed to give them a place within society. Nevertheless the ex-slave and others, such as recently enfranchised provincials, could find themselves occupying uncomfortable positions which left them between social categories.

If upward mobility, however limited, was a reality, was downward movement also possible? It is more difficult to explore this issue, especially since advancement was something marked and celebrated whereas a decline in fortunes was not. Certain features of the Roman system may have mitigated against downward mobility. Legal status and membership of the leading orders were rarely revoked unless an individual fell into criminal ways. Once a freed slave became a citizen he remained one, and a citizen generally passed this status on to his children. The senatorial and equestrian orders were sometimes purged of unworthy members, but the majority held the status for life and passed on the privileges to the next generation. Changes in social rather than legal status were another matter. Authority and respect may have diminished with old age and the passage of time: the elderly were supposed to be respected but failing health could leave even the eminent dependent on others (Valerius Maximus, *Memorable Doings and Sayings* 2, 19; Seneca, *Letters* 12; Pliny, *Letters* 8.18). An individual's financial situation and the power and prestige obtained from this might also fluctuate. Extravagant living could easily diminish a fortune (Juvenal, *Satires* 8). For some the patronage system may have provided a safety net, keeping the individual solvent in terms of both finance and respect. There is some evidence that if senators and their families fell on hard times the emperor would provide assistance (Suetonius, *Augustus* 41; *Vespasian* 17). Admittedly such acts of generosity not only saved the individuals involved from embarrassment but showed the emperor in a favourable light as a benefactor and patron. The dignity of the senatorial order commanded that its members could not be destitute and any indebtedness tied the senator closer to the emperor. For the bulk of the population economic fortune was fundamental in ensuring stability and security, or indeed the lack of it. How frequent or drastic changes in fortune were, whether for the better or the worse, is difficult to gauge. We hear of people living in abject poverty and of others motivated by greed seeking to improve their lot at any cost (Ovid, *Metamorphoses* 9.669–81; Juvenal, *Satires* 3 and 14). But many of these anecdotes are part of the rhetoric of moral decline, of claims that things were no longer as good as they used to be, that morality and virtue had been replaced by avarice and selfishness, that unprincipled foreigners and freedmen prospered while the honest citizen struggled to survive. Once more resentment at the mobility of those perceived as undeserving by some obscures the overall picture.

Evaluating status?

The story of Trimalchio illustrates the difficulty of providing a simple description of the status hierarchy in the Roman environment. In his own home Trimalchio was king, exerting power and authority over all members of his household. He entertained lavishly and was respected by his peers. Yet in the wider world Trimalchio was legally and socially handicapped by his former servitude. He may have been as wealthy as a senator but he could never be a senator. How people would have regarded Trimalchio and reacted to him would have depended on their own status – the evaluation of others was a relative process. Purcell has emphasized how status varied enormously depending on the observer and on the place (Purcell, 1983, p.126). Status itself is a vague word and an imprecise concept (Finley, 1985, p.45). Thus among certain people and in certain situations Trimalchio had high status, while with other people and in other circumstances he had low status. Extreme disparities in status may have caused social difficulties, but many people may have faced inconsistencies in how they were treated and also in how they treated others in the course of their daily lives. A master baker, for example, may have exerted power and authority over a substantial workforce who would view him as a superior, whereas the same man might be despised by others for his association with labour. A wife of a senator might oversee a substantial slave household and be respected by many, yet she was still subordinate to her husband's authority.

Status was multi-dimensional. For some people many dimensions worked in their favour. A senator, for example, was by definition a wealthy adult male, distinguished and a Roman citizen. On this basis the senator could command and expect deferential treatment. His status was physically expressed through his financial ability to afford an extravagant lifestyle and to support a large number of dependants. His superior position was further reinforced through exclusive access to certain status symbols such as distinctive dress and legal privileges. At the other extreme some people commanded very little status. For example, a slave who belonged to a poor peasant was not a citizen, was bereft of his freedom, owned no property and thus had access to no physical status symbols. Many inhabitants of the empire, however, may have rated highly on some status dimensions and lowly on others. An individual might hold citizenship but be poor, or be wealthy but not a citizen and so forth. This combining of factors, as was noted above, could create status dissonance, but it also serves to remind us that the weight or worth attached to differing elements was not constant or consistent. The man who was a father, husband, son, Roman citizen, British, carpenter and ex-slave saw himself and was seen by others as all these things or only some of them depending on circumstances. We need to be particularly aware of this mixing of factors when we assess the impact of legal status. Legal status provides a hierarchical principle that we can readily grasp and use to grade people; in terms of legal status it is apparent that a freed slave was of higher status than a slave, a citizen was of higher status than a *peregrinus* and so forth. In reality many elements such as age, gender, experience, education and wealth ordered people's lives, and legal condition was thus only one factor in a person's status profile. Note how in the social pyramid (Figure 5.3) this is expressed by the use of vertical rather than horizontal lines to mark legal distinctions among the lower strata. This is not to say that legal status did not matter: advantages and disadvantages did accompany the varied legal conditions. These were perhaps most apparent in rules governing marriage and the status of the resulting children. But in many other respects we may wonder how often the issue of legal status came to the fore in the transactions of daily life.

Among the lower strata, *peregrini*, citizens, slaves and ex-slaves intermingled with few observable indicators of their exact legal status. The toga may have been the physical symbol of citizenship, but in everyday life legal status may have found few visible expressions. Seneca noted that if slaves had worn distinctive dress and had thus been able to recognize each other and the strength of their numbers, they might have become a substantial threat (Seneca, *On Clemency* 1.24.1). The fact that confusion could arise over people's exact status suggests that until a crisis involving a legal element arose, legal status often went unrecorded or unobserved. Legal rulings to cover the possibility of people marrying an individual of a lesser legal condition (for example, a Roman citizen woman who had married a male *peregrinus*), through either ignorance or mistake, suggest that people were not always aware of their own legal status or of all the implications concerning that status (Gardner, 1997, p.51). The story of Petronia Iusta indicates how proving legal status could be problematic. This legal case, recorded on tablets found at Herculaneum, involved a young woman calling herself Petronia Iusta. She claimed that she was the freeborn daughter of a freedwoman, but the wife of her mother's former owner claimed that Petronia was born before her mother was freed, and that Petronia had later been freed herself. The two people who could have clarified the legal status of Petronia, her mother and her mother's former master, were both dead. Neither party could produce documents to prove their case and were thus dependent on the contradictory testimony of witnesses. We do not know the outcome of the case or the motives which drove it, but it seems probable that the disagreement over the legal status of Petronia had arisen over an issue of property and/or inheritance rites (Gardner, 1986, pp.1–2; Weaver, 1997, pp.69–71). The majority of the population with little property to argue over probably managed to avoid legal disputes and took their own legal status (and moreover the legal status of others) for granted. In theory documents to prove legal status were available. From Augustus on, for example, a birth register existed for citizens, but this system was not compulsory and did not cover those who gained citizenship later in life. Besides, birth certificates could be lost or forged (Gardner, 1986, pp.4–5). Establishing who and what you were could be a complex issue.

Any overall evaluation of Roman legal and social status also needs to take account of regional and chronological factors. Roman citizenship brought certain privileges and was sought after in the early empire. Yet, as was noted earlier, citizenship may not have been equally valued everywhere in the empire. It was possible to be a citizen of Rome and a citizen of another city. Distinctions based on ethnic and religious affiliations may also have been given greater weight in some areas. St Paul, for example, may have been able to claim the advantages of Roman citizenship, but in the Jewish communities where he lived and worked religious affiliation and religious office were, for the majority of the population, more significant in the assessment of status. This is not to say that Roman citizenship was incompatible with ethnicity or religious beliefs, just that many inhabitants of the empire had diverse facets to their identity. The value of citizenship was also chronologically variable: in the later empire, when citizenship became commonplace, the socio-economic privilege engendered in the *honestiores* and *humiliores* division become more significant. The disadvantages of falling outside the small circle of privilege were striking, especially within the judicial system, where by the end of the second century AD a dual penalty system operated with one set of punishments existing for the *honestiores* and another for the *humiliores*. Definition of membership of the upper and lower strata could also exhibit substantial regional differences. Cities and settlements varied in size and thus also differed in their prerequisites for office holding. In a small and less affluent community the property requirement for joining the *decuriones* may have been considerably less than in a large and thriving community. In a large city such as Comum (Como) in north Italy the minimum property requirement for a decurion was 100,000 sesterces, whereas in the small African municipalities it was only 20,000 (Alföldy, 1988, p.128). People might be rich and important by local standards, but on an empire-wide scale be no more than minnows in a very large pond.

Conclusion

Status mattered in the Roman world, but it is not always possible for us to distinguish which elements of status mattered most and thus create an overall scale on which everyone fits neatly. Too many diverse elements contributed to someone's status profile to make this possible, and the majority of the population did not have their status intricately marked and measured. At times the language and symbols of status seem to have mattered more than the actual status. People could use the language and symbols to present themselves in certain ways: an identity could be constructed that reflected what was important to the individual and how the individual wished to be perceived. With so many diverse elements of status available and few ways of providing proof, it is perhaps unsurprising that sometimes people took this a stage further and pretended to be things that they were not. Some, for example, claimed to be citizens when they were slaves or *peregrini*, others tried to pass themselves off as soldiers or veterans when they had never seen the ranks (Reinhold, 1971). People might wear clothes that suggested senatorial or equestrian status. Pliny the Elder notes that slaves and freedmen often wore gold-plated iron rings in order to pass as members of the equestrian order (Pliny the Elder, *Natural History* 33.6.23). In several epigrams Martial records how people who were not entitled to the honour attempted to sit in theatre seats reserved for equestrians (Martial, *Epigrams* 5.8, 5.14). Such behaviour emphasizes the public side of Roman life and how people were evaluated by what they were seen to be and do; a whole range of factors and status categories allowed the individual to impress or be impressed, to judge and be judged. The very fact that the boundaries between status divisions could be challenged and manipulated also reminds us of the flexibility in how people were defined and the different criteria which could be employed. Discussions and debates recorded in the literature of the first two centuries AD which address issues such as who should sit where in the theatre, social etiquette at dinner parties, the nature of avaricious money-grabbers and the evils of social climbers, all suggest that there were conflicting opinions as to how status should be expressed and defined. Attempts may have been made to systematize the language and symbols of status: legislation, for example, dictated where you could sit in the theatre. But these rules could be and were broken. The very need to introduce such rules suggests that at least some people were uncertain about their own identity and that of others, and that the traditional divisions were inadequate. This uncertainty may have had its roots in the imperial system. With one man in power the value of established status distinctions was questionable and ripe for renegotiation, even if the emperor himself wished to be seen to be promoting the old values that his very position undermined.

In short, the Roman world was a status-conscious place, where a value was put on access to and use of status symbols such as a special seat at the theatre or a detail of dress. But the fact that these things had a value emphasizes how people themselves were rarely so easily defined and categorized. There was a desire, at least in some quarters, to use such outward and visible symbols to evaluate and judge others and to create an identity for oneself. But appearances could be deceptive and did not reveal all aspects of status. Status was multi-dimensional, and across the Roman empire the language and symbols of status were not uniformly employed or uniformly evaluated.

References

ALFÖLDY, G. (1988) *The Social History of Rome* (trans. D. Braund and F. Pollock), London and New York, Routledge.

ALSTON, R. (1996) 'Conquest by text: Juvenal and Plutarch on Egypt' in J. Webster and N. Cooper (eds) *Roman Imperialism: Post-colonial Perspectives*, Leicester Archaeology Monographs 3, pp.99–110.

BERREMAN, G. (1981) 'Social inequality: a cross-cultural analysis' in G. Berreman (ed.) *Social Inequality: Comparative and Development Approaches*, New York, Academic Press.

BRADLEY, K.R. (1987) *Slaves and Masters in the Roman Empire: a Study in Social Control*, Oxford, Oxford University Press.

BRADLEY, K.R. (1994) *Slavery and Society at Rome*, Cambridge, Cambridge University Press.

CROOK, J.A. (1967) *Law and Life of Rome*, London, Thames and Hudson.

D'ARMS, J. (1981) *Commerce and Social Standing in Ancient Rome*, Cambridge, Mass., Harvard University Press.

EDWARDS, C. (1997) 'Unspeakable professions: public performance and prostitution in ancient Rome' in J.P. Hallett and M.B. Skinner (eds) *Roman Sexualities*, Princeton, Princeton University Press, pp.66–95.

FINLEY, M.I. (ed.) (1974) *Studies in Ancient Society*, London, Routledge and Kegan Paul.

FINLEY, M.I. (1985) *The Ancient Economy*, London, Hogarth Press (first published 1973).

GARDNER, J.F. (1986) 'Proofs of status in the Roman world', *Bulletin of the Institute of Classical Studies*, 33, pp.1–14.

GARDNER, J.F. (1993) *Being a Roman Citizen*, London and New York, Routledge.

GARDNER, J.F. (1997) 'Legal stumbling blocks for lower class families in Rome' in B. Rawson and P. Weaver (eds) *The Roman Family in Italy: Status, Sentiment, Space*, Oxford, Clarendon Press, pp.35–53.

GARNSEY, P. (1970) *Social Status and Legal Privilege in the Roman Empire*, Oxford, Clarendon Press.

GARNSEY, P. and SALLER, R. (1987) *The Roman Empire: Economy, Society and Culture*, London, Duckworth.

HOPKINS, K. (1974) 'Elite mobility in the Roman Empire' in Finley (ed.) pp.103–20.

HOPKINS, K. (1978) *Conquerors and Slaves: Sociological Studies in Roman History Vol. 1*, Cambridge, Cambridge University Press.

HOPKINS, K. (1983) *Death and Renewal: Sociological Studies in Roman History Vol. 2*, Cambridge, Cambridge University Press.

KOCKEL, V. (1983) *Grabbauten vor dem Herkulaner Tor in Pompeii*, Mainz, Philip von Zabern.

LEWIS, N. AND REINHOLD, M. (eds) (1990) *Roman Civilization: Selected Readings. Volume II The Empire* (third edition), New York, Columbia University Press.

MACMULLEN, R. (1984) 'The legion as society', *Historia*, 33, pp.440–56.

PURCELL, N. (1983) 'The *apparitores*: a study on social mobility', *Papers of the British School at Rome*, 51, pp.125–73.

RADICE, B. (trans.) (1963) *The Letters of the Younger Pliny*, Harmondsworth, Penguin, The Penguin Classics (reprinted with a select bibliography 1969).

REINHOLD, M. (1971) 'Usurpation of status and status symbols in the Roman Empire', *Historia*, 20, pp.275–302.

SALLER, R. (1987) 'Men's age at marriage and its consequences in the Roman family', *Classical Philology*, 82, pp.21–34.

SHERWIN-WHITE, A.N. (1973) *The Roman Citizenship* (second edition), Oxford, Clarendon Press.

TAYLOR, L.R. (1961) 'Freedmen and freeborn in Imperial Rome', *American Journal of Philology*, 82, pp.231–53.

WASON, P.K. (1994) *The Archaeology of Rank*, Cambridge, Cambridge University Press.

WEAVER, P.R.C. (1974) 'Social mobility in the Early Roman Empire: the evidence of the imperial slaves' in Finley (ed.) pp.121–40.

WEAVER, P.R.C. (1997) 'Children of Junian Latins' in B. Rawson and P. Weaver (eds) *The Roman Family in Italy. Status, Sentiment, Space*, Oxford, Clarendon Press, pp.121–40.

Essay Six
Reading gender in the Roman world

BY DOMINIC MONTSERRAT

Interpreting and studying Roman gender

Gender and power

> To dream of having a beard that is long and thick is auspicious for an orator, a philosopher, and people who are about to undertake a business transaction. It makes the former dignified and the latter formidable. If a woman dreams that she has a beard, she will marry again if she is a widow, but if she has a husband she will be separated from him ... if a very young child dreams that he has a beard, it signifies death for him, because the beard has come before the proper time. But for someone who is an adolescent and who will soon grow a beard of his own, whether he is now a slave or a free man, it signifies that he will be his own master, since the beard shows that he is full-grown and responsible for himself. If a man dreams that his beard has fallen off, or that it has been forcibly shaved off or ripped off by anyone, it signifies harm together with shame.
>
> (Artemidorus of Daldis, *Ways of Interpreting Dreams* 1.30)

The dream interpreter Artemidorus, originally from the town of Daldis in what is now Turkey, lived and worked around the middle of the second century AD. His book *Ways of Interpreting Dreams* (much quoted by Freud) is the most complete example to have survived of what was clearly an influential and important genre of works that once circulated and were consulted by Romans. The satirist Juvenal, for instance, pours scorn on women who are too credulous of dream interpreters and their dubious advice about how to conduct daily life (*Satires* 6.582).

The works of an ancient pseudo-scientist such as Artemidorus may seem an odd place to launch a discussion of gender in the Roman world, but in fact Artemidorus' method of interpreting particular dreams raises some interesting questions about how the Romans might have thought about gender – a concept for which, after all, they had no word. As the interpretation quoted above demonstrates, Artemidorus believes the meanings of dreams to be carefully nuanced. Their meanings will shift in accordance with not only the biological sex of the dreamers, but also other defining factors: their age, their marital position, their status as non-slaves or slaves. When non-male dreamers are made 'male' by dreaming of a beard, they sometimes become empowered. To put it another way, Artemidorus believes that dreams can be read in terms of power and powerlessness, and this is an important idea to take on board when considering the gender systems of the Romans. For them, gender is produced at the place where anatomical sex is intersected by social relations, especially power relations. One might think of it in terms of a diagram like this:

Gender is not a fixed bodily state, but a shifting cultural category in which biological sex may or may not be a determining factor; and the assignment of individuals into particular cultural categories is primarily determined by differences in hierarchy. These notions may seem difficult to grasp now, since there is a predominant model for thinking about humanity as divided into two natural kinds, female and male. But this current paradigm would have seemed equally strange to many Romans. Simone de Beauvoir's famous dictum that 'one is not born a woman, but rather becomes one' may be much closer to the Romans' own notions about the formation of *gender* as opposed to *sex*.

With these ideas in mind, I would like to look a little more carefully at how Artemidorus interprets the dreams about growing a beard. Firstly, the beard is more than an indicator of biological maleness. For the Romans, a man's facial and body hair had immense importance, symbolically placing him at the top of the ascending scale of body hierarchies concocted by the ancient medical writers who followed the lead of Aristotle's pupil Hippocrates. As a sign of the internal bodily heat which women were believed to lack, facial hair is a visible marker of man's inherent claim to superiority and authority over women and other subordinate groups (for a summary see King, 1997, p.621; for its use in other power discourses see Zanker, 1995, pp.217–26). Artemidorus' use of the beard fits within this symbology. It is a signifier of power and a barometer of different states of authority or powerlessness undetermined by anatomical sex. In some circumstances, dreaming of having a beard can bestow (male) power and authority on the dreamers, such as those who are about to undertake business transactions, for whom it indicates success, or slaves, for whom it indicates autonomy and the end of subjection. This autonomy is what some modern gender historians call *agency*. By the same token, it can portend disaster – men who dream of losing their beards will be robbed of their pre-eminence. Artemidorus' interpretation of this dream, then, can be said to articulate many Roman ideas about gender, if gender is considered to be how power and agency are related to biology. As the symbolic beard moves across the faces of Artemidorus' dreaming women, men, children, adolescents and slaves, it elaborates on the idea that gender itself, which was all about hierarchies of power, was not something physically determined but culturally bestowed. The social stratifications that structured the Roman world – men, women, pre-adults, slaves – are all present in his interpretation. Furthermore, Artemidorus implies that biological sex can be transformed into a gender system, built through social practice, a specialized vocabulary or discourse, and ways of seeing. Contemporary cultural historians now think of these as modes of representation, or the way that meanings are made in any particular society or culture. The gender system thus formed only functions in relation to other categories, such as age, class, profession and ethnicity. The concept of gender is a modern one, and many historians would criticize me for even attempting to overlay it on to the Roman world. But it is still worth trying to consider such modern concepts in the light of Roman thought, literature, and material culture, which is my purpose in this essay. What I hope will become clear is that the process of transforming biological sex into a cultural category is concerned with creating *meanings about power*, and about the creation and maintenance of power hierarchies.

In this context, the human body is an obvious location for mapping the shifting boundaries of gender, and ancient physiological ideas enabled this process. The human body was thought to be constituted from the four elements of air, water, earth and fire, and it was necessary for the body to have these elements in the correct equilibrium. Women were believed to be cold and wet (male medical writers often compare them to marshes and bogs), men to be hot and dry like deserts. Any imbalance of bodily elements could result in assuming the traits of another sex. But how did the Romans make the conceptual move from linking such theories about human reproductive organs and secondary sex characteristics into elaborated systems of assumptions about gendered behaviour? Another second-century writer, Marcus Antonius Polemo (*c.* AD 88–144) provides a clue. He practised the science (some would call it a pseudo-science) of physiognomics, which taught that the external appearance of a person could be read quite literally to reveal the hidden depths within:

> You may obtain indications of masculinity and femininity from your subject's glance, movement, and voice, and then, from among these signs, compare one with another until you determine to your satisfaction which of the two sexes prevails. For in the masculine there is something feminine, and in the feminine something masculine, but the designation masculine or feminine is assigned according to which of the two prevails.
>
> (Polemo, *On Physiognomics* 2.1.192F, adapted from Gleason, 1995, p.58)

So masculinity or femininity may be assigned not only according to the body, but also according to behaviour. To illustrate this, I would like to examine an anecdote which is something of a trope, or standard theme, in Roman writing about 'bad' emperors: that they have excessive relationships with male lovers, culminating in attempts to transform the body of one of the partners, whether the emperor or the loved one, into a woman. (See, for another example, Suetonius, *Nero* 28–29.) In AD 218 the youthful Elagabalus became emperor. Of non-Roman origin and religious affiliation, supposedly much dominated by his female relatives, he was an obvious target for the opprobrium of conservative Roman writers such as the early third-century historian Cassius Dio. Dio describes how Elagabalus, among many other gender-bending activities such as spinning wool and wearing eye make-up and female attire, eventually fell in love with a young man from Smyrna called Zoticus. Zoticus had not only 'a body that was beautiful all over because of his athletic training', but also an outsize penis. He was brought to Rome and introduced to Elagabalus:

> When Zoticus greeted him with the usual salutation, 'Hail, My Lord Emperor!', Elagabalus bent his neck so as to assume a ravishing feminine posture, and answered without any hesitation, 'Do not call me Lord: I am a Lady.' ... Later he joined him in the bath, and finding Zoticus when stripped equal to his reputation, he burned with even greater desire for him, and later took dinner in his embrace, reclining like some beloved mistress on his chest.
>
> (Cassius Dio, *Roman History* 80.16.2–6)

Then, according to Dio, Elagabalus sought to take his infatuation for Zoticus to its logical conclusion:

> He carried his excessive licentiousness to such a point that he requested his physicians to contrive a woman's vagina in his body by means of an incision.

Of course, the conservative Dio might be mocking the emperor for trying to alter something as unalterable as biological sex, which implies that Elagabalus thought of himself as divine. But I prefer to see in this story a sophisticated Roman way of defining the difference between sex and gender. Dio offers us a manifestation of what I mean by the *constructed* quality of gender. Instead of it being something natural, inevitable and permanent, gender comes into being and lives via social customs, practices, ideals and norms, and individual desires. Here Dio also calls into question the *naturalness* of gender. For him, gender is transient – a matter of clothing, gesture and behaviour – and sex is mutable, something that can change by human or, more frequently in Roman sources, divine intervention (for an example of the latter, see Ovid's story of Iphis and Ianthe in *Metamorphoses* 9.666–797). So Dio presents a tale of physical transformation that changes the unnatural (gender) into something natural (sex). For all its excess, what underpins his anecdote is that gender and sex need to be in harmony for things to function properly. Although Dio's story plays ironically with fabrications of what is natural and unnatural, its outcome is a conventional insistence on the right alignment and ordering of the Roman world – the very ordering which Elagabalus' activities challenged (see further Kampen, 1996, pp.14–25; Edwards, 1993, pp.63–97).

Elagabalus' attempt to transform himself into a woman so that he could more completely enjoy Zoticus' favours prepares the modern reader for another way in which constructed Roman gender categories differ very much from contemporary ones. What gender category would Elagabalus have inhabited for the Romans after his 'op'? From a modern standpoint, Elagabalus' gender position is problematic. I am reminded of the two cases brought (unsuccessfully) in 1997 to the European Court of Justice by male-to-female transsexuals to have their so-called gender reassignment recognized, so that they could legally *become* women in spite of being *born* men. For the Romans, however, legal action might not have been necessary, because their gender system allowed for the possibility of Elagabalus inhabiting a third gender status that was neither female nor male. There is a certain amount of medicalized discussion of this in the medical writers of the Roman period. Galen, the Greek-trained court physician to the emperor Marcus Aurelius in the late second century, came closest to describing a third gender in his famous discussion of the pigs of Cappadocia (Galen, *On the Seed* 1: *Opera Omnia* 4.569) (Kühn, 1964–5). He describes how the Cappadocians 'castrate' sows (presumably by removing their ovaries) in order to produce an animal that has more palatable flesh than other sows, in the same way that castrated male pigs have tastier flesh than uncastrated ones. Galen goes on to explain how the operation has this effect:

> That which was removed in each case [i.e. of the boars and sows] was that part of the body which was responsible for the masculine and feminine in each. When this operation had been completed, the creature that was left had for itself a *nature* of such a kind as if it had been neither male nor female from the beginning, but a third being different from both.

Galen's terminology here includes a telling pun. The Greek word I have translated as 'nature', *physis*, is also a generic term for genitals, as though the essential element of a living thing is located in its reproductive organs. It serves to underscore Galen's point that removal of testicles or ovaries is thought to produce an intermediate being which is defined by its absence of generative capacity. Although Galen is talking about non-humans, it might be possible to see his argument as a logical product of a patriarchally structured society such as Rome, where the ability to procreate was important in defining both sex and gender, and loss or denial of the reproductive functions placed certain individuals outside the logic of conventional, family-derived social categories. Therefore the Roman third sex could encompass individuals who could not procreate or did not wish to: genetic hermaphrodites and eunuchs, medically castrated men like the Galli (priests of the Syrian goddess Cybele), and celibates such as Vestal virgins might all be seen as members of the Roman third gender. Significantly, Roman authors sometimes talk about these diverse individuals as though they had some inherent connection. There is, for instance, the famous story that seems to link the Vestal virgins with the Galli, related by the early third-century historian Herodian (*Histories* 1.11.4–5). He describes how the cult of Cybele, the *Magna Mater* or Great Mother, was introduced into Rome from Asia Minor in *c.* 204 BC. The vessel transporting the cult image of the goddess and her priests ran aground on a sandbank outside Ostia, the port of Rome, and could only be dislodged and the cult image brought into the city by the miraculous activity of the Vestal Claudia Quinta, who hauled the ship off the sandbank. This passage of Herodian seems to imply that the Galli and the Vestals are somehow conceptually linked: it was only possible for a Vestal, a member of the third gender, to be the agent of entry into Rome for other members of her special gender category, the Galli (Beard, 1995, p.171).

Hermaphrodites and other gender-ambiguous individuals are often represented in Roman literature and in domestic and even funerary art. From the houses of Pompeii and Herculaneum come many examples of wall paintings and statues of hermaphrodites, usually depicted as reclining or turning to one side, so that the male genitalia are not immediately apparent to the viewer, who sees the feminine upper torso and hips first (Figure 6.1). In the funerary sphere, an interesting type of commemorative statue from the early third century AD (Figure 6.2) shows the deceased woman as the mythical Omphale, Queen of Lydia (a region in what is now western Turkey), wearing the attributes of Hercules. A legend often recounted by Roman period poets and mythographers tells how Hercules allowed himself to be sold as a slave in expiation of his blood-guilt after a murder, and was purchased by Omphale, who humiliated him. She forced him to wear women's clothes and set him to spinning wool with her maids, while assuming his traditional attire of lionskin and club herself. Roman poets and visual artists revel in this paradox, especially in describing the hypermasculine Hercules in drag in the luxurious eastern garments and trinkets appropriate for the Queen of Lydia. (See, for example, Ovid, *Fasti* 2.283–358, *Heroides* 9.101–118; Propertius 3.11.17–21 and 4.9.45–50.) But it is significant that the myth of Omphale and Hercules, with its shaming inversion of gender identity, is alluded to in Roman funerary contexts. Perhaps, as Kampen (1996) has suggested, the elastic gender status of Omphale and Hercules in the myth is used by the monumental artists as a metaphor for the uncertain boundaries between life and death and the permeability of those boundaries, in which the mythic figures may act as agents of transfiguration for the dead.

This is not to suggest, however, that third gender individuals were necessarily regarded positively by the Romans: quite the opposite, in fact. This is particularly true of males who had (according to Roman

Figure 6.1   *A hermaphrodite. Wall painting from Pompeii, house of Holconius Rufus. (Deutsches Archäologisches Institut, Rome)*

Figure 6.2 Hercules and Omphale. Museo Nazionale Archeologico, Naples. (Photo: Alinari)

ideas) slipped several points down the gender barometer towards femaleness while still inhabiting male bodies. Maleness is always the optimum state. And violence against third gender individuals could also go beyond the verbal. This is illustrated by a curious book compiled by an obscure author, Julius Obsequens, in the fourth or early fifth centuries AD, but utilizing much earlier material. It is called *The Book of Omens*. Obsequens' work is a sort of anthology of inexplicable events seen as having a predictive or an otherwise portentous quality. The birth or discovery of hermaphrodites is a recurrent theme of these portents:

> In the consulship of Spurius Postumus Albinus and Quintus Marcius Philippus [186 BC]. In Umbria a hermaphrodite about twelve years old was discovered and put to death on the advice of the seers.

> In the consulship of Lucius Metellus and Quintus Fabius Maximus [142 BC]. The plague was so severe at Luna that corpses lay everywhere in the open for lack of people to bury them. At Luna a hermaphrodite was born and on the instruction of the seers was consigned to the sea.

> In the consulship of Gnaeus Domitius and Gaius Fannius [122 BC]. At Forum Vessanum a hermaphrodite was born and thrown into the sea.

Obsequens lists many other examples from all periods of Roman history. The hermaphrodites are clearly seen as disastrous inversions of nature, manifestations of divine displeasure only fit to be destroyed by fire or water so that they do not contaminate the earth. They sometimes seem to be scapegoats for other catastrophes in the community – it is surely no coincidence that when the plague was raging at Luna, a hermaphrodite was found locally on whose baleful influence it could be blamed. Other mentions of hermaphrodites as bad omens interestingly link them with Greekness. Livy, in a discussion of the portents that took place in 209 BC, says that most people called individuals 'born of uncertain sex, between male and female' by the Greek loan-word *androgyne* or 'man-woman', because it was easier to coin these double words in the Greek language (Livy, *Histories* 27.11.4). Once again, as with emperor Elagabalus, gender difference can be equated with foreignness – Livy implies that only the tricksy, slippery Greek language can coin a word for such a monstrous thing as the hermaphrodite, unlike pure, dignified Latin.

Roman gender, Roman women

There is an illuminating entry under 'gender' in the most recent version of the *Oxford Classical Dictionary* (1996), that encyclopaedic treasure trove of received wisdom about Greek and Roman civilization. There is no essay on gender as such, merely a series of cross-references to six other entries. These are to the essays on gynaecology, heterosexuality, homosexuality, marriage, sexuality and women! This desire by the Dictionary's editors to locate gender firmly in the sphere of *women* indicates a particularly topical, late twentieth-century usage of the word. Currently there is something of a tendency to use the words 'sex' and 'gender' as though they were synonyms. There is also an assumption that gender refers principally to women: when people talk of the 'gender balance' of an institution or a committee, they mean the number of women represented on it. I have already suggested that these ways of thinking about gender are not helpful in the Roman context. But if gender is not principally about women, what then is the position of Roman women in discourses about gender? Books on women in ancient Rome have a venerable lineage dating back at least as far as the early nineteenth century, but the academic study of *gender* in the Roman world is a relatively recent phenomenon which in many ways goes hand in hand with the study of Roman women. It is worth considering for a moment how the study of gender in Roman culture has developed in relation to this, and the problems and pitfalls of interpretation that this study has raised. After all, how else can gender in the Roman world be accessed by most individuals in contemporary societies other than through the work of contemporary historians?

From the mid 1970s historians, influenced to varying degrees by feminism, have sought to reinstate women into the mainstream narratives of Roman history. Sarah Pomeroy's hugely influential book *Goddesses, Whores, Wives, and Slaves*, first published in 1975 and still in print two decades later (Pomeroy, 1994), was one of the first scholarly works to attempt to redress this balance. She posed herself the question: what did women do while men were active in all the areas traditionally privileged by (male) classical scholars? Pomeroy's lead was followed in 1982 by an important source history, *Women's Life in Greece and Rome*, which has also gone into a second edition (Lefkowitz and Fant, 1992). But even such pioneering studies addressing questions to do with women and gender in the ancient world are largely based on the idea that there is a homogeneous and unproblematic category called 'women'. These studies also tend to divide the Roman world into compartments that may be meaningful to Euro-Americans in the late twentieth century, but would not necessarily have been so to people in the Roman world. Religion, economy, law, marriage, family life and so on are separated out as discrete topics, so that contemporary systems are conflated with Roman ones. As a result of this approach, such narratives can smooth over the difference and variability between the modern and the Roman worlds, ultimately making the Romans more like 'us'. There is a telling illustration in a slightly earlier example of such a book, Charles Seltman's *Women in Antiquity*, first published in 1956. Seltman, as a fellow of Queen's College Cambridge, curator of the Archaeology

Museum there and an editor of *The Cambridge Ancient History*, was very much in the mainstream of conventional classics in the United Kingdom. The chapter in his book entitled 'The new woman' (about female athletes in ancient Greece and Rome) was illustrated by two photographs of details from fourth-century AD mosaics from Piazza Armerina in Sicily, depicting female athletes carrying symbols of victory. Underneath these is a photograph of the whole mosaic, standing on which is a perky blonde model wearing a black bikini identical to those worn by the women in the mosaic (Figure 6.3). Its symbolism seems clear: ancient experience can be read off against modern, and the athletic 1950s model in her bikini is somehow the 'sister' of her fourth-century AD counterparts. Interestingly, a photograph of exactly the same mosaic is used on the cover of the 1994 British edition of Pomeroy's book, suggesting that such identifications are still considered relevant. For me, this is what Roman gender studies are *not* about – taking contemporary models and projecting them back into the past.

Figure 6.3 *Model posed on the Piazza Armerina mosaic. (Photo: Pictorial Press)*

So the first wave of Roman gender scholarship concentrated on redressing the balance, and bringing to light the information about women that had previously been marginalized, albeit sometimes in an essentialist way which implied that 'woman' was an unchanging, transhistorical category in which all women were the same. As work on Roman women progressed in the 1980s, it soon became clear that 'accessing women's lives' was going to be a major problem given the male origin of most of the sources. It was only then that the focus started to move towards a consideration of the discourses which discussed gender rather than women. Scholars began to realize that 'male' or 'masculine' was as problematic a category as 'woman', and more research began to be undertaken on analysing the complexity and variability of Roman masculinity. From the late 1980s Roman gender research shifted once again, towards elevating the human body as a theoretical space for mapped and inscribed social relations, especially negotiations of power and gender dynamics (Wyke, 1997). This change in emphasis has had the effect of problematizing Roman gender further, by examining the interplay between gendered bodies and the formulation of ethnic identities: Romans and their ethnic opposites did not inhabit the same kind of bodies, according to Roman ideas. Again, foreign eunuch priests (the Galli and the devotees of the Dea Syria) are good examples of gendered and radically different bodies. They are un-Roman for reasons other than their genital mutilations, since their dress, mannerisms, accents and behaviour all set them apart as foreign and different. Some Roman anecdotes present them as having a slang of their own, addressing each other using female adjectival endings and words. They also dress up in female garments, and are hypersexual, with their main attraction being towards men, whom they refer to as their 'husbands' (Apuleius, *The Golden Ass* 8.24–30).

Thinking about gender in the Roman world, then, is not about finding women's (or men's) voices or accessing women's (or men's) lives, but an attempt to understand how gender was a process of constantly renegotiated meanings which structured every aspect of Roman life. In a complicated and stratified society such as ancient Rome, gender and status are continually in dialogue and reconfigure each other in response to that dialogue. On every level of society, power differentials were not necessarily based on sex. Women who had once been slaves might be freed and come to own their own slaves. Ruling-class women often had the connections and money to administer their own property, endow public buildings, perform civic functions, buy slaves over whom they had the power of life and death, exercise authority over their families and dependents, and enjoy themselves in ways of which their male relations disapproved but were powerless to do anything about. A good example of such a woman appears in a story related by Pliny the Younger (died *c.* AD 112) about his friend

Quadratus, a member of the Roman élite. Quadratus lived with his rich widowed grandmother Ummidia Quadratilla. According to Pliny, she liked amusing herself in disreputable ways, which included maintaining a troupe of effeminate actors whom 'she thought far more of than was suitable for a woman from a leading family'. Quadratus did not like the way his grandmother carried on, but could not do much about it, and so tried to keep out of her way as far as possible. His rectitude and probity received due reward, Pliny tells us with satisfaction: when Quadratilla died Quadratus inherited two-thirds of her estate, while his younger sister only got a third (Pliny the Younger, *Letters* 7.24).

From a modern perspective it is heartening to read of women like Ummidia Quadratilla, who had not only the cash but also the strength of character to ignore their male relatives and do what they themselves wanted. But women like her are exceptional. And bear in mind that Pliny only tells Quadratilla's story at all because he wanted to contrast her rackety lifestyle with the fine Roman (male) virtues exhibited by her grandson in such an unpromising ambience. Moreover, it is crucial to remember other factors when considering the gender status of women with economic or even political power. A foreign queen like Boudicca, while an enemy of Rome, can still be credited with traditional Roman male values such as military leadership. In the same way, a rich woman from a local élite family such as Plancia Magna from Perge in Asia Minor (see Essay 4) might experience a real loss of privileged gendered status when she travels to Rome and is deprived of the infrastructure which enables her to function, to many intents and purposes, like a man in her home territory. Indeed, the ways that she has been allowed to act as a 'male' back home may be seen as an index of the extent to which she has colluded with a dominant masculinist ideology, keen to exploit her wealth but unwilling to grant her executive power (van Bremen, 1996, pp.298–302). As members of the dominant group, the Romans could map their diverse empire through the medium of gender. The conquered Germans, the 'noble savages' of the Roman world, have a gender system whose austerity is a model to which the Roman élite should aspire (Tacitus, *Germania* 18–21); at the other end of the spectrum, Greek men are regularly criticized for their effeminacy and lust (see, for example, Juvenal, *Satires* 2.93–99 and 3.58–80). 'Gender, thus, speaks constantly in the languages of age, status, ethnicity, and they in the language of gender; it exists only and always in relation to other social categories. And power can only be understood as it is generated through these complexes of categories' (Kampen, 1996, p.14).

All in all, a gendered approach is certainly useful for modern people trying to unravel something as diverse and complex as the culture of the Roman world (which up to now I have been discussing as though it were something undifferentiated and constant). A nuanced and thoughtful consideration of gender in Roman culture can give an inkling of how much cultural adjustment is required to understand the Roman world, and how very different were its political, social, religious and ideological underpinnings. In other words, the study of *gender* can give us an idea of the uniqueness of Roman culture in a way that the study of *women* cannot. But by the same token, it is crucial neither to write women out of such gendered narratives, nor to use the current interest in masculinity, other genders and the broader picture of Roman gender relations as an excuse for relegating women to the periphery once again, or implying their presence rather than giving them explicit historical existence (Scott, 1993). Take, for instance, another passage from the letters of Pliny the Younger, which is often quoted in discussions of marital relationships among Roman élites. After praising his young second wife Calpurnia, mostly in terms of how worthy she is of her male ancestors, Pliny goes on to remark:

> To all these virtues is added an interest in literature, which she has taken up out of fondness for me. She has copies of my own works, repeatedly reads them, and even learns them by heart. What tension she feels when I am about to speak in court! What joy she feels when I have finished!
> (Pliny the Younger, *Letters* 4.19)

Eleanor Scott (1993) argues fiercely against the gender blindness of some modern scholars who have seen this passage as a vignette of the emotional realities of an actual marriage conducted according to the principles of 'conjugality', which stressed the mutually harmonious and affective relationship of the couple. For the scholars Scott critiques, Calpurnia's having a motive other than pleasing her husband in taking up literature does not even seem to be a possibility.

Gender and material culture

Most of the classicists and ancient historians whose research on gender is outlined above worked primarily on written textual sources, albeit of a wide variety – inscriptions, papyrus documents, graffiti have all been called into play alongside the canonical male-authored texts. Perhaps yet another way of accessing Roman gender is offered by a Roman archaeology which is sensitive to the nuances of gender of the kind that I have sketched above. For a while, I would like to move away from Italy to consider how one might interpret some objects of traditionally 'female' type from Romano-British contexts within the framework of a gender-sensitive archaeology (see Allason-Jones, 1995). For instance, military buildings in the area of Hadrian's Wall have yielded large numbers of earrings, a type of object that Roman archaeologists tend to associate with women. Many of these earrings did not have secure findspots and could therefore have come from parts of the fort where women might conceivably be present. Other earrings, however, were recovered from dates and contexts where one might not expect to see women. The fort at Longthorpe, near Peterborough, was only occupied by the military from *c.* AD 48–62, an early period in the occupation of Britain for women to be present; yet two earrings were excavated from the fort area here. It is, of course, possible that the Longthorpe earrings did belong to women: although officers on postings with families were apparently frowned on by the military authorities, the evidence from Vindolanda on Hadrian's Wall shows clearly that women did sometimes accompany their husbands. Indeed, why assume marriage? Maybe the earrings belonged to local women who had informal relationships with the soldiers. But rather than make the knee-jerk response that the presence of earrings must indicate the presence of women, one needs to consider other explanations according to the shifting criteria of Roman gender. Perhaps the earrings were the possessions of soldiers of non-Roman origin, who came from cultures where it was acceptable to wear earrings: we know of Syrian and North African units serving on the frontier. Or maybe they had been bought and stored as presents for loved ones – of any gender.

On the other hand, the plasticity of the gender significance of objects in certain contexts does not imply that items of material culture were not strongly gendered in the Roman world. Jewellery is seen to be gendered in another corpus of objects long considered marginal to the study of Roman culture – the mummy portraits painted in Roman Egypt between about AD 40 and 275 (Figures 6.4 and 6.5). These portraits were placed over the face of the mummy and incorporated into the mummy wrappings, and were part of a complex iconographic and symbological scheme intended to enable the rebirth of the deceased in the most perfect and vital form. Although the subjects of the mummy portraits are strongly individualized, assignment of gender in them can be a matter of conventional details added to a unisex human face ungendered by signifiers such as a specific bone structure or skin tone (unlike Greek art). This is demonstrated by the second-century child's portrait (Figure 6.4), which displays an interesting array of seemingly contradictory gender signals. The name on the inscription, which simply reads 'Didyme, aged 7', clearly identifies the deceased as a female child, but the hairstyle and clothing are standard for portraits of young boys, and are completely unlike the types of garment shown on other mummy portraits of girls. The addition of the identifying inscription and a necklace was evidently enough to transform a male portrait, perhaps purchased from stock, into an image appropriate for a young girl – even at the supremely important moment of transition between life and death. The significance of jewellery in demarcating gender is suggested by other second-century portraits, such as the example in Figure 6.5.

This unidentified woman's earrings and necklaces, carefully added to the image in gold leaf and coloured paint, are as much the object of detailed representation as the woman herself. What her jewellery's precise significance may have been is unknown. Perhaps it was a tangible representation of prestige dowry objects to indicate that high social standing during life was to be replicated after death, or it may be connected with indigenous Egyptian funerary beliefs which linked gold with the divinized flesh of the reborn. For the Hellenized élite of Roman Egypt, there seems to have been some link perceived between women and jewellery that was important enough to make its representation an integral part of the iconography of women's funerary portraits (Montserrat, 1996, pp.48–53).

Gendering the Roman world

The first part of this essay has suggested some of the ways in which the Romans looked at the gender systems of their culture, and how these have been interpreted by modern scholars. The second part aims to consider in more detail how the Romans might actually have *experienced* gender. It employs some different sets of data while still bearing in mind the general framework already outlined, and is divided into two sections. The first section below considers gendered aspects of the Roman physical environment, while the second attempts to consider the experiential reality of individual gendered bodies moving through those environments. The overall purpose is to think harder about the roles played by power and identity in the Roman gendered experience.

Gender and the environment: microcosm and macrocosm

I have so far stressed that it may be useful for a modern individual trying to access gender in Roman culture to keep an open mind about what signifies gender. However, it is also important to recall that there was much that was male-centred in the Roman world, particularly in the kind of official male-produced sources that have survived to the present day. Roman society may be said to be male-centred or androcentric in the ways that it privileged manhood and masculinity, especially in terms of military and political virtues. It is therefore unsurprising that many scholars have interpreted the Roman built environment as the physical expression of a system-wide male-orientedness. After all, since most Roman architecture was designed and built by men, one might expect it to express masculinist ideologies and aspirations, even if (or especially because) women, children, slaves and non-Romans might all be expected to use some of its structures at different times. Many modern scholars believe that the Roman world was phallocentric, in that it privileged representations of the phallus as a central cultural symbol of male power. And such phallocentricity may have been very literally expressed. For instance, it has recently been argued (Kellum, 1996, pp.170–3) that the Forum Augustum at Rome can be interpreted as a phallus, with its two semi-circular galleries or *exedrae* as the testicles and its long projecting forecourt as the shaft. This forecourt even extends into the Forum of Julius Caesar, with its temple of Venus Genetrix, ancestress of the Julio-Claudian imperial dynasty, in such a way that the buildings could be imagined to be having sexual intercourse. The Forum Augustum also contained the shrine of Mars Ultor (Mars the Avenger), the god to whom Augustus had made a vow before the battle of Actium, at which Antony and Cleopatra were defeated. The decorative

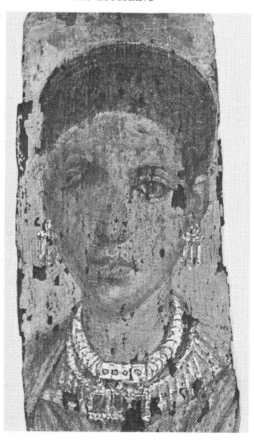

Figure 6.4 *Mummy portrait of Didyme from Egypt. Fitzwillian Museum, Cambridge. (© Fitzwilliam Museum, University of Cambridge)*

Figure 6.5 *Mummy portrait from Egypt. Kelsey Museum of Archaeology, University of Michigan, Ann Arbor. (Reproduced by permission of the Kelsey Museum)*

schemes of this temple stressed the links between military victory, the imperial family and its patron gods and deified ancestors – Anchises, Aeneas, Romulus and so on.

The building may have been utilized to articulate and assert Roman notions of masculinity in other ways. It was used for performing the rites of maturity for élite adolescent boys: the first facial hair was shaved off and dedicated to a god, and the purple-striped *toga praetexta* of childhood was laid aside in favour of the all-white adult toga (see text references in Kellum, 1996, and Persius, *Satires* 5.30.2; cf. Suetonius, *Caligula* 10, *Nero* 12.4). Such a phallocentric reading of the Forum Augustum would argue that its form and function combine to present a coherent ideology of Roman manhood, associated with military service and the male family lineage. What can only be imagined is how one would experience this building, so redolent of ruling-class male values, if one were not part of the group the Forum sought to validate and reproduce.

Such readings of major Roman public building projects may seem fanciful, born out of the late twentieth-century fascination with sexuality which wishes to see everything refracted through its prism. Certainly it is impossible to reconstruct now what was going through the minds of Augustus and his architects, consciously or otherwise, when the Forum Augustum was commissioned and built. Moreover, the Forum Augustum could be said to be unique, fabricated out of Augustus' need for a potent symbol of dynastic power in particular historical circumstances. More prosaically, there is also the question of the extent to which the ordinary 'Roman in the street' was able to perceive a building as a ground plan (though one could argue that in a world replete with phallic images, one might be more likely to recognize a phallus). But such structures as the Forum were also used as performance space for the rituals of achieving masculinity, so the phallic analogy may not be as improbable as it seems. In any case, it does not alter the basic point that the phallocracy of Roman society was replicated in the physical environment. Phalli created in various media were literally stamped all over the material world, and now their ubiquity is sometimes difficult to comprehend. Urban Romans would have seen the phallus, walked under the phallus, and touched the phallus continually in the course of their daily lives. The scale of these ranged from the very large and immovable – such as a heavy stone block to mark the location of a house – to the minute and transportable, such as a tiny *intaglio* engraved on the stone of a signet ring, or a bronze amulet attached to a horse's harness. The physical expression of phallocracy was thus at all times potentially monumental, tangible or ubiquitous. Sometimes, of course, the phallus did have overtly sexual connotations. It could serve as a sign to places where sex might be for sale, such as over a brothel door, or to the *cauponae* or bars of Pompeii; but it could also appear in sexually neutral contexts – on coins and ovens, for instance, or on the mosaics of baths, at military sites, and especially over doors, portals and gateways. Thresholds in particular were regarded by the Romans as dangerous and vulnerable to attack by inimical supernatural powers, and therefore in need of magical protection. And in a male-oriented world, what better protection could there be than the phallus? Hung with numerous bells, phallic door amulets (*tintinnabula*) appealed to the senses of both sight *and* sound to assert their presence and protective powers against unseen hostile forces.

Representing the phallus could also provide good luck. A stone house marker from Pompeii is inscribed with the words *HIC HABITAT FELICITAS*, 'good fortune dwells here', written in two lines above and below a giant phallus. The phallus also rears its head on innumerable household and domestic items: tablewares; wall paintings of Priapus, the garden god, from whose outsize erection a basket of garden produce is suspended; mirror cases decorated with scenes of acrobatic love-making where the lovers are carefully posed so that the penetration is visible; thousands of terracotta statuettes of uncertain function; and lamps cheekily designed so that the wick burns in a nozzle placed at the tip of the penis. Sadly, the sources are silent as to whether Roman men and women felt differently when confronted by these sorts of images. Did women feel alienated and intimidated by them, while men felt a warm glow at the sight of this material affirmation of their own power? And perhaps one needs to be wary about overestimating the symbolism of objects which seem to have sexual meanings. Some of them are probably little more than vehicles for crude humour, like the pottery lamp in the shape of the satyr Silenus, one of the entourage of Bacchus, shown in Figure 6.7. Viewed from above as one fills the lamp, Silenus holds two pots, one on his stomach (the filling hole) and one between his feet (the nozzle for the wick). When placed on a flat surface and seen from the side, however, Silenus seems to be equipped with a

Figure 6.6
Phallic bronze
tintinnabulum
from Pompeii.
British Museum.
(© *The British*
Museum)

huge phallus, topped by a burning wick when the lamp was alight. One wonders whether this was designed with any intention more profound than to amuse.

Up to now I have emphasized the pre-eminence of the phallus, but I do not mean to imply that women's sexual power is never acknowledged in Roman material culture – far from it. Roman terracotta figurines are a good case in point. As Figure 6.7 suggests, it is true that many of them depict the phallic gods and demi-gods of the Graeco-Roman pantheon such as Priapus, Pan and Silenus, but there are also a significant number which depict goddesses displaying their reproductive organs. Aphrodite pulls up her dress to reveal her magically charged genitalia in the gesture known as *anasyrmene*, and the naked Isis as the patroness of the corn harvest impales herself on the pointed bottom of a wheat basket (Figure 6.8). Female reproductive power is certainly an iconographic issue in these images: the question is, what do they mean in relation to gender? As with the question of how women and men regarded images of the phallus, it is not going to be easy to come to any conclusions. Because the archaeological context for most of these statuettes is

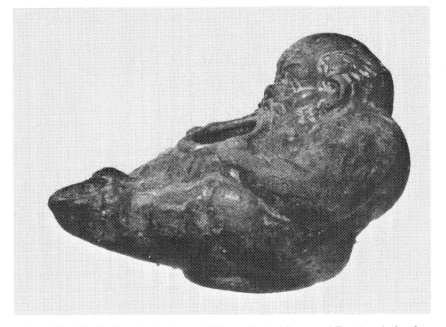

Figure 6.7 *Phallic lamp in the form of Silenus. Petrie Museum of Egyptian Archaeology, University College, London. (© Petrie Museum)*

missing, their meaning is difficult to reconstruct given the mutable meanings of gender according to who looks at the object and in what circumstances. An image like that of Isis straddling the corn basket could have assumed several completely different meanings which were entirely contingent on viewer and context. This figurine would convey something quite different if it were found (say) on the niche of a granary in Ostia, as a votive deposit to a goddess connected with female fertility in Egypt, as an offering in the grave of a pre-adult female from Asia Minor, or in a Pompeian household shrine.

The same questions of context are also pertinent to another aspect of how the physical environment – the social space of the private house – may be responsive to gender. Objects such as the Silenus lamp or the Isis statuette may have signified different things at different times of day, according to

Figure 6.8
Terracotta figure of Isis straddling a corn basket, from Egypt. Museu de Montserrat. (Photo: Institut Amatller d'Art Hispànic, Barcelona)

who was inhabiting the house. For a long time, archaeologists and ancient historians thought that Roman élite houses could be divided up in terms of exclusive male and female spaces, but Romans themselves do not seem to have found male/female spatial distinction meaningful. Recent work rejects the idea of rigid sex-segregation and considers the whole house as a location for gendered social relationships revolving around the now familiar principle of social rank rather than sex. Instead of specific rooms being assigned to male and female functions, the gendered feel of an élite house might shift radically during the daily routines of the household (Laurence, 1994, pp.127–8, 131–2). For most of the day, from the second to the eighth or ninth hours (i.e. from about 7 a.m. to 2 p.m.), the male members of the household were outside the home engaged in the public activities which helped to define their status as members of the élite. The day started and ended with two male-dominated rituals for which the house provided particular spaces: the morning *salutatio*, or meeting with clients and dependents held in the complex of rooms around the atrium, and the afternoon dinner held in the *triclinium*. The gendered feel of the house thus responded to the cadences of the male day, in which women moved about 'in the middle of male life, both in terms of physical space and social occasion' (Wallace-Hadrill, 1988, p.51). Of course, this kind of pattern only appertained to the households of the urban élite. For the huge majority of Romans there would have been less of a distinction between home and workplace than tends to be assumed as the norm in post-industrial societies, perhaps making gender even less of a consideration in the houses of non-élites.

The Roman built environment affected the day-to-day experience of gender in some varied, and perhaps unexpected, ways. But the man-made world of houses, temples, and material artefacts was not the only one upon which the Romans believed gender could be inscribed: it was also an important part of the larger universe, the macrocosm. Roman period astrological texts (of which there are very many, especially written in Greek) can be useful sources for concepts of gender. As with the Romans' physiology, a basic principle underlying their astrology is that there is an affinity between stars and humans, the so-called 'cosmic sympathy' principle. Humans and planets have in common the four elemental qualities of heat, cold, dryness and moisture, and since bodies such as the sun and moon can have observable effects on the earth, it follows that other planets can affect humans, whose qualities they share. 'On this basis people predict everything that will happen in the universe concerning every single person, especially regarding his destiny and personality', observed the third-century AD philosopher Plotinus (*Enneads* 3.1.5). Obviously these ideas have possible repercussions for gender, since planets and stars can have an effect on the bodies of individual humans born under them. A good example is the work of the second-century AD astrologer Claudius Ptolemy. He was born in Egypt but practised his art in Rome, and has left behind an elaborate Greek manual for casting horoscopes. Formally titled *The Astrological Influences*, it is usually known as the *Tetrabiblus* or 'four-volume work', because it was published in that format. Ptolemy is particularly informative about gender. So in a passage describing unfavourable conjunctions of Venus and Saturn, Ptolemy observes that men who lose their genitals or women who are *tribades* will be born if the planet Mars is also present (*Tetrabiblus* 4.5.187). *Tribades* (singular *tribas*) is a Greek word meaning literally 'those who rub', and it is often used to describe 'mannish' women who take the active, penetrative role in same-sex relationships (see Lucian, *Dialogues of the Prostitutes* 5). The *tribades* are thus at the opposite end of the gender slippage spectrum to the Galli: mannish women versus effeminate men. In an earlier passage of his astrology manual, Ptolemy discusses how a woman can become a *tribas*, and how she may behave sexually in that role. *Tribades* are produced by Mars in configuration with Venus, which will produce a masculizing effect: males born under this influence will become hypermasculine, but it will also have the same effect on women:

> The males become addicted to normal sexual intercourse, but are adulterous, insatiable, and ready at all times for shameful and excessive sexual acts; while the females are lustful for unnatural unions, and cast inviting glances of the eyes. They are what we call *tribades*; for they have intercourse with females and perform the function of the males. If Venus alone is constituted in a masculine manner, they do these things secretly and not openly. But if Mars is so constituted, they do it without restraint, so that sometimes they even designate the women with whom they are on such terms as their 'wives'.
> (Ptolemy, *Tetrabiblus* 3.14.171)

Ptolemy's rhetoric is familiar by now, with the mannish *tribades* inverting the normal heterosexual rules. They even adopt (and abuse) the vocabulary of marriage by calling their female lovers their 'wives' (Apuleius said exactly the same thing about the eastern eunuch priests: see above, page 164). Though biologically women, the *tribades* look and act like men, thus inhabiting the gender category of male.

The applicability of astrologers such as Ptolemy to the regular experience of people may be questioned, but it may have been more significant than one might imagine. For many Romans, astrological consultations and horoscopes were a widespread and perfectly respectable resource for finding out about an uncertain future. Children had their horoscopes cast at birth, and this information might be recorded on their tombstones, with their lifespans calculated down to the precise number of hours. Whole families went together to consult astrologers (Montserrat, 1996, pp.205–6). In this context, the fallout of astrologers' rhetoric could have been quite widespread – though one wonders how easy astrologers would have found it to tell their clients that they were *tribades*!

Describing gender and the body

Up to now I have been talking fairly generally about the experience of 'people' or 'the Romans', and this has inevitably led me to make many huge generalizations. In this final section I want to examine the gendered experience of some real Roman individuals by looking at how people could be described physically in gender terms. To illustrate this I have chosen two very different sets of data: the *belles-lettres* of the so-called Second Sophistic period (the upsurge of élite Roman interest in Hellenic culture in the mid second century AD), and some papyrus documents from Egypt. While these two groups of texts were produced for different reasons and in different social circumstances, their ways of describing and evaluating gender (especially in terms of power) are remarkably consistent. They suggest to me that the Romans may have had a descriptive language of gender: a discourse through which gender could be defined in relation to the physical traits of the individual. By now it will probably come as no surprise that the assignment of gender in these descriptions does not always have much to do with biological sex, and much more to do with action and appearance. Gender appears as a performance rather than an anatomical given. Physical descriptions of individuals are common in certain kinds of Roman writing, especially historiography. The second-century AD author Suetonius, biographer of the first twelve Roman emperors, frequently enumerates the physical characteristics of his imperial subjects. But this information is included not exactly to convey to the reader the true appearance of the emperor, as with a modern pen-portrait, but to convey an idea of his true character. Suetonius' descriptions are ultimately derived from the ancient (pseudo-) science of physiognomics, the art of reading faces and bodies to discover true character, as described earlier. Within the physiognomic system, physical appearance could also be used to construct and assign gender. Certain characteristics are inherently 'womanish', on whoever's face they might happen to appear, and are used to assign gender accordingly. It is also noteworthy that the physiognomic system is primarily about describing *men*. Texts from the Roman world, be they literary or vernacular, very rarely describe real women (mythological heroines are another matter). Hence the wives of Suetonius' emperors never get a look in. So while the sources that follow describe different categories of men, occupying different positions on the masculinity scale, in the course of those descriptions a certain amount is inevitably implied about femininity too. This is particularly noticeable with my first case study – Favorinus the sophist (see further Gleason, 1995, pp.3–19).

Favorinus was born in the reign of Domitian into a wealthy family from Arelate in Gallia Narbonensis (modern Arles in France), and died *c.* AD 155. Highly educated (although a native Latin speaker he wrote mostly in Greek), he made his mark on the philhellenic literary world of the second century: he was a friend of Plutarch and Herodes Atticus, and is often mentioned by important littérateurs of the day such as Lucian and Aulus Gellius. Apart from his successful literary career, Favorinus also had a public one, ending up as high priest of Augustus in his home town. In gender terms, he is interesting because his contemporaries describe him as double-sexed or a eunuch, which affected his external appearance in a way that was of considerable interest to them. What did his strange looks suggest about his gender status? In a world informed by the works of physiognomists, Favorinus' status is ambiguous and confounds categorization. He looks like somebody effeminate, but is in fact all man:

> Favorinus ... was a philosopher whose facility with words proclaimed him a sophist ... He was born double-sexed, both male and female, as his appearance made plain: his face remained beardless even into old age. His voice revealed the same ambiguity, for it was penetrating, shrill, and high-pitched, the way nature tunes the voices of eunuchs. Yet he was so hot-blooded that he was actually charged with adultery by a man of consular rank.
>
> (Philostratus, *Lives of the Sophists* 489)

Modern scholars suggest that Favorinus may have suffered from cryptorchidism, or undescended testicles, rather than being a eunuch or hermaphrodite. In another pen-portrait of Favorinus, by the rhetorician and physiognomist Marcus Antonius Polemo (whose work has already been cited), Philostratus' description is taken one step further. Favorinus' womanish physical traits are equated with moral turpitude, in accordance with the physiognomic principle of the surface mirroring the depths:

> He was libidinous and dissolute beyond bounds ... he had a bulbous forehead, flabby cheeks, wide mouth, a gangling scraggy neck, fat calves, and fleshy feet. His voice was like a woman's, and likewise his extremities and other bodily parts were equally soft, nor did he walk with an erect posture: his joints and limbs were lax. He paid regular attention to grooming, with the use of hair-dye, and massaged his body with ointments, and cultivated everything that excites desire for intercourse and lust ... he used to go about cities and market-places, gathering crowds in order to display his wickedness and indulge his taste for sexual excess ... he made men believe that he could compel women to pursue men in the way that men pursue women, using a hidden voice to make himself sound plausible.
>
> (Polemo, *On Physiognomics* 1.160–4, adapted from Gleason, 1995, p.7)

One needs to be careful about using this: Polemo was a professional rival of Favorinus, with his own reasons for slandering him, and their long public rivalry was notorious. It has been compared to the way that the personal rivalries of opera divas are acted out on stage. Yet although his physical shortcomings were regarded with such suspicion, Favorinus was still able to make his way in the male Roman world, and not purely because of his wealth and status. In spite of his ambiguously gendered body, it was still possible for Favorinus to *perform* manhood: that is, by the practice of rhetoric, which included training in voice, body and deportment, he could transcend his bodily state as a not-quite man to become unequivocally male. Once again, the idea that gender does not necessarily have anything to do with the body is apparent. For Favorinus, masculinity is a state achieved through words (Gleason, 1995, pp.131–58).

For my second case study, I move from the literature of the Roman élite to papyrus documents of the same date from the province of Egypt. Although these were written in Greek, and the general cultural framework in Egypt was a mixture of Hellenistic and indigenous elements rather than Roman, such documents still reflect many aspects of the Roman mind-set. They also illustrate the filtering down of gender discourse from 'high' into 'popular' culture, as we have already seen with astrology. Of course, there are problems about using such data to write a social history of gender: in many ways they are as contentious as the literary sources. But it still seems to me that they can give us a good sense of the day-to-day operation of gender in terms of a constantly negotiated and renegotiated dynamic structuring of everyday life. As with the physiognomic evidence already surveyed, it is maleness that is the yardstick by which Roman definitions of gender are measured.

The papyrus documents from Roman Egypt contain numerous body descriptors, though full-scale descriptions of the body are uncommon. The most interesting and thorough descriptions are those of slaves, and people (usually, but not invariably, men) who have been the victims of violence. The circumstances in which verbal description of the gendered body took place suggest to me that the only time it was appropriate to talk about a body in its entirety was when it was a passive object, such as a slave, who was in a 'womanish' state of passivity and subjection until manumission. Similarly, somebody who had been assaulted and needed to have their injuries assessed to get appropriate reparation could also be said to be slavish, because they did not exhibit agency and autonomy, a major component of constructed Roman masculinity. The papyri describe free and slave bodies quite differently when functioning in the same situations, thus emphasizing their qualitative, gendered difference. Hence, documents that aim to apprehend fugitive slaves go into a great deal of detail about the appearance of the runaways. Apart from their very vividness and poignancy about how these subject individuals wore their own bodies, they are informative about the gendered differences between the slavish and the free male. It is also instructive to compare their vocabulary, and the kind of body they evoke, with Polemo's picture of Favorinus.

The most detailed of these word portraits is found in a third-century AD document from Oxyrhynchus, a provincial city in central Egypt. Written on a piece of papyrus, it may be the actual notice which was publicly posted. The fugitive, whose name is lost in a hole in the papyrus, is described as:

> an Egyptian from the village of Chenres in the Arthribite Nome, utterly ignorant of Greek, tall, skinny, clean-shaven, with a [small] wound on the left side of the head, honey-complexioned, rather pale, with a wispy beard

– in fact, with no hair at all to his beard – smooth-skinned, narrow in the jaws, long-nosed. By trade a weaver, he swaggers around as if he were someone of note, chattering in a shrill voice. He is about thirty-two years old.

(*P. Oxy.* LI 3617)

Naturally, some of the bodily details are included here for entirely practical purposes, but there may be a subtext to their inclusion. Because he is a slave, this anonymous person cannot be a 'real man', and the adjectives applied to his body serve both to set him physically apart and render him ridiculous. He is ugly and beardless. His beardlessness perhaps marks him out as potentially penetrable, since the visible growth of facial hair is one of the demarcators in the ancient world of being masculine and unavailable for penetration. His lack of beard also renders him infantile, although thirty-two years old; and like a child he goes around jabbering away, ignorant of civilized languages. The collocation of slaves and children is a very common one in the ancient world – free children lose their infantile status with maturation, but slaves do not, at least as long as they remain slaves. It is no coincidence that the Greek words for slave and child, *pais*, are the same. It is even implied that he has ideas above his station: 'he swaggers around as if he were someone of note'.

Significantly, the bodies of free people are described quite differently in the same circumstances; or rather, they are not described at all. Documents ordering the apprehension and arrest of free individuals give no physical details whatever, merely saying 'apprehend so-and-so'. It may have been thought that the act of description increased powerlessness and was seen as additionally demeaning or objectifying. In fact, the only free individuals whose bodies are the subject of descriptions are those who have been subjected to violence. The context is usually a report written by a public physician ordered by a civic official to examine the injuries of somebody who has been beaten up and has lodged an official complaint against the attacker. Another document from Oxyrhynchus illustrates this: although from the fourth century AD it is representative of a type known from as early as the second century AD, but less well preserved. On 14 June AD 331 the public doctors Theoninus, Heron, Silvanus and Didymus reported that:

> we were instructed ... in response to a petition handed in by Aurelius Paesius, son of Senenuphis, of the village of Pela, to examine his condition and make a written report. Whereupon we examined the man on a bunk in the public office building; he had gashes on the right side of his head ... and a swelling on the right side of his forehead and a contusion with a skin wound on his left forearm, and a slight contusion on the right forearm.

(*P. Oxy.* XLIV 3195.31–49)

Another doctor's report from Oxyrhynchus, dated AD 316, describes a similar train of events. This papyrus (*P. Oxy.* VI 983) is unfortunately too damaged to give a consecutive translation, but its general gist is clear. The public doctor Aurelius Apion son of Herodotus was summoned to examine the injuries of the guard Moueis. He found him bedridden with, among many other injuries, two wounds on his crown, others to the right side of his head and the left temple, swellings and bruises on his left ear, a wound on the right shoulder-blade, his right hand crushed and swollen as far as the middle finger, swellings and contusions on his left hand, and wounds from blows to other parts of his body. In this document the emphasis lies on one aspect of the man's body – the wounds that rendered him passive and vulnerable, unable to fight back physically. The image of the doctors finding the injured men Paesius and Moueis lying prostrate and helpless on a bed, and the enumeration of the wounds inflicted on their arms and hands as they tried to ward off blows to the head, stress the passivity and powerlessness of the victims' bodies. Beating was degrading, as was the inability to repulse an attacker, and the wounded male body in these contexts seems deprived of its masculinity. The ministrations of the doctors perhaps underscored the feelings of disempowerment the men were surely already experiencing. As well as general physical examinations, the medical reports describe the doctors probing individual wounds, penetrating the body. Another report, from the town of Karanis in northern Egypt and dated 22 August AD 130, details how the doctor Gaius Menecius Valerianus went to examine a man with a severe head wound. Probing the wound deeply with his fingers and perhaps a surgical instrument, Valerianus found embedded in it some of the fragments of the missile that had caused the injury, and extracted them.

Whether or not we are to read these wounds almost as metaphorical vaginas which feminize the male body, making it passive and penetrable, the very immediacy and poignancy of the situations described in the papyri take the modern reader on to another level of the Roman gendered experience. Anyone who has been sick and lain on a doctor's couch waiting for a physical examination is able to empathize with the apprehension and pain of men like Paesius and Moueis – pain and apprehension which may have been made worse by the further ignominy the gender system of their culture conferred on being wounded. Perhaps it is in everyday documents like these doctors' reports, unaffected by rhetorical flourishes or literary conceits, that it is easiest to access the gendered experience of the Romans, and to acknowledge not only their closeness to but also their difference from ourselves.

References

Citations of papyrus texts are in accordance with the standard set of abbreviations by J.F.Oates (1992) *A Checklist of Editions of Greek and Latin Papyri, Ostraca and Tablets* (fourth edition, first published 1974), Atlanta, Ga., Scholars' Press.

ALLASON-JONES, L. (1995) 'Sexing small finds' in P. Rush (ed.) *Theoretical Roman Archaeology: Second Conference Proceedings*, Aldershot, Avebury Press, pp.22–32.

BEARD, M. (1995) 'Re-reading (Vestal) virginity' in R. Hawley and B. Levick (eds) *Women in Antiquity: New Assessments*, London and New York, Routledge, pp.166–77.

EDWARDS, C. (1993) *The Politics of Immorality in Ancient Rome*, Cambridge, Cambridge University Press.

GLEASON, M.W. (1995) *Making Men: Sophists and Self-Presentation in Ancient Rome*, Princeton, N.J., Princeton University Press.

KAMPEN, N.B. (1996) 'Gender theory in Roman art' in D.E. Kleiner and S.B. Matheson (eds) *I Claudia: Women in Ancient Rome*, New Haven, Conn., Yale University Art Gallery, pp.14–25.

KELLUM, B. (1996) 'The phallus as signifier: the forum of Augustus and rituals of masculinity' in N.B. Kampen (ed.) *Sexuality in Ancient Art*, Cambridge, Cambridge University Press, pp.170–83.

KING, H. (1997) 'Reading the female body' in Wyke (ed.) pp.620–4.

KÜHN, C.G. (ed. and trans.) (1964–5) *Galen, Opera Omnia* (first published 1821–33), Georg Olms Verlagsbuchhandlung, Hildesheim.

LAURENCE, R. (1994) *Roman Pompeii: Space and Society*, London and New York, Routledge.

LEFKOWITZ, M.R. AND FANT, M.B. (1992) *Women's Life in Greece and Rome: a Sourcebook in Translation* (second edition, first published 1982), London, Duckworth.

MONTSERRAT, D. (1996) *Sex and Society in Graeco-Roman Egypt*, London, Kegan Paul International.

POMEROY, S.B. (1994) *Goddesses, Whores, Wives, and Slaves: Women in Classical Antiquity* (first published 1975), London, Pimlico.

SCOTT, E. (1993) 'Writing the Roman empire' in E. Scott (ed.) *Theoretical Roman Archaeology: First Conference Proceedings*, Aldershot, Avebury Press, pp.5–22.

SELTMAN, C.T. (1956) *Women in Antiquity*, London, Thames and Hudson.

VAN BREMEN, R. (1996) *The Limits of Participation: Women and Civic Life in the Greek East in the Hellenistic and Roman Periods*, Amsterdam, J.C. Gieben.

WALLACE-HADRILL, A. (1988) 'The social structure of the Roman house', *Papers of the British School at Rome*, 56, pp.43–97.

WYKE, M. (ed.) (1997) *Gender & History Special Issue: Gender and the Body in Mediterranean Antiquity*, Gender & History, vol.9, no.3.

ZANKER, P. (1995) *The Mask of Socrates: the Image of the Intellectual in Antiquity*, trans. A. Shapiro, Berkeley, Calif., University of California Press.

Essay Seven
Power, culture and identity in the Roman economy

BY PHIL PERKINS

This essay aims to provide some examples of how power, culture and identity can be located in the Roman economy. It will not be a systematic analysis of the Roman economy, but rather a collection of illustrations and a consideration of the themes. Many different topics could also be used to further illustrate the themes in the Roman economy, for example coinage, imperial expenditure, mining and quarrying and building projects.

Some of the relationships between the Roman economy and power, culture and identity are readily apparent because they are familiar relationships which can be identified in the modern world. So, for example, the Roman state had the power to raise and spend taxes, just as modern states do; likewise wealth often conferred high social status and political power, just as today. However, modern economic terms such as per capita income, gross domestic product, balance of payments and the like are not words that were used in the Roman world. Whether this means that Romans did not have similar concepts or processes that could be described in this way is a different matter. One thing that is certain is that a recognized sector of human activity and awareness directly equivalent to what we now generalize as 'the economy' did not exist. But then there were also many other areas of life that we recognize today which do not have a direct analogy in the Roman world, for example 'society' or 'the subconscious'. So we should not necessarily be discouraged if we cannot readily find something that the Romans themselves called 'the economy'. There is clearly a tension between what we might understand as the economy and what went on in the Roman world. So perhaps we should look at what we ourselves mean by 'the economy', and then go on to look at evidence from the Roman period that relates to our definition.

A simple definition of 'economy' is difficult to provide because the word has a complex meaning. It derives from the ancient Greek word *oikonomia*, which meant household or estate management, and this origin provides its first meaning – the management of expenses, for example 'rural economy' or even 'home economics'. This concept can be extended from household management to 'political economy', the management of the resources and wealth of a people and of its government. Good management requires an understanding of the production and distribution of resources, so 'economy' can be further extended to include the study of productive activity such as farming or manufacturing and also trade and transport of commodities, hence 'economics'. Management also implies making choices about how to dispose limited resources, and so 'economic' also takes on the meaning of careful or frugal use. So in general terms we can think of the economy as a range of activities to do with the production and supply of material needs and the careful management of the resources required to satisfy those needs.

This definition provides some possible indications of where we might begin to look in the Roman world for power, culture and identity in the economy. A study of households and estates along with their management certainly fits in with this definition, and this essay will consider first some literary ideas about estate management and then go on to look at an archaeological example of an excavated villa, at Settefinestre in Tuscany. From the example of an estate the discussion will then move on to a consideration of evidence for the management of the political economy, particularly imperial intervention in economic affairs. This leads to a discussion of some aspects of the production and distribution of food supplies. The final theme considered in detail is how manufacturing within the Roman economy shaped material conditions as well as contributed to Roman identity in the first century AD.

Culture of good management

The notion that good management was a good thing was a firmly established part of élite cultural values in late republican and early imperial Roman society. Furthermore, good management of resources would have been necessary to ensure the generation of wealth to maintain an élite lifestyle, or to rise in status to join that élite since wealth was a qualifying factor in equestrian or senatorial status (for instance one million *sestertii*[1] under Augustus). One of the principal sources for élite wealth was land ownership, and there is good evidence for the operation of the more powerful members of society in estate management and agricultural production (Garnsey and Saller, 1987, pp.64–82). A series of agricultural treatises written by Cato, Varro and Columella provide detailed instruction to the élite on how to organize

---

1 A unit of accounting and a coin. Four tunics could be cleaned for one sestertius in the first century AD.

and manage an estate. Some are prose manuals providing information, but others are poetry. *On Agriculture* by Cato (234–149 BC) is the earliest lengthy Latin prose work to survive; it covers buying a farm, the duties of the owner, manager and staff, working the soil and raising livestock. *On Country Matters* by Varro (116–27 BC) is written as conversations, some of which are dramatic, and provides instruction on the farm, farm buildings and equipment and agricultural work, livestock and the raising of small animals such as poultry and fish. The poet Virgil (70–19 BC) wrote on many topics, but his *Georgics* are poems set in the countryside; a strong theme is the struggle between people and nature, and much of their content derives from folklore and Hellenistic literary traditions. Topics covered include the weather, raising crops, and trees, animals and bees. Columella (*c.* AD 65) was influenced by Virgil, but wrote a more prosaic account (*On Agriculture*) of farm work, farms, livestock, small animals and gardens along with an account of the duties of a farm manager and his wife.

Between them these authors provide a mass of information about the agricultural economy, but it has to be put into context. Their writings come from a period of over 300 years, and the natural temptation is to collapse this timespan and use them to illustrate Roman period farming as a whole, ignoring the potentially huge changes which may have taken place in the time between the first and last writings. In addition to time, space also has to be considered: the agricultural authors were all writing about farming in central Italy, and so what they say is unlikely to be valid throughout the Mediterranean as a whole, let alone temperate parts of Europe, where vines are difficult to grow and the olive cannot survive. A further consideration is that they were all writing from the viewpoint of the land-owning élite: we do not get the point of view of the agricultural labourer, or even the professional farm manager. A final point is that each idealizes rural life in one way or another and country life is seen as pure, simple and worthy rather than uncertain, difficult and very hard work. Most of these writings go beyond the purely didactic and also have ethical and ideological aims, which suggests they can only cautiously be used to describe actual Roman farming techniques.

Columella (*On Agriculture* 1.6–9, in Lewis and Reinhold, 1990, pp.86–92), for example, provides an unlikely mixture of idealized instruction – the villa 'should be divided into three parts' – and attention to practical detail – the farmhouse should have 'two manure pits ... shelving with a gentle slope ... so as not to let the moisture drain away'. The emphasis is on good management, especially management of estate workers and slaves. This is laced with a good dose of prejudice and stereotyping of inferiors as a 'lazy and sleepy-headed class of slaves, accustomed to idling ... to gambling ... to bawdy houses', which adds a moralizing tone to good management). There was also a strong tradition that land ownership and farming were suitable and fitting occupations for the upper classes. Cicero (106–43 BC), with characteristic pomposity, states: 'For of all gainful professions, nothing is better, nothing more pleasing, nothing more delightful, nothing better becomes a well-bred man than agriculture'. This is a quotation from a moralizing set of instructions given by Cicero to his son (*On Duties* 1.151.42); it follows on from a flat condemnation of retailers, manual workers, caterers and entertainers who are, to Cicero, worse than tax gatherers and money lenders. This statement, and others like it, has often been used to suggest that higher class Romans, senators, did not engage in commerce and industry but invested in the land and lived from its profits as 'gentleman farmers'. However, the passage also has to be kept in context: it is moralizing and idealizing, not a description either of how Cicero himself behaved (he borrowed money, for example) or of the real world (Finley, 1979, pp.50– 8), even if it is how Cicero wanted to present himself.

So if the literary sources need to be read with due caution and cannot be treated as literal descriptions, how can we look further into the world of the rich landowner and begin to see how agriculture and land owning were an integral part of élite culture in the early empire? One avenue of approach is to move away from the literary and philosophical attitudes we have just considered and look at some material manifestations of culture by examining some archaeological evidence. If we do this we may gain a broader vision of the realities of the Roman economy.

Settefinestre: a Roman villa in central Italy

At Settefinestre a large Roman villa has been excavated near the Roman colony[2] at Cosa, about 140 kilometres north-west of Rome (Carandini, 1984; 1988). The villa sits on the side of a small hill overlooking the ancient Via Aurelia (the main route from Rome to Gaul (Figures 7.1, 7.2, 7.3). At the front is a turreted wall, making the boundary of the villa look like a city wall. This monumental façade can itself be considered a cultural expression of wealth and power: the power of humans over the environment (remodelling a hillside), and the power of the owner (a large private property having a fortified wall). The main block of the villa was large (50 × 50 metres), and there was also a courtyard and further outbuildings. Together these factors suggest that the villa belonged to a member of the élite, possibly a Roman senator. The name of the owner of the Settefinestre villa is not known for certain, but some roof tiles were stamped with 'LS', possibly a Lucius Sestius who was

2 A colony was a settlement of (usually) Roman citizens, often retired soldiers, comprising a city and a territory divided into lots for the colonists. Later the title became honorary and was a mark of high status for a city.

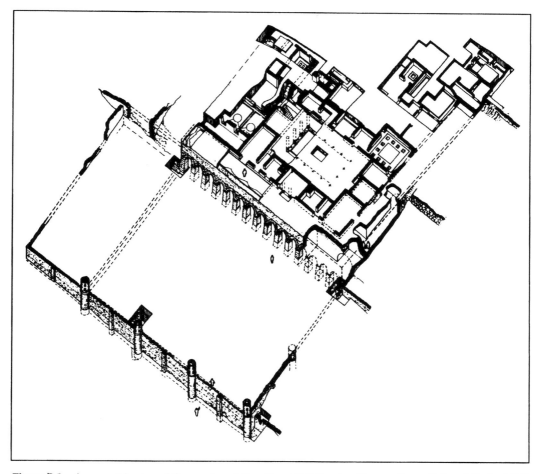

Figure 7.1 *Axonometric view of the remains of the villa at Settefinestre. (Source: Carandini and Settis, 1979, p.139)*

consul – a chief magistrate of the Roman state who presided over the senate – in 23 BC (close to the date of the building of the villa), and whose family had property in the territory of Cosa (Cicero, *Letters to Atticus* 15.27.1).

The villa was entered from the top of the hill where a gate and a passage led into an open courtyard or farmyard. On the far side of this was the main block of the villa. Around the other sides were stores, a cowshed and accommodation and kitchens for the slaves who worked at the villa and on the surrounding estate. The main villa block had two entrances from the courtyard: one led into the main living area for the villa owner and his family (the *pars urbana* – the urbane part) and the

187

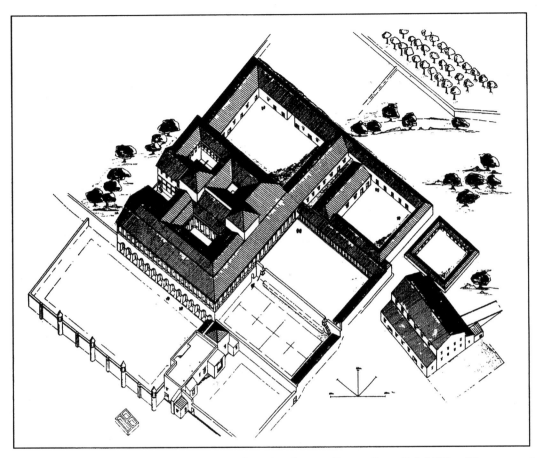

Figure 7.2 *Axonometric reconstruction of the villa at Settefinestre. (Source: Carandini, 1985, p.29; courtesy of the Electa Archive)*

other led into the working part of the villa (the *pars rustica* – the rustic part, where crop processing took place and the slaves and animals lived) (Figure 7.3). The basic layout of the *pars urbana* is similar to some of the axially planned houses at Pompeii, with a set of rooms arranged around an atrium or open courtyard behind the entrance, and a second set of rooms around a peristyle – another open courtyard surrounded by a columned portico framing a garden (Figure 7.4). In contrast to the city houses the villa also has rooms which face out from this central core towards the countryside. All of these rooms have remains of high quality wall and floor decorations, and together they form a well-organized set of rooms suitable for a Roman family of high status. All in all, the villa

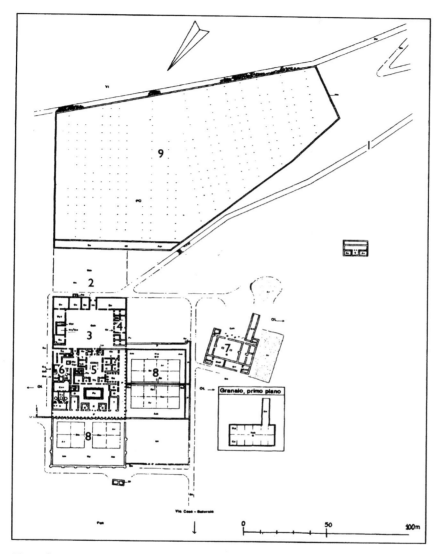

Figure 7.3 *General plan of the villa at Settefinestre. Key: 1 Road; 2 External farmyard; 3 Courtyard; 4 Slave quarters; 5 Pars urbana; 6 Pars rustica; 7 Granary; 8 Garden; 9 Orchard. (Source: Carandini, 1985, p.159; courtesy of the Electa Archive)*

can be seen as a well-appointed residence in the country which gave its owners all the physical comforts of city living and provided a dwelling which was not dissimilar to a town house (*domus*). As such it may be considered as bringing Roman urban-style living into the context of the

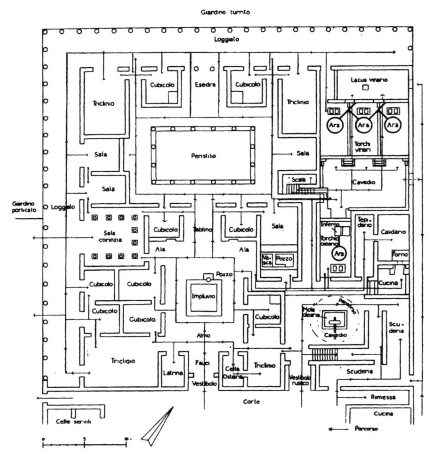

Figure 7.4 *Plan of the* pars urbana *and* pars rustica *of the villa at Settefinestre.*
(Source: Carandini, 1988, p.136)

countryside to some extent, perhaps paralleling the urban view of the
countryside presented in the literature.

The rooms on the north-west side of the building were linked to the
main atrium–peristyle axis of the *pars urbana* by five different routes and
so were closely integrated with the refined, mosaic floors and painted
walls of the living quarters. However, they held the agricultural machines
of the estate: an olive mill, an oil press and three wine presses which
together make up part of the *pars rustica* of the villa. The basic structure
of the *pars rustica* mimics the *pars urbana*: from the courtyard a corridor
led to a small open courtyard, similar to the atrium, but housing a
donkey-powered olive mill; a further corridor led to a courtyard

paralleling the peristyle, with the wine and oil presses on either side. These were beam presses operated by a screw; the grape juice from the pressing was channelled to a cellar by a hole in the floor to ferment in large ceramic jars called *dolia*, before being bottled in the large two-handled amphorae.

The main courtyard, a further part of the *pars rustica*, housed the slaves in a series of twelve rooms each of about 3 × 3 metres, a striking contrast to the owner's quarters. It has been estimated that altogether fifty-two slaves were kept here and were used to provide labour on the estate. Their muscle power would have maintained the villa, worked the presses and other equipment, cultivated the gardens, orchards, vineyards, olive groves and fields which surrounded the villa and tended the sheep, goats and cattle housed in a separate animal house and granary. Here we can see the material conditions the slaves lived in even if we cannot hear their voices in the literary agricultural sources.

The excavator of the villa suggested that this building and its organization closely matched a villa of the type described by Varro (*On Country Matters* 1, written in about 37 BC) and Columella (*On Agriculture* 1) (Carandini, 1988, p.121). In this 'perfect' literary villa the estate is run by a steward, who lives in a corner of the *pars urbana* in the rooms to the east of the atrium; the owner, who visits the estate occasionally, stays in the luxurious rooms of the *pars urbana*. However, according to the instructions of the agricultural manuals, the owner was closely involved in managing the economy of the villa, and this closeness may be reflected in the way that the working parts and the luxurious parts of the villa at Settefinestre were closely integrated. We can imagine a benign, slave-owning, senatorial landowner retiring to his estate at Settefinestre and paying close attention to the running of the villa, with a close match between the literary descriptions and the excavated villa (Purcell, 1988).

The closeness of the fit between the idealized villa and Settefinestre encourages the extension of the analogy to other aspects of the villa's production and organization. The study of the villa showed that it produced a variety of animal produce and crops, perhaps with an emphasis on wine (three presses). In line with the recommendations of the agricultural manuals the productive capacity of the villa should have been balanced, so that the slave labour force was self-sufficient and produced a surplus of marketable produce to provide a cash income for the owner. Putting together all the pieces of evidence from the villa and the Roman writers, it is possible to draw up an estimate of how much the villa produced and consumed and so to gauge how much profit it may have brought to its owner from the work of its slaves. There is obviously a fair degree of estimation and speculation in the figures, but the excavator suggests that the villa could have produced about 100,000 litres of wine worth about 60,000 *sestertii*. Other produce of the villa, such as cheese, eggs, poultry, game birds, geese, ducks, wild animals, snails, dormice, honey and fish, could have provided twice this sum, bringing in a total of 180,000 *sestertii* (Carandini, 1988, pp.173–7). The sale of surplus olive oil and grain could have raised the income further. The total is a very large amount, and comparison with the annual pay of a Roman soldier (900 *sestertii* per annum in the first century AD) suggests that the estate income could have paid for 200 soldiers a year (Jones, 1974, p.192).

The villa at Settefinestre was not static, and at the beginning of the second century AD in the reign of Trajan (98–117) it was reorganized and structural changes made it less like the ideal villas of literature. In the main block the old *pars rustica* was dismantled and the rooms converted into stores, and some of the routes between the two parts of the villa were blocked off. The *pars urbana* was redecorated and became less sumptuous, and a large extension was built in the porticoed garden for a sophisticated complex of hot and cold baths. The rooms around the courtyard were reorganized and to the south-west of this a new set of structures was built around a second courtyard with only two narrow entrances, one of which was later blocked up to further restrict entry and exit. Around three sides of this courtyard were rows of small rooms about 3 metres square, all of which opened on to the courtyard; the walls were unplastered and no flooring was found. The fourth side of the block had a double row of rooms, most of which opened on to a corridor between the old buildings and this new block rather than the new courtyard. This block has been identified as a new set of cells for the slaves (Carandini, 1988, pp.173–7). This new accommodation could have raised the total number of slaves to about 100. The excavator suggests that this represents a fundamental shift in the organization of the labour force of the villa, and that since the empire had stopped expanding the supply of new slaves captured as prisoners had dried up. In response to this the villa had started 'farming' slaves, and females were now kept for breeding purposes, any children not required for labour being sold at market, along with other livestock produced at the villa. The implication is that by the first century AD slaves had become a commodity and could be considered to be produce of an estate just like anything else.

Further changes in the economy of the villa are indicated by the fact the wine and oil presses had been removed. This does not necessarily mean that vines and olives were no longer grown on the estate, but it does mean that they were no longer processed in the villa and so may have been less important. To the south-west of the new slave block another new and similar structure was built. Once again a series of cells were arranged around a courtyard. The cells were smaller than the slave quarters and had well-made plaster walls; each had a narrow entrance which could be closed by a shutter. The building matches the descriptions by Varro and Columella of a pigsty (Carandini, 1988, pp.198–206). It would seem that pig and slave rearing may have replaced wine production.

All of this suggests a change in the management and organization of the estate involving a shift from traditional crops to producing livestock, possibly for the urban market in Rome. Back in the *pars urbana* the definitive separation from the *pars rustica*, represented by the removal of the connection between the wine and oil presses and the dwelling area, may also indicate a changed relationship between the landowner and the production of the estate. Perhaps the close involvement and good management of the landowner was not such a strong cultural imperative in the second century as it had been earlier, and the villa had become more of a productive investment than an integral facet of élite life (Carandini, 1988, pp.213–4).

We do not know for certain who owned the villa or whether the changes in its use might be linked with a change in ownership, but what we can see is the deliberate modification of the organization of production at the villa. This might have been a response to a changed economic climate or a change in the demand for produce, but there is no direct evidence for this possibility. The next issue we shall consider is whether similar interventions in economic activity can be attributed to the emperor's attempting to manage economic affairs.

Power to the imperial sheep

High in the Apennine mountains of southern Italy, at an altitude of 553 metres, lies the Roman town of Saepinum. On the gate of the city, on the road to Bovianum, a set of inscriptions is preserved (Corbier, 1983). The gate in the city walls is a single arch set between two circular towers (Figure 7.5). A large inscription set in a rectangular panel above the arch reads 'Tiberius Claudius Nero, son of Tiberius, Pontifex, Consul for the second time, Imperator for the second time with tribunicial powers for the fifth time and Nero Claudius Drusus Germanicus, son of Tiberius, Augur, Consul, Imperator for the second time had the walls, gates and towers built at their own expense'[3]. The inscription states in large, clear capital letters that Tiberius (later the emperor) and his

3 Pontifex was the highest rank of priest; Imperator denotes a military commander; and an Augur was a high-ranking priest, originally with fortune-telling skills and duties. 'Tribunicial power' refers to the power of the tribune, the highest state official, usually a rank held by the emperor.

Figure 7.5 *City gate of Saepinum, Italy. (Source: Barker, 1995, p.220; photo Graeme Barker)*

brother Drusus, with all their grand titles, powers and priesthoods listed, paid for the impressive fortifications and monumental entrance you are looking at.

Immediately below the inscription in the centre of the arch is a bust of Hercules, famous for his heroic labours, and clearly lending his heroic powers to Tiberius and Drusus. To either side of the inscription are statues of conquered barbarians representing Germania (the Rhineland) and Pannonia (east of the Alps and south of the Danube), provinces where the brothers had recently won military victories over barbaric tribes. The monumental gate is an unequivocal statement of imperial power in the walls of a small town in the hills of Italy. Its form even evokes monumental triumphal arches such as the well-preserved arch of Titus in Rome (Figure 3.8). On the large stone at the lower right-hand side of the arch is a smaller and later inscription dating to AD 169–172, and bearing in mind its context we can examine in detail the text of the three letters it presents:

Bassaeus Rufus and Macrinius Vindex to the magistrates of Saepinum, greeting. We have appended a copy of a letter written to us by Cosmus, freedman of the emperor and financial secretary, together with that which was subjoined to his, and we warn you to refrain from abusing the lessees of the flocks of sheep to the serious detriment of the imperial treasury, lest it be necessary to investigate the matter and punish the act, if the facts are as reported.

Letter of Cosmus, freedman of the emperor and financial secretary, written to Bassaeus Rufus and Macrinius Vindex, prefects of the Praetorian Guard, most eminent men: I have appended a copy of a letter written to me by Septimianus, my fellow freedman and assistant, and I beg that you be good enough to write to the magistrates of Saepinum and Bovianum to refrain from abusing the lessees of the flocks of sheep, who are under my supervision, so that by your kindness the account of the imperial treasury may be secured against loss.

Letter written by Septimianus to Cosmus: since the lessees of the flocks of sheep, who are under your supervision, are now repeatedly complaining to me that they frequently suffer injury along the paths of the mountain pasturages at the hands of security guards and magistrates at Saepinum and Bovianum, inasmuch as they detain in transit draught animals and shepherds that they have hired, saying that they are runaway slaves and have stolen draught animals, and under this pretext even sheep belonging to the emperor are lost to them in such disturbances, we considered it necessary to write to them again and again to act more temperately, so that the imperial property might suffer no loss. And since they persist in the same insolence, saying that they will pay no attention to my letters and that it will do no good even if you write to them, I request, my lord, that, if you deem fit, you notify Bassaeus Rufus and Macrinius Vindex, commanders of the the the emperor's bodyguards, most eminent men, to issue letters to the said magistrates and police ...

(*Corpus Inscriptionum Latinarum*, vol.9, no.2438; in Lewis and Reinhold, 1990, pp.100–1)

The inscription is a public showing of the contents of three letters. It makes public an imperial 'telling off' of the magistrates who ran the local governments of the towns of Saepinum and Bovianum. To have it chiselled in stone above the entrance to their city must have been humiliating for the magistrates. The original letter (the third in the sequence) tells how Septimianus has been ignored by the magistrates and how the magistrates and their security guards are harassing the shepherds of flocks of sheep which belong to the emperor and have been leased out. Septimianus writes to his superior Cosmus who forwards the letter to his superiors Bassaeus Rufus and Macrinius Vindex in Rome. These two, who are superior to the magistrates, send the open letter of reprimand back to Saepinum. Their concern is not that the shepherds are being abused, rather that the imperial treasury is losing money. The hierarchical imperial administration can be seen at work, protecting the economic interests of the emperor by good management and enforcing the authority of the emperor, which has been ignored by the magistrates when they refused to comply with Septimianus' request. The inscription is much later than the commemoration of the building of the gate by Tiberius and Drusus, but placing the letters from the imperial civil servants near to the inscription by the adopted sons of Augustus is clearly and publicly reinforcing the imperial power and authority behind the reprimand. Although sheep farming would only have generated a small fraction of imperial income, the inscription is a clear demonstration of imperial power being used to protect the imperial economic interest. It is, however, imperial management of imperial assets, not management of state economic policy.

The power of good management

This case of municipal malpractice is only one particular instance of the wielding of imperial power in the interest of economic good management. The more general good management of production, supply and taxation was considered part of good government by an emperor, as in this example concerning the Emperor Tiberius, written in the second century AD by Tacitus (*Annals* 4.6).

> To prevent the consequences of unproductive seasons, or losses at sea, he spared neither money nor attention. In the provinces no new burdens were imposed, and the old taxes were collected without cruelty or extortion. Corporal punishment was never inflicted, and confiscation of property was a thing unknown.
>
> In Italy the land property of the emperor was inconsiderable. Good order prevailed among his slaves. Freedmen in his household were few.

This good practice by Tiberius is cited by Tacitus to establish his good conduct as an emperor using his imperial power for the economic benefit of the citizens, but as so often with Tacitus, it has a sting in the tail and the next but one sentence reads: 'And yet to this equitable system he did not know how to add a gracious manner: the austerity of his countenance struck men with terror'. Tacitus is implying that the management was good but the public relations were bad.

The preceding extract mentions two forms of imperial income: taxes which were low and difficult to raise because they would be unpopular, and private imperial estates which might generate a profit on agricultural produce. These resources, along with plunder from war and the produce of imperial gold and silver mines, were the main source of cash income for the emperors, which was needed to pay the army, army contractors, the civil administration and imperial gifts of buildings or amenities to communities. The distinction between which of these was private imperial income or expenditure and which actually belonged to the Roman state was often blurred, but it is in these areas that we can most clearly see imperial manipulation of economic affairs. For example, if the emperor was short of cash there were three main sources of additional money: selling imperial property; condemning wealthy senators and seizing their wealth; and debasing coinage, that is, mixing base metals with the gold or silver for coins to make it go further (Jones, 1974, pp.189–90). There is evidence for such attempts at manipulation of economic affairs which were rather stretching the limits of good management. It is possible to trace the falling actual silver content of silver coinage throughout the first three centuries AD, through either analysis of written sources or chemical analyses of the coins. Nero reduced silver coins to 90 per cent pure silver in AD 64 and later Trajan further reduced them to 85 per cent pure silver. The manipulation of silver content had the effect of increasing the number of coins that could be made from a given weight of silver while keeping the same face value on the coins. Marcus Aurelius reduced the silver content to 75 per cent and Septimius Severus to 50 per cent, and by the time of Gallienus (AD 260–68) the silver content was down to 5 per cent. The void which had opened between the face value of the coin and the intrinsic value of the silver led to inflation in the prices of commodities valued in silver coin (Jones, 1974, pp.197–227; Rathbone, 1996). This difference also led to what we might term devaluations, where the face value of coin was realigned with the silver content as in the vivid example preserved in part of a letter on papyrus found in Egypt and dating to c.300: 'The divine fortune of our masters has given orders that the Italian coinage be reduced to half a *sestertius*. So make haste therefore to spend all the Italian money you have and purchase me all kinds of goods at whatever price you find them' (Lewis and Reinhold, 1990, p.421).

Managed production and consumption

One area where the emperor was required to exercise good management was in the provision of the *annona*. This was the supply of a ration of free grain to citizens living in the city of Rome. Later the provision was extended to include other foodstuffs, particularly olive oil (which provided protein as well as lighting). Much of the grain for the *annona* was acquired from the provinces of Africa and Egypt in the form of a tax on agricultural produce. The grain was shipped to Rome by private contractors until the mid second century, when an imperial fleet of freighters was established to transport it to Rome. The provision of the grain dole was the duty of a senior imperial official (*Praefectus Annonae*), and if the supply was not effectively delivered unrest and rioting might occur in the city and the emperor would certainly lose favour with the people. Conversely, an emperor might improve his reputation by providing additional rations or a new commodity to the people of Rome (Rickman, 1980).

The *annona* stimulated the development of a series of major trade routes: grain flowed from Egypt and modern-day Tunisia (Africa Proconsularis) to Rome and olive oil was transported from Baetica (the Guadalquivir valley between Seville and Cordoba in southern Spain), southern Tunisia and the coast of Libya to Rome. Olive oil from Spain was transported in distinctive globular amphorae (known as Dressel 20 amphorae – see Figures 7.6(a) and (b)) across the western Mediterranean to Rome from the first to the mid third century AD. There a dump of these amphorae some 50 metres high, Monte Testaccio

– 'the mountain of old crocks' – is testimony to the volume of the trade. Large quantities of Spanish oil were also shipped to the Roman legions posted on the Rhine frontier and in the militarized areas of Britain. This connection with the army provides a further area where the emperor was required to see to the management of a sector of the economy. Although the provision of olive oil for the city of Rome does not seem to be part of the duties of the *Praefectus Annonae* until the reign of Septimius Severus (AD 193–212), it is possible that this branch of the imperial administration was responsible for the supply of the army at an earlier period (Remesal Rodríguez, 1986, pp.81ff.). Whether or not this was the case, the good management of the production and shipping of supplies to the troops was vital to the maintenance of the power of the imperial army and the security of the empire.

The trade routes which linked productive areas with areas of high consumption, military zones and the city of Rome were stimulated by imperial control of supplies for the *annona*, even though private individuals were involved in all stages of the production and shipping of the oil, as demonstrated by stamps and *tituli picti* (titles or labels written in ink or paint) on the amphorae. However, the oil, or indeed grain, was collected as tax in kind, requisitioned or purchased at market prices. This both created an assured buyer for agricultural produce and gave producers a stimulus to grow crops so that they could pay taxes and also sell further surplus to the state. So produce was exported not solely via the markets in individual towns and cities but also through taxation and supplying the state. The prices may well have been fixed in the urban markets, but the existence of a parallel means of redistributing agricultural produce, the *annona*, enabled a specialized 'agro-industry' to develop, as the Guadalquivir valley and north Africa became enmeshed in supplying the city of Rome and the army. The supply of the army and Rome created a powerful demand for grain and oil which was met by an imperially organized system of tax, exaction and market purchase which influenced the systems of agricultural production and even settlement pattern in the grain- and oil-producing parts of the empire.

This relationship of supply and demand may also be seen as one of the forces which held the Roman empire together. Productive provinces were bound to Rome and provinces with a heavy military presence were bound to provinces which supplied needs that could not be provided locally. So Baetica and Africa Proconsularis can be seen as productive provinces, whereas Britain and Germany demanded supplies to feed the legions while Rome attracted imports to Italy (Remesal Rodríguez, 1995, pp.358–9). Looked at in this way, the very existence of the empire and its structures can be seen to shape the Roman economy, in addition to the actions of individual emperors.

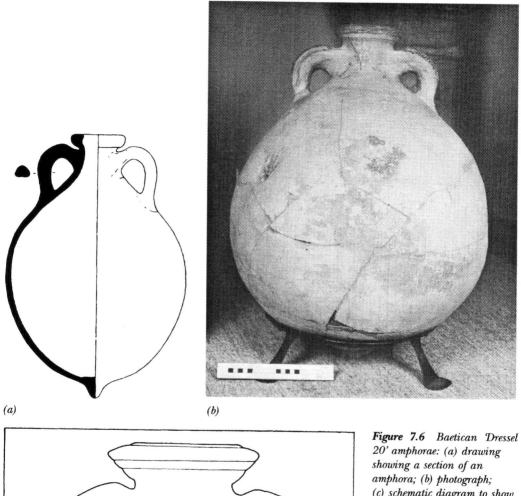

(a)

(b)

(c)

Figure 7.6 *Baetican 'Dressel 20' amphorae: (a) drawing showing a section of an amphora; (b) photograph; (c) schematic diagram to show the arrangement of* tituli picti. *(Source: Peacock and Williams, 1986, p.139, courtesy Winchester Museums Service; p.5, reproduced by permission of Addison Wesley Longman Ltd)*

Manufacturing and Roman identity

Material culture and the economy

'Material culture' is a term used by archaeologists to denote the artefacts used and produced by people at a particular place and point in time. So modern, west European material culture includes Tupperware, beer cans, the Sony Walkman and particular combinations of items of clothing. This may seem a rather modern idea, but the power of material culture to shape an identity was known at least to Tacitus, when he wrote about attempts to make Britain more civilized following the conquest: Agricola was 'encouraging the natives ... to build temples, law courts and comfortable houses ... The Roman apparel was seen without prejudice and the toga became a fashionable part of dress' (*Agricola* 21). The kinds of things people use and own can carry a variety of types of information, for example an expensive car can be a status symbol and intend to signify that its owner is wealthy and successful. As with other sources of evidence, this needs to be carefully weighed because it is perfectly possible that a millionaire might own a rusting Morris Minor as a preferred means of transport. Likewise, in a Roman cultural context a toga signified citizenship or a ring equestrian status. Dinner with the fictional Trimalchio as described by Petronius (*Satyricon* 26–78), discussed in Essay Four, is full of caricatures of status symbols, starting with the porter at the door shelling peas into a silver dish; Trimalchio tastelessly flaunts his wealth at almost every possible opportunity.

As with status, material culture can also play a part in defining identity. So, for example, distinctive artefacts like the Jewish *menorah* (multi-branched candlestick) or terracotta lamps decorated with Christian symbols can be closely associated with a particular identity. If we are to ascribe an active role to material culture, rather than to view it simply as the things we use, the availability and cost of a particular artefact will clearly affect the extent to which it can act as a defining element in culture and society. This is where the operation of the economy becomes important in understanding the roles performed by different artefacts in establishing and defining culture, denoting identity and displaying power, because it is the functioning of the economy that determines the supply and value of commodities. At one extreme the Roman concept of *luxuria* – extravagant living – is an example of what can be called conspicuous consumption, the very public display and disposal of great wealth in order to achieve or maintain the highest social status. On a smaller scale, the ability or power to acquire and use Roman artefacts in a non-Roman context can be seen as an indication of participating in Roman culture and perhaps also gaining some aspects of a Roman identity. Thus both wealth and participation in Roman trade networks, that is, being a part of the Roman economy, contribute to the creation and maintenance of a Roman identity and culture. To explore this direction further we can look in detail at the supply, distribution and ownership of Roman tableware in the early empire.

Tracing and interpreting the uses of Roman-style pottery

Pottery is a privileged form of evidence in archaeology because it is nearly indestructible and is very commonly found in excavations, and so it often receives more attention than its original importance would have commanded. Nevertheless, this does mean that some forms of Roman pottery have been studied in great detail: one such is *terra sigillata* or Samian ware, as it is commonly known in the United Kingdom (Figure 7.7).

This distinctive pottery has a shiny dark red surface and was mostly used to make cups, bowls and plates. The particular style of pottery was probably first made in the town of Arezzo in central Italy around about 40 BC when potters began to experiment with firing techniques and discovered that a shiny red finish could be achieved, in contrast to the shiny black finish that had been in use for at least the previous 400 years. At this time the style of tableware in use was remarkably uniform, and over much of the Mediterranean area shiny black plates and bowls were the norm. In the space of about fifty years, up to about AD 10, this completely changed and the red pottery style came to dominate most of the Mediterranean area. Some of the pottery was also decorated with low reliefs which carried very classical images of mythological scenes, natural abundance and theatrical productions reminiscent of the sculptures of the Ara Pacis and other Augustan period art in Rome. Some of the shapes of the vessels, particularly plates and relief decorated bowls were similar to gold and silver vessels suggesting further links between high culture and low tableware.

Initially much of the pottery was made in Arezzo and exported to other areas, presumably down the river Arno to Pisa or down the Tiber to Rome, from where it was shipped around the Mediterranean. But soon the technology spread and workshops producing the new style of pottery developed in other parts of Italy, Gaul, Spain, and Asia Minor (Figure 7.7(b)). It is one thing to say that the technology spread to other areas, but that begs the question, 'Why?' One possibility might be that the new production techniques brought a functional improvement to the plates and bowls. However, the red wares do not seem to have any functional superiority over the black wares, and in some areas, for example Campania and Sicily, the black wares (Campana A and C wares) continued in use into the first century AD. But it was not simply a matter

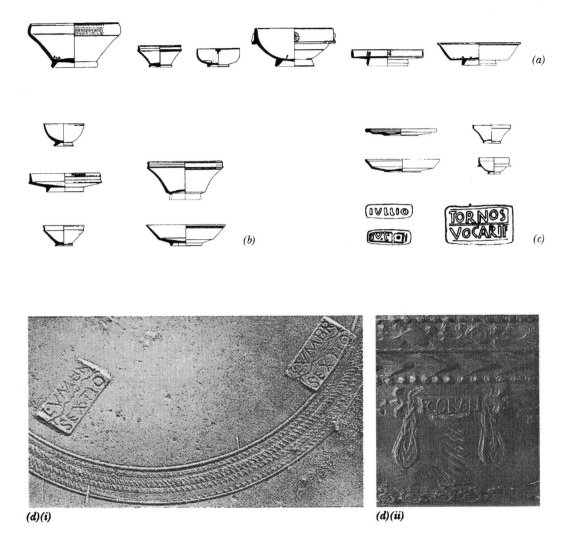

Figure 7.7 (a) Italian terra sigillata *plates, dishes and bowls.* (b) Eastern terra sigillata *plates, dishes and bowls.* (c) Gallo-Belgic tablewares imitating Italian terra sigillata *plates, dishes and bowls, examples of stamps below.* (d) Italian terra sigillata *stamps: (i) L[ucius] Vmbr[icii] Sextio; (ii) P. Corneli[us]. (Sources: Hayes, 1997, pp.46–7; p.55; © The British Museum; Rigby, 1973, p.18; by permission of Valerie Rigby and the Council for British Archaeology; Hayes, 1997, pl.18; © The British Museum)*

of the colour of the pottery changing. For example, in Asia Minor tableware had commonly been red since *c.*150 BC, but in the Augustan period the shape of the locally produced tableware began to imitate the shapes and details of the tableware made in Arezzo (Hayes, 1997) (see Figure 7.7(b)). The production of shiny red tableware also started (around 10 BC) in the areas of Gaul that had recently been conquered by Julius Caesar, at Lyons, and at La Graufesenque near Millau, where a large production centre developed. Later production also spread to places further north and east in Gaul. Meanwhile, in northern Europe the red pottery has been found at Augustan-period army camps along the Rhine and the Danube and would seem to have been brought into these areas by the Roman armies supplied from Italy as they conquered new territories. This history would seem to suggest that the Roman conquest of Gaul and Germania brought with it new Italian-style shiny red tableware that was used by soldiers and conquered peoples alike. However, it is not simply the case that Roman merchants and traders began to operate in conquered areas, and producers found that establishing new pottery workshops in Gaul made supplying local markets easier. Some of these new Gaulish products were traded back into the Mediterranean area and some Italian products were even traded outside the empire to barbarian areas such as Britain before the Roman conquest. This led to a situation where Roman-style material culture was partially adopted in areas which were strictly not Roman, and so the products of the Roman economy began to be traded outside the limits of the Roman world.

The production and trade of Italian-style red pottery can therefore be seen as a mechanism for both spreading and defining a 'Roman' material culture and indeed a Roman identity. This spread cannot be seen as being driven purely by economic factors. Other factors can also be invoked: for example the pottery would have been used in eating and drinking and this too was a culturally determined activity. Augustan *terra sigillata* seems to have been used in a 'set' with a matching cup and plate forming a personal set of tableware, and the vessels were presumably suited to eating Roman food in the Roman fashion. The new style of pottery may even have taken on a cultural value, as being identified as 'Roman' pottery, and we may see this in the so-called Gallo-Belgic wares which were common in north-east Gaul and south-eastern Britain. Here a tradition of pottery with 'Celtic' influences began to produce red cups and plates similar to the *terra sigillata*, but preserved the traditional clays and finishes of the earlier style (Figure 7.7(c)). So without an apparent disruption of the pre-Roman organization of pottery production and distribution, Roman styles and models of pottery were adopted and Roman-style material culture became a part of the material culture of non-Roman, or recently conquered, peoples. By considering these everyday items as a manifestation of Roman culture, we can see that the adoption and spread of that Roman culture was intimately connected to the functioning and organization of the Roman economy.

Identity in the economy

The preceding discussion has focused on material culture that has a distinctive 'Roman' identity, but if it is possible to see a 'Roman' identity in the products of the Roman economy, can we look at it another way round and see the identity of individuals operating in the Roman economy? Well, we have already encountered a number of individuals, appearing in inscriptions, on stamped artefacts or as authors writing about aspects of the economy. There are many other instances of individuals whose names have survived, but we often do not know very much more about them. The names themselves may contain information, for example a triple name (*tria nomina*) usually implies a Roman citizen and a single name usually identifies a slave (see Essay Five). Very often, and especially on stamped ceramics, several names appear in conjunction (Figure 7.7(d)), for example a series of stamps on *terra sigillata* link the name of P. Cornelius with sixty-nine other names, such as 'Apollo' and 'P. Corne'; 'P. Corn' and 'Faustus'; or 'Menolaus' and 'P. Corneli' (Fülle, 1997). In some cases the name is abbreviated and in others the use of the genitive suggests ownership; so in the third example the stamp could read 'Menolaus of P. Cornelius', suggesting that the stamp identifies Menolaus the slave of the freeborn or freedman P. Cornelius.

The most straightforward interpretation of such stamps is that they identify the slave who made the pot, working for a particular master. But we should also consider why the name of the slave and master should be recorded on a plate or bowl. Could the stamp be like a modern trademark, guaranteeing quality and providing information about the manufacturer in case the pot had manufacturing defects? This is a possibility, but it requires a high degree of specialized knowledge on the part of the Roman consumer to differentiate between a plate marked 'Apollo P. Corne' and one marked 'P. Corn Faustus'. The use of written names also suggests that the consumer would have to be literate enough to read the names and understand the information they are conveying. Furthermore, the mechanism for a consumer on the German frontier to attempt to get an exchange or refund for a defective plate from a producer in distant Arezzo is hard to imagine. If the stamps did perform a trademark function it would seem much more likely that the presence of the stamp was more a part of the overall style of the red shiny Italian pottery rather than a detailed information provider. Two further considerations may support this suggestion: the stamps are usually in the centre of the bowl or plate and so highly visible to someone who would have been using it – one might add that they would also have acted as food traps and prevented easy cleaning. The second point is that some of the marks are not written names; rather, they are illiterate attempts at producing a written stamp. These stamps are more common in the vessels imitating *terra sigillata* from Arezzo. For example, in the Gallo-Belgic wares that imitate the shapes of the Italian products, about a quarter bear illiterate marks (Rigby, 1973, p.13). This observation suggests that in these cases the form and presence of the stamp are more important than the actual wording of it.

Another possible explanation is that the identifications in the stamps are not intended for the consumers at all, but rather are a result of the controls used to monitor production in the pottery workshops, perhaps so that pots could be differentiated when they were removed from shared kilns, or to distinguish the work of one slave from another. A further possibility is that the stamps record a contract of letting and hiring (*locatio et conductio*) between the people named on the stamp, concerning the lease of production facilities, raw material or labour: such contracts concerning pottery have survived on Egyptian papyri and provide a model for interpreting the stamps (Fülle, 1997, pp.121–4). This possible interpretation suggests that the identities of the individuals on the stamps were recorded in order to provide legal proof of fulfilment of the contract.

Another area where identity is explicitly linked with economic activity is on gravestones. A job or trade is commonly recorded on gravestones either by name or by a representation of tools or items associated with that trade. One very grand example is the tomb of the baker Eurysaces and his wife Atistia, outside the Porta Maggiore in Rome (Figure 7.8). The whole tomb was built with forms mimicking the shape of bread ovens (the circular holes above) and kneading troughs (the cylinders below) and the frieze near the top of the tomb shows scenes from the whole process of breadmaking from preparing the grain and making bread to baking and distributing the loaves. The inscription reads: 'This is the monument to Marcus Vergilius Eurysaces, baker, contractor and magistrate's attendant.' Eurysaces seems to have been a freedman who prospered as a baker, possibly contracting with the state to supply bread. The frieze supplies images of how a large-scale bakery may have been organized: the work is done by many figures wearing tunics, probably slaves, and overseen by a figure wearing a toga – possibly Eurysaces himself. Their equipment is also informative: similar grain mills have been found at many sites, including Ostia and Pompeii, and some items are otherwise unknown, for example the donkey-driven kneading trough (Figure 7.8(b)(ii), right).

Figure 7.8 (a) Tomb of Eurysaces. (Photo: Alinari) (b) Drawings of the frieze: (i) Buying grain, milling grain w̶ donkey mills, sieving flour, checking flour; (ii) Kneading or mixing dough with a donkey, making loaves, baki̶ (iii) Weighing and checking loaves. (Source: Rostovetzeff, 1957, pl. IV; by permission of Oxford University Pr̶ (c) Portrait of Eurysaces and his wife Atistia, originally part of the main façade of the tomb (now demolish̶ c.30 BC. (Photo: Fototeca Unione, Rome)

Figure 7.9 *Tomb reliefs from Sens. (a) A hardware shop with a scene where a customer is comparing a large and a small pan; (b) A man with a stylus and writing tablets, a hooded cloak hanging on the wall behind; (c) A fuller treading cloth to wash or felt it. (Photo: Musées de Sens, Elie)*

Other examples of individuals using their trade to express their identities are less monumental, but a series of reliefs from tombs at Agedincum Senones (modern Sens in northern France) show individuals performing their trades (Figure 7.9). Further examples from the Isola Sacra cemetery near Ostia show a blacksmith and a water seller at work on funerary monuments. A tombstone represents a unique opportunity to represent an identity to others, and for these tradesmen their economic role was clearly an important, if not a defining, part of their identity. Linking of identity and economy can also be discerned in the range of activities considered suitable for Roman senators in the passage from Cicero's *On Duties* quoted above, so that an economic reality like land owning can form part of an identity for a senator, just as baking can contribute to the identity of a baker.

Locating the Roman economy

In this essay we have considered the management and organization of a Roman villa and its estate in Italy; imperial overseeing of transport, food supply and manipulation of coinage; the organization of food supply to the city of Rome and the army; the spread and development of *terra sigillata* manufacture and use; material culture as a product of the Roman economy helping to define Roman identity; and individuals expressing their identity through their economic activity. To conclude I would like to consider some of the comparisons and differences that can be seen in these apparently disparate areas of the Roman economy and to attempt to locate the economy in the Roman world.

As we have seen, the privileged place in Roman culture of agriculture and land ownership was a result of its association with wealth, élite values and culture in late republican and early imperial Italy, and the model of the villa-dwelling landowner was a potent cultural and economic part of the Romanization of the empire. This model of living along with producing was spread to many provinces of the Roman empire by colonists and settlers, and was also adopted by local élites, so becoming an integral part of the process of Romanization. The Roman-style villa, a substantial building with both residential and productive parts acting as an estate centre, became a common feature of many areas of the countryside in the Roman empire (Percival, 1976). However, the major part of the model that was replicated in provincial areas was probably the physical and spatial aspects of the villa. Just because large and well-appointed buildings can be identified in the Roman provinces we cannot automatically assume that the same slave-powered system of production aimed at producing wine and other foods as a cash crop was instituted throughout the empire. The kind of estate described by the ancient authors and excavated at Settefinestre originated in a set of historical and cultural circumstances which included a wealthy élite competing for status and political power in Rome, a ready supply of slaves from military conquests, the environmental conditions in central Italy, a market for wine in Rome, Italy and the western provinces, and a cultural climate which idealized and valued rural life but not an individual's freedom from slavery.

A Roman senator in the early empire, for example Pliny the Younger (*c.* AD 61–114), was participating in the prevalent élite culture by owning a country estate in Italy rather than owning it simply to provide a profitable economic return. Elsewhere, in Baetica or Africa Proconsularis for example, the economic imperatives were different. Although there were no doubt slave-run private and imperial estates in the provinces, the driving force in the economy was not fuelling the élite in Rome, but supplying the army and people of Rome with food as well as paying imperial taxes and maintaining a local urban infrastructure and local political activities. People living in the provinces, with lower social status than the élite in Rome, were probably more concerned at meeting the demands of the tax collector and hoping to profit enough from their produce to be able to emulate their social superiors and at least raise the outward appearance of their status. This model could apply to colonists from Italy, who would have had every reason to establish *their* way of living as opposed to the customs of the indigenous peoples, and to represent *their own* economic success in the form of Roman material culture and buildings. It could equally apply to indigenous élites who could preserve their status by associating themselves with the dominant political and cultural force by participating in the Roman economy.

In the case of southern Spain, and indeed north Africa, it is possible to see how the mechanism of supplying the central city of Rome and the army, through taxation in kind along with requisition without payment and market-based exchange, led to the development of an agricultural economy which did not operate in isolation. The province of Baetica produced large quantities of olive oil because it could do so, and could also find a guaranteed market in the city of Rome. The strategy of growing olives to pay taxes and exactions, as well as make a profit to invest in developing a dense pattern of urban settlement in Baetica, was bound to the fact that the province was operating within the context of the larger Mediterranean world that was the Roman empire (see Essay Eight). Indeed, the very possibility of participating in inter-regional exchange, and the fact that the city of Rome and the army depended on receiving produce from the provinces, can be seen as a form of economic power that effectively shaped agricultural practice and the generation of wealth in the province. And so just as in Italy the economic organization of these provinces can be seen as contingent on a wide set of cultural, political, social and historical circumstances.

This configuration brings into question the nature of the economic relationship between the centre of the empire in Rome and its periphery. We can ask, was the periphery (such as Baetica) being exploited by the centre because its agricultural produce was taxed and requisitioned? Or was the centre providing the periphery with a market place which enabled the establishment of a veritable agro-industry producing olive oil that could enrich the provincial population? Questions of exploitation depend on the viewpoint of the observer: a slave tending an olive grove may well have been exploited or oppressed by the state or landowner, but from the point of view of an oil dealer the demands of the state provided plenty of opportunity for profit and exploitation of the wealth of the city of Rome. On a broader scale, the province of Baetica may well have been exploited by the imperial administration, extracting oil to feed and illuminate the army, but then the army was also protecting Baetica from raiding barbarians and ensuring the stability required for economic activity. Ultimately, the state and city of Rome existed in a symbiotic relationship with productive provinces like Baetica or Africa Proconsularis, and both the central city and the peripheral province benefited from the economic ties that bound them.

If we can see economic connections between Rome and the provinces on the broad scale of inter-regional exchange, we can also see it on a small scale with the import and export of tableware between Italy and the provinces. We can also see this trade as evidence of participation in Roman culture, with tableware bearing quintessentially classical decoration and made in Italy being used around much of the western Mediterranean and continental Europe. This style of tableware is then reproduced in provincial workshops as local economies become integrated with the wider Roman economy, and can reach markets and trade routes which were previously inaccessible. As discussed above, the Roman economy can be seen as one of the channels through which Roman culture and identity spread to the provinces of the empire. Participating in that economy as a consumer, a trader or a producer can also be seen as participating in the Roman world.

The production and exchange of commodities such as foodstuffs, often over a long distance, and the transference of models for particular commodities such as tableware or wine amphorae, are characteristics of the Roman economy, and this economy functioned within the context of the Roman empire in its geographical and environmental setting. The fact of political unity combined with the distribution of population and variability of the Mediterranean growing season made the organized trade in foodstuffs both possible and necessary. Further indirect effects of Roman rule were more unified legal and monetary systems, peace, roads, exposure to strong centralizing Roman culture and, at yet another remove, the economic demands created by urbanization, all of which added to the potential for wide-ranging networks of production, exchange and consumption to develop through the Roman world. Within these networks it is possible to see identity, culture and power in operation.

References

BARKER, G. (1995) *A Mediterranean Valley: Landscape Archaeology and* Annales *History in the Biferno Valley*, London, Leicester University Press.

CARANDINI, A. (1984) *Settefinestre. Una Villa Schiavistica nell'Etruria Romana*, Modena, Pannini.

CARANDINI, A. (1985) *La Romanizzazione dell'Etruria: il Territorio di Vulci*, Milan, Electa Editrice.

CARANDINI, A. (1988) *Schiavi in Italia. Gli Strumenti Pensanti dei Romani fra Tarda Repubblica e Medio Impero*, Rome, La Nuova Italia Scientifica.

CARANDINI, A. and SETTIS, S. (1979) *Schiavi e Padroni nell'Etruria Romana*, Bari, De Donato Editore.

CORBIER, M. (1983) '*Fiscus* and *Patrimonium*: the Saepinum inscription and transhumance in the Abruzzi', *Journal of Roman Studies*, LXXIII, pp.126–31.

FINLEY, M.I. (1979) *The Ancient Economy*, London, Chatto & Windus.

FÜLLE, G. (1997) 'The internal organisation of the Arretine *terra sigillata* industry: problems of evidence and interpretation', *Journal of Roman Studies*, 87, pp.111–55.

GARNSEY, P. and SALLER, R. (1987) *The Roman Empire: Economy, Society and Culture*, London, Duckworth.

HAYES, J.W. (1997) *Handbook of Mediterranean Roman Pottery*, London, British Museum Press.

JONES, A.H.M. (1974) *The Roman Economy*, London, Basil Blackwell.

LEWIS, N. and REINHOLD, M. (eds) (1990) *Roman Civilization: Selected Readings. Volume II The Empire* (third edition), New York, Columbia University Press.

PEACOCK, D.P.S AND WILLIAMS, D.F. (1986) *Amphorae and the Roman Economy: an Introductory Guide*, Harlow, Longman.

PERCIVAL, J. (1976) *The Roman Villa*, London, Batsford.

PURCELL, N. (1988) 'Review of Tchernia and Carandini (eds)', *Journal of Roman Studies*, 78, pp.194–8.

RATHBONE, D.W. (1996) 'The imperial finances' in A.K. Bowman, E. Champlin and A. Lintott (eds) *The Cambridge Ancient History* (second edition), vol. 10, Cambridge, Cambridge University Press.

REMESAL RODRÍGUEZ, J. (1986) *La* Annona Militaris *y la Exportación de Aceite Bético a Germania, con un Corpus de Sellos de Ánforas Dressel 20 Halladas en Nimega, Colonia, Mainz, Saalburg, Zugmantel y Nida.* Madrid, Editorial de la Universidad Complutense.

REMESAL RODRÍGUEZ, J. (1995) 'El sistema annonario como base de la evolución económica del Imperio romano', *PACT,* 27, 1990, pp.355–67.

RICKMAN, G. (1980) *The Corn Supply of Ancient Rome,* Oxford, Clarendon Press.

RIGBY, V. (1973) 'Potters' stamps on *Terra Nigra* and *Terra Rubra* found in Britain', in A. Detsicas (ed.) *Current Research in Romano-British Coarse Pottery,* CBA Research Report 10, London, Council for British Archaeology, pp.7–24.

ROSTOVETZEFF, M. (1957) *The Social and Economic History of the Roman Empire,* vol.I, Oxford, Clarendon Press.

Essay Eight
Urbanism and urbanization in the Roman world

BY PHIL PERKINS AND LISA NEVETT

In antiquity the term city (Latin *urbs* or *civitas* or Greek *polis* or *asty*) carried with it a range of assumptions about the settlements to which it referred. A striking example of this is a passage in which Pausanias, writing in Greek during the second century AD, describes the city of Panopaeus in Phocis (central Greece):

> if you can even give the name city to those which have no civic buildings, no gymnasium, no theatre and no market, and no water coming down to a fountain; and the inhabitants live in bare shelters like mountain huts, on the edge of a ravine. All the same, there are boundaries marking off their territory from those of their neighbours, and they send their own representatives to the assembly of Phocis.
>
> (Pausanias, *Guide to Greece* 10.4.1–4)

For Pausanias there were clearly two factors which were key indicators of a settlement's urban status: the first was the provision of a range of public buildings which enhanced its appearance and offered amenities to the inhabitants. These buildings are readily identifiable through archaeological work across the Roman world today, and they constituted the physical setting for the life of the city. But a second, equally important element was the way in which the city related politically to the outside world, possessing a clearly defined territory of its own and participating in regional politics. In the case of Panopaeus the settlement's territory and political status confirmed its urban identity, even though it lacked what Pausanias regarded as the outward signs of urban culture.

Ancient authors frequently considered cities to be centres of learning and culture, and a prerequisite for a civilized society (for example, Tacitus, *Annals* 2.52). The civilizing influence of cities was noted in the first century AD by Strabo, who wrote of the Allobroges, a tribe in central France:

> Once, the Allobroges had tens of thousands of men under arms. Today they farm the plains and valleys of the Alps ... and some live in villages, while the most important stay in Vienne. This was once a village, although it was called the capital of the tribe, and they have made it a town.
>
> (Strabo, *Geography* 4.1.11)

This passage introduces the idea that there were close ties between population, territoriality, agriculture and urbanism. Like Pausanias, Strabo believed that a territory was an important and defining part of a city, and he considered that the city acted as a centre for a people. In addition, Strabo indicates that the élite of the tribe lived in the city. The passage also introduces the binary opposition of 'absence of city = savagery, war and unsettled times' and 'city = peace and civilization' (Goudineau, 1980, pp.66–7). This opposition of savagery and Roman civilization devalues the degree of social and political development in the indigenous 'savage' societies, but this attitude towards the 'barbarian' was typical of classical élite culture. The association of the city with civilization was also an assertion that the Roman way of living – in cities – was superior to a 'barbarian' way of life in villages. Another ancient author, Tacitus, showed an awareness of the way in which the foundation of new cities in areas which were previously not urbanized – in this case Britain – led to the promotion of Roman culture:

> And so that these savage, unsettled and warlike people would become accustomed to the pleasures of peace and leisure, Agricola encouraged them ... to build temples, law courts and houses ... And so the population gradually fell into the seductive vices of arcades, baths, and sumptuous banquets. This was called culture [*humanitas*] by the ignorant, while it was actually part of their enslavement.
>
> (Tacitus, *Agricola* 2.21)

An integral part of civilization is good government, and in the Roman empire the city was the seat of government. In theory each city and its people had its own city council (*boule* in Greek) and an oligarchic ruling class (*ordo* in Latin) from which magistrates and officials were selected. The origin and culture of the élite who constituted this urban ruling class clearly would have had an influence on the development and character of the city. If they were established urban dwellers with hundreds of years of urban tradition behind them, as in the Greek east, they would have had a different attitude and traditions from the newly conquered tribal leaders of Gaul. This would have been manifested in their image of both what a city might be like and how it should function politically. It might be expected that an area with ancient urban traditions would have been more conservative in its adoption of overtly Roman models, whereas a society encountering urban life for the first time might more readily have adopted Roman customs and urban forms. However, as highlighted in the extract from Pausanias, urbanism was not solely concerned with the physical structure of the city and the activities of its citizens, but also influenced the wider political role of the community.

In the political and administrative sphere the Roman empire was built from cities. Cities controlled and administered the territory around them, and together those territories formed the provinces of the empire. Each province had a capital where the provincial governor performed military, judicial and administrative duties, and this was the primary point of contact between Roman imperial rule and the élites of the cities and territories which constituted the provinces. The empire itself, as a collection of provinces, had its capital in Rome, the ultimate source of government. Thus the cities provided a framework through which the empire was governed. Theoretically there was a hierarchy of status of cities relating to the legal rights and privileges of the inhabitants (for example, tax exemptions). In this hierarchy, Rome was at the top, followed by provincial capitals, *coloniae, municipia, civitates,* and finally *oppida* at the lower end.

Originally the definition of a *colonia* was straightforward, since it was a colony of Romans or Latins who were sent from Rome to build a city and settle in newly conquered areas, as for example at Cosa or Alba Fucens founded in 273 BC in central Italy (Map 3). Later the *colonia* became a settlement founded for soldiers who received citizenship and land upon retirement: thus, a city like Aosta in the Alps was founded in the time of Augustus for veteran Praetorian Guards and formed a Roman settlement of people who had received a military training in the conquered lands of the Salassi, an indigenous tribe. Aosta was founded on virgin territory but other colonies could be created in pre-existing centres, such as Nîmes, Colonia Augusta Nemausus, also known as Nemausum Arecomicorum – that is, Nemausus of the Arecomici tribe in southern France (Map 2). These cities received the status of *colonia* as a result of either the circumstances of their original foundation or the resettlement of veterans or citizens in existing towns. Through the second and third centuries the nature of the title changed so that it could also be achieved: thus, a community might acquire promotion to the status of *colonia* by virtue of its prestige or imperial benefaction rather than the circumstances of its foundation.

The definitions of other levels in the hierarchy of cities also changed with time. Originally a *municipium* was a self-governing community allied to Rome whose citizens had rights equal to those of the citizens of Rome. Later, in the empire, it became an honorific title indicating high status. *Oppida* were lesser towns, as were the *civitates* – a term which could also be used for a people as well as cities. Although it was generally the larger towns with the most amenities and facilities which were the *coloniae* and *municipia,* it is not possible to equate directly the size or the number of public buildings with the legal status or title of a city. Very often the status of a city has been identified through inscriptions or from references in ancient authors, but in some cases the status remains uncertain.

In addition to the literary and epigraphic sources, we also have archaeological evidence for the nature of the physical fabric of the Roman city. In some cases Roman public buildings have survived: for example, the basilica in Pompeii or the Colosseum in Rome. Others have not survived so well, but there are excavated remains of parts of hundreds of Roman cities from around the empire, some extremely well preserved as at Pompeii, Ostia or Timgad in Algeria. In some cities which have been continuously occupied, features of the Roman city, such as the street plan, are preserved in the modern streets even if the ancient buildings are no more. Studies of the remains of Roman cities have frequently focused upon monumental buildings such as theatres, temples or baths, but more recently attention has been paid to domestic buildings and also to the territories of cities, for example at Cosa (Brown, 1980; Carandini, 1985) and Tarraco (Carreté et al., 1996). Such studies have revealed similarities in the buildings which are found in Roman cities and have enabled the construction of models of an 'ideal Roman city' which can then be used as a standard against which to compare actual cities (Goudineau, 1980, p.67). So, for example, a Roman city will typically have a forum as a market place and focus for urban activities. Close to this will be a basilica for justice and administration, a *curia* (city council building), and a large temple. Roman cities also often contained a market building, a theatre, an amphitheatre, a circus and public baths. Many cities had fortification walls and aqueducts. Although Roman cities may share a range of buildings and amenities, each one did not necessarily have all of the buildings listed. Some buildings are more common in different parts of the empire: amphitheatres are frequent in Italy and Gallia Narbonensis but rare in the east; theatres are widespread but particularly common in Gaul and rare in Britain. Even if the same building types performing the same social and civic functions recur, the details of the building design and decoration are always different. Also the position in the city and the relationships between different buildings constantly varied. Some generalizations may be attempted, such as amphitheatres are often on the edges of cities, but they may also be found close to the forum as at Paestum or Amiens. The basilica and *curia* are almost invariably found in close proximity to the forum.

The fact that Roman cities in widely separated geographical regions of the empire tend to contain a similar range of structural elements – such as roads, walls, temples, theatres, baths and other public buildings – can be taken as an example of the unity of the Roman empire. The presence of such features has often been seen as marking the spread of a distinctively Roman culture across the empire, so as territories are taken into the empire Roman structural elements may be seen to appear in settlements (Millett, 1990, pp.69–103). The degree of closeness to a notional 'ideal' city might be taken as an indication of the degree to which Roman customs and traditions were accepted in new territories. Attractive as this idea is, it is limited by the fact that it concentrates upon the monumental remains of the city and the supposition that there was such a thing as an 'ideal' or even 'typical' Roman city. Nevertheless, it is possible to see the buildings as elements which recur in different combinations in Roman cities throughout Italy and the provinces, and as symbols of Roman culture and government which would instantly be recognizable to visitors upon entering a strange city. An active role for the public buildings of the Roman city is also suggested by the first-century author Vitruvius, who states that 'the majesty of the empire was also expressed through the eminent dignity of its public buildings' (*On Architecture* 1, Preface 2).

So far we have been considering the city as an exclusively Roman phenomenon, but attention should also be given to historical precedents – for example, the Greek city – and to the contribution made by the indigenous cultures of various provinces to the process of creating Roman culture (Woolf, 1995, 1997, 1998). In many areas of the empire cities existed before the Roman conquest, and Roman elements may be thought of as additions to and developments of the pre-existing urban order. In other areas where there was not a strong pre-Roman urban tradition, we should perhaps consider how much the city was a Roman imposition and how much the indigenous societies contributed to the formation and development of the city. These issues can be approached through the study of the material remains themselves and also the social contexts within which they were built, since the city constituted a location where local élites might demonstrate their social status and mobility, identity, cultural values and political loyalties (Veyne, 1990).

In the sections which follow, we investigate the extent to which such a two-way process of acculturation is visible in the creation and history of urban culture by exploring examples from a selection of different regions of the early empire. We look for Roman and indigenous traditions in the urban history of several regions in order to investigate this process. We focus in particular on the creation of new cities and the appearance of Roman elements in the cityscape, and look at examples of cities within their regional contexts in order to explore some of the factors which contributed to the formation of urban culture and identity. The cities we shall discuss developed, or were founded, in different social and political contexts. Regardless of their geographical location, the development of these cities, or rather networks of cities with their associated settlement patterns, can be situated in the context of a dialogue between Roman and non-Roman social, cultural and political traditions. If we polarize the issues, Roman cities were either set in areas which had an earlier urban civilization or set in areas which were not previously urbanized. In some areas of western Asia Minor, for example, Roman cities were set against a background of a long-established urban system consisting of city states (self-governing cities controlling a territory), typically the Greek *polis*, while other parts of the region were more tribal and less urbanized. This forms the first of our examples. In the second example different areas of Gaul will be considered. In the south, bordering the Mediterranean, indigenous society already displayed some manifestations of urbanism when Roman control of the area was developing, and there was a long tradition of contact with Greek colonial urbanism. Following the Roman conquest many of these settlements became Roman colonies. In the north and west Roman cities were the first manifestations of urbanism in tribal areas, and the Roman cities are the beginning of urban history. Here we can think of Roman urbanization as a new phenomenon rather than as resulting from a transformation of pre-existing settlements and societies.

However, Roman urbanism was not simply determined by pre-existing conditions but had its own dynamic force. It is possible to see different processes of urbanization at work. These range from overt colonization, where settlers moved into an area and brought with them Roman institutions and models of urbanism, to a more gradual development of urban living with a less strong Roman influence. A combination of these different processes can be seen in our first example, Asia Minor.

Urban culture and identity in Asia Minor

The western coast of Asia Minor was home to a flourishing urban culture which developed following the arrival of Greek colonists from early in the first millennium BC. Cities were the centre of political and cultural life and the focus of a strong sense of local identity. At various times during the second and early first centuries BC these cities and their territories fell under Roman control. Their value to Rome was considerable since the territories of many cities included land rich in agricultural potential and in mineral resources. The coastal locations of many of these cities meant that they played a significant role in long-distance maritime trade, and their integration into these trading networks meant that they were exposed to a variety of cultural influences, some of which were adopted while others were not. Equally, communication was a two-way process, and the role of these cities as trading centres and providers of income is likely to have meant that influence also passed from this region to other parts of the empire.

The effects of Roman control on these cities can be observed indirectly through textual sources and also more directly, both through the changes made to the architecture and organization of the urban centres themselves, and from the inscriptions and coins they produced. In general terms, it seems that the approach Rome took was to insert itself into the pre-existing civic administrative framework (Garnsey and Saller, 1987, p.26). One indication of the extent to which urban culture was affected by Roman domination is the adoption of the emperor cult (Price, 1984). At Pergamum (Map 4) a temple to Rome and Augustus was erected as early as 29 BC, and although its exact location is now unknown, parallels with other cities in the region suggest that it is likely to have occupied a prominent position in the civic centre (Price, 1984, pp.56, 136). The overall effect was a fusion of local Greek with wider imperial culture, and this interweaving of different cultural traditions is visible in the urban landscapes of many cities, where public buildings of Roman date stand alongside the monumental structures of the Hellenistic period. At Ephesus, for instance, a temple to Augustus was placed in the centre of one of the city's two squares (Price, 1984, pp.139–40), while a later temple to Domitian must effectively have dominated the nearby *bouleuterion* (council building) and *prytaneion* (magistrates' offices) through its sheer size and monumentality (Friesen, 1993, pp.59–73). These and the other new buildings, at Ephesus and elsewhere, were distinctive in their adoption of Roman architectural styles, and the eclectic mixture of structures which had accumulated through time was given a new appearance and a sense of architectural unity by another Roman architectural device, the use of colonnaded streets, which linked the various buildings lying behind them. The effect of these developments must have been to change radically the appearance of the city centre.

During the earlier centuries of Roman rule, then, the civic landscapes of Ephesus and other Greek cities along the west coast of Asia Minor were partially transformed so that they came in some respects to resemble the cities of other provinces of the empire. Nevertheless, this does not mean that local culture was lost or that local identities were forgotten. At Ephesus the traditional Artemis cult continued to be popular and flourished alongside the cult of the emperor: for example, in a lengthy inscription dating to the early second century AD, Salutaris, a local benefactor, laid down conditions for a procession in Artemis' honour, in which her image was to be carried alongside busts of the emperor (Rogers, 1991). Other traditions also seem to have survived from earlier centuries until well into the period of Roman rule. This is illustrated by the frieze of uncertain date ultimately displayed on a temple to the emperor Hadrian which stood on the city's main street, but originally came from another location (Thür, 1995). The frieze shows the city's patron goddess, Artemis, along with a reminder of the city's mythical past – its legendary Greek founder Androclus.

A different pattern of cultural interaction is found in the continent's vast interior, away from Asia Minor's western shores. (For comprehensive treatment of the nature of settlement and society in much of this area, and of the impact of Roman rule, see Mitchell, 1993, vol.1.) In the region of Pisidia, for example, the landscape is rough and mountainous, and some areas are relatively inaccessible even today. Here, although there was considerable Greek and Roman influence, a major role in shaping culture was also played by the indigenous people, who seem to have made up the majority of the population, and cities were founded at a later date than on the west coast. This region therefore offers an insight into the phenomenon of urbanization in the context of a triangular relationship between Greek, Roman and indigenous peoples; it also offers an opportunity to study the process of acculturation – and in some instances colonization – in a region which was relatively remote from the main communication networks of the Roman empire.

According to ancient writers many of the inhabitants of Pisidia were lawless, war-like tribes who were governed by tyrannical leaders (Strabo, *Geography* 12.7.3). These tribes seem to have been resistant to outside control, either from the Hellenistic monarchs of the neighbouring regions or subsequently from Rome. (For details of the way in which Rome gradually pacified the area, see Syme, 1995, pp.204–15.) In 6 BC, however, this area was incorporated into the province of Galatia and a number of Roman *coloniae* were established (Jones, 1971, pp.133–4). It has been suggested that Rome operated a deliberate policy of urbanization in this area in order to establish what was viewed as a civilized society and to pacify the indigenous inhabitants (Macro, 1980, p.673).

Despite the unfavourable impression of this area given by the ancient sources, recent archaeological work has shown that the cultures and settlement system of Pisidia were, in fact, relatively complex. A limited number of literary sources together with epigraphic and numismatic evidence suggest that in the Hellenistic period some cities had already been founded in the area, including colonies established by the Seleucid dynasty at Antioch in Pisidia (the subject of recent archaeological investigation – see Mitchell and Waelkens, 1998) and Apollonia. Nevertheless, other parts of the region remained without large urban settlements even after Roman control had been established (Jones, 1940, p.68). Outside the cities much of the population lived in loose tribal groupings (Jones, 1971, p.145), almost untouched by external influence (Bracke, 1993, p.28). Under Roman rule different patterns of development seem to have been followed in different parts of the area: for example, the region of Milyas seems to have been without substantial urban settlements (Jones, 1971, pp.142–3). Similarly, epigraphic evidence reveals that the more northerly settlement, Tymandus, which had been a village, was elevated to the status of *civitas*, probably during the reign of Diocletian in the late third century (Jones, 1971, p.141). In contrast, the city of Pogla further to the south seems to have suffered the opposite fate, losing its status of city during the Roman period (Jones, 1971, p.143).

The overall pattern of settlement organization and political control in the region is therefore one of great diversity, and the process of urbanization and consolidation under Roman domination took a variety of forms in different locations. Recent archaeological research on two particular cities, Cremna and Sagalassus, provides a basis for detailed discussion of two different models of urban formation in the area: at Sagalassus the Hellenistic city continued to flourish into the Roman period, while at Cremna an Augustan colony was imposed upon an earlier settlement.

Sagalassus

Sagalassus came under Roman control in 25 BC (Waelkens, 1993b, p.45). The city was one of the most prominent in Pisidia and seems to have had control of a large territory (Jones, 1971, pp.141–2; Waelkens, 1993b, p.39). The architectural remains, which have been the subject of recent archaeological survey and excavation, reveal that before the arrival of the Romans the city had many of the formal characteristics of a Greek *polis* (Figure 8.1). By the late Hellenistic period the monuments around the civic centre included an agora or market, a *bouleuterion* or council building, and civic and private monuments such as the Doric-style temple and the elaborate heroon or cenotaph (Waelkens, 1993b, pp.42–5). The excavators see the architectural style of some of these structures as being influenced by the architecture of the larger cities of Asia Minor. At the same time, however, the masons who were responsible for decorative mouldings on various public buildings worked in a characteristic local style, giving the buildings a distinctive regional flavour. It therefore appears that during the Hellenistic period Sagalassus was tied into a wider cultural *koine* (network of shared cultural attributes and practices), which may have helped to shape the identity of the city. Sagalassus also seems to have played some role as a regional centre, although it has been debated how far the presence of such buildings indicates that the city was governed in a similar manner to a Greek *polis* (see Bracke, 1993, p.22).

During the imperial period the area covered by the city expanded and numerous new monuments were constructed (Waelkens, 1993b, p.45). From the mid first century onwards, the additions and alterations made

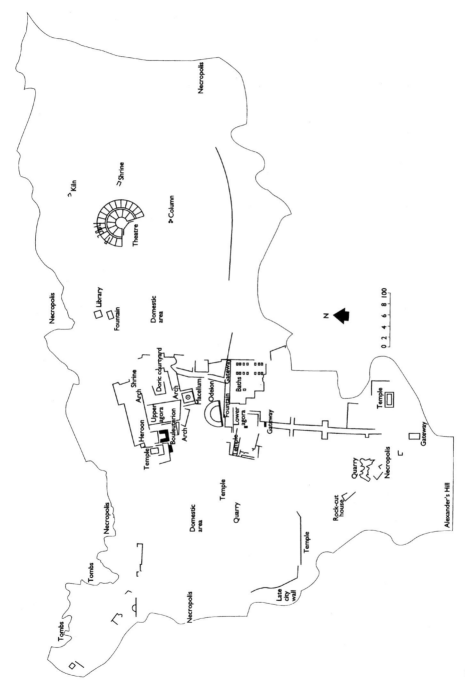

Figure 8.1 Plan of Sagalassus. (Adapted from Waelkens, 1993b, fig.14, p.52)

to the urban environment were influenced by ideas also seen in other parts of the empire. For example, embellishments were made to the upper agora: porticoes were built around the edges of the agora so that it came to resemble city squares (fora) elsewhere in the empire, and new archways were constructed at the entrance which are comparable with the triumphal arches constructed in Rome and some areas of the Roman west during this period (Waelkens, 1993b, p.46; cf. Wallace-Hadrill, 1990). The range of civic amenities was also increased, with the addition of an *odeion* (a covered performance space), and later also a Greek-style theatre, bath house and two temples to the emperor cult (Waelkens, 1993b, pp.46–7).

Although the range of new facilities provided at this time are of a type commonly found in Roman cities across the empire, the decorative style used on many of the monuments continued to feature the vivid floral motifs which had been characteristic of the local Hellenistic building style (Bracke, 1993, pp.26–7). As elsewhere, both in Asia Minor and in the wider empire, this construction activity seems to have been at least partly funded by wealthy local benefactors, like those whose statues – dating from the early to mid first century – have been found in and around the civic centre (Waelkens, 1993b, p.45).

At Sagalassus, then, the architectural evidence reveals a thriving city which was already tied into the wider cultural milieu of the Hellenistic world on the arrival of the Romans. During the early imperial period the civic centre underwent considerable change, with an increase in the number of public buildings and facilities, and this may reflect an increase in the importance of the urban centre relative to its rural hinterland and/or in relation to neighbouring settlements. In some respects the new facilities parallel those constructed at a similar time elsewhere in the empire, and seem to have been funded through a similar mechanism – the patronage of local notables. Nevertheless, at least some of these structures continued to have something of a local flavour, rather than adopting wholesale the styles of decoration common in the larger cities of the empire. It seems that the cultural life of the city continued, and that although changes did take place, Sagalassus managed to retain something of its own identity in the face of Roman influence. This interpretation is supported by the continued minting of coins which bear symbols related to the individual character of the city.

Cremna

The topography of Cremna is known from a recent project which has mapped its surface remains and enabled something of the history of the site to be reconstructed (Mitchell, 1995), although systematic excavation has been limited (Figure 8.2). The rock plateau on which the city stands

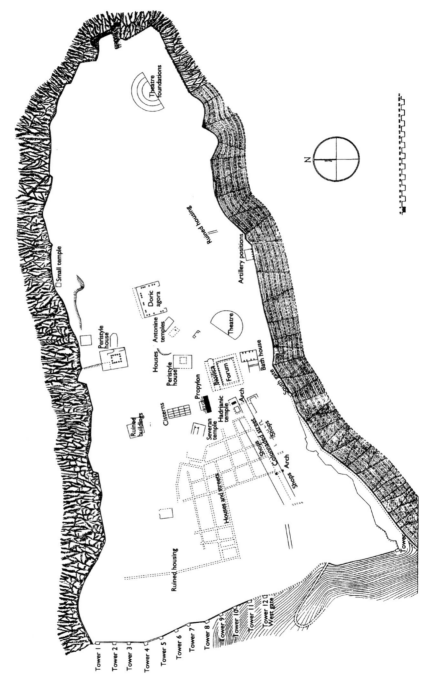

Figure 8.2 Plan of Cremna. (Adapted from Mitchell, 1995; by permission of Duckworth in association with the Classical Press of Wales)

is known to have been settled before the arrival of the Romans: one of
the few references to Cremna in the ancient sources pinpoints this as
the location of a fortress belonging to one of the indigenous groups of
the area (Strabo, *Geography* 12.6.4–5). As Strabo suggests, this was clearly
a stronghold: the city stands on a rocky promontory and the remains of
Hellenistic fortification walls still remain (Mitchell, 1995, pp.46–50).
Nevertheless, this must have been more than simply a military garrison:
the ruins of an early market place have been identified, suggesting that
even by the Hellenistic period there were public amenities comparable
with those of other settlements in the area (Mitchell, 1995, pp.29–41).
Cremna is also known to have minted its own coins at this time
(Mitchell, 1995, pp.44–5). These two facts imply that the location was
occupied by a sizeable community which had the developed political and
cultural life characteristic of a Hellenistic city (Mitchell, 1995, p.33). The
title used for the city in inscriptions shows that it became an Augustan
colony, and Strabo also refers to it as an *apoikia* (colony) (*Geography*
12.6.4).

A remarkable aspect of the refoundation of the city as an Augustan
colony is the apparent lack of any major public buildings datable to the
first century AD (Mitchell, 1995, p.53). Without excavation it is difficult
to be sure of the reason for this, but it has been suggested that the
inhabitants continued to use the civic buildings of the Hellenistic centre
(Mitchell, 1995, pp.53–4), confining new building projects to the
construction of an additional housing area, which in its orthogonal plan
parallels Roman colonies from a number of provinces (Mitchell, 1995,
p.160). Interestingly, an inscribed relief of approximately this date which
probably comes from the site shows that elements of the indigenous
culture continued alongside Greek and Roman influences: the
inscription is in Greek and records a dedication to the Ephesian goddess
Artemis, but among the eight names included on the monument, all but
one seem to be of indigenous origin (Horsley, 1992, p.128).

It was not until the reign of Hadrian that widespread construction of
Roman-style public buildings seems to have taken place at Cremna, with
the laying out of a monumental forum and basilica which are very
similar in plan to the larger forum and basilica at Cyrene (Libya) and to
similar complexes in the north-western provinces of the empire
(Ballance and Ward-Perkins, 1958; Mitchell, 1995, p.68). The date of the
structure is confirmed by an inscription dedicating the building to the
emperor Hadrian (*Corpus Inscriptionum Latinarum* 3.6874). At this period
the city centre was also transformed by the construction of the type of
colonnaded street mentioned above as a typically Roman feature.

At Cremna, then, present evidence suggests that far from
transforming the Hellenistic city, the advent of Roman control left the
urban environment relatively unchanged, and it was only two centuries

later that buildings of a characteristically Roman design began to appear in the civic centre and to transform it into a recognizable Roman city, emulating developments taking place in urban centres elsewhere in the empire.

During the second century, the appearance of structures like the forum and basilica – which reflect Roman ideology and in some cases were actually dedicated to the emperor – suggests that Cremna became visibly and symbolically tied in to the culture of the wider empire. Furthermore, the period at which this investment was made in the civic facilities of the city parallels a widespread pattern of new investment in major building projects which took place in a variety of cities during the reign of Hadrian. The practice of private patronage, which was especially prominent elsewhere in the Roman world during this period, appears to have funded the construction of a number of other new buildings in the civic centre that are dated to this period on stylistic grounds (Mitchell, 1995, pp.85–8). None the less, in their style the forum and basilica did not fully live up to these aspirations: the traditional Doric order which governed their construction and decoration was much plainer than the new, more elaborate styles being used in the coastal cities of Asia Minor and in other cities throughout the empire (Mitchell, 1995, p.63).

In sum, these examples give a brief glimpse of some of the diversity of urban settlements in Asia Minor during the Roman period, ranging from small, relatively isolated cities such as Cremna to large, cosmopolitan centres like Ephesus. They also cover a number of different processes of incorporation into the Roman world, involving varying amounts of reorganization of the pre-existing settlement patterns and of the cultural and political systems which went with them. Cremna and Sagalassus exemplify different policies on the part of Rome: one a colony, the other subject to less direct Roman interference. Although more archaeological work will clarify the situation, current evidence suggests that there is an important difference between Cremna and Sagalassus. Perhaps surprisingly, despite its status as an official *colonia*, it is Cremna which seems to have been slower to take on some of the physical characteristics of a Roman city. A possible explanation for this lies in the relative roles of the two settlements in pre-Roman times, when Sagalassus seems to have been a major regional centre able to draw on an extensive hinterland. If this situation continued into the period of Roman rule, the wealth provided by the city's hinterland may have enabled the occupants of Sagalassus to remodel their civic centre. This scenario emphasizes the extent to which urban development under Roman rule is likely to have been influenced by the pre-Roman settlement structure, and reinforces the point made by the passage of Pausanias quoted at the start of this essay that a gulf may exist between the official status of a city and its physical appearance and facilities.

In the longer term, however, a similar form of urban culture seems ultimately to have developed. The material remains of these cities indicate that several centuries after Roman arrival in the area, they retained their own local culture and identity which coexisted alongside, and to some extent fused with, other elements introduced by the Romans. In both locations Greek seems to have continued to be commonly used, and this is reflected by epigraphic finds from elsewhere in the region: even where Roman titles are given, such as to magistrates, these are expressed in Greek (for example, the inscription from Cretopolis cited by Mitchell, 1994, pp.133–4). It is therefore evident that the processes taking place represented a complex mixture of adoption of some cultural traits and retention of others. The ultimate result was that although in some respects these cities resembled their counterparts in other provinces of the empire, they also maintained their own unique features and the adoption of Roman forms of urbanism was sometimes a gradual process.

Similar transformations may be observed in other provinces. For example, in Africa Proconsularis the pre-Roman, Numidian city of Dougga (Thugga) was well established by 46 BC when the area came under Roman control (Map 2). The settlement received a community of Roman citizens (*pagus*) who lived alongside the Numidians (the *civitas*). During the 30s AD a temple to Caesar was built by a local notable who also built a forum. Various temples were constructed, including those dedicated to Concordia and Roman Minerva, and a market was built by a member of the Roman community. During the second century the pace of building work increased, and among many other structures the city received a capitol, a theatre, temples and a porticoed square. In the reign of Marcus Aurelius the city received the title *Civitas Aurelia*, indicating imperial favour. In the third century a circus and more temples were added along with a triumphal arch to commemorate the granting of the title of *municipium* by Septimius Severus; a bath building and another arch followed, along with more temples. In the reign of Gallienus (261–8) the title of *colonia* was achieved. This gradual accretion of Roman-style buildings transformed the city, but much of the earlier street plan and some of the city walls survived. Virtually all of the building in Dougga was paid for by the local élite, and it is through their donations in the first, second and third centuries that the city developed a range of buildings and amenities typical of cities in Roman Africa and elsewhere in the empire, and eventually achieved the highest civic status (Duncan-Jones, 1990, pp.178–81).

Roman power, urban culture and indigenous identity in Gaul: transition

In the south-eastern parts of France on the shores of the Mediterranean, there was a developing urban tradition before the Roman conquest of the area in the latter part of the second century BC. According to the classical authors a Greek colony was founded at Massilia (Marseilles) in 600 BC and other satellite settlements followed, for example at St Blaise, Olbia and at Glanum (St Rémy de Provence) (Goudineau et al., 1980, pp.76–7; King, 1990, pp.11–25). To the west in Languedoc, the Greek influence was less marked and indigenous peoples occupied fortified hilltops, which had many of the characteristics of urban centres including planned streets, fortifications with towers, and public and sacred buildings. Examples of these settlements include Nages, Nîmes, Entremont, Ambrussum and Ensérune (Goudineau and Kruta, 1980; Février, 1973; Woolf, 1998, pp.106–12).

Probably in 118 BC a colony, the first to be built outside of Italy, was founded at Narbo, near to a pre-existing hilltop settlement at Montlaurès (Map 2). The new city and its Italian inhabitants became a focus of trade between Gaul and Italy (King, 1990, pp.35–9), but seems to have co-existed peacefully with the neighbouring settlement, which continued to be inhabited until the end of the first century BC. The only other new Roman settlement known to have been founded in this period was Aquae Sextiae (Aix-en-Provence), following the destruction of the pre-Roman settlement at Entremont, but its status and importance are not clear. This limited evidence indicates that there was not a widespread founding of Roman cities and massive influx of settlers in this period. It may be that the relatively sophisticated network of settlements already performed many of the functions of Roman cities, and so new settlements were not necessary to administer and control the newly conquered province. Nevertheless Italian, or rather Italo-Greek, influence can be detected in some of the indigenous settlements. For example, some houses at Ensérune and Glanum built around 100 BC show a ground plan very similar to contemporary houses at Pompeii, with rooms arranged around an atrium and/or peristyle (Figure 8.3) (Rolland, 1946, pp.78–104; Goudineau and Kruta, 1980, pp.187–9). At the same time these indigenous settlements also began to use Roman-style material culture – for example, black gloss pottery and amphorae containing Italian wine.

The details of the transition from the pre-Roman to the Roman settlement pattern during the first century BC are not clear, but a hierarchy of cities does seem to have been developing in southern France, particularly at the time when Julius Caesar was conquering the north and west of Gaul and in the reign of Augustus. During this period

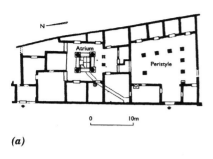
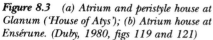
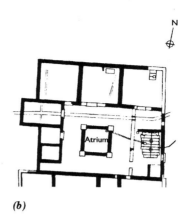

(a)

Figure 8.3   *(a) Atrium and peristyle house at*
Glanum ('House of Atys'); (b) Atrium house at
Enserune. (Duby, 1980, figs 119 and 121)   *(b)*

a number of colonies were established, particularly along the Rhône
valley and the shores of the Mediterranean. These colonies were of
different types. Some had Roman legal rights – these were mainly the
sites where veteran soldiers or civilian citizens were settled. Other
settlements received only the lesser Latin legal rights (*oppida Latina*).
Pliny the Elder (*Natural History* 4.36), writing before AD 79, provides the
names of twenty-nine such settlements. Most are in the form of a city
name and the name of the tribe it belonged to, e.g. Nemausum
Arecomicorum (Nemausus of the Arecomici), and eleven of them
received the title of *colonia* at some point (Goudineau et al., 1980,
pp.91–3). The boundaries and city territories were probably laid down
creating a network of cities in 27 BC, the year that Augustus visited the
province. The gradual development of a settlement pattern consisting of
settlements with a Roman appearance and legal status, whose citizens
had legal rights, can be further illustrated by looking in detail at the
archaeological remains of one of the major cities: Nemausum
Arecomicorum – modern Nîmes.

Nemausum Arecomicorum – Nîmes

Nîmes lies on the slopes of a hill overlooking the coastal plain to the
west of the mouths of the Rhône (Figure 8.4). The modern town is in
the same location as the Roman city and the pre-Roman oppidum. (An
oppidum is an archaeological term for a hilltop pre-Roman Iron Age
fortified settlement or hill-fort, whereas an *oppidum* (pl. *oppida*) is a Latin
term for a lower-status urban settlement.) The town is dominated by a
hilltop upon which sits a Roman tower surviving to 33 metres tall, known
as the Tour Magne, which is visible from afar. The tower is faced with
well-cut ashlar limestone and the main part is octagonal in shape (Figure
8.5). The upper part has four Tuscan pilasters on each face, and above

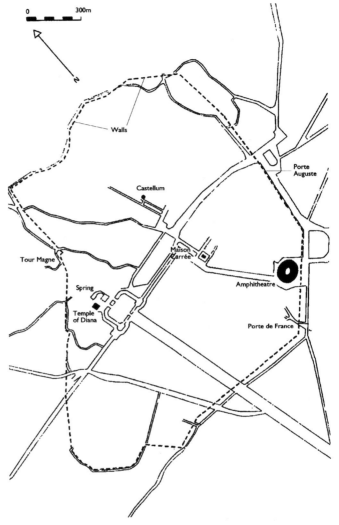

Figure 8.4 *Plan of Nemausum (Nîmes). Roads shown are modern.*
(Adapted from Duby, 1980, fig.172)

this was originally another story faced with engaged columns.[1] The
Tuscan architectural order is typically Italian, and the monument looks
as if it fits in with a Roman tradition of building monuments at
significant landscape features, for example, the Tropaeum Alpium (La

1 An engaged column is attached to the wall and not free-standing.

Figure 8.5   *Tour Magne, Nîmes. (Photo: Lauros-Giraudon)*

Figure 8.6   *Porte Auguste, Nîmes. (Photo: Bildarchiv Foto Marburg)*

Turbie) or the Summum Pyrenaeum. However, the exterior of the tower conceals a pre-Roman conical tower built of rough stone at least 18 metres tall, which seems to have formed a conspicuous part of the defences of the oppidum that preceded the Roman colony. Here we can see the explicit, physical Romanization of an indigenous landmark which had been built in the third century BC and the replacement of a monument built in the indigenous cultural tradition with a Roman monument displaying Roman cultural features. The date of this Romanization is not certain, but it occurred before 16 BC when Augustus paid for a 6 kilometre circuit of defensive walls and gates around the city of Nemausum (Figure 8.6).

The tall Tour Magne at the top of the hill overlooks a large spring further down the slope. This spring was sacred to the water god Nemausus and next to the pool was a Celtic-style temple (a rectangular room with verandahs on all four sides); nearby was a small theatre. The spring was known for the healing properties of the waters, and the shrine may have functioned in a similar way to the famous Sanctuary of Aesculapius at Pergamum in Asia Minor. A second pool nearby had a platform in its centre and on this was probably an altar. The structures are Augustan in date, and they probably relate to a shrine to the Spirit of Augustus (an Augusteum) and so associate the power of Augustus with the power of the indigenous water god Nemausus (Gros, 1984). The whole sanctuary was surrounded by a rectangular portico, on one side of which was the cult building. So here we have another overt example of Romanization with the appropriation and assimilation of an indigenous healing sanctuary by the construction of a portico and imperial shrine, to give an indigenous holy place a Roman appearance and religious function. However, the shrine was not completely converted into a Roman-style shrine, for the spring itself retained its irregular shape and the Celtic-style temple continued in use by the pool.

The most spectacular monument in the city is the Maison Carrée, an almost perfectly preserved Roman Corinthian temple. The temple was originally built in AD 2–3 and dedicated to Gaius and Lucius, two adopted sons of Augustus who died young. This temple dedicated to deceased members of the imperial family can be seen as an expression of loyalty to Augustus and also as an expression of Romanness. The temple was set in the corner of a new forum, and remains of a *curia* have been found nearby.

Other physical remains which illustrate the development of the Roman city are the well-preserved amphitheatre (Flavian), a circus, baths and an aqueduct (possibly 90s AD). In addition, the major Augustan buildings have an orientation similar to some of the rural tracks and field boundaries in the territory of the city, suggesting a simultaneous reorganization of both the city and the territory.

The city seems first to have received the status of *colonia* at the time of Julius Caesar, but was further enhanced by a colony of veteran soldiers around 30 BC, though there is little evidence for development of the city in this period. None the less, the city does seem to have developed rapidly during the reign of Augustus through imperial patronage: the walls and gates were paid for by Augustus, the temple was dedicated to his sons, the Augusteum was built, Gaius Caesar was a patron of the city, and some of Augustus' other sons also donated buildings (Gros and Torelli, 1988, p.275). The reasons for this intense imperial patronage at Nîmes are not known, but it does illustrate a rapid and far-reaching transformation of the earlier settlement and the creation of a Roman cityscape, even if some of its elements were shaped by pre-Roman features.

Some further processes of transition

An example of a more gradual transformation can be seen at the small town of Glanum, near modern St Rémy-de-Provence (Roth Congès, 1992). Up to the early first century BC a city centre developed with a trapezoidal paved area surrounded by a portico, a council building (*bouleuterion*) in a Greek style, a fortified gate and water shrine, and various other buildings and houses set in an irregular street plan. The trapezoidal court was decorated with columns which extended the traditional form of the Corinthian order by inserting a typically Gallic motif – a severed head – between the volutes of the capitals. During this period several houses were built around colonnaded courtyards in the Hellenistic fashion. The settlement seems to been rebuilt in the middle of the century and to have included a mix of Hellenistic and indigenous cultural elements. One house also had an atrium recalling those at Pompeii (Figure 8.3a). Gradually during the latter part of the first century BC Roman-style buildings began to appear. Perhaps the most impressive monument is a mausoleum in the form of an ornamental tower dedicated to the Julii family in *c.* 30 BC. Slightly later a Roman-style temple was built close to the town centre, and a second was built beside it in the 20s BC. Around 25 BC a bath complex was built to the north of the centre of the settlement. This had a common Hellenistic form, familiar from Pompeii, with hot, warm and cold baths arranged along one side of an open courtyard for exercise (Ward-Perkins, 1981, pp.234–5). The town centre was rebuilt in Roman style in 20 BC, and a forum and basilica were constructed covering the area of the trapezoidal courtyard. These were again rebuilt in AD 15–30, and a *curia* and imperial cult building were built on to the basilica in the Flavian period, replacing the function of the Hellenistic *bouleuterion*. Overall, in the century or so from the time of Julius Caesar, the centre of the town had been completely remodelled and the city transformed from an indigenous settlement with profound Hellenistic influence to a Roman town. However, the city did not flourish: there is little evidence of activity in the second century and it was abandoned by the end of the third century.

Away from the Mediterranean coast and the Rhône valley the network of urban centres becomes much thinner, and the cities are smaller, less monumental and more widely separated. Spectacular amphitheatres, triumphal arches and temples in the classical style become less common in the three remaining provinces of Gaul. That is to say, the individual centres of settlement become less like the ideal of a Roman city. Nevertheless, theatres and amphitheatres are quite common. Their remains may not be as spectacular as those of the south, but that is because they were often built of wood and earthworks and so have not survived as monuments. Another problem with evidence is in the dating of the remains because inscriptions providing dates are not common. The provinces seem to have been administratively organized into tribal groups under Augustus, but there does not seem to have been widespread imperial patronage as seen at Nîmes (Woolf, 1998, pp.126–35).

Bibracte and Augustodunum: radical change

The oppidum (hill-fort) at Bibracte (Le mont Beuvray) was the tribal capital of the Aedui, a powerful tribe dominating a large area of central Gaul and allied to the Romans. During the pre-Roman Iron Age it developed into a hill-fort with earthwork fortifications and gates. In the interior there were an industrial quarter, an area of élite housing (including a house with an atrium) and probably a sanctuary; Julius Caesar wrote that it had a 'forum' (Figure 8.7). It thus had many of the formal attributes of an urban centre, even if their physical form did not match a Roman ideal. Following the establishment of Roman control in the area, this settlement did not develop into the Roman tribal capital city (as at Vienne). A Celtic temple survived on the hilltop, but a new town, Augustodunum (modern Autun), was established nearby in a more accessible location 25 kilometres away. This city does appear to have developed most of the physical attributes of a Roman city – a planned grid of streets, monumental gates, city walls, a theatre, amphitheatre, aqueducts, cult centres and cemeteries outside the walls (Figure 8.8). This discontinuity in location was not caused by warfare or the establishment of a colony. Instead, it seems to have been a matter of moving a centre of political power and providing it with a Romanized setting and title. Although the city was provided by Augustus with a massive wall 6 kilometres long and enclosing an area one-tenth the size

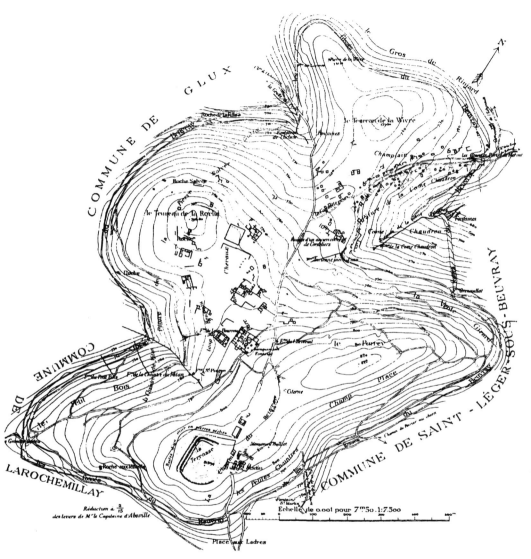

Figure 8.7 *Plan of Bibracte. (Reproduced from* Autun, Augustodunum: capitale des Éduens, *Autun, Musée Rolin;* © *Musée Rolin)*

of Rome, it seems that the development of the buildings was a gradual
process. The walls, gates and streets may have been planned in the
Augustan period, but the theatre, amphitheatre and aqueduct date to
the latter part of the first century AD, and many residential and

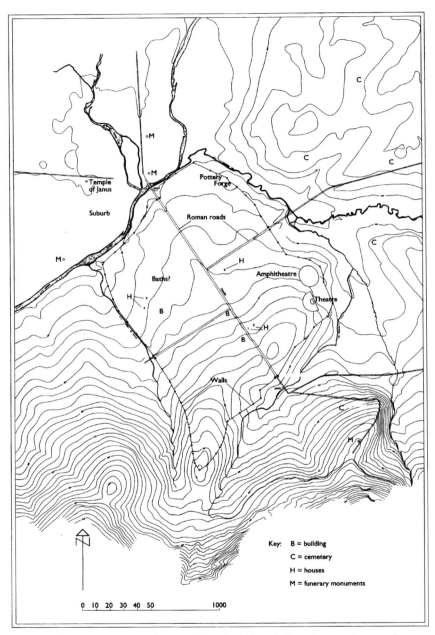

Figure 8.8 *Plan of Augustodunum (Autun). (Adapted from* Autun, Augustodunum: capitale des Éduens, *Autun, Musée Rolin;* © *Musée Rolin)*

industrial parts of the city only seem to have been occupied in this same period. Few of the structures found date to the second century, but many of the sculptures, mosaics and tombstones from the city date to this century, suggesting continued development. The growth may not have continued in the third century, a period of political and economic turmoil in Gaul, and it is possible that the city never grew to fill the area enclosed by its walls (Pinette and Rebourg, 1986; *Autun, Augustodunum*, 1987).

Imposed urbanism in Gallia Belgica

In the most northerly and westerly parts of Gaul there does not seem to have been a strong tradition of urban settlement before the Roman conquest. Following this, development seems to have been slow and gradual. Imperial benefaction and urban development projects by members of a local élite seem to be almost absent. However, urban settlements did occur in a recognizable form. Many settlements have provided evidence for a gridded street plan, indicating some form of planning in their development and the implementation of an ordered model of urban design (King, 1990, pp.3–5). However, they were not founded as colonies, and we know little about the legal or social status of the inhabitants. An example is the city of Bavay, where a grid of eight blocks was laid out *c.* 20 BC covering a tiny area of 8 hectares. Through the first century AD the city developed, and by the end of the century it had a forum, baths, an aqueduct 20 kilometres long, and other, possibly public buildings. The city grew and a further area was developed, with a grid of at least twenty-five new blocks on a different alignment enlarging the area to 40 hectares. In the second century a large forum, temple and basilica complex was built that occupied two city blocks (Figure 8.9). Here these three typical elements of the Roman city appear fused into one architectural block in a pattern similar to other settlements, both in Gallia Belgica (for example, Trier) and elsewhere (such as Paris or Conimbriga in Portugal). The building can be seen as a cultural expression of a typically Roman city-centre complex imposed on a small town. This expression was also powerful since the forum was remarkable for its size: at 98 metres long it was one of the largest in the western empire. However, we do not know why or how such an ambitious development was undertaken: is it a proud expression of local identity, or an imposition of the provincial administration and a show of imperial power? Despite the grandeur of the forum complex, the city remained small and did not flourish (Thollard et al., 1996).

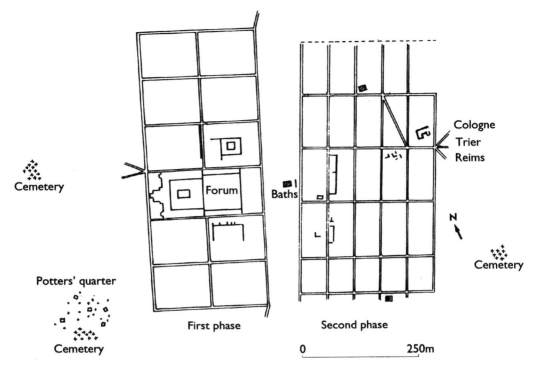

Figure 8.9 *Plan of Bavay. (Adapted from Gros and Torelli, 1994, fig.159)*

The extent of urbanism

So far the examples mentioned have all illustrated the establishment and/or expansion of cities under Roman control. From Asia Minor to Gallia Belgica, the impression we have given is of growing cities either being transformed or being created with Roman-style buildings and urban features. However, this does not provide a complete and balanced picture of the empire as a whole. In some areas the early and mid empire was not a period of urban growth and development. In Sicily, for example, the archaeological record suggests that the first two centuries AD were a period of stagnation and abandonment for many cities in the interior such as Iatas or Morgantina and the smaller coastal cities such as Soluntum or Helorus, even if the major coastal cities like Syracusa or Catania continued to flourish into the fourth century (Wilson, 1990, pp.143–88) (Map 3). One factor in this abandonment may have been that the defensive qualities of the hilltop locations first settled by

Phoenicians and Greeks were not required in the peaceful times of the pax romana (Wilson, 1990, p.188). This cannot, however, be a compelling reason for we have seen examples in other areas, such as Dougga, where a city flourished in an elevated location in a relatively settled area, or at Bibracte and Autun, where a hilltop location was abandoned but a new lowland city established to take its place.

At this point it is as well to note that the city was only one part of the entire Roman settlement pattern and that smaller settlements (*vici*) and rural settlements also existed. In the interior of Sicily it seems that it was this part of the settlement hierarchy which developed rather than the cities (Wilson, 1990, pp.188, 234–6). Presumably the functions of government and administration were continued from the major coastal cities, while the earlier cities lost their political positions and their roles as centres of population.

Sicily, then, provides an example of de-urbanization, and this was not the only alternative trajectory to urban development. In other parts of the empire there is little evidence for significant urban development in any period. In Sardinia, for example, cities do not seem to have developed in the interior, as they did in Sicily during the Archaic and Classical periods. All of the cities seem to have been coastal, and those settlements which were in the interior seem to have been cities in name only. For example, at the Colonia Iulia Augusta Uselis at modern Usullus there is virtually no evidence for monumental public buildings, and most of the people seem to have lived in pre-Roman-style settlements, the *nuraghi* (Dyson, 1992). A similar, or even more minimal, urbanism could also be suggested for northern and western Britain or north-western Spain.

Concluding considerations

By studying the process of urbanization in a number of regions from different parts of the empire, it is clear that the changes taking place in cities were intimately dependent on the local conditions prevailing in different areas, and that urban settlements across the empire were very diverse. It is also apparent that the nature of the pre-existing settlement structure in any one area had a key role to play in determining the form subsequently taken by Roman urban culture in that region. From a broader perspective, viewing Roman cities within their regional contexts and looking at the phenomenon of urban change under Roman rule, it seems that cities were flexible institutions capable of many different forms and of varied processes of development. Furthermore, they were not the only solution to the problem of how the human population could be organized across a landscape (Jones, 1987), since non-urban settlement was a feature of some parts of the Roman empire.

If we acknowledge this diversity, is it possible to identify clearly 'the Roman city' and to use it as an index of the spread of Roman power, culture and identity, and of all the other aspects of life which we might associate with 'Romanization'? Certainly, we can identify a Roman-style forum, basilica or temple in a city, whether in an old-established centre or a new foundation, but can we take this as an indication of similarly 'Roman' social and political institutions existing in the city? There are cities where there is evidence for such institutions – for example, the imperial cult at Nîmes – but we should be careful about over-emphasizing the extent to which Roman culture replaced indigenous culture in all areas of life. The transformations in the early empire were radical, usually including the remodelling of pre-existing city centres by the creation of a new forum and basilica or the establishment of entirely new urban centres in areas which were previously without fully urban settlements. However, it is still possible to see the modification and creation of cities as a gradual process of acculturation which operated in some places faster than others. The new Roman-style buildings, when they appeared, may indicate that the settlements were emulating Roman models in Rome or elsewhere, but other areas of culture and society held more strongly to the pre-Roman traditions, so Celtic temples survived in the cities of Gaul and Greek language and architectural decoration survived in Asia Minor.

Change may have varied in its extent and speed, but the ultimate similarities between settlements in different parts of the empire which followed different developmental trajectories surely reflect the assimilative forces of the Roman empire. Some of these forces – which led to comparable facilities (forum, basilica and capitol) being required by each city as it participated in Roman forms of administration, justice and trade – derive from the imposition of Roman forms of government. But other buildings – such as temples, theatres, amphitheatres, circuses and bath buildings – can be taken as indicative of some level of participation in more general Roman cultural practice. The detailed process of the adoption or acceptance of Roman culture and the extent to which indigenous traditions survived are variable through the empire. The impetus for change also varied. One motivation is the exercise of power, both local and imperial. Take the hypothetical case of a temple dedicated to the imperial cult (an Augusteum) or a forum temple dedicated to the typically Roman Capitoline Triad of Jupiter Optimus Maximus, Juno and Minerva, a frequent and clearly Roman addition to a city. If such temples were donated by members of a local élite, this may be seen, by contemporaries and moderns, as an indication of loyalty to Rome and to imperial power, thereby assimilating local élite power with

Roman power. If, on the other hand, it was donated by the emperor or occupied the physical location of an earlier sanctuary, it may be seen as an expression of Roman power and as assimilating the powers of pre-existing deities. The parallels between imperial and divine power became clearly expressed in the second century, not only at Ephesus as mentioned above, but also more widely. For example, at the city of Dougga the apotheosis of the emperor Antoninus Pius appears in the pediment of the capitoline temple, paid for by a local notable, forging a link between the local élite, the centre of the city, the emperor and the divine.

If it is possible to see the appearance of Roman buildings as an indication of acceptance of Roman power or as expression of that power itself, is it then possible to see the persistence of pre-Roman buildings and institutions as evidence either for resistance or for a lack of Romanization? We have already seen how the development of a Roman city could be a slow and gradual process of accretion, but can the speed of that change be equated with the acceptance or rejection of Roman cultural models? The pace of acculturation would clearly have had its own individual historical circumstances: an agora might continue in use until it was near collapse and then be rebuilt by a city in the form of a Roman forum as a straightforward up-to-date replacement rather than part of a deliberate policy of Romanization. Conversely, a local élite might simply not have the resources to build an amphitheatre for a city, even if there was a desire to emulate the Colosseum. These kinds of considerations might help to inform the understanding of the development of centres such as Cremna. We can readily imagine a 'civilized' and pragmatic transition in areas of the empire with a long urban tradition, but is this possible in newly conquered and previously 'barbaric' areas? It is here that we encounter a more militant aspect of Roman urbanism and the elements of Roman cities are more of an imposition. At Bavay, for example, a preformed set of capitol, forum and basilica was constructed within an imposed grid plan for a city. The framework of streets was laid and the monumental centre created, but we should also ask about what went on around this skeleton of a Roman city.

All too often studies of Roman cities have focused upon public buildings alone, and these have been used to track the development of cities. This, however, needs to be balanced by considering the parallel development of residential, commercial, industrial and even suburban areas. So, for example, at cities such as Pompeii or Ostia large areas of housing are known, whereas in most cities, including the examples discussed here, this evidence is lacking. One result of this has been a general tendency to equate periods of urban development with periods when public buildings were dedicated. If we consider some of our examples, Nîmes seems to have experienced intensive development during the Augustan period, but we have little, if any, information about whether housing and commercial premises also flourished in this period: likewise at Sagalassus and Cremna. At Autun we have some evidence that part of the housing at least developed considerably later than the monumental parts of the city, but we still only have fragmentary evidence and we lack a detailed overall picture. Moving beyond the structural remains of the city, we may also ask to what extent the people who used the Roman city and lived there adopted Roman customs and traditions and how they learned them. Incomers from more 'civilized' parts of the empire or retired soldiers may have settled in new cities, but how 'Roman' were they, with origins potentially far from Rome in Batavia or Syria, even if their urban setting was replete with Roman urban structures? How 'civilized' did they become in their new cities, and how 'civilized' did the indigenous people become? In some areas there is evidence to suggest that the transformation was effective: for Tacitus, Agricola effectively converted the Britons to civil society, and likewise the Allobroges of Vienne. In other areas, such as coastal Asia Minor perhaps, cultural traditions may have been more resilient and Roman features may have taken root more slowly, but generalizations are hazardous. In some parts of the empire cultural fusion and layering of different cultural traits seem to have occurred, as at Cremna with the dedication to Artemis discussed above, or at Dougga where both Numidians and Romans seem to have lived in harmony and built a city with both indigenous and Roman characteristics. Meanwhile, in some more remote areas, city life failed to become established or there was never an attempt to impose it in the first place. It is here, in these parts of the Roman empire, that we encounter the problem of how we study the non-Romanized world from the perspective of Roman classical studies, for if Roman forms of city are absent and Roman authors did not write of them, can we call settlements Roman at all?

References

Autun, Augustodunum: capitale des Éduens (1987) Autun, Musée Rolin.

BALLANCE, M. and WARD-PERKINS, J. (1958) 'The *caesareum* at Cyrene and the basilica at Cremna', *Papers of the British School at Rome*, 26, pp.137–94.

BRACKE, H. (1993) 'Pisidia in Hellenistic times' in Waelkens (ed.).

BROWN, F.E. (1980) *Cosa: the Making of a Roman Town*, Ann Arbor, University of Michigan Press.

CARANDINI, A. (ed.) (1985) *La romanizzazione dell'Etruria: il territorio di Vulci*, Milan, Electa.

CARRETÉ, J.-M., KEAY, S. and MILLETT, M. (1996) 'A Roman provincial capital and its hinterland: the survey of the territory of Tarragona, Spain, 1985–90', *Journal of Roman Archaeology*, Supplementary Series 15.

DUBY, G. (ed.) (1980) *Histoire de la France urbaine, vol.I: La Ville antique dès origines au IXe siècle*, Paris, Seuil.

DUNCAN-JONES, R. (1990) *Structure and Scale in the Roman Economy*, Cambridge, Cambridge University Press.

DYSON, S.L. (1992) 'Roman Sardinia and Roman Britain' in R.H. Tykot and T.K. Andrews, *Sardinia in the Mediterranean: a Footprint in the Sea*, Sheffield, Sheffield Academic Press, pp.484–92.

FÉVRIER, P.A. (1973) 'The origin and growth of the cities of southern Gaul to the third century AD', *Journal of Roman Studies*, LXIII, pp.1–28.

FRIESEN, S. (1993) *Twice Neokoros: Ephesus, Asia and the Cult of the Flavian Imperial Family*, Leiden, Brill.

GARNSEY, P. and SALLER, R. (1987) *The Roman Empire: Economy, Society and Culture*, London, Duckworth.

GOUDINEAU, C. (1980) 'Sources et problèmes' in Duby (ed.), pp.46–69.

GOUDINEAU, C., FÉVRIER, P.A. and FIXOT, M. (1980) 'Le réseau urbain' in Duby (ed.), pp.71–137.

GOUDINEAU, C. and KRUTA, V. (1980) 'Les antécédents: y a-t-il une ville protohistorique' in Duby (ed.), pp.139–231.

GROS, P. (1984) 'L'Augusteum de Nîmes', *Revue Archéologique de Narbonnaise*, 17, pp.123–43.

GROS, P. and TORELLI, M. (1988, third edn 1994) *Storia dell'urbanistica: il mondo romano*, Rome, Laterza.

HORSLEY, G.H.R. (1992) 'The mysteries of Artemis Ephesia in Pisidia: a new inscription', *Anatolian Studies*, 42, pp.119–50.

JONES, A.H.M. (1940) *The Greek City from Alexander to Justinian*, Oxford, Clarendon Press.

JONES, A.H.M. (1971) *Cities of the Eastern Roman Provinces* (second edition), Oxford, Clarendon Press.

JONES, R.F.J. (1987) 'A false start? The Roman urbanisation of western Europe', *World Archaeology*, 19, pp.47–57.

KING, A. (1990) *Roman Gaul and Germany*, Berkeley, University of California Press.

MACRO, A. (1980) 'The cities of Asia Minor under the Roman Imperium', *Aufstieg und Niedergang des Römischen Welt*, vol.II, no.7.2, pp.658–97.

MILLETT, M. (1990) *The Romanization of Britain*, Cambridge, Cambridge University Press.

MITCHELL, S. (1993) *Anatolia: Land, Men and Gods in Asia Minor*, 2 vols, Oxford, Clarendon Press.

MITCHELL, S. (1994) 'Three cities in Pisidia', *Anatolian Studies*, 44, pp.129–48.

MITCHELL, S. (1995) *Cremna in Pisidia: an Ancient City in Peace and in War*, London, Duckworth in association with the Classical Press of Wales.

MITCHELL, S. and WAELKENS, M. (1998) *Pisidian Antioch*, London, Duckworth.

PINETTE, M. and REBOURG, A. (1986) *Autun (Saône-et-Loire): ville gallo-romaine, Musée Rolin et Musée lapidaire*, Paris, Imprimerie Nationale Editions.

PRICE, S.R.F. (1984) *Rituals and Power: the Roman Imperial Cult in Asia Minor*, Cambridge, Cambridge University Press.

ROGERS, G. (1991) *The Sacred Identity of Ephesos*, London and New York, Routledge.

ROLLAND, H. (1946) *Fouilles de Glanum: Gallia Supplement 1*, Paris, Centre National de la Recherche Scientifique.

ROTH CONGÈS, A. (1992) 'Nouvelles fouilles à Glanum (1982–1990)', *Journal of Roman Archaeology*, 5, pp.39–55.

SYME, R. (1995) *Anatolica: Studies in Strabo*, Oxford, Clarendon Press.

THOLLARD, P., CARMELEZ, J.-C. and LEMAN, P. (1996) *Bavay antique*, Paris, Imprimerie Nationale Editions.

THÜR, H. (1995) 'Der ephesische Ktistes Androclus und (s)ein Heröon am Embolos', *Jahreshefte des Österreichischen Archäologischen Institutes in Wien*, 64, pp.63–103.

VEYNE, P. (1990) *Bread and Circuses: Historical Sociology and Political Pluralism* (trans. B. Pearce), London, Allan Lane.

WAELKENS, M. (ed.) (1993a) *Sagalassos 1: First General Report on the Survey (1986–1989) and Excavations (1990–1991)*, Leuven, Leuven University Press.

WAELKENS, M. (1993b) 'Sagalassos, history and archaeology', in Waelkens (ed.).

WALLACE-HADRILL, A. (1990) 'Roman arches and Greek honours: the language of power at Rome', *Proceedings of the Cambridge Philological Society*, 36, pp.143–81.

WARD-PERKINS, J.B. (1981) *Roman Imperial Architecture*, Harmondsworth, Penguin.

WILSON, R. (1990) *Sicily under the Roman Empire*, Warminster, Aris and Phillips.

WOOLF, G. (1995) 'The formation of Roman provincial cultures' in J. Metzler, M. Millett, N. Roymans and J. Slofstra (eds) *Integration in the Early Roman West: the Role of Culture and Ideology*, Luxembourg, Musée Nationale d'Histoire et d'Art, pp.9–18.

WOOLF, G. (1997) 'Beyond Romans and natives', *World Archaeology*, 28, pp.339–50.

WOOLF, G. (1998) *Becoming Roman: the Origins of Provincial Civilization in Gaul*, Cambridge, Cambridge University Press.

Essay Nine
Religion in the Roman empire

BY JAMES RIVES

That religion is closely tied to issues of culture, identity, and power is obvious from contemporary British society. For example, British culture is closely identified with Christianity, regardless of the relatively low number of practising Christians; Islam, in contrast, is often identified with an alien culture, despite the growing number of British Muslims. Similarly, a person's religion is generally regarded as an important part of his or her identity: being a Christian, a Jew, or a Muslim has important implications both for a person's own self-perception and for the way other people view that person. As for connections with power, although the Church of England is no longer as powerful as it once was, the very fact that it remains the Established Church guarantees its role in the ruling structures of the country.

How can these connections be explained? Most people would probably agree that religion is an integral part of culture, in the broad sense. The anthropologist Clifford Geertz defined religion as 'a system of symbols which acts to establish powerful, pervasive and long-lasting moods and motivations in men by formulating conceptions of a general order of existence' (Geertz, 1973, p.90). In other words, religion is very closely bound up with the way a person views the world and his or her own place within it; it both shapes and reflects the system of values according to which a person lives his or her life. For this reason it also plays an important role in defining a person's identity. This is particularly true in a multicultural society: when there is a wide range of religious options, including that of not being religious at all, the religious identity that someone grows up with or adopts becomes an important distinguishing mark. Lastly, the power of the Church originated with its claim to be a necessary intercessor with the divine. If one accepts the premise that there is a divine power that can and does affect one's life, then access to that power is obviously important. Any group or institution that can establish its claim to have sole or privileged access to this divine power can thereby acquire its own social power.

How does all this work in the Roman empire? Before trying to answer this question, I need to point out two major aspects of religion in the Roman empire. First, there was no single 'religion of the Roman empire'. Every people and tribe, in certain ways every town, had its own traditions.

In this respect the Roman empire resembled current multicultural societies like those of Britain or the USA. As I shall argue, it is possible to define a 'normative' religion, a set of generalized features that the élite considered normal. But this was very much a matter of finding and creating common ground between different traditions, resulting from complex cultural interactions and, to a certain extent, simply from the need to get along. Secondly, and even more importantly, 'religion', in the sense in which the term is used today, did not really exist at all. Most people tend to think of a religion as a system of belief in and responses to the divine, a system that is both internally coherent and also separated from other, 'secular', aspects of human life. This was not the case in the Roman empire. There was instead a wide range of ways in which people could interact with and talk about the divine world: ritual, myth, iconography, philosophy. These different modes influenced each other and interacted in important ways, but they did not form a coherent system. Nor were they clearly separated from other aspects of human experience and grouped together as something distinct: poetry about the gods, for example, remained poetry, while public cult was a responsibility of the élite no different from political and financial administration. There was, in short, no widely recognized distinction between 'religious' and 'secular'. For all these reasons it can be somewhat anachronistic and misleading to talk about 'religion' in the Roman world, although for the sake of convenience I will continue to do so.

Given these complications, approaching the topic of religion in the Roman empire may seem like heading into a morass. In order to provide some solid ground, I will start by discussing traditional religion in the city of Rome. This will provide a specific context in which to consider the differences between ancient polytheism and modern monotheism, particularly the central importance of ritual and the close connections between public religion and ethnic or political identity. I will then consider religion in the context of the empire as a whole, discussing in particular the attitudes of Roman authorities towards other religious traditions, the interactions between the Roman and Greek traditions and their role in establishing religious norms, the significance of religious cults focusing on the figure of the emperor, the interactions between Roman traditions and the local cults of the western empire, and lastly some of the cases in which Roman authorities took an active role in suppressing particular religious activities.

Roman religion

Ritual and belief

Roman religion was based not on the revelation of divine truths in a set of sacred scriptures, as are Judaism, Christianity and Islam, but rather on a group of traditional practices that were thought to establish contact between mortals and the gods, and so to enable mortals to win divine favour. Although these practices could be elaborated and combined in any number of ways, so that it was not uncommon for people to create new rituals and ceremonies, the basic practices remained the same. The most important of these were prayer and sacrifice. A prayer was essentially a request: a typical prayer began with an invocation of a particular god, continued with reasons why the god should grant the request (usually the fact that the petitioner honoured the god), and climaxed with the request itself; the Roman prayer form is fairly well attested in literary sources. There were also hymns, which consisted simply of praise without any specific request; these were often associated with particular rituals, and became an important literary genre. Prayer, however, was a much more central cult act. Closely associated with prayers were offerings: one of the best reasons why a deity should grant a request was that the petitioner brought gifts in turn. Sometimes supplicants would recall earlier offerings, or make an offering at the same time as the prayer. Most commonly, however, they would promise a specific gift to be offered after the god had granted their request. This type of promise was known as a vow (from Latin *votum*), and was fundamental to the exchange between the human and divine spheres as the Romans conceived it.

Offerings to the gods took a wide range of forms, from the simple and inexpensive to the costly and elaborate. At one end of the scale were offerings of little cakes and flowers, while a slightly more expensive option was to burn a bit of incense.

Liquids constituted an entire class of offerings known as libations, and included wine, water, milk, honey and oil. Offerings could also be made of durable materials: people often dedicated (that is, handed over to a god) statues, reliefs, inscribed altars, enemy spoils, and even memorabilia.

The offering par excellence, however, was the blood sacrifice, the ritual slaughter of anything from a small bird to a full-grown bull. Whatever the animal, a sacrifice was always a complex cult act, involving additional libations and small offerings, ritual prayers and invocations, and a sequence of prescribed actions that had to be followed meticulously.

Figure 9.1 *A second-century votive dedication to the Germanic goddess Vagdavercustis showing a worshipper burning incense on an altar; at left is a boy holding the box of incense, and behind him a man playing the pipes in order to drown out inauspicious noises. (Photo: Römisch-Germanisches Museum, Köln)*

Despite its importance and complexity, a sacrifice was something anyone could perform: it did not require the involvement of a priest or other religious specialist. This is an important feature of the Roman religious tradition, since it meant that interaction with the divine was open to all, and not monopolized by a powerful priestly class. As I shall discuss below, Roman priests were more a type of public official than anything else, and derived their power more from their civic position than from their role as intermediaries with the divine.

It is possible to deduce from these rituals a set of beliefs about the divine world and its relation to humanity. Briefly put, this would be that there was a multitude of divine forces that could affect human life for better or worse but could in turn be affected by human actions; by honouring these divinities, chiefly by offering them gifts, people could hope to win their favour and obtain help in achieving their goals. But while this might be considered a rudimentary theology, it remained implicit in the rituals and was never really articulated, much less formulated as a doctrine or worked out into a system. Traditional religion, so far as the evidence goes, did not involve any creeds about the nature of the divine or any exegesis of basic rituals. The rituals were performed

Figure 9.2 *A late second-century stele dedicated to the African Saturn, a god of agricultural prosperity. He is shown in the centre of the top panel, seated on a bull and holding a sickle. The panel immediately below depicts the dedicator and his family performing a sacrifice; the two bottom panels show scenes of prosperous farm life, no doubt the reason for this gift to the god. (Photo: Bardo Museum, Tunis, reproduced in MacKendrick, 1980, Figure 3.13)*

Figure 9.3 *A second-century relief showing the rituals preliminary to the sacrifice of a bull. The chief officiant, the emperor Marcus Aurelius, has his toga folded over his head in the manner prescribed by tradition; to the right is the pipe-player (see Figure 9.1) and the* victimarius *who will perform the actual slaughter. The bull looks on from behind. (Museo Nuovo dei Conservatori, Rome. Photo: Alinari)*

because they had always been performed and because they seemed to work. Hence it is fair to conclude that the centre of Roman religion lay in ritual, not in belief: it was what people did that was important, not what they thought.

This is not to say that the Romans never thought about their gods or cult practices. On the contrary, under Greek influence they developed a number of ways to describe the divine world and to discuss their religious traditions. Greek myths affected how the Romans conceived of their gods from a very early date (Feeney, 1998, pp.50–1). It is largely the result of Greek influence that Virgil in his *Aeneid* can describe the gods as playing active roles in the foundation of Rome, with Venus aiding her son Aeneas and Juno stirring up trouble, and that Ovid in his *Metamorphoses* can weave together a complex mythological tapestry of cosmic history from the creation of the world down to his own day. During the first century BC, some Romans also adopted the Greek philosophical tradition of speculating about the nature of the divine. Cicero, for example, wrote a lengthy philosophical dialogue, *On the Nature of the Gods*, in which he presents in turn the Epicurean viewpoint, according to which the gods were completely unconcerned with human affairs, the Stoic position, which accepted that the gods cared for humanity but which also had a strong pantheistic element, and lastly, the sceptical Academic position, which denied that any certain knowledge about the divine world was possible at all. Lastly, the first century BC also saw the rise of the antiquarian study of traditional religion. The great scholar Marcus Terentius Varro, for example, wrote a major work in sixteen books, now unfortunately known only from citations by later writers, that gathered together much obscure information about the traditional priests, cult places, festivals, rituals and deities of the Roman people.

All these things – iconography, myth, philosophy and antiquarianism – were important ways of understanding and dealing with the divine world. But they all had their own dynamic, and although they certainly interacted with each other and with traditional ritual, they were not incorporated into a system. Thus, the ways one talked about the divine world remained fundamentally separate from the rituals one used to interact with it. This situation resulted in juxtapositions that to modern observers seem bizarre or hypocritical. So, for example, Ovid in his *Fasti*, a poetic exposition of the Roman calendar, presents a *mélange* of Roman antiquarianism and Greek mythology along with bits of philosophical speculation and even astronomy. Although many scholars have tried to distinguish what parts of this are 'real' Roman religion, it seems best to conclude that, in different ways, all of it is. Cicero provides an even more intriguing example: although he concludes his dialogue about the gods with strong sceptical arguments, he also served as a public priest and was proud to do so. For this some modern scholars have accused him of hypocrisy, or even a cynical exploitation of religion. Moreover, in another work, *The Dream of Scipio*, he suggests that men who bestowed great benefits on the Roman state enjoy immortality among the stars, while in his letters he reveals that he seriously contemplated building a temple to his deceased daughter (*Letters to Atticus* 12.18.1). Was Cicero a hypocrite, or was he just mixed up? It seems best to regard his various opinions as simply the result of what Denis Feeney, following Paul Veyne, has called 'brain-balkanization':

> ... the capacity of educated Greeks and Romans of the post-classical period to entertain different kinds of assent and criteria of judgement in different contexts ...

> These people are involved in very different activities when they sacrifice outside a temple, talk to the custodian of a temple, read the aretalogy [i.e. the record of the god's powers and blessings] inscribed outside the temple, read the scholar Apollodorus' book *On the Gods*, listen to hymns, read Homer allegorized or Homer rationalized, read an epic on Heracles, or read about Heracles the supreme commander in a history.

> (Feeney, 1998, pp.14–15)

In short, it is not so much that belief was not important to the Romans, but that it simply did not operate in the way that modern westerners expect it to. Religious belief is, of course, a notoriously difficult thing to pin down, and close scrutiny of anyone's statements and behaviour would almost certainly reveal fundamental inconsistencies. The difference is rather that in modern western culture the ideal is that religious belief should be coherent, while in the Roman world such an idea would not even have occurred to most people.

A related issue is the connection between religion and morality. In Judaism, Christianity and Islam, this connection is intimate. The observation of certain ethical principles is considered an important, even the most important, way of honouring God, and anyone who professes one of those faiths is expected to live his or her life in accordance with those ethical principles. In the Roman tradition, however, this close bond between the worship of the gods and ethical behaviour simply did not exist: people won the good will of the gods by showing them honour and giving them gifts, not through acts of justice or charity. Again, it would be wrong to suppose that there was no connection whatsoever. There was certainly a general sense that the gods looked with approval on justice, and poets and philosophers sometimes put considerable weight on the gods' concern for proper behaviour. But this belief had relatively little effect on cult practice, which for the most part continued to reflect a quid pro quo view of the relations between gods and mortals. There was nothing comparable to the Ten Commandments or the Sermon on the Mount, no sacred texts that made the observation of particular moral principles a fundamental obligation to the gods. Nor was there an agreed upon view of the afterlife, in which the virtuous would enjoy their rewards and the wicked suffer punishments. So in this respect also, ritual rather than belief lay at the centre of Roman religion.

Public and private religion

Since the good will of the gods was necessary to any success, it was obviously important that the community as a whole win their favour and support. The Romans did this by using the basic rituals discussed above to establish permanent relationships between the community and selected gods: in return for the blessings of a particular deity, representatives of the community would vow to establish a permanent public cult, with a public shrine and the regular performance of sacrifices and other specified rituals. This was essentially a sort of contractual agreement, in which each party was expected to fulfil its obligations: so long as the Romans carried out their promises, they assumed that the gods would favour them. Yet they also acknowledged that they might inadvertently do something to incur divine displeasure, and they generally interpreted misfortunes such as plagues, droughts or military defeats as indications that the gods were angry. On such occasions they tried to determine the exact cause and correct it, and sometimes as a result established a public cult for a new deity. The gods for whom the Romans set up public cults were in a very specific sense 'their' gods, and were thought to have particular care for them. The most important were Jupiter Optimus Maximus, Juno and Minerva, whose temple was on the Capitoline hill and who are consequently known as the Capitoline Triad. Public religion was thus essentially the sum of the rituals employed by public representatives to maintain good relations between the community and its gods.

A public cult involved three things: a cult place, regularly performed rituals, and public representatives to perform these rituals. Although a cult place could be simply an altar, most public cults centred on temples, monumental and increasingly elaborate buildings that would house the cult statue as well as various gifts dedicated to the deity.

The rituals, which generally took place every year on a fixed date, could vary from a relatively simple sacrifice to very elaborate festivals. The great Ludi Romani, for example, the 'Roman Games' celebrated in honour of Jupiter Optimus Maximus, began with an elaborate procession to the Circus Maximus consisting of magistrates, performers and statues of the gods, and climaxing in a series of sacrifices; it then continued for sixteen days of chariot races, athletic contests and

Figure 9.4 *A small but well-preserved Roman temple of Augustan date in Nîmes, in the south of France. (Photo: Maison Carrée, Nîmes)*

theatrical displays. We can reconstruct the religious year of Rome in great detail thanks to the partial survival of a number of calendars inscribed on public monuments during the reign of Augustus. From these it appears that numerous public rituals were performed over the course of the year: some seventy or eighty sacrifices, six or more sets of games, and some thirty-five other festivals of various sorts.

Lastly, since these rituals were performed on behalf of the community as a whole, it made sense for them to be managed by representatives of the community. In a few cases these were people who were attached to the worship of a particular deity, such as the six Vestal Virgins who served the goddess Vesta. But specialized priests of this sort were the exception rather than the rule. It was much more common for magistrates to supervise the rites of the public cult. The consuls, for example, as chief executive magistrates, performed the annual vows to Jupiter Optimus Maximus every January 1st, while the aediles, lesser magistrates responsible for public buildings and markets, presided over the Ludi Romani. The most important public priests were organized into colleges and acted primarily as specialist advisors on matters of ritual. So, for example, the augurs maintained the traditional lore for interpreting signs sent by the gods, while the pontifices were responsible for the correct performance of rituals and for such quasi-religious matters as burial law. These priesthoods were held for life, but were not exclusive positions: men served as augurs and pontifices in addition to acting as senators and holding the usual annual magistracies. And men they mostly were, since apart from the Vestals women held very few priestly offices.

It seems natural to assume that these priests were the ones who controlled public religion in Rome, but that was not in fact the case. Priests had an important advisory role and were at times required to perform particular rituals, but it was the senate as a whole that made the actual decisions concerning public religion – for example, what new cults to establish and what rites these would involve, when to consult religious specialists and when to take their advice. The colleges of augurs and pontifices were in many ways more like standing sub-committees of the senate than independent religious authorities. In Rome, then, public religion was organized and maintained by the political and economic élite: the senate made all the important decisions while the priests and magistrates (who were themselves also senators) maintained the traditional religious prescriptions and performed the rituals. In this respect public religion was no different from foreign policy or the governance of the city: to the Romans it seemed only natural that the same people should oversee all important matters of public concern, those involving the divine sphere as well as those involving human affairs.

Along with public religion there was also private religion: it was, of course, just as important to individuals to obtain the support of the gods for their private concerns as it was for the community as a whole to obtain public blessings. The means in both cases were the same: prayers and offerings. People would pray for help for themselves and their loved ones in all the circumstances that one would expect: for recovery from illness or successful childbirth, for success in love and prosperity in business, for favourable outcomes to their endeavours. They might choose a deity thought to have particular power in the area with which they were concerned (for example, Venus for love, Mercury for business, Juno or Diana for childbirth), or one to whom they happened to be personally devoted. They also would make vows, promising a sacrifice or offering in the event that their request was answered. In the imperial period it became popular to record the fulfilment of a vow in an inscription, such as this simple one found near Verona: 'To Vesta;

Quintus Cassius Varus gladly and deservedly fulfilled his vow'
(*Inscriptiones Latinae Selectae* 3317). The number and variety of extant
examples attest to the importance of such vows in private life. People
could also have small household shrines that were typically dedicated to
the household gods (the Penates and Lares) but which might also
include any deity in whom they had particular interest.

There was little connection, however, between public and private
worship: the two did not form parts of a single whole, as in the
monotheistic religions of today. The authorities who oversaw public
religion were generally concerned with it alone, and had little interest in
private religion. On the one hand, they did not require private
individuals to participate in public rites. As long as the appropriate
public official correctly performed the ritual at the proper time and
place, public responsibility to the deity was fulfilled, and the number of
Romans who witnessed it was usually irrelevant. The only general
obligation individuals had towards public religion was to abstain from
business during religious festivals. Of course, certain public rites,
particularly the great games, tended to attract big crowds because they
provided entertainment. Some of them were also invested with considerable patriotic sentiment, in so far as they gave public expression to
the bond between the Roman community and its gods. But participation
was never enforced or necessarily expected, in the way that regular
attendance at church, for example, is expected of good Christians.

On the other hand, public authorities did not for the most part
restrict or control people's private religious lives. This was particularly
true when it was a question of what people thought. Although
mythology, philosophical speculation and antiquarian investigation were
all important parts of Roman religion, they were left entirely up to
individuals to pursue or ignore as they pleased. There was never a sense
that the public authorities should determine which ways of thinking
about the gods were acceptable and which were not. Although exegesis
of public rituals might be an important part of the total experience of
religion, public officials were concerned only with the rituals themselves,
and left exegesis to be debated by private individuals. This is yet another
indication that ritual and not belief was the centre of Roman religion. As
for private ritual, the situation is a little more complex. In general the
public authorities seem to have been little concerned with private cult,
but action was sometimes taken against certain private religious
associations. The cult of Isis, for example, was banned from Rome on
several occasions, the last time by Tiberius in AD 19. The most dramatic
example of these actions was the repression of the worshippers of
Bacchus in 186 BC, many of whom were killed and whose cult was strictly
controlled for the future. It is thus clear that public authorities could
exert some control over private cult when they wanted, but did so only

rarely. Otherwise, individuals seem to have been free to conduct their private religious lives as they pleased.

Culture, identity and power in Roman religion

It is now time to summarize what I have said about religion in Rome, and to highlight some of the ways it interacted with culture, identity and power. First, it should be clear enough that Roman religion was an important aspect of Roman cultural identity. But it functioned in a very different way from how Islam or Christianity functions in contemporary western society. Since private religion was largely uncontrolled, individuals in a sense had the freedom to construct their own religious identities, in so far as in their private lives they were not obligated to worship any particular set of deities or adhere to any particular doctrine. Moreover, the public religion of Rome was not in any significant respect distinct from that of other Italic peoples; most of its important deities, institutions and rituals were in fact part of a general Italic religious tradition. At the same time, however, different cities drew on this common tradition to create different combinations of deities and rituals, so that each city had its own distinct pantheon and set of public rites. As a result, public religion was an important focus for civic and ethnic identity. Identification with and participation in the public cults of Rome created a sense of community with one's fellow citizens and reinforced one's own sense of being Roman. The Roman people would gather to observe the consuls perform the annual vows to Jupiter Optimus Maximus not because their attendance was necessary, but because it was an opportunity to take pride in their identity as Romans, the people whom Jupiter had blessed above all others.

At this point I must address an aspect of ancient religion that is extremely important, but rather difficult for people raised in monotheistic traditions to understand. Since there were traditional cults of Jupiter in many cities besides Rome, how could his worship be so distinctively Roman? Here again the lack of an articulated religious system that integrated both ritual and belief is important. The difference between the Jupiter of Rome and the Jupiters worshipped elsewhere in Italy was essentially one of cult: they had different cult titles and were honoured in different places through different sets of rituals. Thus it was only in Rome that Jupiter was worshipped together with Juno and Minerva as Jupiter Optimus Maximus, the 'best and greatest' Jupiter, and it was only in Rome that the Ludi Romani were performed in his honour. In myth, by contrast, there was only a single Jupiter, the ruler of heaven and the king of the gods, as he appears in Virgil's *Aeneid* and Ovid's *Metamorphoses*. Was myth then less important than cult, not something that people really believed? It seems instead that the Romans were simply not interested in resolving the relation between the different Jupiters of cult and the single Jupiter of myth. On the contrary, they were apparently quite content to accept that things worked differently in cult from how they did in myth, even if that meant that a god could simultaneously be multiple and singular, local and universal. It was as a consequence of this type of thinking that the public cults of Rome could serve as a focus for Roman identity even when there were other cults of the 'same' gods in other cities.

Secondly, it should also be clear that Roman religion was intimately bound up with power relationships. The basic cult acts that I described above were themselves instrumental in shaping what the Romans conceived as one of the most important and basic power relationships, that between mortals and gods. Through these cult acts, people acknowledged the superior power of the gods and their own subordinate status, but were also able to establish a reasonably stable and mutually satisfactory quid pro quo relationship, with the gods receiving honour and people receiving practical help in their affairs. Religion was also closely connected with power relationships between people, but these connections took a very specific form. There was no priestly class that monopolized access to the divine and used that monopoly as the basis for social or political power, as happened with the Christian church. In their private lives, people could to a large extent worship whatever gods they chose in whatever way they pleased. Public religion, however, was another thing entirely. The élite, as embodied in the senate, were the ones who decided which gods the Roman people as a whole would worship and in what ways, and who were responsible for performing the required cult acts. They were in short the mediators between the community and the divine world, and this mediating role was both a source and an expression of their power within the community.

As I noted above, in certain circumstances the senate might intervene in private worship as well. It is useful to consider what the concerns were that led to such actions. It is likely that the cult of Bacchus provoked such a strong reaction from the senate because it had 'a structure of authority and organization and asked of its members a high degree of commitment and obedience, as well as regular worship' (North, 1992, p.182); in other words, it served almost as an alternative, rather than a supplement, to public religion. Although the senate allowed people to pursue their private religious interests as they wished, it seems to have drawn a line at the point where these private pursuits began to affect people's public identities or where private religious specialists began to acquire independent social power. Roman culture thus involved a crucial nexus between religion, Roman identity and public power.

Religion in the Roman empire

Roman religious policy

Given the nature of Roman religion, it is understandable that it did not spread with the expansion of the empire, at least in the same way that Islam spread with the Arab conquests or Christianity spread with European imperialism. Since Roman authorities did not require adherence to a defined set of beliefs even from Roman citizens, they naturally did not expect it of the peoples they conquered. The lack of any doctrine meant that the very ideas of mission and conversion are inapplicable to Roman religion. As I have pointed out, however, rituals are something else. Although the Romans could not have imposed a set of beliefs on their subjects, they might have demanded or encouraged the observance of some cults and prohibited others. On first sight, there seems ample evidence that this was in fact the case. Particularly in the western provinces, Roman religious practices and the worship of Roman deities became very widespread, while the cult of the emperor was ubiquitous throughout the empire (see 'Imperial cult' and 'Romanization and local identity' below). Roman historians tend to describe these as the 'official cults' of the empire, suggesting that they were somehow imposed by imperial authorities. Likewise, Roman officials at times did prohibit particular cults and religious practices, most famously in the persecution of Christians (see 'Religious conflict' below). But while it is tempting to see these developments as the effects of a formal religious policy, it is better to view them as resulting from the complex interactions between religion, identity and power that characterized Roman culture.

As a first approach to this problem, I will consider whether Roman citizens were required to observe Roman cults. I have already noted that individual citizens in Rome were not required to participate in them, but what about citizens outside Rome? The Romans from an early date had the custom of extending citizenship en masse to entire communities. Since Roman public cults were such an integral part of what it meant to be Roman, one might expect that these new Roman communities would be obliged to abandon their own cults and adopt those of Rome. Some evidence does seem to point in that direction. For example, the fact that copies of the Roman religious calendar have been found in many cities of Italy suggests that the cults of Rome did in a sense become standard. There is also archaeological evidence in many Italian cities for temples to Roman gods, most strikingly *capitolia*, temples of the Capitoline Triad. Other evidence, however, proves that local communities also maintained their traditional cults. In a few cases, these even appear in copies of the Roman religious calendar: that from Praeneste, modern Palestrina, includes a sacrifice to the local goddess Fortuna Primigenia, 'First-Born Fortune', while that from present-day Guidizzolo, a small town northwest of Mantua, includes one to the Celtic goddess Epona. It thus seems that as the cities of Italy became communities of Roman citizens, they combined their traditional local cults with distinctively Roman cults. This process closely mirrored the changes in their civic identities: the people of Tusculum and Pompeii, for example, did not lose their attachment to their own city on becoming Roman citizens, but added to it an identification with Rome. So too they retained their traditional local cults as markers of their local identity, and at the same time adopted Roman cults as markers of their Roman identity.

Another case to consider is that of Roman colonies, self-governing communities of Roman citizens who had emigrated from Italy. These were in many respects intended to be copies of Rome itself, and were established by charters that outlined their organization and public institutions. We are fortunate to have extensive remains of one such charter, from a colony founded in 44 BC at Urso (modern Osuna in Spain, some 60 miles east of Seville). The organization of public religion in Urso was much like that in Rome itself: local magistrates were apparently responsible for at least some public sacrifices, and there were colleges of augurs and pontifices. There were also provisions for public games in honour of the Capitoline Triad and of Venus. Otherwise, the town council, the local equivalent of the Roman senate, was explicitly charged with deciding 'the dates and numbers of festal days, the sacrifices to be publicly performed, and the persons to perform such sacrifices' (Rives, 1995, pp.29–33). Just as in Rome, then, the political élite was responsible for selecting and overseeing public cults. But this in itself suggests that, apart from the two cults specified in the charter, they were not obligated to copy the cults of Rome, but could worship whatever gods they pleased. The evidence suggests that they generally chose typical Roman deities, but in unique configurations. In Carthage, for example, refounded as a Roman colony at the same time as Urso, the first public cults apparently included those of the Capitoline Triad, Ceres, and Concordia, all of whom were worshipped in Rome. But while the Capitoline deities were pre-eminently Roman, the latter two were not. Details of organization also differed: a prestigious annual priesthood of Ceres was not based on anything found in Rome but seems instead to have copied Greek models (Rives, 1995, pp.39–51). The specifically Carthaginian character of the colony's public religion increased over time, as some traditional local deities like the goddess Caelestis were introduced into the pantheon. The public cults of Roman colonies, then, like those of enfranchised cities, were both Roman and local, and so suited a civic identity that was simultaneously Roman and local.

If Roman citizens were not limited to Roman cults, it seems safe to assume that the non-citizen subjects of the empire were even less restricted. In fact, there is abundant evidence that the worship of local deities continued and often flourished. The Christian writer Tertullian claimed that 'each province and city has its own god: Astarte in Syria, Dusares in Arabia, Belenus in Noricum, Caelestis in Africa': these provinces are Roman, he adds, but their gods are not *(Apology* 24.7–8). All these gods and hundreds more are attested in inscriptions, which constitute the most important source of information about local deities. A quick scan of the index of gods in a major collection of Latin inscriptions turns up Abaddir (in modern Algeria), Abellio (near the French Pyrenees), Abinius (near Paris), Abnoba (in the Black Forest), Acaunus (near Vienna), and Adido (south-west of Lyons); a scan in a similar collection of Greek inscriptions from the empire reveals Aglibolos (eastern Syria), Aeichala (Lebanon), Aminibis (southern Egypt), and Angdistis (west-central Turkey). By now it hardly needs pointing out that cults of this sort reinforced ethnic or local identity: just as the cult of Jupiter Optimus Maximus was an important part of being a Roman, so too an important part of being an Arab was worshipping Dusares and the other traditional gods of Arabia.

There was little reason for Roman authorities to prohibit or discourage the worship of these local gods. The Romans were used to the idea that religion was tied very closely to a specific city or ethnic group and took this to be the norm. Since they had their own deities and public rites, they thought it only natural that other cities and peoples had theirs as well and did not expect them to replace them with those of the Romans. If anything, the opposite was true: Roman authorities were actually more likely to want subject peoples to maintain their traditional cults. On the one hand, devotion to ancestral cults was something they could understand, since they believed that their own devotion to ancestral deities had been a major factor in their success. On the other hand, when they conquered other peoples and incorporated them into their empire, they also in a sense incorporated their gods; it was thus in their interest that people continue to maintain the goodwill of these local gods. Roman officials were ready to honour local gods themselves whenever appropriate; Figure 9.1, for example, shows a dedication to the Germanic goddess Vagdavercustis by the military officer Titus Flavius Constans. Even Roman governors and generals sometimes made offerings to the gods of the areas in which they were serving.

There was thus no pressure to abandon the worship of traditional deities, and little overt pressure to adopt Roman cults. Nevertheless, the nature of ancient religion meant that there were indirect pressures and powerful incentives to devise some cultic connection with Rome. Since religion played such a key role in both defining civic identity and structuring relationships of power within a community, it provided an excellent medium for forging symbolic ties between local communities and the centre of power in Rome. Local élites and ambitious provincials could use religion in this way to maintain or advance their own positions in the hierarchy of power relationships that extended throughout the empire. Their strategies, however, differed considerably in the eastern and western parts of the empire. In the west, they generally tended to make religion more Roman, both by adopting Roman cults and by Romanizing traditional local ones. In the east, by contrast, Roman cults had relatively little impact, and local élites instead created symbolic links to Rome by devising cults that centred on the figure of the emperor. But before I discuss these developments, it will be useful to examine more broadly the relationship between the Roman and Greek religious traditions.

The Greek tradition and normative religion

One of the key differences between the western and eastern parts of the Roman empire was that Greek culture had tremendous prestige among the Romans as well as other peoples, whereas the indigenous cultures of the west did not. The Romans were accordingly willing to accept the Greek religious tradition as virtually equivalent to their own; moreover, the extensive similarities between the two traditions made it easy to do so.

These similarities were due in large part to the profound influence of Greek traditions on those of Rome, some of which I have already mentioned. This influence, which began in the earliest period of Roman history, had a significant effect on the gods the Romans worshipped, the way they worshipped them, and above all the way they thought about them. The Romans introduced some Greek gods directly into their own pantheon, notably Hercules (by the sixth century BC), Apollo (in 431 BC), and Aesculapius (in 291 BC). More commonly, they often identified a native deity with a similar Greek figure, and thereby attributed to the former many characteristics of the latter. This process is generally known as *interpretatio Romana*, literally, 'Roman translation'. It was particularly through *interpretatio* that Greek traditions had such a tremendous impact on the ways that the Romans thought about their gods. So, for example, the standard iconography of Roman deities derived substantially from that of their Greek counterparts: Jupiter was depicted like Zeus as a mature man with a full beard; Minerva, like Athena, as a young woman in martial dress (see Figure 9.5).

Gradually the whole apparatus of Greek mythology was adopted, and expressed in literature as well as iconography: Latin literature begins with a rendering of the *Odyssey* in which 'Zeus' and 'Athena' are translated by 'Jupiter' and 'Minerva', and reaches a peak with the elaborate mythologizing of the *Aeneid*. This process of *interpretatio* depended on the ability simultaneously to distinguish and identify deities in different traditions. Thus Jupiter was the same as Zeus for the purposes of mythology, philosophy, and general iconography, but remained distinct in cult, just as Jupiter Optimus Maximus was distinguished from other Jupiters. Culturally, however, the Romans had by the imperial period long been accustomed to view the Greek pantheon as equivalent to their own, and to see 'Hera' and 'Juno', for example, simply as the Greek and Latin names of the same goddess.

Greek influence affected Roman religious tradition in many other respects. As I noted above, philosophical speculation about the divine came to Rome from the Greek world, while the Romans even adopted some Greek rituals: for example, certain sacrifices

Figure 9.5 *A statue of the Roman goddess Minerva, depicted with the usual attributes of the Greek goddess Athena. She wears a Greek helmet, carries a shield and a spear (now lost), and wears the* aegis, *or goatskin, adorned with the Gorgon's head. (Museo Capitolino, Rome. Photo: Alinari)*

had to be performed *ritu Graeco*, 'according to the Greek rite'. The most important similarities, however, concern the basic structures of religion. Just as in the Roman tradition, Greek religion centred on ritual rather than belief, and these rituals defined a relationship of power between the gods and their mortal adherents. Although mythology and philosophy were also very important, they were only loosely tied to cult and remained outside the organization of public religion. Public cults in the Greek world as in Rome were an aspect of civic life, closely associated with particular cities and serving to define and reinforce civic identity. Important cults centred on public temples that housed the cult statue of the deity. There was again no separate priestly class: local Greek élites selected, organized, and celebrated the public cults, and so acted as mediators between their communities and the divine world in the same way that the senate did in Rome. It was thus not merely the Greek pantheon that seemed familiar to the Romans, but the general structure of the religion as a whole.

This is not to say that there were no differences: there were, and both Romans and Greeks remained keenly aware and even proud of them. There were no Greek priesthoods that corresponded to the augurs and pontifices of Rome: most Greek priests and priestesses served as individuals rather than as members of a college, and generally did not act as religious advisors but were instead attached to the cults of specific deities. The public cults of Greek cities tended to involve more popular participation than did those of Rome: the populace at large might be expected to take part in religious processions or even perform individual sacrifices during a festival. In the Greek tradition there seems to have been a closer connection between myth and ritual; for example, in the second century AD the travel writer Pausanias collected dozens of myths related to him by local priests that were intended to explain peculiar local rituals. The role of myth was also much more important than in Rome: Homer, Hesiod, and other poets had used myth to articulate a Panhellenic pantheon as early as the late eighth century BC, and in doing so had defined a common Greek religion in a way that had never been done for the Italic religious tradition. Roman political domination did nothing to eradicate these distinctive features of the Greek tradition. Nor did the Romans have any desire to assimilate their own tradition entirely with that of the Greeks. On the contrary, they often explicitly marked the elements borrowed from Greek tradition in order to distinguish them from native traditions, as for example in the very term 'according to the Greek rite' (Feeney, 1998, pp.25–31).

But although the Greeks and Romans remained keenly aware of the differences in their religious traditions, the similarities were such that each could accept the other's tradition as normal rather than alien. Since theirs were the two most prestigious religious traditions of the empire, the one for political reasons and the other for cultural reasons, the common ground between them tended to define an implicit model of normative religion – that is, religion that the élite of the empire recognized as 'normal'. It is important to stress that this model remained implicit, and was never worked out or given explicit form. But certain aspects of it appear in the comments Greek and Roman writers make about the traditions of other peoples. For example, it was common to sneer at the Egyptian custom of depicting gods in animal or mixed animal/human form, since the 'normal' thing was to imagine the gods in anthropomorphic guise. Several writers also remark on the Jewish and Persian refusal to represent gods with statues, or on the Persian and German rejection of temples, because it was 'normal' for a cult to centre on a cult statue in a temple. Other writers comment with surprise that other peoples required religious specialists for sacrifices and other basic rituals, as the Persians required Magi or the Celts required Druids: the 'norm' was that anyone could make an offering. Other aspects of this normative religion are not mentioned even to this extent, but can be deduced from general trends: that public religion was a part of civic life, and that religious identity was closely bound up with civic or ethnic identity. Lastly, it is important to notice that this normative religion was very much what the élite considered normal, and generally excluded popular beliefs and practices that had not been integrated into public religion or made respectable by poets or philosophers. The élite in fact tended to associate such practices and beliefs with foreign traditions, and dismiss them all as superstition or magic.

Since the Romans acknowledged the prestige of the Greek religious tradition and regarded it as at least the equivalent of their own, there was little incentive for the élites of Greek cities to adopt Roman cults or religious practices. In the east, as a result, Roman gods were only worshipped in Roman colonies and army camps, and even in the colonies Greek cults gradually came to dominate. Elsewhere Roman cults are hardly visible: there are occasional dedications to Zeus Kapitolios, the Greek name for Jupiter Optimus Maximus, but little else. In general, Greek cities maintained their traditional civic cults, as Athens did with the cult of Athena and Ephesus with that of Artemis. These cults continued to provide a strong focus for local identity, as they had always done. Yet it was none the less important for the élites of these cities to give some religious expression to their links with the centre of power in Rome. They were able to do this through cults of the emperor, which defined their roles as mediators between the community and imperial power in the same way that traditional civic cults cast them as mediators between the community and the divine.

Imperial cult

Imperial cult had its origin in the kingdoms of the Hellenistic period, when Greek cities for the first time had to deal with rulers who were Greek rather than foreign and yet not part of the city-state. As Rome gradually displaced the Hellenistic kings as the greatest power in the Greek world, cities began to devise new cults. Sometimes these were directed towards the senate or individual Roman leaders, but much more often to the goddess Roma, the personification of the city. But once the republican constitution gave way to the principate, the emperor naturally became the chief focus of such cults. Under Augustus, they quickly spread to the western part of the empire, and by the end of the first century AD were pervasive throughout the empire on all levels.

The most common form of imperial cult was civic in organization, analogous to traditional public cults. These civic cults typically involved a public temple, at least one but usually several sacrifices or festivals marking imperial anniversaries, and one or more priesthoods usually held on an annual basis by members of the local élite. There were also provincial cults of the emperor; this was a noteworthy phenomenon, since no other cult had any significant organization on a level higher than that of the individual city or shrine. In a provincial cult, all the cities of the province would send representatives to a common sanctuary, where they would perform rituals in honour of the emperors and choose a provincial priest. This priesthood was a very prestigious position, and held only by the most illustrious men of the province.

Although the political dimension of imperial cult is obvious enough, its status as a genuine form of religion may seem more dubious. Modern views on the subject tend to be shaped by the monotheistic traditions of Judaism, Christianity and Islam, all of which stress the fundamental and virtually absolute division between the human and divine spheres. In this context, the worship of a man as a god can only be explained by megalomania on the part of the emperors and gross flattery on the part of their subjects: otherwise, how could anyone really believe that a man was a god? But it is important once again to remember that religious 'belief' did not function in the ancient world in the same way that it does in our own. There was no explicit theology or organized doctrine to which people were expected to adhere; instead, imperial cult centred on ritual. As I have suggested, the basic cult practices of sacrifice and prayer articulated a relationship of power between gods and mortals. It was for this reason that they could also serve to articulate the relationship between the emperor and his subjects: 'using their traditional symbolic system, [Greek cities] represented the emperor to themselves in the familiar terms of divine power. The imperial cult, like the cults of the traditional gods, created a relationship of power between subject and ruler' (Price, 1984, p.248). Imperial cult was thus not so much an object of belief as a way of understanding and dealing with the world; in this respect it fits quite well with the definition of religion proposed by Clifford Geertz, quoted at the start of this essay.

A second point is that the term 'imperial cult' is somewhat misleading, since it implies that there was a single comprehensive cult of the emperor. The term is in fact a modern one, used for the sake of convenience to denote any association of the emperor and his family with the divine sphere. Given the tremendous variety of ancient religion, the range of ways this was done was not surprisingly extremely wide, both in terms of the medium employed (for example, ritual, iconography, poetry) and in the type of association. One could for example depict the emperor with the attributes of a specific deity, describe him as the representative of a god, pray to the gods for his well-being, honour him as a god after his death, or worship collectively all past and present emperors. All these strategies were fairly common and are usually included under what is meant by imperial cult, even though to current thinking they were not strictly compatible.

Lastly, many of these devices for associating the emperor with the divine sphere did not entirely equate him with the traditional gods. For example, an inscription from Narbo (modern Narbonne in southern France) records a whole series of imperial anniversaries on which offerings were to be made. These offerings, however, were directed not to the emperor himself, but rather to his *numen*, which means something like 'divine power'. Although a *numen* was something that a god had, people did not normally make offerings to a god's *numen*, but to the god

Figure 9.6   *The emperor Claudius in the guise of Jupiter, holding aloft the sceptre and with the eagle, the bird of Jupiter, at his feet. (Museo Vaticano, Rome. Photo: Alinari)*

himself; hence worshipping an emperor's *numen* marked him as similar to, yet different from, a traditional god. A similar inscription from the town of Gytheum in the Peloponnese describes its imperial festival. This included a public procession to the temple of the emperor, where the local magistrates sacrificed a bull 'on behalf of the safety of the rulers and gods and the eternal duration of their rule'. It is striking that although the emperor is described as a god, the sacrifice is not directed towards him but merely performed on his behalf: in terms of cult, he is treated more like a man than a god. Evidence suggests that most imperial sacrifices were celebrated on behalf of, rather than to, the emperor (Price, 1984, pp.210–15). Similar ambiguity existed in the context of iconography and poetry. When the emperor Claudius, for example, was depicted with the eagle and sceptre of Jupiter (see Figure 9.6), that was a way of expressing his power: just as Jupiter ruled over heaven, so Claudius ruled over earth. But whether this meant that Claudius was an actual manifestation of Jupiter, or his terrestrial representative, or merely in some way 'like' him, was not spelled out. In all these cases, emperors were treated like gods, yet not exactly like the traditional gods.

One final point about imperial cult requires some attention. It is often implied that, because imperial cult was an official cult of the empire, everyone was required to observe it. But I have suggested that this for the most part was simply not the way religion worked in the Roman empire; this is as true of imperial cult as of any other. Roman officials hardly ever imposed the worship of the emperor, although they did at times encourage it. Instead, the initiative more often lay with the local élites. For example, the city of Tarraco (modern Tarragona in southern Spain) sought and received permission from the emperor Tiberius to build a temple for his deified predecessor Augustus. So too the magistrates of Gytheion wrote to gain approval for their cult in honour of Tiberius and other members of the imperial family along with Augustus. In this case, Tiberius replied that although it was proper to worship the deified Augustus, he was himself satisfied with the honours appropriate to mortals. Nevertheless, the magistrates of Gytheion went ahead with the cult as planned, and even inscribed their exchange with Tiberius on a public monument. The reason for such enthusiasm was that local élites benefited from imperial cult as much as, if not more than, the emperor himself: through it they could place themselves in a close if symbolic relation to the centre of power, and so reinforce their local status. The only context in which emperors took the initiative in organizing imperial cult was on the provincial level. But in this context imperial involvement was crucial: an emperor simply could not allow the leading men of a province to assemble at will without any oversight by the central government. Hence some emperors seem to have taken the initiative to organize provincial cults in order to maintain some control over them. Otherwise, the advantages of creating a symbolic link to the emperor provided sufficient incentive for people to establish imperial cults on their own.

Romanization and local identity

In the western empire, unlike the east, Roman cults and religious practices did become very widespread. I have suggested that the reason for this lies in the fact that the cultures of the west lacked the prestige of Greek culture, and so could not compete as well with the culture of the conquerors. Consequently, local élites in the west tended to refashion themselves as Romans, so that by identifying with the dominant culture they could use its prestige to reinforce their own social positions. Since Roman cults were so intrinsic a part of Roman identity, it was only natural that the élites adopted them. But the situation was more complex than this analysis would suggest. Although Roman cults did spread, they did not wipe out the worship of local deities, as I have already noted. And as elsewhere in the empire, local cults were an important part of local ethnic or political identity. At the same time, these cults did not simply continue unchanged alongside the newly adopted Roman cults, but instead became much more Roman themselves.

Roman influence on religious practice in the western empire is obvious. The very custom of erecting inscribed dedications, thanks to which these local cults are known, was essentially a Graeco-Roman practice; the same was true of constructing stone temples or depicting deities in anthropomorphic form. Both Roman officials and locals élites tended to adopt Graeco-Roman practices like this for local religious traditions. But were traditions modified in this way still genuinely local? A useful context in which to consider this issue is that of *interpretatio Romana*. The practice of identifying deities from different cultures (see 'The Greek tradition and normative religion' above) was not limited to Greek and Italic deities but extended to all those with whom Romans or Greeks came into contact. What did it mean for someone to invoke a local deity under a Roman name? Jane Webster has argued forcefully that it was an instrument of Roman cultural imperialism: 'the process of "translating" an alien deity by equating it with a Classical one ultimately constitutes the superimposition of one belief system on another' (Webster, 1995, p.157). In this view, the native tradition was essentially buried underneath the Roman one. This is certainly an important aspect of what was going on, and must in many cases have been intentional: when either a native or a Roman honoured a traditional local god under Roman guise, he or she was in certain respects suppressing that god's traditional character. But there were other aspects to this process as well, as a brief consideration of *interpretatio* in two different areas, northern Africa and Gaul, will suggest.

In Gaul, it was fairly common to add the name of a local god to that of the Roman god with whom he was identified. So for example there are dedications to Mars Albiorix, Mars Belado, Mars Camulus, Mars Giarinus, Mars Intarabus, and dozens more. These inscriptions reveal the assimilation of a number of local gods with the Roman Mars. At the same time, however, the process was not entirely one sided, but affected the Roman god as well as the local one: when Mars was identified with Albiorix and Belado and Intarabus, the very meaning of the name 'Mars' shifted and expanded. Furthermore, although these local gods 'became' Mars, they were local versions of Mars and hence could still serve as the focus for local identity, just as the local cults of Jupiter or Juno did in Italy. As I suggested above, it was an inherent feature of Roman polytheism that the same god could in different contexts be both local and universal.

In Africa, by contrast, the practice of using double names was very rare, and it was common for Graeco-Roman divine names to replace local names completely. Yet in some cases the change of name seems to have had little effect on the conception of the god. So, for example, the African Saturn, who is thought to represent the Punic god Ba'al but whose non-Roman name is not recorded, remains strikingly distinct from the Roman Saturn in terms of epithets, iconography and cult (see Figure 9.2). In other cases, the *interpretatio* is not simply the substitution of a Roman divine name for a local one, but something more subtle. So, for example, the goddess Caelestis, the 'Heavenly One', whose cult

Figure 9.7 *The goddess Caelestis shown riding through the heavens on the back of a lion, in a first century relief from Rome. (Museo Capitolino, Rome. Photo: Maria Teresa Natale)*

continued that of the Punic goddess Tanit: many scholars treat this name simply as an epithet of Juno, but although the identification of the great goddess of Carthage as Juno was well established in poetry (for example, Virgil's *Aeneid*), it was largely ignored in the actual cults of Roman Africa. Worshippers instead preferred to use the descriptive name 'Caelestis' on its own, and so in effect developed their own distinctive Latin name for their goddess (Rives, 1995, pp.151–2). And as with Saturn, the iconography of Caelestis clearly distinguished her from the Roman Juno.

As these examples suggest, what happened in the western part of the empire was not simply the submerging of indigenous religious traditions under the Roman one, but a more complex process of assimilation and appropriation resulting in new cults that were simultaneously local and Roman. It is difficult to generalize about this process. Because Roman officials exercised at most an indirect influence over these developments, people largely did as they pleased. Consequently, Romanizing elements in religious traditions meant different things in different contexts. It is easy to imagine that motives must have been extremely varied: some people wanting to assimilate to Roman standards, others wanting to resist them, still others wishing to be both Roman and local. The only generalization possible is that the maintenance and transformation of local religious traditions was a consistently important locus for working out issues of identity and relationships of power.

One further issue needs to be raised here, on a different but related topic. The dichotomy that I have presented between 'local' and 'Roman' does not account for all the varieties of cult within the empire. There were also cults that, while not originating in Rome, nevertheless spread throughout most of the Roman world. One particularly well-known example is the cult of the goddess Isis. Although in origin an ancient Egyptian deity, her cult began to spread through the Greek world in the Hellenistic period, and in the process became thoroughly Hellenized. Nevertheless, it retained very strong associations with Egypt: the temples were Egyptian in décor, the cult personnel displayed Egyptian trappings (for example, the shaven heads and linen robes of the priests), and there was considerable emphasis on allegedly ancient Egyptian wisdom.

Despite initial opposition from authorities in Rome, the cult of Isis became very widespread in both east and west. Because of its very specific cultural associations, it was neither local nor Roman. Moreover, although there were many public temples of Isis, it was characteristically celebrated by private or semi-private religious associations. On the other hand, it was held in honour by many of the élite, who tended to regard it as part of the common religious inheritance of the empire. It was thus both non-Roman and Roman at the same time.

Figure 9.8 *A relief from Rome showing a procession of worshippers of Isis. The two men have the shaven heads associated with Egyptian priests; the woman at left carries a* sistrum, *a type of rattle used in the cult, and the woman at right has a snake entwined around her arm. (Museo Vaticano, Rome. Photo: Alinari)*

Religious conflict

Given the fluid nature of ancient religion, the traditional lack of public control over religious belief and private cult, and the tendency for religious tensions to be worked out in a cultural rather than a political context, one would not expect any legal restriction or persecution of particular religious activities. Yet this clearly did occur: the persecution of Christians is the best-known instance, but there were others as well. Roman authorities banned the Druids of Gaul and succeeded in driving them underground, while some religious activities were defined as magic and made liable to capital punishment. Although the problems involved in these episodes are too complex to address fully in this essay, they are closely bound up with issues of power and identity and so merit a brief discussion.

As I mentioned above, one aspect of what I have called normative religion was that access to the divine was not under the control of religious specialists, but instead open to all. In so far as there was control over religion, it was that exercised by the local socio-economic élite over public cult. The Druids, however, did not fit this model at all. Although the evidence is uncertain and open to debate, it seems that they derived their authority not from wealth but from the command of arcane traditional wisdom, acquired over many years of study. It was because of this knowledge that they had important roles in cult, education and the resolution of disputes. Roman officials, however, were accustomed to religious authority lying in the hands of the political and economic élite. They thus found it very difficult to understand the social role of the Druids, and accordingly viewed them with suspicion. The arcane nature of Druidic lore only increased their mistrust, since religious authority that was not exercised in the open was a potential source of resistance and unrest.

Similar issues seem to have been involved in the laws against magic. What exactly counted as magic was never explicitly defined, although it tended to include old folk beliefs in potions and spells as well as exotic religious traditions: the lore of the Druids, for example, was at times described as magic. But while issues of culture and class were closely bound up with the criminalization of magic, the most important issue was perhaps the fear that magic allowed for a privileged access to the divine, a type of access that was not available to everyone but only to those with the requisite secret knowledge. This sort of privileged access could provide a basis for social power that did not exist in normative religion, in that the people who claimed it were thought able to bestow benefits and inflict harm in ways that most people could not. In this respect magic not only conflicted with the normal pattern of religious authority in the Roman empire, but by serving as an alternative and uncontrolled source of social power also posed a potential threat to the established political and social hierarchy.

With Christianity, on the other hand, one of the central problems concerned issues of identity. In normative religion, the political or ethnic unit was the centre of public religion and an important focus for a person's religious identity. Although a person might have whatever private religious attachments and beliefs that he or she desired, these were not allowed to overshadow public cults. As I noted above, one of the reasons that Roman leaders in the second century BC viewed the worshippers of Bacchus as such a threat was that this cult became an alternative focus of religious identity. This was even more true of Christianity, which claimed the highest level of allegiance from its adherents and explicitly forbade them to participate in traditional public religion: it thus completely severed the normal ties between religious identity and civic identity. This seems to have been one of the chief underlying reasons for the persecution of Christians, although its mechanics were in practice more complex than this would suggest.

Conclusion

In this essay I have tried to sketch out some of the basic features of ancient religion that made it different from the monotheistic traditions normal in western society, and also to suggest some of the important ways in which religion interacted with culture, identity and power. These connections were as important as in modern western society, if not more so, but took forms that modern observers might not always expect. Religion was most definitely an aspect of culture in the ancient world, both in shaping the way people understood the world and in being a distinguishing characteristic of different cultural traditions: hence the prestige of Roman culture in the western empire guaranteed the spread of Roman and Romanizing cults, while the prestige of Greek culture in the eastern empire meant that there Roman cults were an insignificant part of the religious landscape.

For these same reasons religion was an important element of a person's identity. But while the Roman empire was in certain respects a multicultural society similar to modern western ones, religious identity functioned in a very different way. In the contemporary world, a person can be a Christian, a Muslim or a Jew without that also determining whether he or she is also British, French, American or Indian. In the ancient world, by contrast, religious identity was inextricably linked to ethnic and political identity, so that these tended to shift together. This was true primarily of public religion; private religion, which had only a loose connection with public religion, was generally left up to the individual and so might be much more varied. For this reason a person's religious identity might be much more disparate than today, with part tied to his or her city or people, part directed towards Rome and the emperor, and part reflecting personal inclinations and interests.

Lastly, the connections between religion and power were very important but very different from those that exist in modern society. There was no church or religious hierarchy that derived its power from a monopoly on access to the divine, and that exercised authority even over the private lives of individuals. Religious authority lay instead primarily with the political and economic élite. But their concern was especially with public cult, and extended to private cult only when this seemed to threaten the status quo. Moreover, because the standard model of public cult in the ancient world was one in which it was tied very closely to the particular city or tribe, there was no 'official' religion that was imposed or organized by the imperial authorities. There was instead an implicit and undefined 'normative' religion which served as a model for local élites to adopt in their attempts to reinforce their own positions within the empire. Because of all these varied connections, religion was one of the most important areas in which issues of culture, identity and power were played out.

References

FEENEY, D. (1998) *Literature and Religion at Rome*, Cambridge, Cambridge University Press.

GEERTZ, C. (1973) *The Interpretation of Cultures*, New York, Basic Books Inc.

MACKENDRICK, P. (1980) *The North African Stones Speak*, Chapel Hill, The University of North Carolina Press.

NORTH, J. (1992) 'The development of religious pluralism' in J. Lieu, J. North and T. Rajak (eds) *The Jews among Pagans and Christians*, London and New York, Routledge.

PRICE, S.R.F. (1984) *Rituals and Power: the Roman Imperial Cult in Asia Minor*, Cambridge, Cambridge University Press.

RIVES, J.B. (1995) *Religion and Authority in Roman Carthage from Augustus to Constantine*, Oxford, Clarendon Press.

WEBSTER, J. (1995) '*Interpretatio*: Roman word power and the Celtic gods', *Britannia*, 26, pp.153–61.

Essay Ten
The language of dissent

BY PAULA JAMES

Addressing the issues

An investigation of dissent in the Roman empire has to view it as a reality to be demonstrated and a concept to be defined. It would be a tall order and also beyond the compass of this contribution to discuss each and every manifestation of discontent within the Roman imperial boundaries, whether it emanated from individuals close to the emperor or involved collective disaffection at home and abroad. So this study concentrates on the conceptualization of dissent rather than provides a checklist of its occurrences. The aim is to tease out some of the patterns in the *discourse* of dissent, how it was defined and articulated by the Romans themselves. Reconstructing an ideology of dissent, or at least finding some philosophical underpinning to the various trends, was a challenge taken up by Macmullen (1967). He surveyed oppositional forces and categorized individuals and groups who were perceived as threats, distinguishing various ideological standpoints. More recently Rudich (1993, p.239) concluded that the term 'ideology' was not well suited to defining dissident sentiments at the time of Nero, on the grounds that senatorial dissidents did not have a coherent system of views and that their dissident activities could not be fully explained in terms of the tenets of republicanism or Stoicism.

Whatever the approach and compass of the discussion, we need to be aware that our twenty-first century perspective influences the way we frame our questions. Our conclusions will, in turn, reflect pre-occupations specific to modern times, even if our intention has been to lay bare the essence of a foreign or 'alien' identity. There are other pitfalls to studies of this kind. Elsewhere in this volume you are alerted to the fragmentary nature of the evidence, whatever aspect of Roman society you are studying. Caution has to be exercised at every stage of analysis, whether the source is archaeological, artistic or literary. Archaeological evidence traces the impact of Roman occupation by reading the landscape rather than the writers who inhabited that landscape and who selected, emphasized and evaluated with various agendas. The 'informative dustbin' (a concept borrowed from Branigan,

1991, p.92) and other material remains are testimony to local lifestyles in the provinces, and Branigan champions their relative integrity. It is interesting that using this sort of evidence he still subscribes to the belief that 'many natives of the northwestern provinces, from all points on the social ladder, perceived the Romans and their empire to be broadly beneficial' (p.104).

In a study of Latin and Greek literature, the loudest and sometimes the only voice we hear is that of the educated male élite who were fully literate and likely to be writing from the perspective of Roman rule and its legitimacy. Essay Two explores the issue of the power and cachet of literacy in detail.

The existence of dissent in the Roman empire is a complex territory to map, not just because the clearest and most coherent accounts of unrest, whether at the centre of political and administrative life in Rome, or further afield among the military or the provinces they policed, emanate from the ruling culture. An additional challenge is the tendency of those operating within the dominant power structures and loyal to the Roman empire to speak simultaneously for those with a critical agenda. In other words, they appear to view events from both sides. The pages of Tacitus provide us with persuasive critiques of Roman hegemony put into the mouths of barbarian chieftains. I believe that it is important to value this kind of contemporary source even though on the surface it creates an occupational hazard for historians of the ancient world. The aim of this essay is to exploit the evidence we do have and to read one or two of the key sources in a spirit of intellectual optimism.

Tacitus was an early second century AD historian. He is himself famous for his dissonant if not dissident tendencies. Tacitus' critique of the Roman emperors from Augustus onwards is a harsh one. He lived much of his life under Domitian, who made little attempt to disguise the iron fist of power within the velvet glove of diplomacy, at least as far as his relationships with his senatorial administration were concerned. Senators such as Tacitus kept their counsel if they wanted to retain their position or, in the worst case scenario, to keep out of mortal danger. However, Tacitus writes as a representative and beneficiary of Roman *imperium*. In his biography of his father-in-law, the general Agricola, he wants simultaneously to champion the Roman right to conquest and occupation and to let the reader know that under Domitian the Roman destiny to rule was being distorted and falling into disrepute. Tacitus demonstrates in his writing how educated Romans might interpret motivations and manifestations of opposition by projecting their own agendas and models of freedom on to the sentiments of their enemies. He gives highly charged and colourful accounts of the challenges to Rome's imperial destiny on the peripheries of the empire, the occasions when there was outright opposition to Roman expansionism. The rhetoric of resistance, as reconstructed by the Romans themselves, is informative for a number of reasons. Firstly, this reconstruction throws light on where and why the Romans decided against absorption and went instead for annihilation (there was not one simple strategy for their expansion); secondly, it says significant things about how critics close to home, who had difficulty compromising with certain regimes, might form and frame their reservations about autocratic power and its excesses.

A literary example from Tacitus – the rallying speech of the British chieftain Calgacus to his troops when facing Agricola – will illustrate how the spokesmen for empire effectively redefined and refined the discourse of dissent by investing the opposing culture with a pronounced Roman character. This may be received by the modern reader as propaganda, but in the Roman context its purpose was subtly different. Roman rule and the Roman right to rule was a given. Crediting the malcontents with a critique of imperial expansionism could paradoxically strengthen the validity of the destiny and identity that was the Roman empire. It could also provide a subtext of dissent nearer to home, an implied critique of an emperor who had silenced all opposition and was therefore having a damaging effect on that very destiny and identity.

The rhetoric of resistance: the rallying speech of Calgacus

The context of this dramatic reconstruction is highly significant. Tacitus' *Agricola* is a celebration of his highly successful life as a Roman commander during the reign of Domitian when senators were terrorized into passivity and inertia. Macmullen (1967, pp.79–80) sets the work firmly in a tradition of eulogy which commemorates not just a man, but a man who operated with dignity and integrity under an autocratic and unpopular emperor. Agricola campaigned and conquered parts of Britain under the regime of Domitian. Tacitus depicts this as a time of severe restrictions when the senators lived in fear of a cruel and capricious master, but Agricola's virtues – moderation, discretion, obedience, self-control, hard work and vitality – mollified even this quick-tempered emperor (Mellor, 1993, p.98).

The biography of Agricola was probably completed in the 'happy times of Trajan' (described thus in *Agricola* 3). Tacitus can now safely publish the celebration of his father-in-law and connect him with other men of integrity who possessed the traditional republican virtues and were deserving of immortalization. Under Domitian the authors of works on the lives of courageous opponents to earlier imperial regimes were charged with capital offences and had their books publicly burned. Tacitus' condemnation of this repression is forthright after the event:

> They [Domitian and his court] even went on to banish the professors of philosophy and exile all honourable accomplishments so that nothing decent might anywhere confront them. We have indeed set up a record of subservience. Rome of old explored the utmost limits of freedom; we have plumbed the depths of slavery, robbed as we are by informers even of the right to exchange ideas in conversation. We should have lost our memories as well as our tongues had it been as easy to forget as to be silent.
>
> (*Agricola* 2, trans. Mattingly, 1976)

Ironically, those who retired from public life could be viewed with deep suspicion by paranoid emperors. Romans who favoured the Greek Stoic philosophy had always interpreted its principles and practices elastically. They did not generally live a higher life in private, keeping their distance from affairs of the state. 'The work of a good citizen is never in vain. By being heard and seen, by his expression, gesture, silent stubbornness, and, by his very walk, he helps' (Macmullen, 1967, p.51). Stoic senators from the time of Tiberius onwards found that silence was construed as dissent and that 'it was part of the formal charges against them that they had withdrawn from politics' (Macmullen, 1967, p.51). Seneca wrote in *Epistles* 14.8 that 'a part of safety lies in not seeking it openly'. Agricola, the man of action, was not open to such accusations, nor did he make any stand against Domitian but, in time, even he was demoted and (according to Tacitus) died in suspicious circumstances, perhaps because he constituted the threat of a good example.

In his discussion of Tacitus as a political analyst, Mellor (1993) assesses Tacitus' attitudes to the emperors past and present and his judgements on those in the senatorial ranks who took up critical positions or formed conspiracies against the rulers. Tacitus viewed autocratic behaviour as something that came with the imperial territory, both in the individual actions of the emperor and in the conduct of his army abroad. The best policy for the old ruling class, who now relied on the emperor for all favours and promotion, was to acquiesce with as much dignity as possible. According to Mellor's interpretation, Tacitus was equally contemptuous towards those of high rank who planned an overthrow of a tyrannical emperor, for they were themselves ambitious, vainglorious and likely to be as totalitarian in their approach if given the same opportunities.

Tacitus admired Seneca, who tried when in a position of influence to guide the young emperor Nero towards best practice. In spite of this, Nero turned out to be one of those emperors destined to behave spectacularly badly. Seneca eventually fell from favour and chose to make an honourable exit by committing suicide. It was typical of Tacitus to record noble gestures in the face of autocracy. Elsewhere he was critical of Seneca's source of wealth (family money), but Tacitus liked to spotlight heroic exemplars, men of the moment. He reports how Cremutius Cordus had been prosecuted in AD 25 for praising Brutus and Cassius in his history. Mellor (1993, p.101) points out that neither the Praetorian Guard nor a single rebellious legion was ever inspired by the writings of intellectuals. Cremutius' memory survives because of Tacitus' indictment of Tiberius' role in the prosecution. The historian's account of Cremutius' speech in the senate before he takes himself off to an inevitable and courageous suicide has Cremutius defending himself on the grounds that he recognizes that the republic is dead and buried, and asks what possible threat his work could constitute in an established principate.

Tacitus seems to be drawing distinctions between those wishing to retain the right to speak out, to criticize tyrannical actions, and those who formed conspiracies and allied with the like-minded men of action in the ranks of the army to remove the emperors or to assassinate them. '*Libertas*' was the watchword of those planning to restore the republic, and embodied the power of the old senatorial stratum who had run Rome; *libertas* was a guarantee of all their former privileges.

In fact it was invariably the army, perhaps aided by imperial freedmen, who disposed of extreme rulers. Their agenda was not the restoration of the republic, but a better candidate to take on the mantle of emperor. If Mellor's reading is accurate, Tacitus shared this sense of realism. He reports approvingly of men in the élite classes who defended freedom of speech – the legitimacy of the written word without censure – even if republican sentiments were uttered, and who were courageous enough to advise limits to the imperial power.

It is with this background in mind that the speech of Calgacus should be read. Not only a worthy opponent of the great general Agricola in military terms, he is also used as an object lesson in courage when faced with the loss of liberty and when forced to confront tyranny and fight against subjugation. The fact that Tacitus was part of that tyranny and would have perceived it as the right and destiny of Rome to rule over a vast empire does not inhibit him as a historian from viewing it objectively. As Goodman says (1991, pp.222–3), 'Tacitus' sympathy for Calgacus did not prevent him treating the compulsive militarism of Agricola as the acme of virtuous behaviour for a senatorial Roman.' Calgacus' exhortation is paralleled by Agricola's speech to the Roman troops, and the whole scene is reminiscent of the oratorical exercises that formed a regular part of higher education in the empire, the 'present both sides of a situation' practice piece. However, it has a more complex function than that of dramatic decoration.

Tacitus claims to be basing Calgacus' *tour de force* on a verbal account: 'This is the substance of what he is reported to have said.' During the course of the speech Calgacus is given certain perceptions of Roman expansion which were not necessarily that far from the truth. Having forcefully stated that there was no option but to make this last stand for liberty (now the native Britons had come to the attention of Rome, Rome was determined to enslave them), Calgacus paints a vivid picture of the degradation and exploitation they will continue to suffer under such masters. Across the empire there were tribes and tribal localities which did not have the social structures or material lifestyle which could be adapted to or could benefit from the *pax romana*. Moreover, the patterns of their existence were seriously disrupted by the programmes of urbanization the Roman authority had put into practice and by the agricultural support systems the successful towns required to sustain themselves. For communities and leaders like Calgacus, outside the margins of stable settlements, the Roman policy was truly 'to make a devastation and call it peace'. Essay Twelve unravels this aspect of the *pax romana* in more detail.

Dyson, in his survey of native revolt patterns (1975), makes a convincing case for Roman land hunger as the underlying cause of much of the discontent throughout the provinces. Calgacus' accusation seems to confirm this: 'Now the farthest bounds of Britain lie open to our enemies, what men know nothing about they always assume to be a valuable prize.' Dyson argues that once suitable land had been annexed, Roman agricultural settlements grew and then steadily advanced into the pasturage areas used by nomadic societies, and this was the cause of further tensions. These sorts of boundaries had not necessarily been extended by formal conquest: the expansion was more of a spontaneous process of encroachment than a policy decision backed up by the strong arm of the military. In Dyson's critique Africa provides good examples of this sort of encroachment.

Britain presented a different sort of problem when it came to the securing of frontiers in the north and Scotland. Agricola's defeat of Calgacus opened up Caledonia for conquest but the Romans moved back south. Herm says that the emperor, Domitian, probably did not see the point of annexing barren land 'the administration of which would cost more than the income it would provide' (Herm, 1976, p.224). However, Tacitus portrays the truncating of the Caledonian campaign as Domitian's jealous manoeuvre against his general Agricola. Tacitus comments on and makes the most of the campaign – as far as it went. In the speech that Tacitus attributes to the British chieftain, Calgacus talks about the brutal retaliation from Rome, as one would expect from an army with such a fearsome reputation. Such words enhance the image of the Roman enemy. Moreover, it does Agricola no harm to be the symbol of uncompromising Roman rule and it makes Domitian's subsequent order to withdraw from Caledonia look quite shameful and un-Roman. The events that follow the battle are an anticlimax to Calgacus' picture of intensive Roman exploitation, their boldly going after the prize of more territory and so on.

Putting such a construction on Calgacus' speech suggests that Tacitus was adding his own agenda to the established literary canon. Tacitus goes beyond the tradition of giving the opponents of empire a rhetorical case against imperialism. Ogilvie and Richmond note that the impulse towards world domination was a traditional way of rationalizing and characterizing empire building from the time of Alexander and was an established motif in political philosophy. They also summarize the speech's Roman colouring in the following way:

> Tacitus does not attempt to give arguments which Calgacus might actually have used, although he does convey something of a barbarian's boastfulness ... but contents himself with the traditional Roman criticisms of imperialism such as were voiced in the schools. Calgacus could not have known and would not have denounced the world-wide character of Roman power ... nor would he have been familiar with the cosmopolitan organization of the Roman army. ... The attack on *avaritia* ... and the contract between freedom and slavery are typically Roman attitudes. Above all, the example drawn from the position of slaves in a household ... presupposes Roman society.
>
> (Ogilvie and Richmond, 1967, pp.253–4)

There is another reason for the very Roman colour of these sentiments. The spirit shown by the barbarian chieftain and his description of tyranny, albeit the collective might of the Roman empire, is an object lesson for the cowardly and slavish silence that Tacitus identifies in the senate even when emperors had clearly overstepped the mark. Ironically, Calgacus is attacking an illegitimate target, because Rome in the eyes of Romans like Tacitus was both destined and divinely supported to expand *without limits*, the famous prediction Virgil put into the mouth of Jupiter in his epic poem, the *Aeneid* (1.279). When emperors attempt to rule without restriction, good men and true should point out that there are recognized ethical limits to autocracy, even if the Roman empire itself is boundless.

The concerns bestowed on Calgacus and the model of oppression he is constructing and opposing represent a Roman-style discomfort with the abuse of power. Calgacus is 'telling it how it is' in the tradition of a Stoic voice of conscience. For the Stoic 'servitude was no more than ignorance of the truth', a failure to describe reality accurately. A Stoic philosopher was duty bound to speak out against tyranny in all its forms (Macmullen, 1967, p.64). The upright man of integrity would unhesitatingly remind wayward emperors about appropriate behaviour and the exercise of antique virtues. It is Tacitus who reports Tiberius' exasperation with the senate because of its slavish compliance with his wishes (*Annals* 3.65). Fine speeches condemning the excesses of the powerful became the prerogative of Rome's external enemies, demonstrating that in this sphere too it was the barbarian outsiders who best preserved the Roman spirit and moral fibre of earlier and hardier times.

Figure 10.1 *Statue of a Gallic farmer. Museum Calvet, Avignon.*

Calgacus addresses his non-Roman troops with an instinctive grasp of the difference between liberty and enslavement. He unpacks Roman rhetoric about peace and reveals not only what it means for those who do not compromise with the invaders, but also the realities of *pax romana* for local peoples who attempt some kind of accommodation: children conscripted to be slaves abroad, wives raped or seduced (in Greek and Roman eyes, the latter was the worse fate as the affections of the women were then alienated), goods and money consumed by taxation and land stripped of its harvest (*Agricola* 31).

If the reader is eagerly awaiting a dynamic display of Roman eloquence from the book's 'hero', the commander Agricola, then the rallying speech is a disappointment. Although Agricola reiterates reasons for past and future successes in battle – factors such as the disorganized and uncultured barbarian foe facing a disciplined Roman army, to say nothing of his own military skills as a general – he makes only a cursory case for the natural superiority of the Romans: 'Where the modern reader may find Calgacus exciting and Agricola dull, the moralistic Roman reader would more probably consider Calgacus rash and Agricola sound' (Braund, 1996, p.169). Tacitus makes Agricola a man of fewer (rhetorical) words than the barbarian leader, but the battle demonstrates the Romans' strength and is the real story of their success.

There are one or two ironies lurking here, however. Archaeological evidence contradicts the ancient historian's assumptions about the composition of the Roman army: 'The size of the Celtic units serving under Roman standards can be gauged from finds made on former battlefields. So few items of Roman equipment have been found that we can assume that in Britain it was mainly Celt who met Celt in battle' (Herm, 1976, p.219). Of course, if Tacitus was aware of a considerable Celtic contingent (and Herm's interpretation may exaggerate the proportions), this may have influenced his approach to reconstructing Agricola's address to the troops. It would be interesting to reinterpret the exhortation with mainly Celtic troops in mind. A more subtle reading might explain Agricola's slightly downbeat approach to rallying the troops as part of the demoralization to come with Domitian's apparently defeatist tactics. Agricola is a servant of a ruler who freezes military initiative and muzzles free speech, so the paradoxes proliferate.

Disarming tactics

It is possible to draw out another set of Roman preoccupations with their own loss of identity (the former days of freedom are mentioned nostalgically by Tacitus in his introduction to the *Agricola*), by looking at another famous extract from this history. Tacitus has Calgacus describe brutal enslavement as the fate the Britons will suffer. In a passage extolling the astute policies of Agricola in winning over British leaders, Tacitus also talks of enslavement to the Roman way of life, its luxuries and leisure styles. This statement by Tacitus is a much-discussed one (see Essays Four and Eight). The local élites were not even aware that they had been subdued, so subtle was the process and so insidious the strategy:

> Agricola had to deal with people living in isolation and ignorance and therefore prone to fight; and his object was to accustom them to a life of peace and quiet by the provision of amenities. He therefore gave private encouragement and official assistance to the building of temples, public squares and good houses. He praised the energetic and scolded the slack; and competition for honour proved as effective as compulsion. Furthermore, he educated the sons of the chiefs in the liberal arts, and expressed a preference for British ability as compared with the trained skills of the Gauls. The result was that instead of loathing the Latin language they became eager to speak it-effectively. In the same way, our national dress came into favour and the toga was everywhere to be seen. And so the population was gradually led into the demoralizing temptations of arcades, baths and sumptuous banquets. The unsuspecting Britons

spoke of such novelties as 'civilization', when in fact they were only a feature of their enslavement.

(Tacitus, *Agricola* 21, trans. Mattingly, 1976)

An interesting aspect of this statement is the connection made implicitly between adopting the luxuries imperial Rome could offer and compromising one's own cultural identity, especially barbaric vigour and simplicity. Tacitus echoes a number of educated observers of trends in Roman society and of the dilution of its stern and stalwart character by just such benefits of civilization. Cassius Dio (*Roman History* 62.6.4) gives Boudicca a speech which highlights the degeneracy of the sons of Rome:

Men who are aggressive, dishonest, avaricious and irreligious, if that is we can call them men who take warm water baths, eat exotic meals, drink undiluted wine, smear themselves with oil, recline on soft cushions, and sleep with boys (who are actually past their prime!). These men are slaves to the lyre player – and not necessarily a good lyre player!

Tacitus describes barbarian customs and hardy lifestyles which from his perspective evoke the healthy and beneficial practices of early Roman society, now sadly lost in the sophistication of its imperial period. He admires German family life (*Germania* 18–20). He describes the acclimatizing of local chieftains in Britain to Roman civilization as seduction. Is there a tinge of regret here?

As well as drawing a moral lesson about luxury in his admiration of Agricola's tactics for guaranteeing the loyalty of local leaders, Tacitus, it seems to me, is also suggesting a parallel with the 'enslavement' of Roman society from the time of the first emperor, Augustus. Braund (1996, p.163) comes to a similar conclusion. From the point of view of the ruling élite in barbarian societies, they gained in status by sharing in Roman conspicuous consumption, just as the senatorial class retained their cachet in the capital and throughout the administrative structures of empire. It is interesting to read Tacitus' account of the origins of this 'enslavement', namely the settlement of Augustus:

He seduced the army with bonuses, and his cheap food policy was successful bait for civilians. Indeed, he attracted everybody's goodwill by the enjoyable gift of peace. Then, he gradually pushed ahead and absorbed the functions of the senate, the officials, and even the law. Opposition did not exist. War or judicial murder had disposed of all men of spirit. Upper-class survivors found that slavish obedience was the way to succeed, both politically and financially. They had profited from the revolution, and so now they liked the security of the existing arrangement better than the dangerous uncertainties of the old regime.

(Tacitus, *Annals* 1.2, trans. Grant, 1989)

Tacitus' assessment of Augustus' consolidation of power is characteristically blunt. Mellor (1993) suggests that Tacitus' political realism prevented him from yearning for a return to republican government but that he did seek to revive republican values. I suggested earlier that *libertas* could be translated as aristocratic privilege. For Tacitus it can be shorthand for the republic itself, the epoch before emperors. Much of the stability of support for imperial rule among the élite classes relied on the masking of the emperor's autocracy or at least a downplaying of their own subservient position. Those expressing republican sentiments were not persecuted by Augustus, and admiration of republican heroes and ideals was more a subject for light-hearted teasing than savage reprisals. Tiberius, according to Tacitus, began his rule with a tolerant connivance at political jibing. Such a state of affairs could not and did not last. Tacitus implies that general paranoia came with the territory once the autocratic institution had been established. Evidence from the time suggests that punitive responses, exile and execution became the norm at any hint of criticism. These tactics created a climate of dissent in Rome which might have been avoided and indeed was partially created by the extension of censorship.

From Tacitus' account, Agricola emerges as a skilled manipulator of the local élites in Britain. He imitates the strategy of Augustus, who had disarmed opposition to his rule by a combination of brute force and bribery. Tacitus relates how Agricola encouraged the barbarians to adopt a Roman lifestyle and this effectively enslaved them to Roman rule. Tacitus emphasizes that this was a gradual and an almost imperceptible submersion. An interesting contrast can be found in Cassius Dio's description of Quinctilius Varus' governorship in Germany at the time of Augustus (*Roman History* 56.18–19). Varus became a byword for tragic defeat at the hands of Arminius and Segimerus (three legions were massacred by them in the forest of Teutoberg). These local leaders and their followers appeared to have accepted Roman rule and customs unreservedly. Cassius Dio, writing much later, criticizes the high-handed and complacent technique of Varus in carrying out what sounds to be a very similar policy to the much later Agricola's:

> ... in the exercise of his powers [Varus] also came to handle the affairs of these peoples, he tried both to hasten and to widen the process of change. He not only gave orders to the Germans as if they were actually slaves of the Romans, but also levied money from them as if they were subject nations. These were demands they would not tolerate. The leaders yearned for their formal ascendancy, and the masses preferred their accustomed condition to foreign domination.
>
> (Cassius Dio, *Roman History* 56.18, trans. Scott-Kilvert, 1987)

An alternative reading (see the entry in the *Oxford Classical Dictionary* for Quinctilius Varus, Publius) is that Varus was a scapegoat and was only carrying out established policies of Romanization which were prompted from above. The errors and vices of individuals on both sides made a ready explanation for what were to the Romans surprise revolts. This was the Roman way of rationalizing opposition in terms of bad rulers and obstinate peoples; the disaster arose from a combination of subjective circumstances because the Romans would not have the inclination nor the sociological data to look for causal factors in the objective material conditions.

Romanized barbarian chieftains such as Arminius became disaffected with Roman rule and were prepared to organize the resistance against it. Arminius' actions were unexpected and his success devastating to the emperor. (Augustus is reputed to have let out anguished cries about his lost legions for the rest of his life.) This was a situation where, cynically speaking, the Roman way of peace was an option as long as the subjugation could be conducted with restraint and diplomacy. Where Roman rule was successful and discontent kept to a minimum, we are likely to find that the local leaders had been guaranteed the continuation of their community in a form that allowed them to retain their positions in the hierarchy. Better still, these positions were enhanced by the wider range of status symbols Roman political culture was able to provide.

The fall of Varus and his legions in the Teutoberg Forest went down in Roman history as a notorious defeat and humiliation. Evidence of other, albeit brief, successes scored against Roman power is not always easy to access, and may have been actively suppressed at the time. The revolt of the Blemmyes on the southern border of the province of Egypt is not nearly so famous an incident and yet this tribe captured the magnificent bronze head of the emperor, Augustus, a real trophy to resistance. The head can now be seen in the British Museum, so it has been restored to its place as a symbol of Roman hegemony (Figure 10.2).

The Roman élite, with the prestige and authority now centred on the imperial image, had plenty of readily adaptable articulations of power and authority. In alliance with native nobility they could secure the co-operation of large areas in even the notoriously troublesome provinces. In contrast, if leaders and their communities were unceremoniously railroaded into a Roman way of life with little attempt at balancing its often nakedly exploitative nature and subsuming all the traditional hierarchies under Roman rule, then opposition was likely to erupt. Similarly, in relation to the senatorial class at Rome, Augustus' successors were not always as adept as the *princeps* or first emperor had been when it came to disguising where the real power lay.

There is a logic to Tacitus' approach when he is both articulating and accounting for the dissent of the disaffected communities in the provinces. He not only employs the élite literary language of Rome but also transfers to those who are geographically and culturally remote from the capital the preoccupations of the 'conscientious objectors' closer to home. These speeches from barbarians have a strong subtext of criticism towards the injustices and excesses of ultimate power. Their words would strike a chord with those of Tacitus' class who periodically smarted under the loss of *libertas*.

Critics, conspirators and casualties

From the emperor's point of view, even cryptic pronouncements from critics could be damaging to the image and carefully stage-managed appearance of the ruler. The most passive and re-strained of opponents might succeed in constructing ideal models of rulership and negative paradigms of tyrannical behaviour against which rulers could be measured and compared. Emperors were highly sensitive to any portrayals of them which hinted that they were unfit to rule, and the ultimate treason was to suggest they were endangering the existence of the empire itself.

Figure 10.2 Bronze head of Augustus (over life size) excavated at Meroë, Sudan. British Museum. (© The British Museum)

Plans to overthrow the ruler could be justified on the basis that the current emperor was damaging the image and the security of the empire. This point is worth stressing because it suggests the technique of 'wedge driving'. While the person of the emperor and the interests of the empire could be portrayed as running in harness, as being in perfect concord, acts of revolt and treason against the individual ruler could be brutally punished as threats to the power and people of Rome. It cannot be emphasized too strongly that the rhetoric of removing emperors who had lost legitimacy had nothing to do with dismantling the empire or obstructing Rome's glorious destiny.

The genuine 'opponents of conscience' to later imperial regimes, whose philosophical (usually specifically Stoic) principles impelled them to speak out against injustice and tyranny, rarely plotted against the emperor's life, resigning themselves to passive resistance and perhaps making personal statements in pamphlets which signed their death warrants. They lived to suffer and they expected ultimately to die nobly for their independent stands against autocratic behaviour. Many victims of imperial paranoia exhibited Stoic-style courage and dignity in the face of death, for instance Thrasea Paetus, who fell foul of the emperor Nero and whose demise and death are related by Tacitus with an eye for the tragic and theatrical effect.

According to Macmullen (1967, pp.82–94), the early Stoic exemplars of courage, forced to suicide for 'speaking as they found', established a discourse of dissenting martyrdom which can be traced unbroken to the later persecution of the Christians. Macmullen suggests that the trials of the Christians are not merely documented but clearly embellished with established traditions of suffering in mind. These reconstructions borrowed much of their oppositional rhetoric from the *Acts of the Pagan Martyrs*, so much so that there was 'a full range of perfectly alien motifs imported into martyrology from pagan writings' (Macmullen, 1967, p.92). A common motif is that of divinely inspired strength and an ability to endure torment to such a degree that the persecutor is exhausted before the victim. Macmullen believes that 'certain stereotypes of superhuman virtue were too deeply fixed in the ancient mind to be eradicated' (1967, p.93). The record of opposition aims to preserve for posterity an eloquence which triumphs over the tyranny, whatever the fate of the accused.

Augustus, who fostered some of the best writers to promote his image, position and social and cultural programme for Rome, did not take kindly to any undermining of his carefully composed ideology, the vision of a new Golden Age for Rome of peace, prosperity and permanence. This is in contrast to his tolerance towards nostalgia for the old idealized republic which did not work against his claims to have created a new and improved model of just such a legendary time.

Ovid, a favoured poet, unwisely undermined the picture of integrated destinies and indivisible symbols uniting the *princeps* with the empire. Augustus developed exile as a handy strategy for dispatching critics and potential rivals from Rome. In the days of the republic exile had quite often been a voluntary and an expedient departure when a statesman's political star had temporarily fallen from ascendancy. Under the emperors it could be both a life and a death sentence and the surroundings were frequently remote and isolated. Exile to a lonely outpost of Rome was the fate of the popular and talented writer Ovid, who seems fatally to have combined some indiscretion with the production of a poem which was out of tune with the regime's legislation against adultery. In his poetry, he espoused the carefree attitudes to sexual *mores* which had characterized Rome for many years. Ovid tells us in his *Laments*, written from his place of banishment, Tomis (Constantsa

Figure 10.3 *Nineteenth-century statue of Ovid, Constantsa. There is a similar statue in Ovid's home town of Sulmona in Italy. (Picture taken by Dr Neil Masuda)*

on the Black Sea coast in Romania), that he committed a crime which was in truth a mistake: witnessing something embarrassing to the imperial family is one of a number of speculations about what it was. Ovid's poem, the *Art of Love* – advice about seduction written in mock didactic tones – suddenly incurred the wrath of Augustus almost a decade after its publication, which indicates a sea change in the limits of toleration.

Are the poems in praise and celebration of the first emperor also subtly equivocal about Augustus' path to power? Gurval (1995) is, at the time of writing this essay, the most recent critic to interpret the poet Propertius as 'damning with faint praise' the emperor's victory over Antony and Cleopatra; he believes there was an active refusal on Propertius' part to glorify the principate (the rule of Augustus) in anything but a tongue-in-cheek manner. More controversially, Virgil's epic the *Aeneid* has been reinterpreted and different 'voices', some with a critical register, have been proposed for even this apparently loyal and optimistic supporter of Augustus' 'new deal'. The final scene of Virgil's poem has Aeneas, the Trojan founder of Rome, mercilessly dispatching the local rival, Turnus, to the Underworld, in spite of the warrior's pleas for his life. This has been viewed as a 'downbeat' finale with an unfortunate focus on suffering and tragedy rather than victory and celebration.

Counter-moves to this reading point to an inevitable dark side to all empire building and consider that contemporary audiences and readers would not view the finale of the *Aeneid* as an undercutting of the empire nor of Augustus. The search for anti-Augustanism in the very poets patronized by the first emperor has not yielded conclusive arguments. It has to be said that if offence was intended, it was rarely taken by the man who mattered, Augustus himself.

There were to our knowledge no reprisals for Propertius, and if Virgil had his doubts about the cost of Rome's greatness, they did not worry Augustus, who insisted the *Aeneid* was published, not quite completed, after the poet's death and expressly against the author's wishes. It is important to note that Virgil's epic poem accepted and promoted Augustus as divinely destined to save and perpetuate the Roman empire, giving his claim to the leadership validation from the past and surrounding it with an aura of aesthetic authorization. From Augustus' point of view, who could ask for anything more?

Ovid suffered for subverting the rhetoric of the Augustan regime. Ovid's intentions were hardly revolutionary. Playing around with the emperor's discourse for moral regeneration is more likely to be an indication that the poet had more wit than wisdom and wrote not wisely but too well. Subsequently serious inner-circle dissidents did deliberately turn the regime's best ideological weapons against the incumbent emperor. This is especially noticeable in the medium of literature. The skilful writers played the Roman emperors or rulers at their own rhetorical game. Seneca, in his satire *The Pumpkinification of Claudius*, depicted the dead emperor Claudius attempting to enter Olympus and become a god. He is summarily dispatched to the Underworld for an ignominious fate, a fitting end for an emperor who in his lifetime had enrolled Gallic aristocrats into the august body of the Roman senate. Many senators had seen this as an attempt to degrade and weaken them and their assembly.

Nero was launched as a Golden Age emperor by the same Seneca, and the influence of Stoic philosophy and ethics was the key selling point for the young successor of Claudius. Nero's opponents, conspirators, and innocent victims of his anxiety about plots and assassinations frequently gave a critique of his regime with Stoic criteria in mind. Thrasea Paetus has already been mentioned. He is quoted in Epictetus (*Dissertations* 1.1.26) as preferring death today rather than banishment tomorrow. Also part of the Stoic opposition were Musonius Rufus, Helvidius Priscus and Paconius Agrippinus. They took the attitude that exile was to and could be endured if one's Stoic principles had any meaning. Priscus was banished a second time under Vespasian for his outspoken criticism, even insults, of the emperor. Epictetus also records an encounter between the two in the *Dissertations* (1.2.19–22):

> *Helvidius Priscus*: You can banish me from the senate, but while I am a member of it, I must go into the house.
>
> *Vespasian*: Well all right, go in but stay silent.
>
> *Helvidius Priscus*: Do not ask for my opinion and then I can keep quiet.
>
> *Vespasian*: But I have to ask you.
>
> *Helvidius Priscus*: Then I must say what seems right to me.
>
> *Vespasian*: But do that and I will execute you.
>
> *Helvidius Priscus*: I have never claimed to you that I was immortal. You do what is your part and I shall do mine. Yours is to kill me and mine to die unafraid. Yours is to banish me and mine to go into exile unsorrowing.

Exporting contradictions

Modern historians of the classical world frequently negotiate Roman hegemony with a salutary angst in case they are condemned for devaluing the culture of the oppressed or for not looking hard enough to find it (see Mattingly, 1967, throughout). On the other hand, the sometimes brutal reality of Roman rule should not be marginalized by this new and valuable focus on 'interpenetration' of cultures. The evidence can also suggest that the imperial identity was being actively and forcefully marketed and disseminated. In the past, scholars whose nations had a history of empire building tended to play down the aspect of coercion in the process of expansion or to reproduce uncritically Roman rhetoric about legitimate cultural hierarchy. Recent scholarship has to tread a cautious path in this respect, to avoid underplaying Roman oppression from the progressive standpoint of celebrating the survival of local identities within the Roman political landscape. The coercive aspect of Roman rule also reveals some of the underlying stresses that made the empire a less than peaceful place both politically and militarily.

Post-colonial studies, studies of power based on the work of thinkers such as Foucault and Gramsci, show that attempts to ring-fence investigations of resistance can end up retracing the contours of hegemonic power. More simply, no space exists for resistance to occur unless it is in the very space generated by domination and already partially occupied by the symbols the resistance is seeking to desecrate or expropriate. I shall discuss – briefly, as many of the areas are given a more rigorous exposition in other essays – the principal fields in which imperial power was exercised and the difficulties in finding a dissenting voice that is not filtered through élite Roman consciousness.

The manipulation of large and lucrative provincial areas by the generals of the late republic is treated in the detailed and now standard work by Badian (1984), *Foreign Clientelae*. This study demonstrates that when Augustus took control, and those known to have access to him and to be his loyal delegates constituted the government and authority over the provinces, the structures and the psychology were already in place for the person of the emperor to be accepted, looked to for protection, obeyed and revered as the ultimate patron.

According to Whittaker (1997, pp.150–1), the imperial rulers did not leave anything to chance in the cities where it mattered, but made sure that the local administration arranged statuary in the main squares to reflect the centrality of the Roman emperor and his bureaucracy in the political and social scheme of things. In the light of new discoveries and new interpretations such as these, certain pieces of literary evidence acquire added value and are being used accordingly. For instance, Cassius Dio indicates that a shrine to the deified Augustus erected at Rome was duplicated across the empire but, revealingly, states: 'some of the communities built these of their own accord, others only under orders' (*Roman History* 56.46, discussed in Whittaker, 1997, p.155). Cassius Dio's text produces further examples of active interference and something close to coercion in the construction of temples to Rome and Caesar across the empire.

On the other hand, archaeology and the evidence of the visual arts can gauge the survival of local cultures throughout the empire in the face of at times aggressive Romanization. Branigan, who has already been cited, would see archaeology as our most powerful way of reading the past and particularly of reading the possible protests of the past. Webster (1997, pp.170–82) alerts us to the open-endedness of such investigations. She shows the alternative ways of interpreting a surviving sculptural relief of the marriage of Roman Mercury to the Celtic goddess, Rosmerta (Figure 10.4). This merger can be seen as the submersion and submission of local deities to the power and religious culture of Rome; alternatively, the placing of the Roman god next to a highly potent mother earth symbol may be a deliberate compromising of Roman hegemony. Webster (p.175) uses the term 'resistant adaptation' to encompass everyday and small-scale acts which could undermine the

Figure 10.4 *Sculptural relief of Mercury and Rosmerta from Shakespeare's Inn, Gloucester. Gloucester City Museum. (© Gloucester City Museum and Art Gallery)*

alien images and ambiences of imperial Rome. The middle way between these two readings is that Rosmerta has been creatively resignified in Roman terms, but has not lost her identity by this process; rather, she has a new and an empowered lease of life. If the native nobility could be persuaded to acquire Roman forms of status and to adopt Roman cultural expressions to enrich or expand their own symbols of power, why should their gods not be invested with new layers of artistic representation to the same end?

Pax romana

The Roman concept of peace is evaluated in Essay Twelve. The baseline of Roman power and control was the existence of a highly professional and, from the time of Augustus, permanent standing army. The prolonged and difficult subjugation of Dacia (modern Romania) was recorded in Trajan's column in a series of very detailed reliefs and with all kinds of battle techniques preserved for posterity. Goodman (1997) discusses the reasons behind the creation of a standing army under Augustus, the first emperor, whose regime set the tone in so many ways for subsequent administrations and styles of leadership. Augustus' priority was to keep his own power base secure from internal challenges and rivals among the senatorial class. The army, whether in Rome in the form of the Praetorian Guard or settled along the borders of the empire, presented a show of strength to the citizens within those borders as much as being a permanent military fixture facing external threats from volatile tribes and disaffected allies:

> It is also possible that Octavian and his successors hung on to a large force primarily to deter rivals within the senatorial elite. Octavian's own early career had demonstrated the ease with which legions could be raised on private initiative by the ambitious, and it was characteristic of Augustus that he viewed Roman politics in the light of his own success.
>
> (Goodman, 1991, p.235)

In the days of the republic the army was an effective troubleshooting outfit, with a fearsome reputation for reacting to rebellion, disaffection and barbarian incursions over the borders. However, most of the troops had to be reconscripted to serve the exigencies of the moment. The army did not need to be on the spot, nor did reprisals have to be immediate in every case. The crucial thing was that they validated an expectation among allies and enemies alike that sooner or later they would be there to deal with dissent and revolt: 'It was only necessary that the enemies of Rome should know that Rome would always retaliate – in time' (Goodman, 1991, p.233).

Goodman believes that 'some revolts that occurred soon after conquest by Rome can best be seen as a final desperate attempt to reverse the political trend by those native leaders who were in the forefront of the changes coming over their society, and thus were in a particularly good position to appreciate the incipient danger that such changes would prove irreversible' (1991, p.227). Whittaker (1997) supports the conclusion that the development of the standing army, itself ensuring enclaves and microcosms of Roman social identity, was the baseline of imperial power and authority. Dissent and revolt in the army was potentially far more effective and dangerous than in any other sphere. It could involve small-scale mutiny or be a manifestation of the army's support for an individual commander – the famous phenomenon of emperors made elsewhere than at Rome. When the latter did occur either it was successful, in so far as a legion's candidate for emperor would take power, or it was rapidly rooted out by the troops of a rival claimant or the incumbent emperor's soldiers.

Tacitus tells the touching story of a mutiny forestalled when Germanicus was campaigning in Germany (*Annals* 1.40). The soldiers were full of remorse at the departure of their general's wife and children, particularly the army 'mascot', Gaius Caligula (later to become emperor), because their safety could not be guaranteed in the camp. This anecdote about sentimental attachments to the imperial family and spontaneous outbursts of affection disguises the fact that the loyalty of troops to empire and emperor was consciously constructed wherever the army was in the provinces. The imperial cult had a high profile in army life: it was linked to the worship of the legionary standards and had its rituals attached to the handing out of donatives. The image of the emperor was omnipresent among the troops even if the emperor in person was not there as a campaigning general. It was hardly surprising that army revolts tended to produce new candidates for ruler and that the soldiers were not agitating to have no ruler at all.

Goodman points out that the very expense of sustaining these military forces, which he estimates at around 250,000 including auxiliaries at the time of the principate, were as likely to foster unrest as to deter it, especially among those peoples in the provinces who were under particular pressure to subsidize these troops by taxes and levies or to accept high-handed requisitions when the military required them (Luttwak, 1976, p.16). Before Augustus, the bulk of the army had been regularly disbanded (there was an ongoing problem of finding land for veterans in return for service). Augustus' organization left half the legions (twenty-eight in number) on permanent duty, with longer years of service for the individual soldiers who now spent up to twenty years in settlements, virtually small towns in some cases, across the empire.

Under the principate the administration of an established army had a considerable impact on the economy of the empire – Goodman (1997, p.82) estimates its cost at half the total spending of the state under Augustus – and the need to raise the resources throughout the empire resulted in a more systematic and intensified exploitation of the provinces, with the resulting protests and manifestations of discontent. However, the structures of military command which had come to stay as part of the administration of the empire provided opportunities for the senators. In other words it provided 'jobs for the boys', the republican oligarchy which had been the governing body of Rome before the emperors and which Augustus made a great show of taking into partnership once he was the established ruler of the empire.

The senatorial class to whom Augustus delegated authority in the army and the administration, along with selected posts for the *equites* class, were given an occupation and a status as well as a stake in the preservation of law and order. Augustus took great pains to enhance the self-esteem of the senators and was prepared to legislate against any loss of prestige they had suffered or brought upon themselves in the last years of the republic. In summary, possible rivals to the emperor's one-man management were given a share in that management, but as a gift, with a corresponding obligation on their part, from Augustus. They exercised control over the troops, but they owed this control to the monopoly of power and authority which rested in the emperor alone. The aim was to encourage loyalty without dissent among the élite classes from which Augustus had sprung. Such a strategy required a great deal of political acumen, a quality not all of his successors had in equal measure.

On the one hand the preservation of imperial rule became bound up with the power base of the emperor, and the need to burden the provinces more heavily to sustain the guarantee of his power, namely the army, was a potential threat to harmony in the provinces. A central aspect of the emperor's image, and one initiated and fostered by Augustus, was how much the glory and destiny of the empire were tied to the emperor himself. The irony does not need much forcing. The empire needed an emperor to orchestrate its defence and guarantee its frontiers, but the existence of the emperor set up its own internal pressures and demonstrations of discontent. On the other hand the concerted programme of urbanization and the emphasis on the place of the emperor at the sacred heart of things, a semi-divine figure with the highest authority to legitimate his rule, actively encouraged loyalty in all the key locations of Rome's imperial sphere.

Tensions from below

Riots and urban unrest in Rome itself (and this is true of a number of large cities, for example Carthage) were not part of international solidarity with oppressed peoples elsewhere in the empire nor were intended to question the need for Roman rule. Alexandria is a case in point, famous for urban riots and particularly anti-Semitic ones (Modrzejewski, 1997). At Rome demonstrations against emperors were commonly reactions to hunger and hardship when grain supplies were held up. Times of discontent among the plebs in the capital occurred when the ruler was patently unable to deliver the goods. The 'goods' were not always material and basic but, certainly in the case of Rome, included 'cultural' consumption, the entertainments the crowds had come to expect at the Circus Maximus or in the amphitheatre. The visible sharing in the benefits of empire has been discussed elsewhere in this volume (see Essay Seven). Essay Three suggests some of the functions of shows and displays in the capital city. Public shows certainly set aside space for the operation of control and consensus. Emperors and people played out a kind of mutual manipulation at the games and at the races. Occasionally, and interestingly, an outburst of feeling at the games in the arena or at the races conveyed discontent with the behaviour of the ruler – an implied critique of his presentation skills perhaps, which suggests to me that the Roman plebs had a conception of appropriate styles for the imperial image. The need for an image and for an emperor was, however, never in question.

Patterns of revolt

I have already discussed possible causes for disaffection in the provinces in the context of Calgacus' speech and using Dyson's study of the trends across the spectrum of empire. I suggested that the kinds of motives that apologists for Roman domination ascribed to those who kicked against imperial power revealed a number of significant concepts in Roman political thought. Goodman (1991) argues against the assumption that religious zeal and a keen sense of national identity drove certain groups into active opposition against their Roman masters. (See also Essay Eleven, on the Jewish question.) He suggests that this impression is one fostered by writers in the Flavian period for propaganda purposes and connected to the 'messianic or other anti-Roman notions to be found in a limited number of Judaic texts surviving from that period' (p.223). Goodman reinforces his point about the Jews' ability to accommodate themselves to Roman rule by citing Josephus and Philo, 'both ostentatiously pious and knowledgeable about their ancestral religions, but both philo-Roman'. Although active revolt of identifiable ethnic groups might take on a religious colour or expression, it is not until the second to third-century *Acts of the Pagan Martyrs* and the *Acts of the Christian Martyrs* that exclusive belief systems and rival deities are counterposed to the pantheon and worship of Roman gods.

A consensus, at least among these scholars, is emerging that in most cases the causes of larger-scale rebellions were much more material than spiritual. Dyson (1975) stresses that the 'lack of a dynamic religion in most of the societies conquered by Rome meant the social and psychological energy often generated by native revolts did not easily channel itself into a religious form' (p.170). This conclusion is not necessarily at odds with the exploration of the role native religious cults seem to have played in sustaining oppositional identities on a day-to-day and not directly confrontational basis, the resistant adaptation theory raised earlier.

The Christians, whose dissent I have somewhat marginalized, relegating them to a place in the traditions of martyrdom, ran into trouble with the authorities principally because they could not venerate the image of the emperor even though they were generally willing to accept his authority and the administration of Roman rule. Acceptance of rule without veneration of the emperor simply was not good enough, since there was a vital *concordia* not just of symbols but also of concepts of hegemony and power, uniting the person of the emperor to the power of the empire. Christians became famous scapegoats and suffered a series of vicious persecutions from the time of Nero. Their dissent could be reconstructed by the ruling ideology so that accusations of disloyalty were connected with assumptions about difference, and Christian beliefs and rituals were painted with a barbarian, even Druidical, hue. It is significant that this would give them a kind of guilt by association with the more outlandish and troublesome tribes in outlying reaches of the empire, peoples who sometimes did translate their discontent into collective attacks on Roman rule. Add to this the conflation of Christian with Judaic beliefs and their commitment to a messianic saviour prince, and their condemnation was assured.

As regards individual dissenters, whether rivals to the title of emperor, hopeful champions of a restored republic or embittered individuals with a personal axe to grind against particular rulers, they can either be judged individually on their 'merits' or alternatively be marshalled into categories and styles of opposition. They rarely challenged the right of Rome to rule and this is why they have to be distinguished from native revolts. Although Macmullen (1967) does have examples of philosophers appealing to the people against the emperor, generally the days when the ambitious élite politician could use the plebs to destabilize his peers and make a personal bid for power were over with the advent of the principate and the monopolizing of such channels by the emperors, direct patrons of the Roman people. I refer the reader to Macmullen, pages 56–7 and note 14 on page 307: 'Thrasea's alleged ambitions for *nova instituta* [new ordinances, but almost the restoration of traditions] and *libertas* ... and his and Helvidius' championing of *vocem populi Romani et libertatem sebatus* [the voice of the people and the freedom of the senate] ... aim at nothing more than the old Republican constitution. The people's *vox* would have been very small.'

Conclusion

> A central problem in the study of imperialism involves comprehending both the broad dynamics of expansion, exploitation and control, and also the multiplicity of local experiences, as each society accommodated itself to the new order. Both conquerors and the conquered have their own stories, and both deserve telling.
>
> (Woolf, 1992, p.349)

This essay has concentrated on the conquerors' story and particularly on how this story was transferred into the mouths of the conquered. The discourse of dissent is simultaneously the description of domination. However empowering the rhetoric of opposition seems to be in the pages of Roman historians, and however sympathetic, or perhaps empathetic, their attitudes are to those facing slavery and subjugation, the preoccupations with liberty and cultural identity are fundamentally Roman ones. That does not mean to say that they are invariably inaccurate interpretations of the responses to Roman rule across the empire.

Rome's capacity to conduct surveillance and exercise constant control must have been limited by low levels of communications technology and significant gaps in administrative bureaucracy. There must have been many occasions when Romanization in practice meant exploiting a commonality of interests. Tacitus certainly assumes that all ruling classes speak the same language. Another famous British chieftain, Caratacus, who rallied his troops in a similar way to Calgacus, is also portrayed by Tacitus as pleading for mercy from the emperor Claudius. (Tacitus' report covers an event which predated the author's own time by about fifty years.) Caratacus presents himself as a worthy opponent of the emperor. It was only natural that he should resist enslavement. Circumstances have rendered him a defeated enemy but he might equally have been a respected ally. Caratacus is spared by Claudius. Caratacus might have been very amenable to receiving the insignia of Rome as long as his position among his own people did not fundamentally alter.

> Had my lineage and rank been accompanied by only moderate success, I should have come to this city as friend rather than prisoner, and you would not have disdained to ally yourself peacefully with one so nobly born, the ruler of so many nations. As it is, humiliation is my lot, glory yours. I had horses, men, arms, wealth. Are you surprised I am sorry to lose them? If you want to rule the world, does it follow that everyone else welcomes enslavement? If I had surrendered without a blow before being brought before you, neither my downfall nor your triumph would have been famous. If you execute me, they will be forgotten. Spare me, and I shall be an everlasting token of your mercy.
>
> (Tactitus, *Annals* 12.33, trans. Grant, 1989)

Claudius spares Caratacus' wife and brothers too. Caratacus' special pleading has somewhat corrupted the Roman principle, articulated by Virgil, that only the submissive could be shown mercy (*Aeneid* 6.853). Caratacus freely confesses to have been numbered among the proud who refused to submit. This may be just another example of a traditional critique of imperialism, and yet Tacitus must have intended some statement about this gesture of pardon. It seems in any case to have been a novel display of a defeated enemy as the freed prisoners gave the same homage to the emperor's wife, Agrippina, as they did to the emperor himself. One wonders if the image of Claudius as an eccentric and uxorious emperor with a weak grasp on public decorum is not being subtly alluded to in this colourful episode. In that case, like the speech of Calgacus, the words given to Caratacus are a prompt for an implied comment about life at the centre and its corrupt court. This is Tacitean rather than native dissent and seems an appropriate place, having come almost full circle, to end the discussion.

References

ALEXANDER, L. (ed.) (1991) *Images of Empire*, Journal for the Study of the Old Testament Supplement Series 122, Sheffield, Journal for the Study of the Old Testament.

BADIAN, E. (1984) *Foreign Clientelae (264–70 BC)* (first published 1958), Oxford, Clarendon Press.

BRANIGAN, K. (1991) 'Images – or mirages – of empire? An archaeological approach to the problem', in Alexander (ed.), pp.91–106.

BRAUND, D. (1996) *Ruling Roman Britain: Kings, Queens and Emperors from Julius Caesar to Agricola*, London, Routledge.

DYSON, S.L. (1975) 'Native revolt patterns in the Roman empire', *Aufstieg und Niedergang der römischen Welt*, vol.II, no.3, pp.138–175.

GOODMAN, M. (1991) 'Opponents of Rome: Jews and others' in Alexander (ed.), pp.222–38.

GOODMAN, M. (1997) *The Roman World: 44 BC – AD 180*, London, Routledge.

GRANT, M. (trans.) (1989) *Tacitus: the Annals of Imperial Rome*, Harmondsworth, Penguin Books.

GURVAL, R.A. (1995) *Actium and Augustus: the Politics and Emotions of Civil War*, Ann Arbor, Mich., University of Michigan Press.

HERM, G. (1976) *The Celts: the People Who Came Out of the Darkness*, London, Weidenfeld & Nicolson.

LUTTWAK, E.N. (1976) *The Grand Strategy of the Roman Empire from the First Century AD to the Third*, Baltimore, Ohio, John Hopkins University Press.

MACMULLEN, R. (1967) *Enemies of the Roman Order*, London, Routledge.

MATTINGLY, D.J. (ed.) (1997) *Dialogues in Roman Imperialism: Power, Discourse, and Discrepant Experience in the Roman Empire*, Journal of Roman Archaeology Supplementary Series no.23, Portsmouth, R.I., Journal of Roman Archaeology.

MATTINGLY, H. (trans.) (1976) *Tacitus: The* Agricola *and the* Germania (revised by S.A. Handford), Harmondsworth, Penguin Books.

MELLOR, R. (1993) *Tacitus*, London, Routledge.

MODRZEJEWSKI, J.M. (1997) *The Jews of Egypt from Rameses II to Emperor Hadrian*, Princeton, N.J., Princeton University Press.

OGILVIE, R.M. and RICHMOND, I.A. (1967) *Tacitus: De Vita Agricolae*, Oxford, Clarendon Press.

RUDICH, V. (1993) *Dissidence and Literature under Nero: the Price of Dissimulation*, London, Routledge.

SCOTT-KILVERT, I. (1987) *Cassius Dio: The Roman History: The Reign of Augustus*, Harmondsworth, Penguin Books.

WEBSTER, J. (1997) 'A negotiated syncretism: readings on the development of Romano-Celtic religion', in Mattingly (ed.), pp.165–84.

WHITTAKER, C.R. (1997) 'Imperialism and culture: the Roman initiative', in Mattingly (ed.), pp.143–64.

WOOLF, G. (1992) 'The unity and the diversity of Romanization', *Journal of Roman Archaeology*, 5, pp.349–52.

Essay Eleven
Jews and Jewish communities in the Roman empire

BY MARGARET WILLIAMS

For the Jews of Judaea, the arrival of the legions of Rome in their country in 63 BC marked the end of an era. Although the physical damage inflicted by Pompey's troops on Jerusalem and its temple in that year was merely temporary, politically Judaea was never to be the same again. Gone for ever was the autonomy that the Jews had been enjoying since the 160s BC under their Hasmonean high priests and kings. Until the Arab conquest of the area *c.* AD 640, Roman power there, exercised variously by puppet princelings, prefects, procurators and legates, was paramount. Few challenges were ever made to that power, and those that were made were invariably unsuccessful (for example, the First Jewish Revolt of AD 66–73/74 and the Bar Kochba Revolt of AD 132–5). Such complete political dominance by Rome, however, does not mean that Jewish culture in Judaea was suppressed or Jewish self-identity destroyed. Though deprived successively by Rome of their priestly rulers (the Hasmoneans, in the person of Hyrcanus II, were replaced by the client dynasty of the Herods in 40 BC), their temple (destroyed by Titus in AD 70), their holy city (the emperor Hadrian banned Jewish access to Jerusalem in AD 135), and even of the distinctively Jewish name of their country (the province of Judaea, literally, the Land of Judah, was renamed Syria Palaestina after the Bar Kochba Revolt), the Jews still had the Torah, the Law of Moses, as enshrined in the Pentateuch, the first five books of the Bible. Their continuing possession of this unique source of law and tradition proved more than adequate for enabling them to retain their cultural identity and refocus their communal life. Henceforth, intensive Torah study came to fill completely the void left by temple ritual, and the rabbinical academy (Beth ha-Midrash) to replace the temple as the dominant institution of Palestinian Jewry. In this refocused and (ultimately) revitalized society, virtually all hope of an imminent coming of the Messiah was abandoned and Roman power was accorded a grudging acceptance.

It was not only in the province of Judaea/Palestine, however, that Jews were to be found in early Roman imperial times. They lived also, and in far larger numbers, throughout the greater part of the Mediterranean world (see Figure 11.1). And it is with these Jews, those of the so-called Diaspora (literally, dispersion or scattering), that I shall be concerned in the rest of this essay. My virtual exclusion of the Jews of Judaea from this discussion may perhaps seem strange, but it is deliberate. Partly it is a question of space, but mainly it is because Diasporan Jewry is of far greater relevance to the issues of culture, identity and power in the Roman empire. That Judaean Jews managed to retain a powerful sense of their Jewish identity under Roman rule is unsurprising. Providing that they were loyal subjects (that is, that they paid the taxes and did not revolt), the Romans, ever pragmatic, were content to allow them to live their lives in accordance with their ancestral customs. And that the great mass of them never became more than superficially acculturated is equally unsurprising. Since they formed a clear majority of the population of the province of Judaea, they felt little pressure to accommodate themselves to the lifestyles of the sundry Gentiles, many of them Greeks and Romans, who lived there as well.

But for Jews living in other parts of the empire the situation was different. Even where they were settled in great numbers, as at Alexandria, Antioch on the Orontes and Rome, they always formed a distinct minority of the local population. And those of them who wished to continue living their lives in accordance with ancestral customs – and such people existed in large numbers – were faced with a number of problems. Fulfilling the requirements of the Law of Moses, as of course they had to do if they were to retain their Jewish identity, put them under immense cultural pressure. Circumcision, for instance, that most fundamental of Jewish rites, was widely derided by Greeks and Romans, who themselves did not practise this 'mutilation of the genitals' (*Augustan History: Hadrian* 14.2). Sabbath observance, an equally alien custom (the seven-day week was not a feature of Graeco-Roman social life), was regularly mocked, as was Jewish abstention from pork. (For the facetious remarks attributed to the emperors Augustus and Gaius (Caligula) on this subject, see Williams, 1998, 2.123–4.) Nor were the difficulties confronting Diasporan Jews merely cultural. Because strict adherence to the cult of Yahweh (the worship of God) of necessity entailed denial of the deities of the Greeks and Romans, the Jews were always open to charges of undermining the community. That they managed, for the most part, to negotiate those problems successfully is a remarkable achievement that has all too rarely received the attention it deserves. Hence my decision to focus upon it in this essay. However, before I discuss Diasporan Jewry in early Roman imperial times in terms of culture, identity and power, the context needs to be established. There follows, therefore, a brief survey of the extent, origins and salient features of the Jewish Mediterranean Diaspora in antiquity, and the more common Graeco-Roman reactions to it.

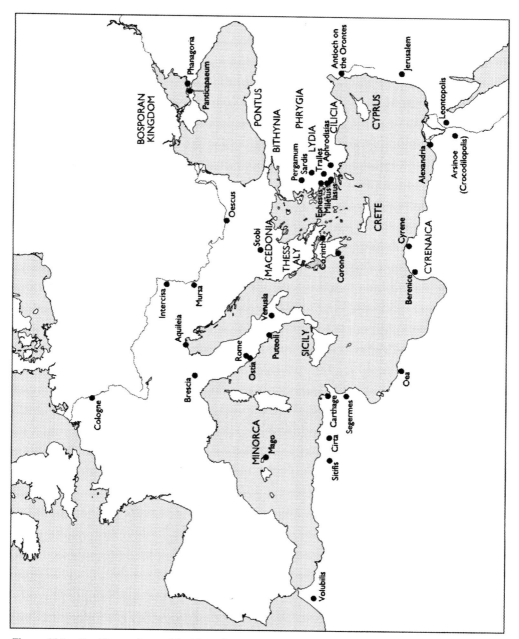

Figure 11.1 *Significant places of Jewish settlement in the Roman empire. Lack of space precludes giving a comprehensive list. There was, however, scarcely a coastal city in the eastern Mediterranean that did not have a Jewish community.*

The Jewish Diaspora: its extent in the first century AD, origins and salient features

> Concerning the Holy City [Jerusalem], there are points to be made that relate to me. It is, as I have said, my native city and the mother city [*metropolis*] of not just one country, Judaea, but the majority, because of the colonies [*apoikiai*] it has sent out from time to time both to the neighbouring lands of Egypt, Phoenicia and Syria – the so-called Coele Syria as well as the rest – and to the distant countries of Pamphylia, Cilicia, most of Asia up to Bithynia and the depths of Pontus, and in the same way also to Europe, to Thessaly, Boeotia, Macedonia, Aetolia, Attica, Argos, Corinth and most of the best parts of the Peloponnese. It is not only the continents that are full of Jewish colonies but the most renowned of the islands, Euboea, Cyprus, Crete. Concerning the lands across the Euphrates, I keep silent. Except for a small part ... they all have Jewish settlers.
>
> (Philo, *Embassy to Gaius* 281–2)

This passage, an extract from a letter allegedly sent to the emperor Gaius (Caligula) in AD 40 by the Jewish ruler, Agrippa I, is one of the best thumbnail sketches to survive from antiquity of the Jewish Diaspora in early imperial times. That the words were entirely Agrippa's own is very doubtful. They belong to the same category of writing as the speech that Tacitus puts in the mouth of Calgacus (see Essay Ten), and as such were probably largely Philo's invention. That, however, does not mean that the information they convey is valueless. To convince his readers, Philo had to produce a plausible description of the contemporary Jewish world. And who more likely to have the knowledge and skill to do that than this well-educated Alexandrian Jew from a family with extensive business interests in the Mediterranean and Near East? But Philo produces more than a plausible description here. It is also accurate, as a whole raft of evidence, literary, archaeological and epigraphic, confirms. In one respect only is it deficient. Philo, for reasons that must remain speculative, makes no mention of contemporary Jewish settlements west of the Adriatic. There was, however, a large Jewish community in first-century Rome, of which he certainly had knowledge – he describes its location and privileges in an earlier section of the same treatise (*Embassy to Gaius* 155–8). And he is likely to have been aware of the substantial Jewish settlements that existed in his day at the ports of Puteoli and Ostia. Apart from the fact that Philo's brother had a business agent at Puteoli, virtually the first thing that Jewish travellers at that time tended to do on arriving in Italy from Alexandria and Judaea was to make contact with the local Jewish communities in those places (Josephus, *Jewish Antiquities* 18.160 and *Life of Josephus* 16). Philo's failure to mention Jews in the western provinces of the empire is not surprising. While there may have been Jewish communities in Spain at that date (some scholars infer that from the Epistle of Paul to the Romans 15.24), hard evidence is lacking. As for Jewish settlements in other parts of the western empire (for example, Africa, Mauretania and Gaul), they enter the historical record only in the second or third centuries AD and thus may not have existed in Philo's day.

To dignify the diffusion of the Jews, Philo, both in the passage quoted above and elsewhere, resorts to the traditional terminology of Greek colonization. The words 'mother city' (*metropolis*) and 'colonies' (*apoikiai*) are deliberately chosen to create the impression that the Jewish Diaspora was a calculated, state-led enterprise, and Diasporan Jews enthusiastic colonists in search of a better life in 'a place away from home' (the literal meaning of *apoikia*). The reality was very different. It was the warfare of the Ptolemies and Seleucids, who for over a century had contested the rulership of southern Syria, that had led to the formation of the Mediterranean Diaspora. Ptolemy I, for example, is alleged to have transported no fewer than 100,000 Jewish prisoners of war from Judaea to Egypt. And it was the security needs of those same dynasties that had led to the wider diffusion of Jews in the west. The Ptolemies, for instance, are known to have settled large numbers of Egyptian Jews in Cyrenaica (Libya) as military colonists (Josephus, *Against Apion* 2.44), and the Seleucid monarch, Antiochus III, to have planted hundreds of his Babylonian Jewish subjects in the unruly areas of Phrygia and Lydia in Asia Minor. Roman military activity in Judaea (for example, Pompey's conquest of that territory in 63 BC and Sosius' recovery of it from the Parthians in 37 BC) caused the numbers of Diasporan Jews to swell even more: the Jewish community at Rome, which in the early first century AD is known to have numbered several thousands (Josephus, *Jewish War* 2.80), was comprised largely of people whose forbears had been brought from Judaea in chains (Smallwood, 1976, p.131). And there was to be a further increase in its size in AD 70 after the capture of Jerusalem and the crushing of the First Jewish Revolt. But it must not be thought that all Diasporan Jews were involuntary exiles. For example, the founders of the Jewish settlement at Leontopolis in Egypt (mid second century BC), with its exact replica of the temple at Jerusalem, had opted for life abroad after losing out in political in-fighting in Judaea (Josephus, *Jewish War* 1.31–3). Removing oneself willingly from 'the promised land', however, was not a course of action that Jews tended to embark upon lightly, and initiatives such as that were rare (Gafni, 1997).

The deracination that foreign captivity involved must have caused some Jews to abandon their ancestral ways. It is hard to see, for instance, how isolated Jewish slaves with unsympathetic Gentile owners can have managed to obtain kosher foodstuffs or observe the commandment against working on the Sabbath. Other Jews would have succumbed to the influence of their new, polytheistic environment and made compromises with paganism. The clearest evidence for this from Graeco-Roman antiquity belongs to the Hellenistic period (Williams, 1998, 5.50; cf. 5.47–9 and 51), and so cannot appropriately be cited here. However, an example of this type of behaviour from early imperial Roman Italy is probably to be seen in the *ex voto* dedication of Annia Juda, widely believed by scholars to have been a Jewish freedwoman. Found at Brescia in northern Italy, it records the offering she made to the local fertility goddesses, the Iunones, on behalf of her family (*CIJ* 1.77*, in Williams, 1998, 6.22).

Many Jews, though, endeavoured to remain faithful to 'the customs of their fathers', and where such people existed in sufficient numbers congregations for that purpose tended to come into being. Frequently those bodies adopted the Greek title *synagoge*, the primary meaning of that word being 'gathering' or 'assembly'. To give a few examples: the congregations (*synagogai*) of the Augustesians and Agrippesians, attested at Rome in the third century AD, are thought to have originated among Jewish slaves and freedmen in the households of Augustus and Agrippa respectively, the *synagoge* of the Tripolitanians to have been founded by Jewish immigrants to Rome from one of the several Mediterranean cities named Tripolis, and the *synagoge Siburesion* to have been comprised of Jews residing in the Subura, a notorious slum area of the capital (Leon, 1960, pp.140–2 and 151–4). Although the simple premises in which congregations such as the last are likely to have met often developed over time into multi-purpose community centres, complete with dining rooms (*triclinia*) and accommodation for travellers, their primary function was always religious. (A fairly elaborate synagogal complex of the imperial period has been found at Ostia; see Figures 11.2 and 11.3.) Here, on the Sabbath in particular, the Torah was studied (Philo, *The Special Laws* 2.62; Acts of the Apostles 17.1–3). Here the contributions required by the Law

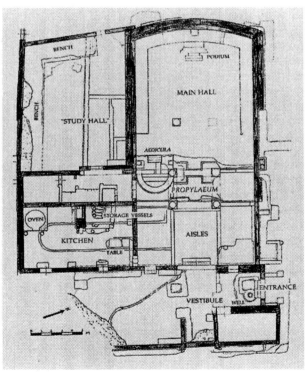

Figure 11.2 *Plan of the synagogue at Ostia. (Reproduced from Fine, 1996)*

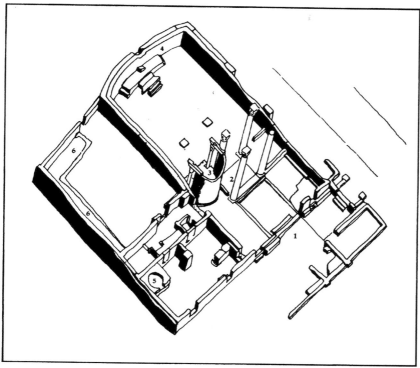

Figure 11.3 *A perspective drawing of the synagogue at Ostia showing (1) the central door, (2) the inner gateway, (3) the Torah Shrine, (4) the curved back wall, (5) the oven and (6) the benches (probably for students of the Law/Torah). (Reproduced from Shanks, 1979, courtesy of Hershel Shanks, Biblical Archaeology Society, Washington DC)*

of Moses for the maintenance of the temple cult and priesthood were deposited for annual despatch to Jerusalem (Philo, *Embassy to Gaius* 156–7), and here prayers were regularly offered up to God – hence the commonest term for the Jewish meeting house in Graeco-Roman antiquity – the 'house of prayer' (Greek/Latin: *proseuche/proseucha*). '*Synagoge*' only became a term for the communal building, as opposed to the congregation that worshipped in it, in the first century AD (see the Berenice inscription cited on p.317) and never enjoyed universal use.

Graeco-Roman attitudes to the synagogue and the Jews

That the Jewish communal buildings discussed above were noticed by local Gentiles is clear from pagan literature and inscriptions. For Juvenal, the synagogues (*proseuchae*) of Rome signified the haunts of beggars (*Satires* 3.296). Ovid, tongue in cheek, hinted that they were good places to pick up girls every seventh day (*The Art of Love* 1.75–6), and for other Romans they served as a kind of address. Thus Publius Corfidius Signinus has come down in history as 'the fruit vendor by the prayer house (*proseuche*) at the Servian Wall' (Williams, 1998, 1.60). Some Greeks and Romans, though, did more than just note the existence of Jewish prayer houses. A recurrent theme of the Acts of the Apostles, a crucially important text for first-century AD Diasporan Judaism, is the attendance of 'Hellenes' (that is, Graeco-Roman Gentiles) at synagogues in the eastern Roman provinces for Sabbath worship. Although there are scholars who argue that these so-called 'God-Fearers' were no more than a theological construct (Kraabel, 1981), this is belied by numerous synagogal inscriptions, most notably from Asia Minor. These not only mention numerous Godfearers (*Theosebeis*) by name but attest to their piety and close links with the synagogue. To give some examples: at Tralles, a town in Caria (south-western Asia Minor), Claudia Capitolina, known to have been the daughter, wife and mother of Gentile Roman senators, paid for, among other things, the mosaics in the prayer house (Trebilco, 1991, pp.157–8 and Williams, 1998, 7.13); at Sardis, at least two Godfearers joined with the full members of the congregation in helping pay for the paving of the synagogue forecourt (Williams, 1998, 7.14–15; see Figure 11.4), and at Aphrodisias (also in Caria) more than fifty of them contributed to a *mnema* (memorial), the precise nature of which is disputed (Reynolds and Tannenbaum, 1987; Williams, 1992).

For some Gentiles, however, not even regular attendance at the synagogue and patronage of the local Jewish community was enough. So great was the attraction of the Jewish way of life that they were not content until they had actually 'crossed the boundary and become Jews' (Cohen, 1989) – a momentous act, which for male converts involved undergoing the socially unacceptable rite of circumcision. The technical name for those converts, who, it is important to realize, were regarded by Jews and Gentiles alike as no less Jewish than those who had been born as such (compare, for instance, Josephus, *Antiquities* 20.38–48 and Cassius Dio, *Roman History* 37.16.5–17.1) was proselytes. Some of them became esteemed members of the synagogal community. Beturia Paulla, for instance, a rich Roman matron who on conversion to Judaism took the Hebrew name Sarah, was awarded by two congregations in the capital the high honour of the title 'Mother of the Community' (*mater synagogae*) (Williams, 1998, 7.30). (This title is discussed further below.)

Significant though it is to find epigraphic confirmation of the existence of Godfearers and proselytes among the Greeks and Romans, the fact remains that such people are likely to have comprised a very small element in the Gentile population of the Roman empire. Jews, unlike Christians, probably did not engage much in missionary activity (for divergent views on this highly controversial subject, see Goodman,

Figure 11.4 *Mosaic inscription from the forecourt of the synagogue at Sardis. Translated from the Greek, it says: Aurelius Eulogius, Godfearer, has fulfilled his vow. (Reproduced from Hanfmann, 1983; © Archaeological Exploration of Sardis/Harvard University)*

1994 and Feldman, 1993), and the number of Godfearers and proselytes known to us by name is very small. (For the nineteen epigraphically attested proselytes, see Horbury, 1997.) Most Greeks and Romans were probably indifferent to Judaism. If they did have any feelings towards the Jews and their religion, those feelings were probably antipathetic. Acts of vandalism against synagogues (for example, the theft of the financial contributions for the temple), as well as petty harassment of Jews (such as requiring them to appear in court on the Sabbath or forfeit their case), are attested on a number of occasions and in a variety of places in the Roman east (for example, Asia Minor and Cyrene (Josephus, *Jewish Antiquities* 16.27–8 and 169–70). And sometimes tension between Greeks and Jews reached such a pitch that serious rioting broke out, as at Alexandria in AD 38 and 66. The large body of Greek and Latin writings on the Jews and Judaism, which is overwhelmingly hostile in character, reflects this widespread antipathy. While detailed examination of this material would be impossible in a short essay such as this, it is necessary to give some idea of its flavour. To that end, I cite here an extract from

313

Tacitus' notorious excursus on the Jews from his *Histories*, Book 5. Though it makes distasteful reading in places, I have chosen to quote it for two reasons. As the core of the most sustained literary attack on the Jews to survive from antiquity it has been enormously influential (primarily through Edward Gibbon's use of it in his *History of the Decline and Fall of the Roman Empire*) in shaping European perceptions of ancient (and not so ancient) Jewry (Hoffmann, 1988, pp.15–18). Secondly, and more mundanely, it provides a useful catalogue of the chief constituent elements of Jewish self-identity, a topic to be discussed in greater depth below. (The translation here, like that of all the other sources quoted in this essay, is my own. Please note that words in parentheses do not represent translated material but are additions that I have made to help clarify the meaning of the text.)

> To retain his hold over the people for ever, Moses established rites that were new and quite contrary to those practised by other mortals. To the Jews, everything is profane which we hold in reverence and what is permissible with them is abhorrent to us ... [Discussion follows of their practice of sacrificing animals sacred to other peoples.] Because the disease to which pigs are prone once disfigured them [a reference to the Jews as lepers], they abstain from the flesh of that animal. They still bear witness with frequent fasts to a protracted famine of long ago and, as proof of the haste with which the grain was seized, no raising agent is used in Jewish bread [a unique reference to the use of unleavened bread at Passover]. They say that they decided to rest on the seventh day because that was the day that brought an end to their struggles. However, because indolence was so attractive, they then gave over to idleness the seventh year as well [a unique reference in Graeco-Roman literature to the Sabbatical Year, the one year in seven when Jews, in the interests of good husbandry, rested the land and left their fields untilled] ...

> These rites, however they were established, are maintained through their antiquity but the rest of the Jews' customs are sinister and abominable and owe their vigour to their depravity. For Jewish wealth has increased because the very worst among other peoples, after spurning their ancestral religions, have channelled tribute and contributions to Jerusalem [as offerings to the Temple]; further, because the Jews' group loyalty is so strong, they are always quick to show compassion towards one another [a reference to Jewish charity] but towards everybody else they display only enmity and hate. In dining and sleeping, they keep themselves strictly apart and, despite the strong proclivity of their race to lust, they abstain from sexual relations with foreign women. Among themselves, however, everything goes. They decided to circumcise their genitals, so that by this difference they might be distinguished from other peoples. Those who go over to their ways observe the same practice and they are barely initiated before they start despising the gods, disowning their native land and holding cheaply their parents, children and brothers. To the increase of

their own numbers, however, considerable attention is paid: it is a crime to make away with any issue [a high-flown allusion to the Jews' abhorrence of infanticide – a common practice among Greeks and Romans] and they consider that the souls of those who die in battle or through capital punishment are immortal. Hence their passion for procreation and their contempt of death. Like the Egyptians, they bury the body rather than cremate it. There is the same concern and the same belief about the nether world but as far as celestial matters are concerned, they are quite different. The Egyptians venerate a host of animals and composite images but the Jews conceive of a sole divinity and that with the mind alone. They consider profane those who, from mortal materials, fashion images of the gods to look like men. In their opinion, that supreme and eternal being cannot be copied and will not perish. And so, they set up no images in their cities, still less in their temples [i.e. their synagogues]. This flattery is not paid to kings, nor this honour to emperors. Because their priests used to chant together to the accompaniment of flute and drums and wreath themselves with ivy and a golden vine was found in the Temple, some have thought that they worshipped father Liber [i.e. Dionysos/Bacchus], the conqueror of the East. But there is no similarity whatsoever between the two cults. For Liber has instituted rites that are festive and joyous but the customs of the Jews are ridiculous and mean.

(Tacitus, *Histories* 5.4–5, in Williams, 1998, 7.2)

This ethnographic description of the Jews by the early Roman empire's most famous historian was not, it is universally agreed, the product of Tacitus' personal observation of the Jewish community at Rome itself. Rather it is a literary construct, based in large part upon the works of Graeco-Egyptian writers, whose anti-Semitic tendencies are notorious. (For a detailed analysis, see Schäfer, 1997.) Its positioning in the narrative is conventional – it was placed immediately before an account of the Jews' overwhelming defeat by Rome in AD 70. And standard, too, is the way in which it portrays the soon-to-be-conquered enemies of Rome – it was customary to depict the mores of such people as the antithesis of Rome's and to imply, by dwelling on their barbarism and 'otherness', that they were suitable candidates for suppression and ultimate civilization. But the fact that this diatribe is conventional does not mean that its facts are wrong. To be sure there are some inexactitudes – circumcision, for instance, which is presented without understanding as a perversity of the period after Moses, was as ancient as Judaism itself. By and large, though, the information that Tacitus transmits is correct and some of it is found in no other Graeco-Roman source (for example, his references to the Sabbatical Year and the use of unleavened bread at Passover). But what about his interpretation of this information and the completeness of his picture of the Jews? In the next section, I shall discuss the evidence that the Jews themselves have left behind for their life in a Graeco-Roman environment. Besides literary works, this consists of papyrus documents of various kinds and inscriptions largely in the form of epitaphs and texts recording benefactions to synagogues. What will emerge is that the Tacitean picture of the Jews is both incomplete and, in parts, seriously distorted. As Stern (1974–84, vol.2, p.1) has justifiably remarked of the passage just cited, were it not for the fact that its author was 'the greatest historian of Rome', it is doubtful if it would have commanded such inordinate attention.

Cultural assimilation

Language

Tacitus, it will have been observed, presents Jewish mores as totally alien and the Jews themselves as stubbornly unaccommodating. By and large, however, the Jews who lived among the Greeks and Romans in his day were extremely adaptable people, who had achieved a high degree of cultural assimilation. Take the languages they generally used. These were not Hebrew (only rarely attested and thought to have been barely known outside Judaea in the early imperial period) nor Aramaic but Greek and Latin. Of the last two, Greek enjoyed the wider currency, since it had long been far more than the language of everyday speech. It also functioned as Diasporan Jewry's sacral tongue and, as such, was the language in which proceedings in the synagogue were regularly conducted. This had been the case since the early Hellenistic period. Already by the reign of Ptolemy II Philadelphus (that is, the second quarter of the third century BC), the Jews in Egypt had become so assimilated that they needed a translation of the Scriptures into Greek, the Hebrew original no longer being sufficiently intelligible to them. Hence the production of the Septuagint, which remained the sole Bible of Diasporan Jewry until two newer and more literal translations from Hebrew into Greek, the versions of Aquila and Theodotion, supplemented it in the second century AD. Nor was Diasporan Jewry's formal use of Greek restricted to the synagogue. Its literature, much of it surviving only in fragmentary form, was written in Greek too. One has only to consider the works of Philo of Alexandria, and Josephus, an aristocratic refugee from Judaea who lived and wrote in Rome throughout most of the Flavian period (AD 70–96). Philo's voluminous oeuvre is entirely in Greek, as are all the works that Josephus composed for circulation within the Roman empire – that is, the second edition of the *Jewish War* (an account of the First Jewish Revolt against Rome), the *Jewish Antiquities* (a history of the Jews from the Creation down to AD 66) and the two apologetic tracts that conventionally (and rather perversely) go by the Latin titles, *Vita* (*Life of Josephus*) and *Contra Apionem* (*Against*

Apion). So prevalent was the use of Greek by Diasporan Jews that even those who detested Graeco-Roman culture (such as the anonymous authors of Third Maccabees and the *Egyptian Sibylline Oracles*) penned their denunciations of its idolatry and immorality in that language. (For these and other culturally antagonistic Jewish works in Greek, see Barclay, 1996, ch.7.)

Nomenclature

The personal names borne by Diasporan Jews also reflect their strong assimilatory tendencies. Jewish inscriptions from all over the Roman world point to a general preference for Latin and Greek names (especially the latter) over Hebrew and Semitic. One of the best pieces of evidence for this is a synagogal decree from the city of Berenice in the Roman province of Cyrenaica (modern Benghazi in Libya). Dating from the second year of Nero's reign (AD 55), it lists in two columns on a marble stele the eighteen members of the congregation who had recently 'contributed to the repair of the synagogue'. I give their names and patronymics below, transliterated exactly from the Greek. Hence the variant spellings of some of the names.

Zenion, son of Zoilos – 10 drachmas

Eisidoros, son of Doseitheos, *archon* – 10 drachmas

Doseitheos, son of Ammonios, *archon* – 10 drachmas

Pratis, son of Ionathas, *archon* – 10 drachmas

Karnedas, son of Kornelios, *archon* – 10 drachmas

Herakleides, son of Heraklides (*sic*), *archon* – 10 drachmas

Thaliarchos, son of Dositheos, *archon* – 10 drachmas

Sosibios, son of Iason, *archon* – 10 drachmas

Pratomedes, son of Sokrates, *archon* – 10 drachmas

Antigon(o)s, son of Straton, *archon* – 10 drachmas

Kartisthenes, son of Archias, priest – 10 drachmas

Lysanias, son of Lysanias – 25 drachmas

Zenodoros, son of Theuphilos – 28 drachmas

Marion, son of [...] – 25 drachmas

Alexander, son of Euphranor – 5 drachmas

Eisidora, daughter of Serap(i)on – 5 drachmas

Zosime, daughter of Terpolios – 5 drachmas

Polon, son of Dositheos – 5 drachmas

(For the full text, see Williams, 1998, 1.107)

The most striking feature of this document is the overwhelmingly Greek character of the names used by this congregation. Hebrew elements are not altogether lacking: Ionathas is a Hellenized form of the Hebrew name Jonathan, and Dositheos, which occurs several times, a literal Greek translation of one of the many Hebrew names meaning 'given by God' (for example, Netanyahu). By and large, though, most of the names are Greek. Also worth pointing out is the occurrence of several pagan theophorics – that is, names derived from those of the pagan gods. While Ammonios, Eisidora/os and Serapion recall the Egyptian deities Ammon, Isis and Sarapis, with Heraklides, Zenodoros and Zenion the references are to the Greek demi-god Herakles and his divine father, Zeus. It would be tempting to conclude that such a preference for Greek names and such indifference to pagan onomastic constructs must have been the product of prolonged residence in polytheistic society; but papyri from Ptolemaic Egypt show that this was not the case. Before the end of the third century BC, Jewish abandonment of Hebrew and Semitic names in favour of Greek ones – some of the latter pagan theophorics such as Herakleia and Diophantos (*Corpus Papyrorum Judaicarum*[1], 1.19 and 22) – was already well advanced (Tcherikover et al., 1957–64, vol.1, pp.27–30). It was not until the re-Hebraization of Diasporan Jewry in the centuries after Constantine that Hebrew and Semitic names were once again used outside Judaea/Palestine on a wide scale. Analysis of the three largest collections of onomastic data for Diasporan Jewry – the epitaphs from Leontopolis in Lower Egypt (second century BC to first century AD), the tax receipts from Apollinopolis Magna/Edfu in Upper Egypt (first to second centuries AD) and the funerary inscriptions from the Jewish catacombs of Rome (third to fourth centuries AD) – has revealed an overwhelming preference for Latin and Greek, especially Greek, names. What is more, in the area of general onomastic practice (such as the formal citation of names), no significant differences between the Jews and their Gentile neighbours have been detected (Rutgers, 1995, ch.4). (The only seriously divergent piece of evidence would appear to be the recently discovered 'Jews and Godfearers' inscription from Aphrodisias in Asia Minor, dated tentatively by its editors, Reynolds and Tannenbaum (1987), to the early third century AD. However, there are strong grounds for arguing that the text may belong to the fourth century or even later.)

Titles and honours

It will have been observed in the Berenice inscription cited above that no fewer than half the donors bore the title *archon*, a common Greek

---

1 Hereafter abbreviated to *CPJ*.

civic term found at Athens and elsewhere, the literal meaning of which is ruler or leader. Its appearance in a synagogal context may seem surprising, but actually it represents typical Diasporan usage (see Figure 11.5). Throughout the Diaspora it was the norm for Jewish community officers to bear titles either borrowed directly from or patterned upon those used in Greek civic and cultic life (Williams, 1998, 2.19–82). Besides *archon*, also to be noted are *grammateus* (secretary), *phrontistes* (manager), *archisynagogos* (leader of the gathering/congregation) and *gerousiarch* (ruler/president of the *gerousia*, the council of Elders). That Greek titles were standard even in the synagogues of Rome and the Latin-speaking west is only to be expected. By the time Jews began to settle in any numbers in the western Mediterranean (that is, in the decades after Pompey's conquest of Judaea in 63 BC), the Diasporan

Figure 11.5   *One of the numerous marble burial plaques from the Jewish catacombs of Rome that mention synagogal archons. (Reproduced courtesy of Simon Wiesenthal Center Library and Archives, Los Angeles, CA)*

319

synagogue, attested epigraphically in Egypt as early as the third century BC, had become a thoroughly mature institution with largely standardized liturgical and administrative procedures conducted mainly in Greek. Given that the institution itself underwent no significant name change on transplantation to the west (Greek *proseuche* and *synagoge* might occasionally be Latinized as *proseucha* and *synagoga/sinagoga*, but that is the extent of innovation), it would be surprising if widespread alterations had been made to the titulature of its core functionaries. Jews in the Latin-speaking west, however, being no less amenable to the influence of Roman culture than their counterparts in the Hellenistic world had been to Greek, came in due course to extend the repertoire of synagogal titles by including in it terms that reflected values peculiar to Roman society – for example, the importance attached to patriarchy and to familial relationships. Hence the prevalence within Jewish communities in Rome, Italy and the western provinces of *pater synagogae* (Father of the Community) and its female equivalent, *mater synagogae* (Mother of the Community) – honorific titles awarded to elderly, wealthy, and hence respected and influential, members of the congregation. Beturia Paulla, the proselyte mentioned earlier, was one person so honoured. (For further examples and discussion, see Williams, 1998, 2.7 and 68–73.)

In one other way synagogal titulature in the west reveals Jewish receptivity to the values of Roman society. In Jewish epitaphs from Rome itself, as well as from the ancient Roman colony of Venusia in south Italy, young boys are sometimes commemorated bearing such titles as *grammateus, archon, mellarchon* (that is, archon-elect) and *archisynagogos*. Given the age of the children concerned, often three years or younger, it is clear that they cannot have been functioning officers of the synagogue. That their titles are purely honorific is to be deduced from general Roman and Italian practice. In the municipalities of Italy, making very young boys *decuriones* (town councillors) was a common way of honouring their families, invariably the most wealthy and prominent in the community. The expectation was that these honoured scions would eventually become leaders and benefactors of the community like their fathers and grandfathers. Ultimately the model for this practice was Roman. In so conspicuously honouring the sons of the more prominent families in their communities and marking them out for 'high-flying' synagogal careers, the Jews of Rome and Italy reveal how thoroughly they had absorbed the values of the 'host' society.

Jewish borrowings from the Greeks and Romans did not stop at titles. Several synagogal decrees survive from the last century of the Roman republic and early empire. In these, Diasporan Jews can be seen bestowing upon their benefactors, both Jewish and non-Jewish, the types of honours current in local Gentile society. While in documents from the Greek east, more specifically Egypt, Cyrenaica and Asia Minor, Greek-style honours (such as gold crowns, gilded shields and the right of privileged seating on public occasions) are mentioned, the solitary synagogal decree from the Latin west (found in the vicinity of Ostia) features an honour common in municipal Italy – the provision, at community expense, of land for the construction of a family tomb. (For this important, but rather fragmentary, text, see Williams, 1998, 6.36). Only one synagogal decree, the longest and best preserved Jewish inscription from Graeco-Roman antiquity, will be cited here by way of example. It emanates from the *politeuma* (Jewish community) of Berenice in Cyrenaica and is to be dated probably to 13 BC (Baldwin Bowsky, 1987). It is important for revealing not only the enormous impact of local civic practice upon the Jews (all the procedures mentioned here are attested in the local Greek community) but also their relationship with the Roman authorities. That is a topic to which I shall be returning in the final part of this essay.

> Year 55, Phaophi 25, at the assembly of the Feast of Tabernacles ... in the archonship of Kleandros, the son of Stratonikos; Euphranor, son of Ariston; Sosigenes, son of Sosippos; Andromachos, son of Andromachos; Markos Lailios Onasion, the son of Apollonios; Philonides, son of Hagemon; Autokles, the son of Zenon; Sonikos, son of Theodotos; Iosepos, son of Straton: because Markos Tittios, son of Sextos, of the Aemilian tribe, a worthy and excellent man, since coming to the province to administer public affairs [probably as the legate of the governor of the province of Crete and Cyrene] has directed their governance with benevolence and skill and in his behaviour consistently shown himself to be of an eirenic [i.e. peaceful] disposition, and has behaved unoppressively both in these (public matters) and with regard to those of the citizens who have approached him privately, and because for the Jews of our *politeuma* both publicly and privately his administration has been useful and he has not ceased to perform deeds in keeping with his own essential nobility of character, therefore the *archons* and the *politeuma* of the Jews in Berenice have decided to laud him and crown him 'by name' at each gathering and each New Moon with a wreath of olive leaves and (a fillet of) wool. The *archons* are to inscribe the decree on a stele of Parian stone (i.e. marble) and to place it in the most conspicuous part of the amphitheatre [thought by scholars to be either an oval Jewish council chamber or possibly the synagogue hall itself, the Greek word *amphitheatron* describing any structure which had seats for spectators in either an oval or a U-shape]. All [voting] (pebbles) white (i.e. decided unanimously).
>
> (Williams, 1998, 5.35)

The principal mechanisms for facilitating cultural assimilation

That Jews living outside the province of Judaea/Palestine exhibited the degree of cultural assimilation illustrated above should come as no surprise. Although Diasporan Jews tended to dwell close to one another in the cities in which they had settled, no compulsion was involved in this, and in some places Jews are known to have lived in a variety of locations alongside Gentiles (see Williams, 1998, 1.56–66 for the evidence relating to Jewish residence at Alexandria, Antioch on the Orontes and Rome). Dwelling among the Greeks and Romans, however, was not the only form of contact between Diasporan Jews and Gentiles. In several cities of the Greek east (Alexandria, Cyrene, Iasus in Asia Minor, Corone in Greece), rich Jews are known to have undergone a gymnasial (that is, a Greek-style) education (Williams, 1998, 5.1–3 and 5.21–3). It was from this, so it is always assumed, that Jews such as Philo of Alexandria derived their deep knowledge of Greek literature and culture. From the Greek east also there is considerable evidence (mainly supplied by Josephus) for Jews dealing with Greek officialdom over Jewish community matters – for example, with the chief city magistrates (*archons*) at Miletus over the infringement of Jewish rights (Josephus, *Antiquities* 14.244), with the *agoranomos* (superintendent of the market) at Sardis over the provision of special foodstuffs (Josephus, *Antiquities* 14.259–61), and with the managers (*phrontistai*) of the water board at Arsinoe in Egypt over supplying the synagogue annually with its ritually essential water (*CPJ* 2.432). No wonder that Diasporan Jews were so familiar with Greek civic titulature! As for their knowledge of Greek civic honours, that would have come from their attendance, attested in both literary and epigraphic sources, at such Greek cultural venues as the theatre, hippodrome and odeon.(For the evidence, see Williams, 1998, 5.20–30.)

In Rome and Italy, by contrast, where the social status of Jews was, in general, lower than in the eastern provinces of the empire, cultural assimilation will have come about mainly through Jews residing as slaves in Gentile households. For many Jews, perhaps the majority, life in the west began in slavery, even if it ended in freedom (Philo, *Embassy to Gaius* 155). As Roman freedmen and freedwomen, these people would have experienced at first hand the workings of that most fundamental feature of Roman society – *clientela*, the formal relationship between weak and strong, under which services (*officia*) rendered by the former, termed clients, almost automatically compelled a paternalistic response (*beneficium*) from the latter, termed patrons. The *synagogai* of the Augustesians and Agrippesians at Rome, mentioned above, reflect the impact upon the Jews of *clientela*. Those congregations were essentially cliental organizations, comprised (originally at least) of slaves and freedmen in the households of Augustus and Agrippa. No different in kind from the many 'in-house clubs' (*collegia domestica*) attested at Rome, each derived its name from its patron – that is, the head of the household (*paterfamilias*) in which it had been founded.

The self-identity of Diasporan Jews

Although clear mechanisms existed in both the eastern and western parts of the Graeco-Roman world for the cultural assimilation of the Jews, only in rare instances, it is generally thought, did that process go so far that Jewish self-identity was lost. One such case is Philo of Alexandria's nephew, Tiberius Julius Alexander, who was procurator (governor) of Judaea under Claudius, prefect of Egypt under Nero, and a key political figure in early Flavian Rome (possibly he was Praetorian Prefect under the emperor Vespasian). Josephus speaks disapprovingly of Tiberius Alexander's abandonment of his ancestral practices, comparing him unfavourably with his rich and pious father, Alexander (Josephus, *Antiquities* 20.100). Indeed, so comprehensive was Tiberius Alexander's loss of his Jewish identity that Tacitus, introducing him in his narrative at *Annals* 15.28.3, describes him simply as *inlustris eques Romanus*, that is, a distinguished member of the equestrian order. Such high-flying apostates, however, were extremely rare and apostasy itself uncommon. (At any rate it is not often attested.) Infinitely more numerous were those Diasporan Jews who managed, despite a high degree of cultural assimilation, to maintain an identifiably Jewish lifestyle.

Among peoples whom Rome had both conquered and deracinated, the ability to operate within two cultures simultaneously was extremely rare. Yet the Jews of the Diaspora managed to do that successfully for as long as the Roman empire lasted. Why? The basic reason for their remarkable achievement was their unique possession of the Torah, a written set of injunctions believed to have been given them by God, the observation of which they regarded as both a sacred obligation and a special privilege (see Figure 11.6). This Law of Moses, however, while furnishing them with a firm framework for their lives in an alien environment and fostering a strong sense of Jewishness, did not prevent their assimilation, since its requirements, in the main, were easily compatible with the practices and values of Graeco-Roman society. Offences such as murder and adultery were no more tolerated by Greeks and Romans than by Jews. And Jewish views on the necessity of honouring parents and providing for the less well-off in society had distinct affinities with Roman ideas of *pietas* (the duty owed by, among others, children to parents) and *clientela*. However, the Law of Moses did enjoin certain practices that most Greeks and Romans, for one reason or another, found odd or unacceptable. (I shall be examining three of them below.) These, while providing the Jews with a special sense of identity, made them appear to be an irremediably alien (and in the case of proselytes, even treacherous) element in Graeco-Roman society.

The extent to which Jews in the Roman empire observed the minutiae of the Torah is impossible to assess. The kinds of texts that Diasporan Jews have left behind (largely epitaphs and dedicatory inscriptions in synagogues) do not disclose that kind of information, and pagan writers who refer to the Jews living in their midst deal in the main only with generalities – and those, very few in number. Tacitus' list of Jewish 'perversities' quoted above is atypical in both its length and its detail. Most references to Jewish practices by early Roman imperial writers (for example, poets such as Horace, Persius, Martial and Juvenal, and men of letters such as Seneca) concern themselves mainly with three topics only – Sabbath observance, circumcision and monotheism. (The taboo on eating pork, though alluded to fairly often, comes a very poor fourth.) And the Graeco-Roman archive material upholding Jewish rights cited at length by Josephus in *Antiquities* 14.190–264 is similarly limited in range. Brief though the list of topics is upon which our sources focus, it is still immensely valuable. Not only does it throw considerable light on how the Romans perceived the Jews, but it enables us to identify the non-negotiable core of Diasporan Judaism. The practices listed above, as will be seen in the discussion to follow, regularly occasioned Diasporan Jews personal inconvenience and embarrassment; and sometimes even involved them in communal conflict. That such a large element of Diasporan Jewry persisted in adhering to them demonstrates their importance. To most Jews, Sabbath observance, circumcision and monotheism with no divine images constituted the *sine qua non* of retaining a Jewish identity.

Figure 11.6   Reconstructed Torah shrine from the synagogue at Sardis. (Reproduced from Hanfmann, 1983; © Archaeological Exploration of Sardis/Harvard University)

Sabbath observance

Sabbath observance is the Jewish practice most frequently mentioned in Roman sources, presumably because it was by far the most conspicuous.

Wherever Jews were settled in any numbers (for example, the Transtiberine and the Suburan districts of Rome), their shops shut down and their living quarters came alight as the Sabbath approached and the Sabbath lamps were lit. The impact of this ritual on non-Jews can be gauged from the extract from Persius' *Satires* quoted below, which describes in graphic terms and (for a Roman source) unusually accurate detail the Sabbath as celebrated in the slums of late Julio-Claudian Rome.

> But when the days of Herod come and all along the greasy window-sills the lamps, wreathed in violets, belch forth their fatty clouds and the floating tail of the tuna encircles the earthenware bowl and the white pot swells with wine [an allusion to two key elements of the Sabbath supper, fish and wine], then silently you move your lips and grow pale at the Sabbath of the circumcised.
>
> (Persius, *Satires* 5.179–84)

But although many Romans were aware of Jewish Sabbath practices, few had any understanding of them. Hence the constant trivialization of the ritual in Roman sources by such writers as Horace, Ovid and Tibullus, and the monotonous attribution of it to Jewish laziness (Seneca, *On Superstition*, cited by Augustine, *City of God* 6.11; Tacitus, *Histories* 5.4.3; Juvenal, *Satires* 14.105–6). The importance to the Jews, however, of obeying the divine injunction to keep the Sabbath holy can be deduced from the inconvenience they allowed its observance to cause them, such as delay in collecting their vital food supplies whenever the distribution of free corn at Rome coincided with the Sabbath (Philo, *Embassy to Gaius* 158), and forfeiting lawsuits when an appearance in court was required on the Sabbath day (Josephus, *Antiquities* 16.163).

Circumcision

But if Sabbath observance was occasionally inconvenient, a perpetual problem was presented by circumcision. For Jews, this rite was symbolic of their Covenant with God and hence their status as the chosen people. As such, its enactment was absolutely essential. Greeks and Romans, by contrast, viewed the practice as barbaric and no different in kind from castration (Williams, 1998, 2.119). In a world where much male social activity was carried on in the nude (the Greek higher educational system centred on the gymnasium and public bathing was an important feature of Roman social life), being circumcised could cause acute embarrassment. Hence a variety of contraptions worn by Jewish males to conceal the condition (these feature in two exceedingly crude poems by Martial, *Epigrams* 7.35 and 82) and, for a minority bent on full assimilation, the painful procedure known as epispasm. In this, the skin surrounding the trunk of the penis was, without benefit of anaesthetic, surgically detached and then stretched. (For a stomach-churning description, see the medical writer Celsus, *On Medicine* 7.25.)

Circumcision, of course, was not uniquely Jewish but practised by other groups in antiquity too, most famously the Egyptian priesthood and the Colchians of the Caucasus. But whereas Greeks and Romans will have come across few Egyptian priests and Colchians in the course of their daily lives, Jews they will have met with frequently. Since that was the case, it is not surprising that they came to believe that circumcision was a uniquely Jewish practice and saw it as the Jews' principal defining characteristic. Hence the references in Roman legal sources to circumcision as the *ritus Iudaicus* (Jewish rite/custom) or the *nota Iudaica* (Jewish mark) (Williams, 1998, 2.120–1).

Monotheism

Sabbath observance and circumcision might cause individual Jews inconvenience or embarrassment, but neither of those practices possessed the capacity to create community-wide conflict between Jews and Gentiles. Jewish monotheism, the first requirement of the Law of Moses, could do this, and sometimes did so in the Greek cities of the eastern Roman provinces. There were two components to this conflict – the Jews' refusal to acknowledge the gods of the Greeks and Romans, and their insistence on meeting their own cult obligations by paying a regular tax to the temple authorities in Jerusalem. (The Torah required that each male Jew over the age of twenty should make a fixed annual contribution towards the maintenance of the temple cult, the central feature of which was daily sacrifice to God/Yahweh.) While Jewish neglect of the pagan gods aroused deep anxiety among the worshippers of those deities (they feared that their *whole* community might suffer in consequence), the conspicuous transfer of gold to Jerusalem caused intense resentment – wealth generated within a community should be used for the benefit of that community, they doubtless felt, not the enrichment of some foreign shrine. So strong were the feelings generated by this issue that the so-called sacred monies were not only frequently stolen from synagogues by individual Greeks, but sometimes even impounded by the city authorities themselves. Time and time again the Jews felt compelled to protest. Appeals were made not just at a civic level but to a whole host of Roman officials, and sometimes even to the emperor himself (Josephus, *Antiquities* 16.27–8, 162–5, 167–8, 169–70). Rome invariably upheld the Jews' ancestral 'right' to collect and despatch to Jerusalem the half-shekel tax but lacked the resources (and will) to do anything more concrete. Not until the temple was destroyed in AD 70 and the tax insultingly converted into a two-denarii impost, payable to Jupiter Capitolinus, did the divisiveness caused between Jew and Greek by this particular way of affirming Jewish identity cease. Greeks could hardly object to their Jewish neighbours upholding, albeit involuntarily, the cult of the chief protecting deity of Rome.

Diasporan Jews and the Roman authorities

The Jews' confidence in appealing over the heads of the Greek civic authorities to Rome sprang from their long-standing 'special relationship' with the latter. From the mid second century BC, when they had first entered into treaty relations with Rome – by then already the paramount power in the eastern Mediterranean – they had always found the Romans at least verbally supportive. (See, for instance, the directive, cited at I Maccabees 15.16–24, that the Romans sent on their behalf to sundry kings and cities in Asia Minor and the Aegean.) And from the time of Julius Caesar, Jews had frequently enjoyed preferential treatment in such areas as military service and the right of assembly for religious purposes (Josephus, *Antiquities* 14.225–7 and 213–16). The reason for these concessions was the client relationship that the Jewish high priest, Hyrcanus II, had managed to establish with Caesar during the latter's successful campaign in Egypt in 48–7 BC, the so-called Alexandrian War. Through Hyrcanus' influence on the Jews of the Egyptian Diaspora and their timely services to Caesar, the latter was henceforth willing to extend his patronage to all Jews everywhere. Since client relationships, once established, tended to assume a hereditary character, the Jews came ultimately to enjoy the patronage of the emperor Augustus, Caesar's adopted son and heir. How useful this relationship was to them can be seen from the edict, cited below, that Augustus sent to the province of Asia around the beginning of the first century AD on their behalf.

> Caesar Augustus, Pontifex Maximus, with tribunician power [a numeral has fallen out of the text here], decrees: since the Jewish nation has been found well disposed towards the Roman people not only at the present time but also in the past, and especially in the time of my father the Imperator Caesar, as has their High Priest Hyrcanus, it has been decided by me and my council under oath, with the consent of the Roman people, that the Jews are to follow their own customs in accordance with their ancestral law, just as they did in the time of Hyrcanus, High Priest of the Most High God, and their sacred monies are to be inviolable and despatched to Jerusalem and handed over to the treasurers in Jerusalem, and they need not give bond [to appear in court] on the Sabbath or on the day of preparation for it after the ninth hour. If anyone is caught stealing their sacred books or their sacred monies from a synagogue or a community hall, he shall be regarded as sacrilegious and his property made over to the public treasury of the Romans. The decree they have given to me in honour of the dutifulness [*pietas*] I show towards all men

and in honour of Gaius Marcius Censorinus [proconsul of Asia in AD 2–3], and this edict here I order to be set up in the most conspicuous part of the temple assigned to me by the federation [*koinon*] of Asia at Ancyra. If anyone contravenes any of the above ordinances, he shall pay a heavy penalty.

(Josephus, *Jewish Antiquities* 16.162–5)

The Roman practice, exemplified here, of upholding appeals made by Diasporan Jews may well have lulled the latter into believing that their observance of their ancestral customs was an inalienable right. It was nothing of the kind. Official protection of the Jewish way of life had simply been a *beneficium* (a kindness) that Rome, as a satisfied patron, had seen fit to bestow on clients who had fulfilled their duties (*officia*). When the latter gave cause for dissatisfaction, as the Jews of the Diaspora, increasingly unsettled by the deteriorating situation in the province of Judaea and the rising militancy of its Jewish inhabitants, were soon to do, emperors such as Tiberius, Claudius, Vespasian, Trajan and Hadrian were to show very quickly what Jewish 'rights' amounted to – concessions by the sovereign power, no more, no less.

The first time that this was made brutally clear to the Jews was in AD 19, just five years into the reign of Augustus' adopted son, heir and successor, Tiberius. In that year, punishment was meted out to the Jews of Rome in the form of the expulsion from the city of their entire community, conservatively estimated at around 25,000 people, the conscription of 4,000 young Jewish males for military duties in Sardinia, and the summary execution of those who refused to serve for 'fear of breaking the Jewish Law' (presumably by being required to fight on the Sabbath and consume non-kosher food). So much for Rome's respect for Jewish ancestral customs and the Jews' much vaunted exemption from military service! Precisely why the Jews of Rome were punished in this manner has been the subject of much debate. (For recent discussions of the question, see, for example, Williams, 1989; Feldman, 1993; Rutgers, 1994; Schäfer, 1997.) But without doubt they were deemed by the Roman authorities to have been guilty of undesirable, even criminal, behaviour and hence judged liable for punishment.

Nor was this the only occasion on which Diasporan Jews fell foul of the Roman authorities. In the AD 40s, the Jewish communities of both Alexandria and Rome managed to get on the wrong side of the emperor Claudius. With regard to the Alexandrian Jews, their offences were two – not only were they virtually at war with the local Greeks when Claudius came to the throne (for the tangled events in Alexandria under Gaius/Caligula and their background, see Tcherikover et al., 1957–64, vol.1, pp.55–74; Smallwood, 1976, ch.10), but they had even encouraged Jews from Syria and other parts of Egypt to come and join in the fight. While Claudius refrained from actual punishment of the Jews, since their responsibility for provoking the unrest was unproven, he delivered a stern and lengthy admonishment to both them and the Greeks, just one sentence of which I quote here: 'I simply tell you that unless you put an end to this destructive and stubborn hatred of each other I shall be forced to show you what a benevolent ruler is like when he has turned to righteous anger.' And to the Jews he gave an additional warning – if they continued to bring in supporters from other parts of the Diaspora, 'I shall proceed against them in every way as fomenting a common plague for the inhabited world' (*CPJ*, vol.2, no.153). While the Alexandrian Jews escaped actual punishment, the Jews of Rome (now back in the capital again) were not so fortunate. Twice during his principate Claudius proceeded against them. In AD 41 he banned them from assembling for religious purposes, since their large and growing numbers had given him cause for concern, and a few years later he expelled them altogether from the city for being involved in constant rioting (Suetonius, *Life of Claudius* 25.4; Acts of the Apostles 18.1–2).

Apart from Tiberius Julius Alexander's ruthless suppression of Jewish rioters in Alexandria under Nero in AD 66, nothing much is heard of Diasporan Jews until after the fall of Jerusalem to the Romans in AD 70. Then several measures were taken against them by the new emperor, Vespasian. Besides closing down the Jewish temple at Leontopolis in Egypt, lest it replace the now destroyed Jerusalem temple as the focus of Jewish resistance to Rome (there were no other Jewish temples besides these), Vespasian also imposed upon all Jews everywhere, male and female over the age of three, an annual tax payable to Jupiter Capitolinus at Rome. Inasmuch as Josephus does not mention any involvement in the First Jewish Revolt by Jews from the Mediterranean Diaspora, Vespasian's measure, a vast extension of the old Temple tax, would seem to be unduly punitive. But Josephus' silence is not to be trusted. Given the strong bonds that had always existed between Jerusalem and the Diaspora (for evidence and discussion, see Safrai and Stern, 1974–76, vol.1, ch.4; Williams, 1998, chapter 3), Diasporan involvement in the rebellion is inherently likely. What is more, there is evidence for it. Cassius Dio, whose account of the Jewish War unfortunately survives only in fragments, informs us in one of them that the rebels in Judaea were assisted by many of their co-religionists 'not only from the Roman empire but also from beyond the Euphrates [that is, the Babylonian Diaspora]' (Cassius Dio, *Roman History* 66.4.3). That would explain the sweeping nature of Vespasian's punishment, as well as his empire-wide humiliation of the Jews. Not only did his coinage celebrate *ad nauseam* Rome's victory over them (see Figure 11.7), but the monuments he and his son, Titus, erected in the major cities of the empire served as permanent reminders to the Jews of their defeat. Noteworthy are the arch of Titus in the main forum at Rome, on which

Figure 11.7 Roman coin celebrating the re-conquest (literally, capture) of Judaea. Dejected Jewish captives are depicted on either side of a date palm, the conventional Roman symbol for Judaea. (© The British Museum)

were depicted triumphant Roman soldiers holding aloft the looted temple treasures (Figure 11.8), the city gate in Antioch on the Orontes on which the golden cherubim from the temple were actually mounted, and the amphitheatre in the same city which was built on the site of a synagogue, deliberately demolished for that purpose, and dedicated thus: 'From the spoils of the Jews' (Williams, 1998, 1.65).

Given the punitive actions just listed for what was probably no more than the participation of a minority of Diasporan Jews in the First Jewish Revolt, it should cause no surprise that when whole Diasporan communities rebelled – as the Jews of Cyrene, Egypt and Cyprus did under Trajan in AD 115–17 – the punishments were extremely severe. Apart from the inevitable loss of life and freedom that accompanied military defeat by Rome, the Jews of Cyrene and Egypt suffered widespread confiscation of property, and those of Cyprus a permanent ban on residence on the island – a ruling that was still in force in Cassius Dio's day, around a century after the revolt (Cassius Dio, *Roman History* 68.32.3).

It might be thought that such a demonstration of the consequences of defying Roman power would have deterred Diasporan Jews henceforth from entertaining any thoughts of rebellion. Notwithstanding the poverty of the sources for the Bar Kochba Revolt (AD 132–5), there is some evidence that Diasporan Jews were involved in it (see the commentary on Cassius Dio, *Roman History* 69.13.1 in Stern, 1974–84, vol.2, pp.402–3). But even if this testimony did not exist, Diasporan participation in the revolt could legitimately be deduced from the empire-wide punishment of the Jews that the emperor Hadrian meted out after its suppression. All Jews everywhere were banned not only from entering Jerusalem but, much more seriously, even from practising circumcision.

Conclusion

Diasporan Jews, no less than their counterparts in Judaea, must have felt utterly devastated after this latest overwhelming display of Roman power. Not only had Jews suffered defeat in the field, but they were forced after AD 137 to witness a systematic attempt to destroy their very sense of identity and change the culture of their homeland. Jerusalem was

Figure 11.8   *One of the two reliefs on the arch of Titus, set up in the Roman forum to commemorate Titus' victory over the Jews in* AD *70. It shows the booty from the temple being carried in his triumphal procession – the seven-branched candelabrum, the trumpets, and behind them the Table of the Shewbread. (Photo: Alinari)*

refounded as a pagan city and renamed Aelia Capitolina after Rome and the emperor (Hadrian's family name was Aelius), Judaea given the non-Jewish name Palestine (Land of the Philistines) and extensively paganized too, and circumcision, the very rite that gave Jews their sense of being a special people, outlawed. However, as indicated in the introduction, the Jews of Palestine did refocus and recover, the Torah being the means of their salvation. Among the milestones on that road to recovery the following three are worth mentioning. By the time the reign of Hadrian's successor, Antoninus Pius, was over (AD 161), they had recovered the right to circumcise their sons (but not their Gentile slaves). (Pius, it seems, while not rescinding the Hadrianic ban on circumcision, granted exemption from it to both Jews and others, such as Egyptian priests, for whom circumcision was of ritual significance. See Williams, 1998, 2.119.) Well before the century had ended, their leading rabbinical family, in the person of Judah I ha-Nasi (the Prince), became recognized as a virtual client dynasty by Rome (Avi-Yonah, 1976, pp.57–60). And finally, sometime around AD 200, this refocused and revitalized society produced the first great compilation of the Jewish oral law, the Mishnah. As for Diasporan Jews, an analogous recovery clearly was made by them too, even though the process itself is unrecoverable because of lack of evidence. The outcome, however, admits of no doubt. That Diasporan Jews had put rebelliousness aside and decided to take their place alongside Greeks and Romans in the administration of the empire is shown by a ruling of the Severan emperors. Sometime during the joint reign of Septimius Severus and Caracalla (AD 198–209) it was decided that the restrictions hitherto preventing observant Jews from serving on city councils should be eased. By ruling that adherents of the Jewish superstition might be permitted to hold office but perform only such duties as did not offend against their religion (Williams, 1998, 5.8), those emperors enabled these rich and highly acculturated members of Roman provincial society to play for the first time a full part in it without sacrificing their Jewish identity. The new ethos pervading Diasporan Jewry is best illustrated by the dedicatory inscriptions, all of them Greek, from the mosaic floor of the Sardis synagogue. What these benefactors stress is not their standing within the synagogal community of which their wealth would have made them important members, but their position within Graeco-Roman society. One example out of many must suffice: 'I, Aurelius Hermogenes [literally, born of Hermes], citizen of Sardis, councillor, goldsmith, have fulfilled my vow' (Williams, 1998, 1.91). Were it not for the fact that the context dictates that this worthy provincial citizen and pious benefactor must have been a Jew, how else could that have been deduced?

References

AVI-YONAH, M. (1976) *The Jews of Palestine: a Political History from the Bar Kokhba War to the Arab Conquest*, Oxford, Basil Blackwell.

BALDWIN BOWSKY, M.W. (1987) 'M. Tittius Sex. F. Aem. and the Jews of Berenice (Cyrenaica)', *American Journal of Philology*, 108, pp.495–510.

BARCLAY, J.M.G. (1996) *Jews in the Mediterranean Diaspora*, Edinburgh, T & T Clark.

COHEN, S.J.D. (1989) 'Crossing the boundary and becoming a Jew', *Harvard Theological Review*, 82, pp.13–33.

FELDMAN, L.H. (1993) *Jew and Gentile in the Ancient World*, Princeton, New Jersey, Princeton University Press.

FINE, S. (1996) *Sacred Realm: the Emergence of the Synagogue in the Ancient World*, New York and Oxford, Yeshiva University Museum and Oxford University Press.

GAFNI, I.M. (1997) *Land, Center and Diaspora: Jewish Constructs in Late Antiquity,* Journal for the Study of the Pseudepigrapha, Supplement Series 21, Sheffield, Sheffield Academic Press.

GOODMAN, M. (1994) *Mission and Conversion,* Oxford, Clarendon Press.

HANFMANN, G.M.A. (1983) *Sardis, from Prehistoric to Roman Times,* Cambridge, Mass., Harvard University Press.

HOFFMANN, C. (1988) *Juden und Judentum im Werk Deutscher Althistoriker des 19. und 20. Jahrhunderts,* Leiden, E.J. Brill.

HORBURY, W. (1997) 'A proselyte's *Heis Theos* inscription near Caesarea', *Palestine Exploration Quarterly,* 129, pp.133–7.

KRAABEL, A.T. (1981) 'The disappearance of the "God-Fearers"', *Numen* 28, pp.113–26.

LEON, H.J. (1960) *The Jews of Ancient Rome,* Philadelphia, The Jewish Publication Society of America.

REYNOLDS, J. and TANNENBAUM, R. (1987) *Jews and Godfearers at Aphrodisias,* Cambridge, The Cambridge Philological Society.

RUTGERS, L.V. (1994) 'Roman policy towards the Jews: expulsions from the city of Rome during the first century C.E.', *Classical Antiquity,* 13, pp.56–74.

RUTGERS, L.V. (1995) *The Jews in Late Ancient Rome: Evidence of Cultural Interaction in the Roman Diaspora,* Leiden, E.J. Brill.

SAFRAI, S. and STERN, M. (1974–76) *The Jewish People in the First Century,* 2 vols., Assen, Van Gorcum.

SCHÄFER, P. (1997) *Judeophobia: Attitudes toward the Jews in the Ancient World,* Cambridge, Mass., Harvard University Press.

SHANKS, H. (1979) *Judaism in Stone: the Archaeology of Ancient Synagogues,* New York and Washington, Harper & Row and Biblical Archaeology Society.

SMALLWOOD, E.M. (1976) *The Jews under Roman Rule from Pompey to Diocletian,* Leiden, E.J. Brill.

STERN, M. (1974–84) *Greek and Latin Authors on Jews and Judaism,* 3 vols., Jerusalem, The Israel Academy of Sciences and Humanities.

TCHERIKOVER, V.A., FUKS, A. and STERN, M. (1957–64) *Corpus Papyrorum Judaicarum,* 3 vols., Cambridge, Mass., Harvard University Press.

TREBILCO, P. (1991) *Jewish Communities in Asia Minor,* Cambridge, Cambridge University Press.

WILLIAMS, M.H. (1989) 'The expulsion of the Jews from Rome in AD 19', *Latomus,* 48, pp.765–84.

WILLIAMS, M.H. (1992) 'The Jews and Godfearers inscription from Aphrodisias – a case of patriarchal interference in early 3rd century Caria?', *Historia,* 41, pp.297–310.

WILLIAMS, M.H. (1998) *The Jews among the Greeks and Romans: a Diasporan Sourcebook,* London, Duckworth and Baltimore, Maryland, The Johns Hopkins University Press.

Essay Twelve
Concepts of peace

BY LORNA HARDWICK

'Peace' is not such an uncomplicated idea as it may sound. The entry under 'peace' in the *Oxford Classical Dictionary* (third edition 1996) offers no definition, but instead directs us to examples of how peace was represented or marked in social and religious practices. For example, in ancient Athens there was a cult of Eirene, peace personified; she was the daughter of Zeus and Themis, divinities associated respectively with power and justice. For the Romans, by the time of Augustus, political peace was personified in the figure of Pax. Another associated divinity was Janus Quirinius, the god of door and gate. His temple marked ceremonies at the beginning and end of military campaigns. The doors were unbolted by the consul and not closed until the end of hostilities (Virgil, *Aeneid* 7.61, describes an imaginary divine disagreement over the procedure). The *OCD* also refers us to the significance of libations: the ritual pouring of water, wine, oil, milk or honey in honour of gods, heroes and other dead. This ceremony, usually with wine, marked the sealing of truces. Additionally, discussion of war in the ancient sources frequently invokes peace in order to emphasize the troubles brought by war. War is a source of profit and glory and as such part of social norms, but it also disturbs these norms. To quote Herodotus, the Greek historian of the fifth century BC:

> ... in peace children bury their fathers, while in war fathers bury their children.
>
> (*The Histories* 1.87.4)

The *Shorter Oxford Dictionary* approaches from a modern perspective, and offers a definition rather than a set of practices and associations. Peace is defined as a state of freedom from war and civil disorder, as involving quiet and tranquillity, a state of friendliness rather than strife. The *SOD* approach emphasizes a combination of emotional and material factors, and draws a distinctly polarized contrast between peace and war.

In this essay I shall argue that in the Roman empire, far from being rigidly separate, peace and war were closely interrelated both as concepts and as experiences. I shall look at examples of the ways in which the Romans marked peace, the language they used, and the contexts in which they discussed it. So the essay will be very much concerned with the question of perspectives – peace for whom and from whom? Who decides how peace is to be defined and achieved? How is peace to be maintained and by whom (that is, by whose agency)? I shall refer to some of the best-known documentary sources which record information about peace, and will use these to try to open up some critical questions about Roman attitudes, administration and propaganda. These lead to questions about the extent to which public and private notions of peace coincide, differ or overlap. I shall also try to discover some clues to the perspectives of non-Romans, and so will include reference to a variety of sources from the point of view of historical/chronological development, geographical location, and religious and cultural standpoint. Of course, it is always difficult to move from the constraints of written evidence to justify generalizations about the experiences and attitudes of ordinary people, but the guiding themes of this book – culture, identity and power – suggest some ways in which judgements may be made.

The essay is in four main sections:

1   the pax Augusta;

2   the pax romana;

3   experiences and reactions of the 'recipients';

4   challenges to the concept of the Roman peace.

The final section will end by considering notions of peace as an index of culture, identity and power.

There are a wide range of relevant sources, most of which represent or discuss the concept of peace in relation to other issues. Therefore, in addressing the sources, it quickly becomes clear that the idea of peace is 'embedded' (and sometimes more problematically 'encoded') in a whole system of interrelated ideas, symbols and allusions. I shall be considering whether some of these are common to more than one conception of peace, as well as asking questions about whether peace is primarily seen as a public affair or a private one and how it is related to other concepts such as order and justice. It is necessary to ask who is speaking in a particular source and to and for whom. Who is silent and can we find other ways of hearing silenced voices? Do notions of peace vary at different points in the power structure? At the end of the essay I will review the extent to which we are justified in generalizing about notions of peace both chronologically and spatially, and comment on what this suggests about other aspects of Roman life and the changes which took place when the geographical empire was controlled by an imperial form of government. So there will be a high degree of interconnection between this essay and some of the others, especially Essay Two, 'Communicating culture, identity and power', and Essay Ten, 'The language of dissent'.

The pax Augusta

In talking about peace it is necessary also to talk about war. In the ancient world, war was a basic fact of life for many and Rome was no exception. What changed across time and place was the types of war, how war was organized, and how attitudes to war were expressed. Of particular importance is the distinction between civil war and war against external enemies. How these outsiders were defined and treated is often important for notions of what constituted peace. To appreciate the concept of the pax Augusta (the peace associated with the first emperor Augustus and derived from a phrase in chapter 12 of the *Res Gestae*), it is helpful to look at events and attitudes in the republic in order to judge how Augustus responded to them and to consider the main changes in circumstances in the early empire. In the key period for Roman expansion in the middle republic – the second century BC – Rome went to war almost every year (Harris, 1979, pp.9–10; Evans, 1991, pp.1–4). The doors of the temple of Janus were rarely closed. Roman influence and power grew (and not always by annexation). From this time the Roman empire began to expand, with important effects on the senate, on citizen soldiers in the army and its commanders, on competition for power, and on agriculture and trade.

Imperial expansion fanned the desire for *laus* (fame, praise) and *gloria* (renown) and for additional benefits to the aristocracy. The career of Octavian/Augustus developed in this context, with civil war as the trigger. Some scholars believe that there is no significant difference in the mentality of particular power seekers, whatever the context for their activities. They follow the generalization recorded by Thucydides, the Greek historian of the fifth century BC, in the Melian Dialogue:

> ... of the gods we believe and of men we know for certain, that by a necessary law of nature they always rule where they can.
>
> (*History of the Peloponnesian War* 5.105)

However, even if this statement is true, it does not necessarily entail the further claim that power is always defined and exercised in the same way. Variables include differing acceptance of the costs/sacrifices involved and variations in willingness to exert power, as well as differing attitudes to the feasibility and legitimacy of the means through which it can be exercised. This means that the practices and attitudes associated with war, imperialism and the exercise of power also have a role to play in the practices and attitudes associated with peace.

Furthermore, the way in which Thucydides' approach has influenced modern analyses of power relations (whether relating to ancient or contemporary situations) has diverted attention from what was radical about his analysis of the fifth-century BC situation: namely, that it brought political and military force to the centre of analysis. This framework has tended to become the norm, and as a result commentators who have drawn on modern conceptual analysis have tended to underplay religious and cultural aspects of the system of social values which underpinned the definition and exercise of power in the Graeco-Roman world (Crane, 1998, p.5). A feature of the range of sources available for the study of Roman cultural history is that, taken as a whole, they do enable study of the interrelationship of different aspects of competition for power, including cultural and religious issues.

In the context of Augustus, peace is presented in a range of sources as having two main aspects – civic accord at home (that is, Rome and Italy) and victory abroad. However, in the *Res Gestae* Augustus did not initially make a distinction between his aims and attitudes in respect of civil and foreign wars:

> **3** I undertook many civil and foreign wars by land and sea throughout the world, and as victor I spared the lives of all citizens who asked for mercy. (2) When foreign peoples could safely be pardoned I preferred to preserve rather than exterminate them.
>
> (*Res Gestae Divi Augusti*; trans. Brunt and Moore, 1967, p.18; all subsequent references are to this edition and translation)

What is common to both kinds of war is Augustus' stress on his status as victor (Figure 12.1) and on the benefits he conferred on the defeated. The next chapter of the *Res Gestae* expands on this aspect by itemizing the ovations, triumphs and salutations which he received as *imperator*, and adds a religious dimension of approval to that of the Roman senate and people: 'On fifty-five occasions the senate decreed that thanksgivings should be offered to the immortal gods on account of the successes on land and sea gained by me or by my legates acting under my auspices' (*Res Gestae* 4, p.21).

The *Res Gestae* was deposited with the Vestal Virgins by Augustus in AD 13, giving it religious authority. Some aspects were updated after his death (when it was reproduced as a monumental inscription for public display – see Figure 2.3), and the text can be taken as good evidence not only of how he wished to be remembered but also of how it was thought appropriate that he should be remembered (see Essay Two). Its ethos is in accordance with the republican tradition of a rich grandee favoured by the gods who, in the ancient world, were generally regarded by the people as being supportive of war. Nevertheless, the *Res Gestae* also affords evidence that respite was needed from the demands of war, and particularly from civil war. For example, in addition to the reference in *Res Gestae* 3 to the pardoning of the defeated, chapter 34 states that 'I extinguished civil wars' and associates this with a (spurious) restoration of the republic and with the virtues of courage, clemency, justice and

Figure 12.1   *Quinarius, eastern mint, 29* BC. *Obverse:* 'CAESAR IMP VII', *head, bare (right). Reverse:* 'ASIA RECEPTA', *Victory standing holding wreath and palm on a* cista mystica *(sacred Dionysiac basket) between two serpents. The coin records the recovery of the province from Antony. British Museum, London. (© British Museum)*

piety. These concepts were inscribed on the Clupeus Virtutis (Shield of Virtue) which was set up in the senate house in 27 BC.

The relief at the ending of civil war is a subtle theme in the Augustan poets. Propertius, whose family had suffered in the proscriptions, refers to 'those ungentle times when feud at home/Hounded to war the citizens of Rome' (*Elegies* 1.22; trans. Watts, 1966, p.65). Even in respect of foreign wars, which he celebrates at the behest of his patron Maecenas, Propertius occasionally suggests that victory has two aspects and that 'war wearied Rome' is 'by her conquests, as by foes, hemmed around' (*Elegies* 2.15; trans. Watts, 1966, p.89). Horace's famous poem on peace of mind examines both individual desire for tranquillity and the longing of Rome's opponents for peace:

> And peace is what the battle-maddened Thracians
> And the fierce Parthians with their painted quivers
> Pray for – the peace no gold or gems or purple,
>> Grosphus, can buy
>
> (*Odes* 2.16; trans. Michie, 1963, p.106)

However, care was needed in commenting on recent events. Civil war had set up dangerous tensions, and the new regime was sensitive to anything which might destabilize it. Augustus' stress in the *Res Gestae* on his clemency to his defeated opponents at home was confirmed, with a shift of focus towards the glories of foreign conquests. A sense of Roman unity towards defeated 'foreigners' helped to paper over cracks within the Roman upper class and encouraged ordinary people to take pride in the new order. Perhaps this underlines Horace's sense of caution, expressed in his 'Ode to Pollio'. (Pollio was writing a history of the years from 60 BC to the supremacy of Augustus.) Horace's opening words soon expose the dangers of what Pollio is doing:

> Your theme is civil warfare ...
>   Pollio: you tread on fire
> Still smouldering underneath deceptive ash.
> ... Our fields are rich with Roman
> Dead and not one lacks graves to speak against our
>   Impious battles.
>
> (*Odes* 2.1; trans. Michie, 1963, pp.73–4)

In the face of these memories, it is no wonder that Augustus had to stress the benefits he had allowed to the defeated, the land he allotted to soldiers, and the prosperity and 'unity' which his supremacy had brought. This tells us a good deal about what was considered a benefit, how peace was defined, and to whom the ideal of Augustan peace was thought to appeal.

The *locus classicus* or prime example for the description of the Augustan peace is in Velleius Paterculus:

> Twenty years of civil war came to an end and abroad all hostilities ceased. Peace was re-established and the madness of armed conflict was assuaged in every quarter. Law and order were restored: the courts and the Senate once more enjoyed authority and prestige ... Agriculture revived, and with it religious observance and security of life and property. There was useful law reform and beneficial legislation.
>
> (*History of Rome* 2.89, in Chisholm and Ferguson, 1981, p.51)

Velleius died sometime after AD 30. It is a commonplace to say that as an acolyte of Tiberius he was an uncritical commentator, but I find in the extract a genuine sense of relief that the turmoils of the previous generation were over. The question remains, however, turmoils for whom? And the answer is: for the upper or at least reasonably prosperous groups, who had lost land or life in the civil wars. Augustan ideology required that Augustus had to be represented not only as victor (essential both in fidelity to republican values and as a concealed threat to any who might still desire to oppose him), but also as a deliverer and as a restorer, so that those who were potentially powerful opponents might feel they had been given back their traditional benefits and way of life. To take a more cynical interpretation, it was also necessary that the changed nature of political supremacy might be, if not concealed, at least mitigated. Augustus' shrewdness in this respect is shown by the persistence of the desire to associate peace with restoration of traditional values. This continued to be an issue in time of civil war, as demonstrated by the issue of coins inscribed *pax et libertas* (peace and liberty) by Vindex, the Praetorian governor of Gallia Lugdunensis, when he attempted to justify his revolt against Nero in AD 68, the year of the

Four Emperors. (*Libertas* was the slogan of the ruling class in the republic. It did not imply freedom for all social groups to share in the exercise of power.)

Alongside the political benefits of peace, there is also a less focused but nevertheless powerful association of the victories of Octavian/Augustus with regeneration. For example, in the invocation to Virgil's *Georgics* 1, Octavian (to whom the poem may have been recited on his return from the east in 29 BC) is linked with the regeneration of the countryside and the reassertion of the lasting foundations and values of Roman life. A visual rhetoric which brings together the ideas of healing and restoration under the aegis of Augustan supremacy is also evident in the Ara Pacis, although interestingly the monument is not frequently mentioned in the ancient sources. The altar was consecrated in 13 BC and dedicated in 9 (Figure 12.2). *Res Gestae* 12 refers to it as an altar of the Augustan peace, and somewhat coyly records that it marked the 'successful arrangement of affairs in the provinces of Spain and Gaul'. The end panels of the upper frieze show the earth (Tellus) or Italy as an abstraction of prosperity (Figure 12.3), with other friezes showing leaves, garlands and fruit (Figure 12.4). All of these are traditional symbols of well-being, stability and prosperity, but are organized into and associated with the primacy of Augustus. As well as exploiting the iconography of plenty, the altar also emphasizes the political aspects of the victory that precedes peace in Roman discourse, for example in the procession of senators, priests and imperial family on the south and north friezes (Figure 12.5).

The altar was perhaps a religious and artistic counterpart to the closing of the gates of the temple of Janus Quirinius:

> ... which our ancestors resolved should be closed whenever peace with victory was secured throughout the empire of the Roman people by land and sea, and which before my birth according to tradition has been closed only twice in all since the foundation of Rome, was ordered by the Senate to be closed three times during my principate.
>
> (*Res Gestae* 13)

In later sources, the closing of the gates of the temple of Janus becomes a *topos*, a rhetorical motif in statements in praise of Augustan stability (Figure 12.6) and in Suetonius, *Augustus* 22. As Suetonius was working under Trajan and Hadrian, this is an indication of the extent to which an idealized notion of the Augustan peace had passed into tradition.

The model, therefore, of the pax Augusta within Italy is victory for Augustus in the civil war, deliverance from internal fighting, and regeneration with a strong bias towards restoration and celebration of prosperity in the countryside, combined with traditional religious legitimation. In *Eclogue* 4 Virgil drew on this nexus of associations to

Figure 12.2 Ara Pacis, view of the west (front) entrance, 13–9 BC, marble, length 11.63 m, height c. 6.3 m. Deutsches Archäologisches Institut, Rome.

Figure 12.3 Ara Pacis, panel from the east end showing earth or Italy in peace and plenty, c. 155 × 237 cm. (Photo: Alinari-Anderson)

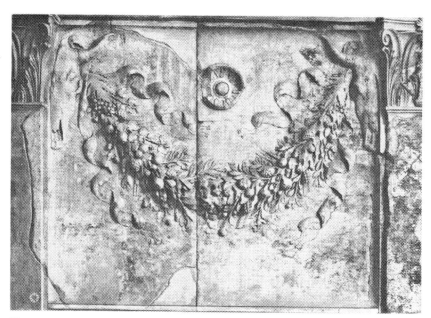

Figure 12.4   *Ara Pacis, detail of the upper internal frieze of the precinct wall. (Photo: Alinari-Anderson)*

Figure 12.5   *Ara Pacis, detail of the south frieze showing a sacrificial procession with members of the imperial family, height c. 183 cm. (Photo: Alinari)*

Figure 12.6 *Aureus of Nero, AD 64–68. Temple of Janus with doors closed to denote the universal peace on land and sea proclaimed by Nero and in the inscription:* 'IANVM CLVSIT PACE PR TERRA MRIQVE PARTA'. *Hunterian Museum, University of Glasgow.*

represent peace as a past happy state which had now returned. The political aspects of this are represented in the *Res Gestae* and in Velleius. For propaganda purposes, in Rome and Italy the pax Augusta also includes successful campaigns abroad. The pax Augusta therefore fits into the concept of the pax romana, a term which applies both to the geographical empire which developed under the republic and the enlarged empire of provincial territories presided over by the emperors.

There is, however, one significant poetic exception to the association of the imperial peace with benefits to Rome. This is in a particularly pessimistic invocation of the situation which faced Rome by the poet Lucan (AD 39–65). Lucan was the nephew of Seneca, and like his uncle a member of Nero's inner circle. The poem (*Pharsalia*, sometimes called *De Bello Civili*) has been described as a virtual anti-*Aeneid*. It depicts the brutality and criminality of the civil wars which led to the fall of the republic, but instead of welcoming the peace brought by the end of civil war, the poet portrays an on-going struggle between liberty and tyranny. The Roman 'suicide' represented by the factions of the civil wars is mirrored by breakdown in the traditional meanings of words, in which *dominus* (ruler) becomes a loathsome word. Lucan situates the conflict in the past, exploring it through astrologers and visionaries. Peace, the normally hoped-for outcome (celebrated by Virgil), is characterized ironically as even worse than the civil war which preceded it ('peace will bring nothing but tyranny in its train', *Pharsalia* 1.669–73; trans. Graves, 1956, p.45). Unlike Virgil and Horace, who were interested in the idea of Concord, Lucan uses the image of Discord ('when the mechanism of the Universe gets thrown out of gear', 1.79–80, p.28). Lucan also picks up the image of dangerous ashes used by Horace and creates an epic scene of the funeral pyre of Pompey the Great, in which Cordus writes Pompey's name in charcoal on the tomb (8.793). In spite of his care in adopting a poetic and historical distance from his own time and a (possibly ironic) panegyric on Nero, Lucan was forced to commit suicide when he was discovered to be part of Piso's conspiracy against Nero in AD 65.

The pax romana

There are long-running debates among scholars about the extent to which the Roman empire was primarily aggressive and voracious in territorial and material terms. There is corresponding disagreement about the extent to which it could be said to have a strategy of defence rather than aggrandisement (see Whittaker, 1994, especially chapters 1–4). I do not intend to go through all the issues and judgements involved, but some aspects of the debate do underlie the problems discussed in this essay. The most important assumptions from which I am working are these:

1   In practice, different kinds of 'frontiers' emerged, adapted to different kinds of conquest, domination or authority, and not necessarily planned or consistent in their development. These frontiers might be material or physical (as represented by fortifications and the presence of the army), they might be socio-economic (represented by people, goods and technology, the mechanisms of exchange), or they might be cultural (including language, religion and philosophical ideas). Or they might combine aspects of all of these – a situation with which Roman administration then had to contend. This plurality of frontiers could vary in combination in different parts of the empire and at different times. I therefore follow Whittaker in thinking in terms of frontier *zones*: physical and cultural spaces within and across which Roman and non-Roman interacted, sometimes by negotiation, sometimes by force – and sometimes, no doubt, by accident. This model is compatible with both the main views – defence and aggrandisement.

2   Nevertheless, it seems a contradiction in terms to say that a developing empire can be defensive. In *Res Gestae* 26, Augustus made the claim:

> I extended the territory of all those provinces of the Roman people on whose borders lay peoples not subject to our government.

The word *fines* (boundaries) or its derivative is used twice in that sentence. The sentence which follows claims that Augustus 'brought peace' (to the Gallic and Spanish provinces). Here, the Latin word used is the verb *pacavi*, which literally means 'I pacified'. This active usage is intensified in the next sentence, which claims that '*I secured the pacification* of the Alps ... yet without waging an unjust war on any people' (my emphasis). So the points to note here are the association between setting new frontiers, pacification and the claim of justice, as well as the exploitation of quasi-diplomatic mechanisms such as client-kingship (in which a local ruler's supremacy was supported by patronage from Rome; this meant that he had obligations to implement Roman policy).

3   It is necessary to unravel the notion of the 'just war'. There was an ancient Roman tradition that for a war to be 'just' it must be officially sanctioned and perhaps, in some sense, 'defensive'. For this reason, the traditional rituals of the *fetiales*, a special group of priests, had to be invoked when war was declared. In *On Duties* Cicero refers to the fact that under this convention 'no war is just, unless it is entered upon after an official demand for satisfaction has been submitted or warning has been given and a formal declaration made' (1.36). Clearly, in this context 'defensive' has a special connotation of implying a response to some disagreement (that is, a demand for satisfaction), rather than necessarily implying that Romans were directly under military attack. The main sources for the rituals are Livy, *Books from the Foundation of the City* 1.24.46, and Dionysius of Halicarnassus, *Roman Antiquities* 2.72.4–9. It seems that a formal request for satisfaction was made (for example, in cases of disputed treaties), and if necessary war was ritually declared at the enemy's boundary. The traditions of the *fetiales* did not cater for civil war, which by implication was to be regarded as lacking religious sanction. After 171 BC the fetial procedures for declaring war seem to have lapsed, partly because they were cumbersome and partly because in an expanding empire remote enemies were unlikely to share the same gods as the Romans, so a religious formula was less appropriate. However, there were some survivals. For example, Cato the Stoic declared to the senate in 55 BC that Julius Caesar's war in Gaul was *iniustum* (unjust) because it was not defensive and not properly justified and that Caesar should be handed over to the enemy to prevent divine punishment falling on Rome (Suetonius, *Divus Julius* (*Julius Caesar*) 24.3, and Plutarch, *Life of Caesar* 22.4). The fetial traditions were revived for his own advantage by Octavian/Augustus (because the procedures appeared to increase control over wars by the senate and people and therefore by himself). The phrasing in *Res Gestae* 26 seems to involve a carefully worded denial of the impropriety of which his adoptive father had been accused. The association between justice and religious sanction is important. The pax deorum (literally 'peace of the gods') required that the Roman state should be in harmony with the gods, honour them and secure their approval. Breaking this special kind of *pax* could bring divine outrage and disaster for the state.

The nexus of the notion of the just war, imperial strategy and the definition and invocation of peace must therefore be seen against this background. It is clear that wars were fought, in the republic and later, both *de imperio* (to exert power) and for the sake of honour, fame and *dignitas* (position, reputation). In the first century AD, Seneca specifically links the pax romana with *imperium*, the exercise of power by the emperor, and claims that peace depended on the emperor/general (*On Clemency* 1.4). If peace was seen as a benefit brought by the emperor, then any threat to its imposition and maintenance could be seen as a grievance justifying war. The pax Augusta expressed this belief internally; the pax romana did so in terms of the wider empire.

This conjunction between the notion of peace and that of justified war has been used by some scholars to construct a link between peace and strategy, notably in an influential book by Edward N. Luttwak (1976). Luttwak (a political adviser to the US President Richard Nixon) wrote from the perspective of strategic analysis and modern international relations. He pointed out how the detailed work of archaeology, epigraphy, numismatics and textual criticism can be undermined by the application of inappropriate modern strategic ideas (for example, nation-state conflicts, total war, war for specific results) and especially argued that study of the ancient world precludes too sharp a distinction between peace and war. From that claim Luttwak went on to draw attention to the importance of images of force and various forms of diplomatic coercion. He argued that Roman strength was derived not merely or even primarily from tactical supremacy on the battlefield or superior generalship, but also from a complex of ideas and traditions informing the organization of military power and its harnessing to political purpose. This included, in his view, the role of engineering in building supply roads, camps and efficient administration rather than open warfare. All these things played a role in pacification and came to be associated with the virtues of peace. Victories may have been won slowly, but the Romans were hard to defeat.

On this basis, Luttwak identified distinct phases of imperial security, each satisfying a distinct set of priorities. These were hegemonic expansion (late republic and Octavian), territorial security (leading to the assurance of the empire in the second century AD), the priority of sheer survival (and so into Decline and Fall). Each phase used a different combination of diplomacy, direct force, management of client states and handling of the infrastructure.

While it has strengths in its awareness of the interrelationship between war and peace, the weakness of Luttwak's general model of the Roman exercise of power is that it is rigid and conceives of the frontier populations as 'an enemy to be intimidated' (Whittaker, 1994, p.7). A different emphasis has been suggested by Isaac (1992), who argues that the role of the Roman army was analogous to that of police.

However, no one model is likely to be satisfactory if one accepts that circumstances varied in different parts of the empire and at different times. For example, Roman domination of Greece differed from that of Judaea, and in Judaea there were differences in periods of client-kingship and administration by Roman officials (procurators). I see the relationship between the pacified populations and the Romans as complex and variable. The diplomatic accoutrements of 'peace with victory', the images of power and negotiation, and the material mechanisms of domination can also generate a double perspective when they become part of a discourse of peace. It is sometimes claimed that Augustus' alleged advice to Tiberius in his will 'that the empire should be kept within its boundary stones' signals a change from offensive to defensive strategy (Tacitus, *Annals* 1.11). However, the suggestion put forward in Tacitus, *Agricola* 13 – that the move away from enlargement of the empire involved neglect rather than positive policy – perhaps indicates that Tacitus was interpreting the situation within his overall assessment of the workings of the imperial system, and gives a salutary warning against neat and tidy interpretations. In my view, much of the comment in the ancient sources about frontiers and imperial strategy is embedded in, and sometimes conceals, the contest between opposing political groups. This is particularly the case with comment about the reception of the Romans and Romanization by subject peoples. The sources point to a number of ways in which the imposition and acceptance of Roman power could be justified as 'peace' or rejected as tyranny.

Some of the best-known examples in this context are speeches composed by Tacitus. He attributes to the Roman general Cerialis a speech to the Gauls after their revolt was suppressed in AD 70:

> Gaul always had its kingdoms and wars till you submitted to our authority. We, though so often provoked, have used the right of conquest to burden you only with the cost of maintaining peace ... Should the Romans be driven out – which the gods forbid! – what will result but wars among all these peoples? ... And yours will be the greatest peril, for you have gold and wealth, which are the chief causes of war. Therefore love and cherish peace and the city in which we enjoy an equal right, conquered and conquerors alike.
>
> (Tacitus, *Histories* 4.74, in Lewis and Reinhold, 1990, p.330)

This is the frank appeal to the prosperous élite among the Gauls. It is the other side of the perception attributed to Boudicca, queen of the Iceni, in her address to the Britons by the Greek historian Cassius Dio: 'deceived by the alluring promises of the Romans ... you have come to realize how much better is poverty with no master than wealth with slavery' (Cassius Dio, *Roman History*, Epitome of LX II.3; trans. Cary, 1925, p.84). Tacitus, too, attributes similar sentiments to Calgacus, the Caledonian chieftain: 'They rob, butcher, plunder, and call it "empire"; and where they make a desolation, they call it "peace"' (*Agricola* 29–30, in Lewis and Reinhold, 1990, p.335). In the same vein he describes the Batavian rebel Civilis, who 'reminded them of their miseries that they had endured so many years while they falsely called their wretched servitude a peace' (*Histories* 4.17). Of course, the sentiments are attributed to leaders of the upper class, and it is unlikely that Tacitus was doing more than project a traditional Roman senatorial perspective based on attachment to *libertas* on to the Caledonian and Batavian resistance. Equally, Dio was steeped in the Greek aversion to being enslaved (as opposed to being the enslaver). However, this type of source (if one digs beneath the noble, freedom-loving barbarian stereotype popularized by Gibbon's analysis) does indicate that the Romans needed the complicity of a majority of the group which had ruled previously in order to ensure a relatively trouble-free continuation of their domination and so 'peace'.

There are some sources which seem to speak on behalf of the conquered and advocate the acceptance of the benefits of the Roman peace. The Greek Plutarch (*c.* AD 50–*c.* 120) wrote:

> ... the greatest blessings that cities can enjoy are peace, prosperity, populousness, and concord. As far as peace is concerned the people have no need of political activity, for all war, both Greek and foreign, has been banished, and has disappeared from among us. Of liberty the people enjoy as much as our rulers allot them, and perhaps more would not be better.
>
> (*Precepts of Statecraft* 32, in Lewis and Reinhold, 1990, p.23)

The title of the work signals its focus. The passage shows the traditional Greek horror of *stasis* (civil strife), and reveals the way in which Greek appeals to concepts like concord and harmony were usually oligarchic. Harmony and concord are opposed to the *agon* (contest) and activity to be found in a democratic assembly. Concord is not about equal partnership but about agreement and complicity. It is one of a range of concepts which sanction inequalities, whether or not resulting from the use of force. So in the Roman period, as in previous ages, there might be an argument for external alliances (even the acceptance of domination) in order to have an internal political and economic system to one's liking.

The development towards the idealized image of stable empire of the second century can be seen, too, in the nauseating *Address to Rome* by Aelius Aristides (29–33, 60, in Lewis and Reinhold, 1990, pp.23–4):

> Extensive and sizeable as the Empire is, perfect policing does much more than territorial boundaries to make it great ... Like a well-swept and fenced-in front yard ... the whole world speaks in unison, more distinctly than a chorus; and so well does it harmonize under this director-in-chief that it joins in praying this Empire may last for all time.

Perhaps Aelius wished to exalt the status of his own city, Smyrna, but undoubtedly the passage attests the continuation of a trend of public adulation in the Greek east which was already emerging under Augustus. An inscription from Priene dated to 9 BC celebrated Augustus as a ruler 'given by providence who has brought war to an end and ordained peace', and another from Halicarnassus celebrated Augustus as 'saviour of the whole human race' because 'land and sea have peace, the cities flourish under a good legal system, in harmony and with an abundance of food' (see Sherk, 1984, no.101). Certainly, empire could be kept and its acceptance induced through benefits as well as force of arms (Wells, 1984, chapter X). Those sources suggest that attitudes to war and peace in the prosperous cities of Asia Minor may have differed from those in newly conquered areas or those subject to direct military control or fortification.

However, there are some extant texts which indicate cultural as well as military resistance to the perceived benefits of the pax romana. A Rabbinic text, the Babylonian Talmud, tells this story:

> Why did they call [Rabbi Judah ben Ilia] the first of the speakers? For once Rabbi Judah and Rabbi Jose and Rabbi Simeon were sitting, and Judah son of proselytes was sitting with them. Rabbi Judah began and said: 'How excellent are the deeds of this nation. They have instituted market places, they have instituted bridges, they have instituted baths.' Rabbi Jose was silent. Rabbi Simeon ben Yohai answered and said: 'All that they have instituted they have instituted only for their own needs. They have instituted market places to place harlots in them; baths, for their own pleasure; bridges, to collect toll.' Judah son of proselytes went and reported their words and they were heard by the government. They said: 'Judah who exalted shall be exalted; Jose who remained silent shall be banished to Sopphoris; Simeon who reproached shall be put to death.'
>
> (*Sabbath* 33b, in Lewis and Reinhold, 1990, pp.333–4)

This story vividly illustrates possible tensions between Jewish and Roman attitudes to material culture, but it has to be borne in mind that the Talmud dates from *c.* AD 550 and that the authors saw themselves as heirs of the Pharisees, strict adherents of Jewish law, and inheritors of the religious authority of Moses. The source has its own perspective as the voice of a tradition which regarded the Romans as the blasphemous destroyers of the Temple of the Jewish faith in Jerusalem in AD 70.

Experiences and reactions of the 'recipients'

I want now to pursue in more detail these questions about who benefited, who suffered and who opposed, and consider how these experiences were expressed in attitudes to peace. So far, the evidence to which I have referred has been almost entirely produced by the upper classes, and the majority of the sources are also directed at the privileged. To identify evidence about the experiences and attitudes of ordinary people is difficult, and it is even harder to discover directly the voices of the ordinary men, women and children who were caught up, willingly or unwillingly, in war, pacification and its aftermath. However, it is to some extent possible to make judgements about the impact of war and peace on the lives of the 'ordinary'. Archaeological evidence yields information about how people lived and how space was used. It can suggest something of the intensity of conflagration, and answer some of our questions about the extent and nature of cultural exchange in and around the frontier zones. Funerary inscriptions give examples of the social and geographical mobility which Roman rule offered to soldiers, and can also indicate places of settlement which they took up on retirement (another indication of a degree of peaceful co-existence with the indigenous population). Numismatics has enabled the identification and classification of coins and study of the iconography of empire in their design: see, for example, the idealization of peace and plenty (Figure 12.7) and compare the stress on Victory in the *Judaea capta* and other series (Figures 12.8–12.10). Coins were designed and minted by the administration, and are therefore an important source for the study of Roman propaganda. However, they were also seen and handled by at least some fairly ordinary people, so they help us to round out some aspects of popular experience by showing the visual images which were a part of everyday life. Both archaeology and written texts attest to the effects of popular disturbances and religious tensions, and suggest indirectly that peace was not always universally desired (see Essays Ten and Eleven).

Nevertheless, it is a big step from evidence about the experiences of ordinary people, with all its problems of interpretation, to questions about whether there is any correlation between the presence or absence of 'peace' and the presence or absence of oppression, misery and suffering, whether under indigenous tyrants, slave owners or Romans.

Figure 12.7 *Silver tetradrachm, eastern mint, c. 27–25* BC. *Reverse: 'AVGVSTVS' with six corn ears, the symbol of plenty. British Museum, London. (© British Museum)*

Figure 12.8 *Victory draped, standing on a globe, holding a wreath in her right hand. The legend reads 'CAESAR DIVI F[ILIUS]' (Caesar son of a god). British Museum, London. (© British Museum)*

351

Figure 12.9 (a) Aureus, eastern mint, 27 BC. Obverse: 'CAESAR DIVI F COS VII', head, bare (right); below, small capricorn (Augustus' natal sign). Reverse: 'AEGVPT [O] CAPTA' with crocodile, symbol of Egypt. The inscription refers to the seizure of Egypt from Cleopatra. The coin was struck for the seventh consulship of Octavian in 27 BC on the eve of his assumption of the name Augustus. British Museum, London. (© British Museum) (b) Aureus, eastern mint, 21–19 BC. Obverse: 'AVGVSTVS', head, bare (right). Reverse: 'ARMENIA CAPTA', winged Victory kneels on a bull and kills it. The inscription refers to the bringing of Armenia under Roman control as a client-kingdom in 20 BC. British Museum, London. (© British Museum)

There is a sense in which we can know nothing of the fears, tears, hopes and joys of the millions who were unknown to historians or at least were not given a place in their histories. For example, the impact of war and peace on women and children is hard to assess because only rarely are they directly represented in the written sources, and there is virtually no evidence which we can be sure was directly created by them. The historian Livy (59 BC– AD 17) does, however, record the impact of war on the bereaved, on the legal status of women in Rome during the republic, on their ownership and use of property, and on the ability and necessity of poorer freeborn women to enter the rural and urban workforce. Women and children were also liable to capture and enslavement. Later

Figure 12.10   Sestertius, Rome, AD 71. 'IVDAEA CAPTA SC'. *The type is the same as in Figure 11.7, except that here Vespasian's son, the future* princeps *Titus (who completed the suppression of the revolt), is shown standing in military dress, foot on helmet, holding spear and parazonium (dagger). British Museum, London. (© British Museum)*

sources refer to imperial legislation to prevent the castration of slave children, and all those captured in war were particularly vulnerable to various kinds of prostitution (for detailed discussions see Evans, 1991). The Column of Marcus Aurelius, which was set up in Rome to commemorate Roman victories in the campaign in Bohemia against the Marcomanni in AD 172, shows that the Romans had no scruples about

Figure 12.11   Column of Marcus Aurelius, from scene 20: devastation of a village. Rome. (Photo: Alinari-Anderson)

Figure 12.12 *Column of Marcus Aurelius, from scene 104: capture of women and children. Rome. (Photo: Deutsches Archäologisches Institut, Rome)*

either the triumphant depiction of suffering caused to the women and children of their enemies or showing themselves inflicting it brutally (Figures 12.11 and 12.12). The enslaved were an important aspect of booty. Yet I do not think that the lack of direct evidence absolves us from the need to look for the possibility of indirect evidence about their experiences. Some modern historians have attempted to reconstruct such experiences; for example, Klaus Wengst (1987) has included chapters on the impact of peace on the defeated, especially in respect of the legal system, culture and economics.

It is usual in the written sources for the imagined reactions of ordinary people to be portrayed, if at all, through the mouths of the élite. Tacitus makes Calgacus say that 'our life and limbs will be used up in building roads through forests and swamps to the accompaniment of gibes and blows' (*Agricola* 31). Now, while it is true that Roman domination brought about forest clearing and road building and increased the demand for forced labour, there would equally be no justification in claiming that prior to conquest Calgacus' people had been free of hard (sometimes literally killing) manual work. This was just a fact of life for ordinary people in the ancient world. Nevertheless, increased building and engineering work needed manpower, as did the movement of foodstuffs and luxuries: there was forced labour in Egypt under Trajan, for example. So while peace may have brought respite from fighting and pillage, it also resulted in other kinds of compulsory activity for those at the bottom of the socio-economic heap. The stress of Tacitus on the enslavement which accompanied the Roman peace usually refers to the loss of political, social and economic dominance by the indigenous rulers. However, in times of instability or food shortage, arguably those who had least suffered the most, whether their suffering came about in war or peace or, most likely, in the grey area in between. As Gibbon put it in the eighteenth century, 'if we are more deeply affected by the ruin of a palace than by the conflagration of a cottage, our humanity must have formed a very erroneous estimate of the miseries of human life' (Gibbon, 1993, chapter 24).

A good deal of the comment in the ancient sources about the effects of war and peace focuses on booty and taxation. Josephus, a Hellenized Jew writing in the first century AD, comments on the extent of the plundering after the storming of the Temple of Jerusalem by Titus in AD 70 and claims that the loot was 'beyond all human expectation and opinion' (*Jewish War* 6.317). Depictions on victory pillars and triumphal arches show what was taken off to Rome – and Josephus also refers to Vespasian's ironically named temple of Peace (*Jewish War* 7.158–60). Because Josephus (who moved from being a defeated general in the Jewish army to living in Rome as a citizen) is ambivalent about the benefits of the pax romana, he is also particularly useful as a source for upper-class reactions. For example, he presents Herod Agrippa, Herod the Great's grandson, as trying to persuade the Jewish people not to revolt on the grounds that it was too late, although it would have been natural to revolt at the moment of provincialization (*Jewish War* 2.345–401). According to Josephus, Herod Agrippa argued that people submit because of the prosperity brought and because of their awe of Roman power (this is almost like the modern theory of deterrent power: that a display of power actually brings about peace, not war, by preventing revolts which are bound to fail). Also, it seemed to him that God was on the side of the Romans. But as Josephus points out elsewhere (*Jewish War* 5.403–6), God could also have changed sides if the Jewish people deserved it.

However, most of the sources concentrate on material reactions. Tacitus says that the troops in Gaul during the disputes of AD 68–9 'preferred to secure rewards rather than mere pay' (*Histories* 1.51). Similarly, the effect of garrisons in time of peace would be to produce wealth for some and misery for others. The garrisons were paid for by taxes, tolls, tributes and levies. The implications of failure to pay taxes might be severe. According to Plutarch, Nero's procurators in Spain caused those in debt over tax to be sold as slaves (Plutarch, *Galba* 4). Tacitus makes links between fair and just administration and the preservation of peace, and regards it as the duty of rulers to prevent corruption and the abuse of taxation. Although his duty as a son-in-law no doubt colours his portrait of the virtuous Agricola, the general point holds good: 'By suppressing these abuses ... Agricola restored the popularity of peace, whereas under his predecessors – thanks to their indifference or arrogance – peace had been dreaded no less than war (*Agricola* 19–21, in Lewis and Reinhold, 1990, p.278). In this way a hint of a 'just peace' emerges to parallel that of the just war.

In most of these sources the dividing line between war and peace is fluid. This is peace resulting from victory. On the one hand, it is characterized by the prosperity of the victors and, on the other, it is 'justified' by the stability it brings to conquerors and conquered alike. In Virgil's words:

> But, Romans, never forget that government is your medium!
> Be this your art: – to practise men in the habit of peace,
> Generosity to the conquered, and firmness against aggressors.
> (*Aeneid* 6.851–3; trans. Day-Lewis, 1966, p.314)

Achieving this balance was necessary to ensure the 'popularity of peace', as Tacitus put it.

Challenges to the concept of the Roman peace

In this section I want to look more closely at some of the more critical responses to the notion of the Roman peace. There is significant evidence to be found in poetry and in philosophical and religious writings. The evidence is not always clear-cut, and at its most interesting shows writers grappling with both benefits and drawbacks of the Roman conceptions of peace. Alternatives to the public notions of peace take two forms. The first is that of a quietist retreat either individually or as part of a small community. The second suggests an alternative 'power' structure through which peace may be achieved. Both forms have an ambivalent relationship to the Augustan peace and Roman peace, in that they challenge their pervasiveness in all aspects of culture and yet require some sort of publicly established 'peace' or order to be able to formulate and cultivate alternatives. The ways in which the Roman authorities reacted to and dealt with such 'challenges' are also instructive.

One example of an apparently quietist approach is found in the philosophical poem *De Rerum Natura* (*On the Nature of the Universe*) by Lucretius (*c.* 94–55 BC). The poet reworks Epicurean ideas concerning psychological tranquillity or peace of mind (*ataraxia*), which can be achieved by turning aside from the anxiety-creating activities associated with public life, strife and competition for glory:

> Consider too the greed and blind lust of power that drive unhappy men to overstep the bounds of right and may even turn them into accomplices or instruments of crime, struggling day and night with unstinted effort to scale the pinnacle of wealth ... so in their greed of gain they amass a fortune out of civil bloodshed: piling wealth on wealth, they heap carnage on carnage.
>
> (3.61f.; trans. Latham, 1951, pp.97–8)

Lucretius, writing during the later part of the republic, shows a particular horror of civil war. Yet he also associates avarice, ambition and violence with fear of death and religious superstition. He claims, 'True piety lies rather in the power to contemplate the universe with a quiet mind' (5.1197; trans. Latham, 1951, p.208). Clearly this world view is subversive of the whole network of Roman values associated with political life, and his notions of peace and piety are at variance with the situations later celebrated in the pax Augusta and the pax romana. Yet his philosophy offered no threat to the established social and political framework. It involved withdrawal and cultivation of the mind (presumably based on the security afforded by personal financial sufficiency and public order). There is no evidence that his views were particularly influential in his own time, but after his death his poem was read and possibly edited by Cicero; later it may have influenced Virgil (70–19 BC) and Horace (65–8 BC) in substance and style.

A combination of these Epicurean approaches with an ironic attitude to the benefits of empire can be seen in Horace's 'Peace Ode', in which, beginning with a conventional imaging of the desire of Rome's enemies for peace, he explicitly contrasts the mechanisms of public order control with the uncontrolled turbulence of the mind:

A pasha's bribes, a consul's rodded lictors
    Can soon disperse a riot of the people,
But not the grey mob of the mind, the worries
    Circling the beams

Of fretted ceilings.

This may seem rather like a withdrawal into psychological introspection, but Horace then moves on to consider the cause of anxieties in phrasing which allows a fluid association between public and private:

Why do we aim so high, when time must foil our
    Brave archery? Why hanker after countries
Heated by foreign suns? What exile ever
    Fled his own mind?

Then, apparently on the brink of public comment in a way contrary to his advice to Pollio, Horace slides into a contrast between public wealth and reputation and his own private contentment. This culminates in a vignette which combines Roman nostalgia for pastoral tradition with an appeal to aesthetic sensibility and a biting comment on current social values:

But I am rich too: Fate, an honest patron,
Has given me a small farm, an ear fine-tuned to
The Grecian Muses, and a mind from vulgar
    Envy aloof.
(*Odes* 2.16; trans. Michie, 1963, p.106)

Although Epicureanism seems to have been assimilated into the prevailing culture in Rome by the early years of the imperial system, it continued to feature in sources from the Hellenized parts of the empire, notably Asia Minor, in the ten cities known as the Decapolis, in Tarsus and in Antioch, and even tried to broaden the social base of its appeal (Long, 1986, p.17). Indeed, there is some commonality in the vocabulary and ideas of Epicureans and early Christians (as demonstrated in the Epistles of Paul). Both groups saw themselves as communities, attacked superstition, criticized political ambition, and (for very different reasons) did not fear death. Probably both communities drew on elements in the eclectic *koine* culture of the eastern Mediterranean, and I shall return to the issue later.

There is, however, one major extant source, the Inscription of Diogenes of Oinoanda, which shows that Epicureanism also had a significant public presence. Oinoanda was a prosperous city of northern Lycia in south-west Asia Minor. The inscription (second century AD), parts of which have been restored, was clearly an important public proclamation of the wealth and public benefaction of Diogenes, who took the opportunity to inscribe quotations from and allusions to the books of Epicurus and Lucretius. For example: 'we can look at other people's possessions [without envy] and experience [purer] pleasure than they can; for [we are free from craving]' (fragment 108; trans. Smith, 1993). Some scholars think that the inscription reflects the continued prominence of Epicureanism in the Hellenized parts of the empire, which is also demonstrated by the request (recorded on inscriptions) of Trajan's widow Plotina to Hadrian in AD 121 to grant new privileges to the Epicurean school in Athens and by Marcus Aurelius' general commitment to philosophy in his endowment of chairs at Stoic, Epicurean, Academic and Peripatetic schools in Athens in the later part of the second century. This publicly recognized role of Epicureanism indicates that it was accepted by the authorities as, at best, complicit and, at least, unthreatening to the nexus of associations in which the pax romana was embedded. Its stress on harmony was compatible with the oligarchic exploitation of concord discussed above.

The most significant Greek philosophical influence on alternative conceptions of peace came via the Stoics. In contrast to the Epicureans, many Roman Stoics were politically involved. Psychological tranquillity and moral rectitude were thought to go together, and were achieved by the cultivation of indifference to externals such as luxury. Freedom from the psychological slavery brought by desire for these was the aim. The individual should be autonomous and uncorrupted by love of riches or even public acclaim. Politically, such attitudes tended to go with an idealized view of the Roman republic as a repository of the values of honesty and simplicity associated with figures such as the Elder Cato ('Cato the Censor', 234–149 BC). This austere, even harsh, aspect of Stoicism had important political implications in its rejection of authority and hierarchy in favour of the autonomy of the individual conscience. However, this generally implied dissent rather than conspiracy (see Essay Ten). Nevertheless, during the early empire, Stoics such as Thrasea Paetus attempted to challenge the excesses of the new regime and yearned for a return to republican ideals of *libertas* (that is, freedom for the traditional senatorial rulers to continue their ascendancy rather than to have to acknowledge the power of the emperor – see Tacitus, *Annals* 16.19). Thrasea was a leading senator. His refusal to take part in public events and rituals was taken as intending a slight on the emperor Nero. For a leading figure to absent himself from formal requirements was equated with a public expression of moral criticisms of the emperor. Tacitus, of course, makes much of this:

> Thrasea's independence made others less servile ...
> (*Annals* 14.48)

and records that part of the accusation against Thrasea was that:

> In every province and army the official Gazette is read with special care –
> to see what Thrasea has refused to do.
>
> (*Annals* 16.19)

At the time of his enforced suicide Thrasea was in the company of the leading Cynic philosopher Demetrius.

Many of the people exiled or killed by Nero combined admiration for republican heroes with Stoic austerity and moral judgements about the emperor's rule, while Domitian came to regard Stoicism as an ideology of opposition. Thus 'peace' was interpreted by these Stoics in terms of mental, moral and political autonomy, and the Augustan peace was not a sufficient response to their requirements because it had undermined the political freedoms of the ruling élite. Even the philosopher Seneca, who was Nero's close adviser, commented on the danger of moral and spiritual slavery (*Moral Epistles* 47, 17). He, too, was excluded from power and eventually killed by enforced suicide.

However, once the imperial regime became firmly established, the 'Old Romans' – as the Stoic dissenters were called – were superseded by a Stoicism which was assimilated more readily into the imperial ethos. In fact, one of the major Stoic works to be produced during the empire was the *Meditations* of the emperor Marcus Aurelius.

At this point, it is perhaps useful to pause and unravel some of the individual strands which have emerged in this account of challenges to the Roman conceptions of peace. Firstly, it is necessary to distinguish between actual and potential challenges. Withdrawal from public life and from the rituals associated with the pax Augusta and pax romana was only a significant challenge if one was a prominent person with public duties to perform. An 'ordinary' person could make a quietist withdrawal. A poet could use figurative language. Those of a philosophical turn of mind could be vulnerable if they participated in politics or wrote in political contexts. Secondly, it does seem that public protest was made primarily by those who had some additional axe to grind – for example, a desire to return to republican political institutions. Thirdly, there is evidence that potential challenges couched in philosophical or moral language which drew on or expressed alternative conceptions of peace could be assimilated over time into the dominant values of the Roman imperial system. From the point of view of the authorities, the crucial point seems to have been whether there was actual challenge to the 'social cement' of public and religious sanctions which underpinned Roman rule. (I leave aside the issue of actual conspiracy or rebellion, which is outside the boundaries of this discussion.)

The concept of peace in early Christian writings

An alternative conception of peace which falls squarely into this problematic area of potential challenge to Roman dominance is to be found in the early Christian writings known as the New Testament and dating from the second half of the first century AD. They are thus an important source for a period in which the Roman empire was itself facing instability after the deaths of Augustus and Tiberius, the failure of Nero, the disasters of the year of the Four Emperors, and the efforts of the new Flavian dynasty to establish its credentials by emphasizing its role in the suppression of the Jewish Revolt, the destruction of the Temple at Jerusalem, and the siege and destruction of Masada. There are three particularly significant features in exploring the idea of peace to be found in the New Testament. The first is the role of the Jewish concept of peace to be found in the Hebrew Bible (of which many books now form the Old Testament and were known to Jews in the Diaspora and subsequently to Christians, including Gentiles, through the Septuagint, the Greek translation of the Hebrew Bible; see the discussion in Essay Eleven). The second feature is the use of the language of warfare to express the Christian concept of peace. This usage is, in my view, derived partly from its roots in Hebrew tradition and partly from the cultural context and vocabulary of the Hellenized Near Eastern Roman province of Asia Minor. The third significant feature is derived from the context and purpose of the New Testament writings and the uneasy relationship of the very early Christians with the Roman powers. In this respect the Christian notion of peace could imply either a potentially quietist retreat into the spiritual sphere or a refusal to comply with the public manifestations of the Roman peace such as public cult (for detailed discussion of the impact of public cult, see Price, 1984).

The Hebrew tradition was that there can be no peace without a covenant with God. See, for example, Psalm 147:14: 'He maketh peace [shalom] in thy borders and filleth thee with the finest of the wheat'; Psalm 29:11: 'The lord will bless his people with peace [shalom]'; or Psalm 128, which speaks of peace as involving divine ordering or attunement in nature and concludes: 'Behold that thus shall the man be blessed that feareth the lord ... thou shalt see thy children's children, and peace [shalom] upon Israel.'

In some texts in the Hebrew Bible this is expressed as an identification of peace with wisdom, as in Proverbs 3:17: 'Her [wisdom's] ways are ways of pleasantness and all her paths are peace.' In Hebrew scripture, because shalom has a number of aspects which are bound together in God's creation, there is a duty to defend it against injustice and oppression. War, therefore, is not the opposite of peace, but may be invoked in order to restore peace.

The New Testament writings represent a meeting point for several of the discourses of peace discussed above (the standard collection of references and discussion is Swartley, 1996, and for Stoicism and Christianity, see Colish, 1992). It has become conventional to point to the language of peace in the letters attributed to Paul as evidence of the way in which the early Christian Church developed a notion of spiritual peace: 'the peace of God which passes all understanding' (Philippians 4:7). This notion is analogous perhaps to Greek ideas of the tranquillity of mind and psyche which could be achieved by withdrawal from the worldly sphere of striving for material benefits and temporal power, but in Christian theology it is achieved through the agency of Jesus Christ (see Wengst, 1987; for the diversity of the cultural influences on Paul, see Wallace and Williams, 1998).

In some of the texts preserved in the New Testament, there is a sense that the spiritual peace of Christianity represents no challenge to the imperial situation represented by the pax romana and can co-exist with it. In contrast to the vision of the eventual divine overthrow of Roman power which is presented in the Book of Revelation and derives from Jewish apocalyptic tradition, the narrative in the Gospel according to St Luke and its companion text, the Acts of the Apostles (which are presented by the author as historical narratives including speeches), seems to imply that Christianity is compatible with the *imperium* of Rome. Representatives of the Roman administration are shown carrying out their duties correctly and conscientiously. The soldiers are presented as guarantors of the pax romana and as necessary protectors of civic order, such as the centurion Cornelius in Acts 10 and the centurion in Luke 7:3–6. In contrast with the Gospel according to Mark, the soldiers in Luke take little part in the mistreatment of Jesus (in Mark 15 the soldiers flog and ridicule Jesus and are said to loot garments), and in Acts 21–2 soldiers treat Paul in accordance with the laws of citizenship. In Luke 20:19–26 Jesus is reported as displaying a *denarius* which had the emperor's head on one side. (In the example in Figure 12.13 there is a representation which is thought to have combined the figure of Augustus' wife Livia (mother of Tiberius) with the goddess of Peace.) In response to hostile questioning Jesus is said to have replied that people had dual obligations: 'Render unto Caesar the things which be Caesar's and render unto God the things which be God's' (Matthew 22:21). The perspectives represented in Luke/Acts have led to debate about whether Luke is simply separating spiritual and political spheres, or whether the texts encode a positive apology for the empire and a legitimation of the status quo. In contrast, in the Pauline letter 1 Thessalonians 5:1–11 and especially verse 3, it seems that reference is being made to a pax

Figure 12.13   *Denarius of Tiberius, Gaul,* AD *14–37. The tribute significance of the* denarius *is referred to in Matthew 22:21. This example is thought to represent Livia, wife of Augustus and mother of Tiberius, as Pax. Hunterian Museum, University of Glasgow.*

romana-type of 'peace' which can be used as a slogan, 'peace and security' (in the Greek text *eirene kai asphaleia*), but which involves unacceptable complicity with Roman religious and social values and is liable to be suddenly overthrown by divine intervention.

However, for the purposes of this essay, the most significant aspect of the discourse of peace in the New Testament is the way in which it employs the vocabulary of war. This phenomenon has proved important historically, in that it perhaps underlies some of the ways in which Christianity has been exploited to justify the waging of war by states and dominant groups. As Raymond Hobbs has put it, 'in spite of the tendency to see the heart of the Gospel in terms of pacifism ... the reality of Christianity has portrayed the opposite. Throughout Christian history there seems to be a ready adoption of the language of warfare in both central and more eccentric forms of theology' (Hobbs, 1995, p.259). Although my concern here is not with the history of Christianity, let alone with theology, the issue usefully focuses attention on the relationship between the concept of the peace of Jesus Christ, which is the overt concern of the Christian texts, and the cultural and material context in which those works were constructed. It is therefore necessary to ask certain questions about the discourse of war, through which some aspects of the idea of the Christian peace were communicated. What kind of language is used? What is its role in the Christian texts? What is its effect on the community to which it is addressed?

Hobbs has made an analysis of the distribution and type of war language used in the New Testament (p.260). Apart from Acts, from which it is largely lacking, the distribution is fairly evenly spread across the Gospels, the works attributed to Paul and his associates, and other writings. Usage is mainly referential and illustrative, along the lines discussed above, in which soldiers are depicted as representatives (positive or negative) of an alien power. In addition, however, the language associated with war is used as exortation and as metaphor, and it is these two categories which have the most significant implications for the discourse of peace.

The best-known example of metaphorical usage is probably that in Ephesians 6:10–18. (Ephesians is a letter attributed to Paul or one of his followers. It was designed to be read as encouragement and exhortation to the congregation of Christians in Ephesus.)

> Put on the whole armour of God, so that you may be able to stand against the wiles of the devil ... Stand therefore, and fasten the belt of truth around your waist and put on the breastplate of righteousness. As shoes for your feet, put on whatever will make you ready to proclaim the gospel of peace. With all of these take the shield of faith, with which you will be able to quench all the flaming arrows of the evil one. Take the helmet of Salvation, and the sword of the Spirit, which is the word of God.
>
> (New Revised Standard Version, 1990)

Christian apologists have tended to suggest that the analogy with the arms and equipment of the Roman legionary soldier serves to emphasize the (defensive) qualities of resistance and solidarity (see Figure 12.14 and the discussion in Court, 1990, pp.313–14). However, Paul's metaphor of the soldier also draws on a Hebrew literary and religious tradition in which God is represented as a mighty warrior. This occurs in the Hebrew Bible and Old Testament book of Isaiah 59:17 ('he put on righteousness like a breastplate ... he put on garments of vengeance for clothing, and wrapped himself in fury like a mantle') and in Wisdom 5:17–23. (Wisdom is a Hellenistic Greek text from the Jewish Apocrypha and originated in Egypt at the end of the first century BC or beginning of the first century AD. It would therefore have been known to Jews of the Diaspora.) One could compare also the vocabulary and imagery of the War Scroll, 1 Qumran, which supported the military-type discipline of the Jewish community at the Dead Sea site and expressed (probably figuratively) its sense of a moral and spiritual battle against evil. (For the War Scroll, see Vermes, 1997, pp.161–8; Campbell, 1996; and Roitman, 1997.)

The additional layer of meaning which draws together these contextual strands within the Christian metaphor above is the suggestion that the armour, its strength and the 'military' qualities it implies are accessible to ordinary people. This is made explicit in another letter attributed to Paul: 'Weak men we may be but it is not as such that we fight our battles ... we compel every human thought to surrender to Christ' (2 Corinthians 10:1–5). Finally, there is one further element: the use in New Testament texts of words advocating valour and courage in conjunction with military metaphors. Examples occur in 1 Corinthians 16:13, Ephesians 6:10, and 2 Timothy 2:1 (Hobbs, 1995, p.260). These

Figure 12.14 *Roman soldiers with weapons and armour, from a first century AD bas relief of the emperor's Praetorian bodyguard. Ephesians 6:10–18 refers most immediately to the Roman soldier and his equipment. (Court, 1990; photo: Mansell Collection/Time, Inc.)*

mix in with the Hebrew and Roman cultural strands the Hellenic tradition of the hero, persistent in the culture of the ancient Mediterranean. Sometimes this is adapted to a notion of heroic suffering (2 Timothy 2:3), but the metaphor consistently communicates the idea of military virtues, moral and spiritual combat, strong leadership, clear boundaries of allegiance and behaviour, and a sense of community. The language of war and heroism serves to associate the Christian notion of peace with victory in a parallel with the Augustan model.

In other words, the effect of this hybrid discourse of war/peace is the self-definition of a community which is both related to the cultural traditions in which it has grown (Hebrew, Hellenistic, Roman) but also apart from them. Its identity is self-proclaimed, but because its language is figurative it can also claim to present no threat to the temporal power of Rome. Metaphorically, the conjunction of the language of war with the image of spiritual peace as a benefit given by Jesus Christ replicates the relationship between client and patron, which was the social cement of Roman society and which had been variously adapted first by Roman military leaders in the republic to express the duty of allegiance owed by their soldiers and the benefits thereby received, and subsequently further refined by the emperors to express their dominant role as patrons of all social strata both in Rome and in the wider empire. The Christian notion of peace and the means of its communication can therefore be seen to follow patterns of relationship between clients and patrons, duties and benefits similar to those identified in the preceding analysis of the pax Augusta and the pax romana. For Christians the special kind of peace available to them and denied to outsiders was embedded in a network of allusion, values and traditions, just as with the other kinds of Roman peace which involved identification with particular kinds of communities.

For Christians and for the Roman authorities, a key issue was whether membership of more than one of these communities and participation in more than one kind of peace were compatible. The correspondence between Pliny and the emperor Trajan (see Essay Two) indicates that the authorities tolerated quietists but regarded challenge to public institutions and public cult as dangerous. Within the Christian communities, too, there were divisions. The New Testament Book of Revelation, probably addressed to the seven churches of Asia in the first century, rebukes Christians who were complicit with Roman power and values, and looks ahead to the imminent overthrow of Rome by the agency of God (see Thompson, 1990). Significantly, the word 'peace' only occurs twice in this text, and one of these is in the liturgical introduction (1:4).

In the Roman empire the discourse surrounding peace and the images associated with it provide some evidence of cultural exchange and also help us to map the processes of acculturation and socialization. The relationship between peace and war, both literally and metaphorically, and the surrounding association with victory, justice, regeneration, benefits, tranquillity, concord, pacification, and sometimes with aspirations of moral and spiritual harmony provide a commentary on the facts of power and the way in which power was perceived and communicated by and to various social and cultural groups. In this sense, power and identity shaped one another.

References

BRUNT, P.A. and MOORE, J.M. (trans.) (1967) *Res Gestae Divi Augusti*, Oxford, Oxford University Press.

CAMPBELL, J. (1996) *Deciphering the Dead Sea Scrolls*, London, Fontana.

CARY, E. (trans., based on H.B. Foster) (1925) *Cassius Dio: Roman History*, Loeb edn, Cambridge, Mass., Harvard University Press.

CHISHOLM, K. and FERGUSON, J. (1981) *Rome: the Augustan Age*, Oxford, Oxford University Press in association with The Open University Press.

COLISH, M.L. (1992) 'Stoicism and the New Testament: an essay in historiography' in W. Haase (ed.) *Aufstieg und Niedergang der Römischen Welt*, vol.II.26.1, Berlin and New York, Walter de Gruyter, pp.334–79.

COURT, J. and K. (1990) *The New Testament World*, Cambridge, Cambridge University Press.

CRANE, G. (1998) *Thucydides and the Ancient Simplicity: the Limits of Political Realism*, Berkeley, Los Angeles and London, University of California Press.

DAY-LEWIS, C. (trans.) (1966) *The Eclogues, Georgics and Aeneid of Virgil*, Oxford, Oxford University Press.

EVANS, J.K. (1991) *War, Women and Children in Ancient Rome*, London and New York, Routledge.

GIBBON, E. (1993) *The Decline and Fall of the Roman Empire*, 3 vols, London, Everyman's Library.

GRAVES, R. (trans.) (1956) *Lucan: Pharsalia: Dramatic Episodes of the Civil Wars*, Harmondsworth, Penguin.

HARRIS, W.V. (1979) *War and Imperialism in Republican Rome*, Oxford, Oxford University Press.

HOBBS, R. (1995) 'The language of warfare in the New Testament' in P.F. Esler (ed.) *Modelling Early Christianity*, London and New York, Routledge, pp.259–73.

ISAAC, B. (1992) *The Limits of Empire: the Roman Army in the East*, Oxford, Oxford University Press.

LATHAM, R.E. (trans.) (1951) *Lucretius: On the Nature of the Universe*, Harmondsworth, Penguin.

LEWIS, N. and REINHOLD, M. (eds) (1990) *Roman Civilization: Selected Readings. Volume II The Empire* (third edition), New York, Columbia University Press.

LONG, A.A. (1986) *Hellenistic Philosophy* (second edition), London, Duckworth.

LUTTWAK, E.N. (1976) *The Grand Strategy of the Roman Empire from the First Century AD to the Third*, Baltimore and London, Johns Hopkins University Press.

MICHIE, J. (trans.) (1963) *Horace: Odes*, The Library of Liberal Arts, Indianapolis, New York and Kansas City, Bobbs-Merrill.

PRICE, S.R.F. (1984) *Rituals and Power*, Cambridge, Cambridge University Press.

ROITMAN, A. (ed.) (1997) *A Day at Qumran: the Dead Sea Sect and its Scrolls*, Jerusalem, The Israel Museum.

SHERK, R.K. (ed. and trans.) (1984) *Rome and the Greek East to the Death of Augustus*, vol.4 of Translated Documents of Greece and Rome series, Cambridge, Cambridge University Press.

SMITH, M.J. (1993) *Diogenes of Oinoanda: the Epicurean Inscription*, Naples, Bibliopolis.

SWARTLEY, W.M. (1996) 'War and peace in the New Testament' in W. Haase (ed.) *Aufstieg und Niedergang des Römischen Welt*, vol.II.26.3, Berlin and New York, Walter de Gruyter, pp.2299–408.

THOMPSON, L.L. (1990) *The Book of Revelation: Apocalypse and Empire*, New York and Oxford, Oxford University Press.

VERMES, G. (1997) *The Complete Dead Sea Scrolls in English*, London, Allen Lane.

WALLACE, R. and WILLIAMS, W. (1998) *The Three Worlds of Paul of Tarsus*, London and New York, Routledge.

WATTS, A.E. (trans.) (1966) *The Poems of Propertius*, Harmondsworth, Penguin.

WELLS, C. (1984) *The Roman Empire*, London, Fontana.

WENGST, K. (1987) *Pax Romana and the Peace of Jesus Christ* (trans. J. Bowden), London, SCM Press.

WHITTAKER, C.R. (1994) *Frontiers of the Roman Empire*, Baltimore and London, Johns Hopkins University Press.

Index

Emperors and writers are indexed under the name by which they are usually known. Place names may be given in their ancient or modern form according to how they appear in the text.